Island in a Puddle

Kei Sanbe

3

CONTENTS

CHAPTER 11: Can't Run Away! ································· 3

CHAPTER 12: Betrayal ································· 43

CHAPTER 13: Footsteps of Revenge ···················· 83

CHAPTER 14: "Minato's" Decision ·················· 123

CHAPTER 15: A Kind Wizard ··························· 163

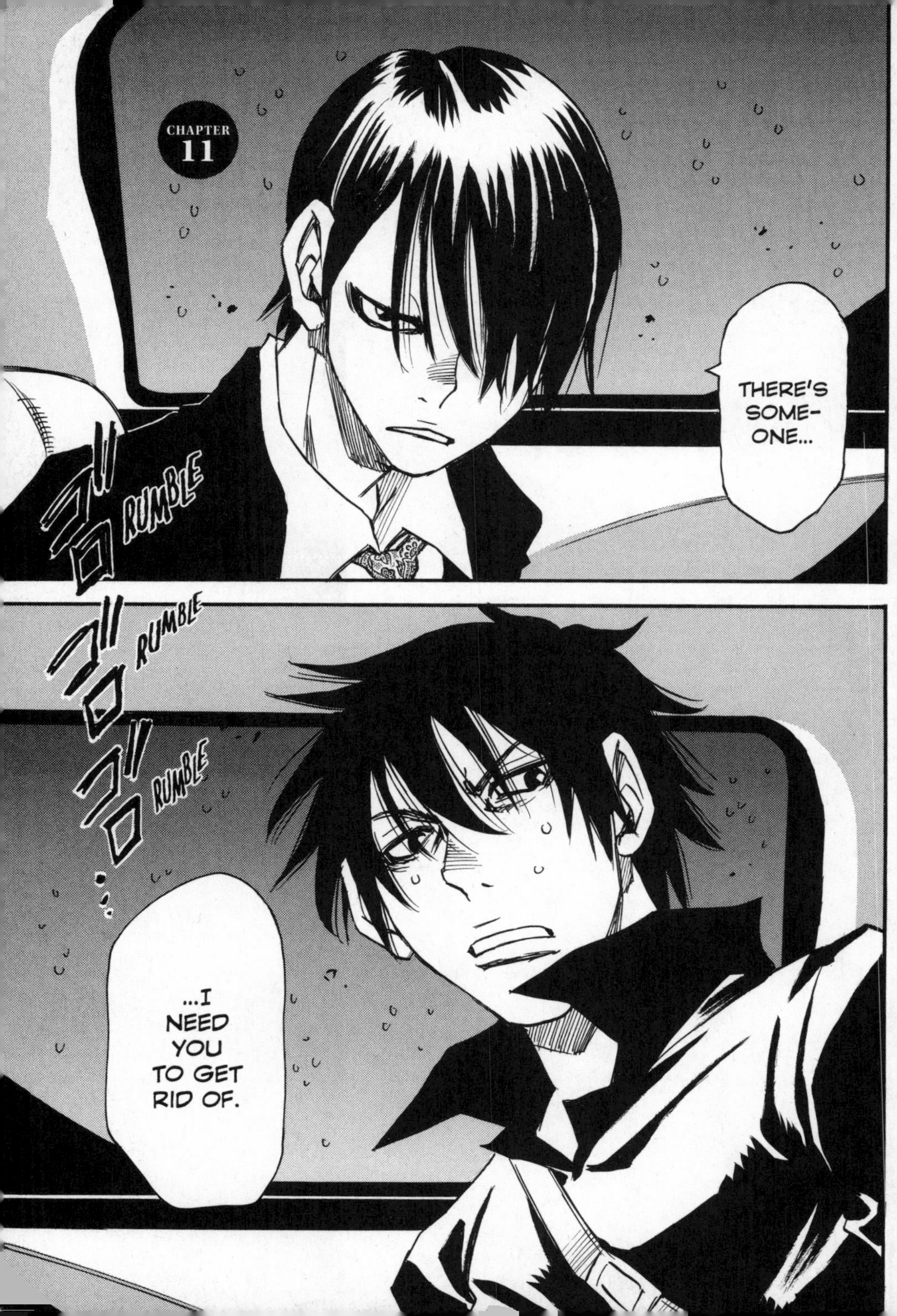
CHAPTER 11
THERE'S SOME-ONE...
RUMBLE
RUMBLE
RUMBLE
...I NEED YOU TO GET RID OF.

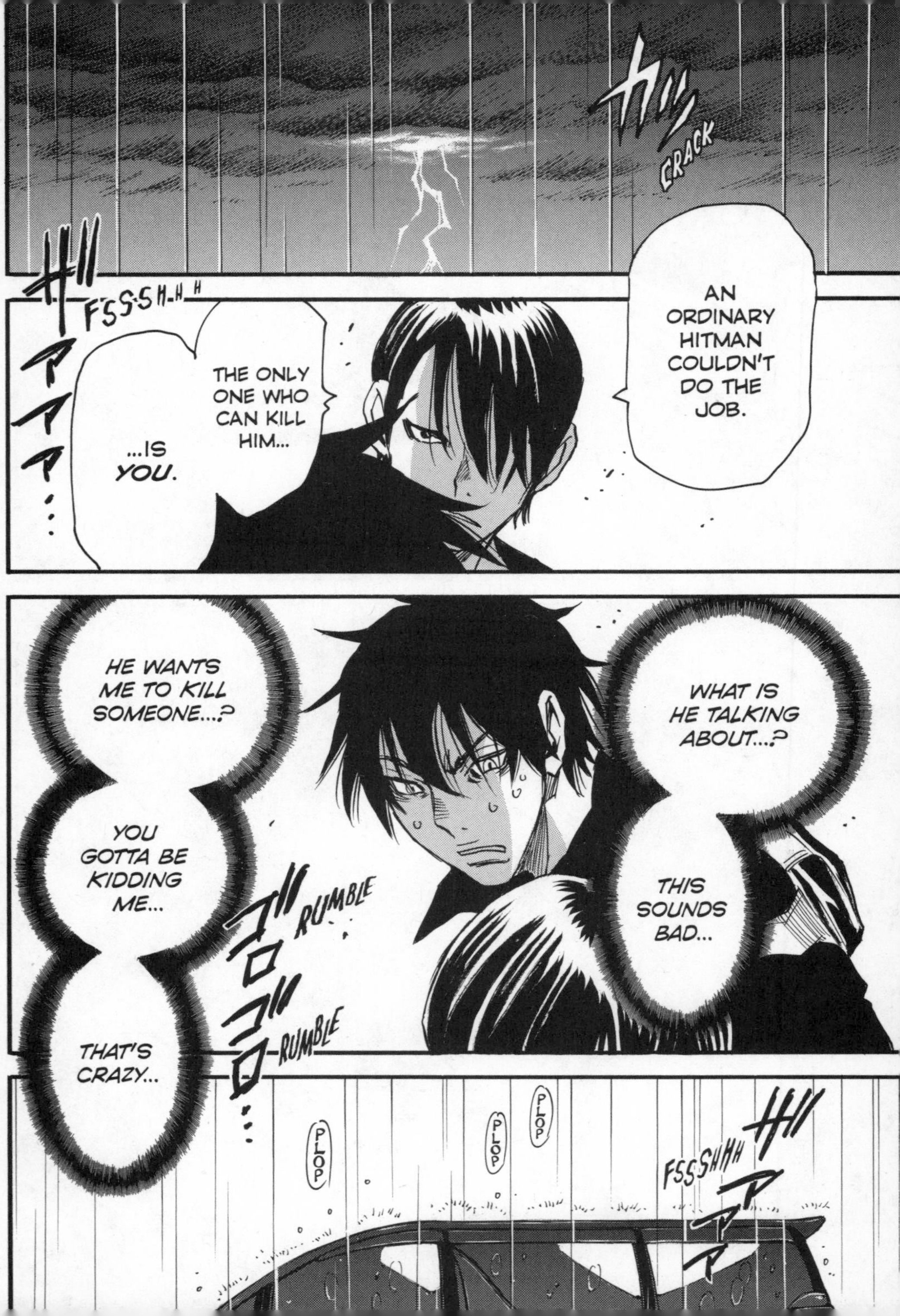
CRACK
AN ORDINARY HITMAN COULDN'T DO THE JOB.
FSS-S-SH-H-H
THE ONLY ONE WHO CAN KILL HIM...
...IS *YOU*.
WHAT IS HE TALKING ABOUT...?
THIS SOUNDS BAD...
HE WANTS ME TO KILL SOMEONE...?
YOU GOTTA BE KIDDING ME...
RUMBLE
RUMBLE
THAT'S CRAZY...
FSSSHHH
PLOP
PLOP
PLOP

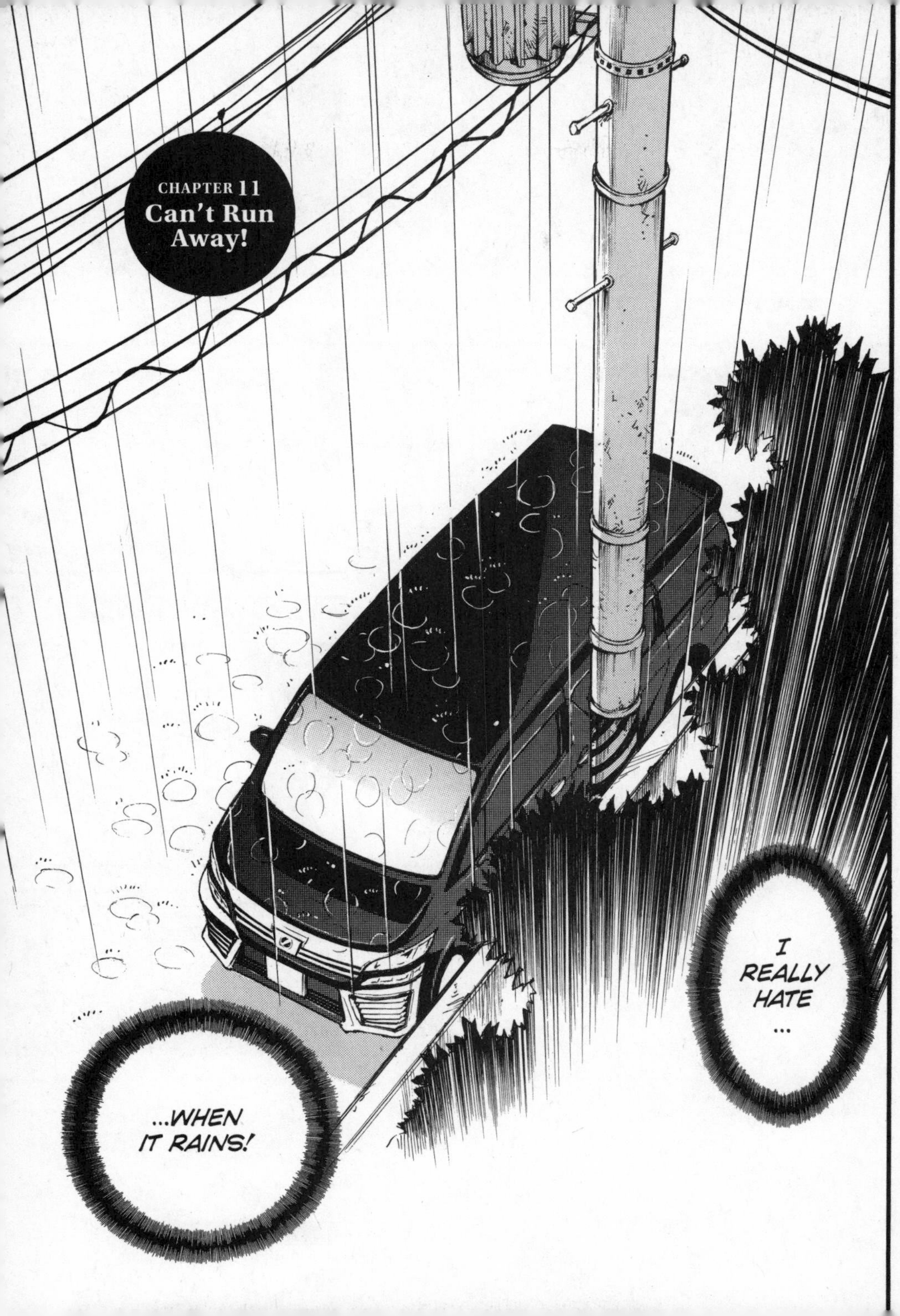
CHAPTER 11
Can't Run Away!
I REALLY HATE ...
...WHEN IT RAINS!

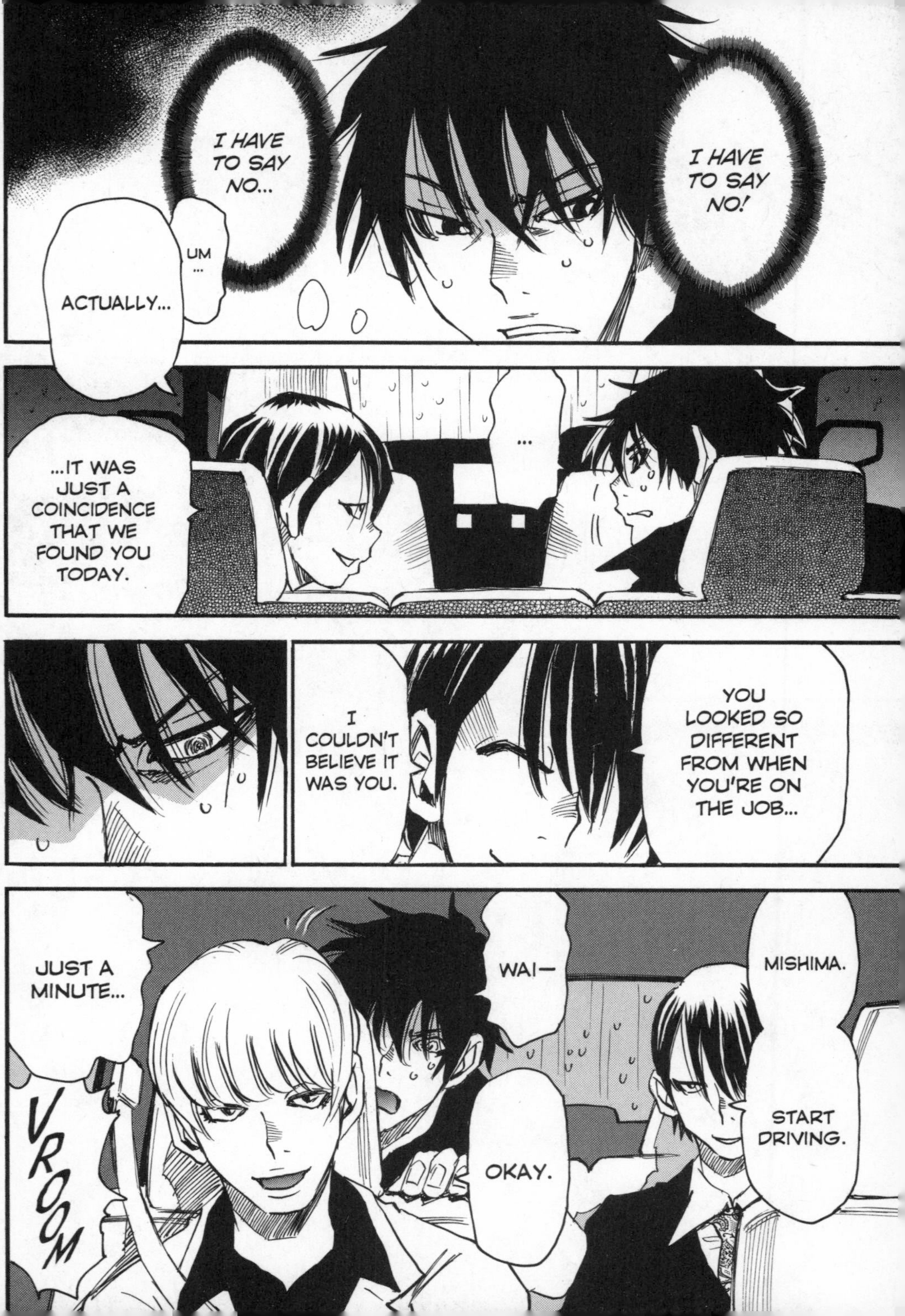
I HAVE TO SAY NO!
I HAVE TO SAY NO...
UM ...
ACTUALLY...
...
...IT WAS JUST A COINCIDENCE THAT WE FOUND YOU TODAY.
YOU LOOKED SO DIFFERENT FROM WHEN YOU'RE ON THE JOB...
I COULDN'T BELIEVE IT WAS YOU.
MISHIMA.
WAI—
JUST A MINUTE...
START DRIVING.
OKAY.
VROOM

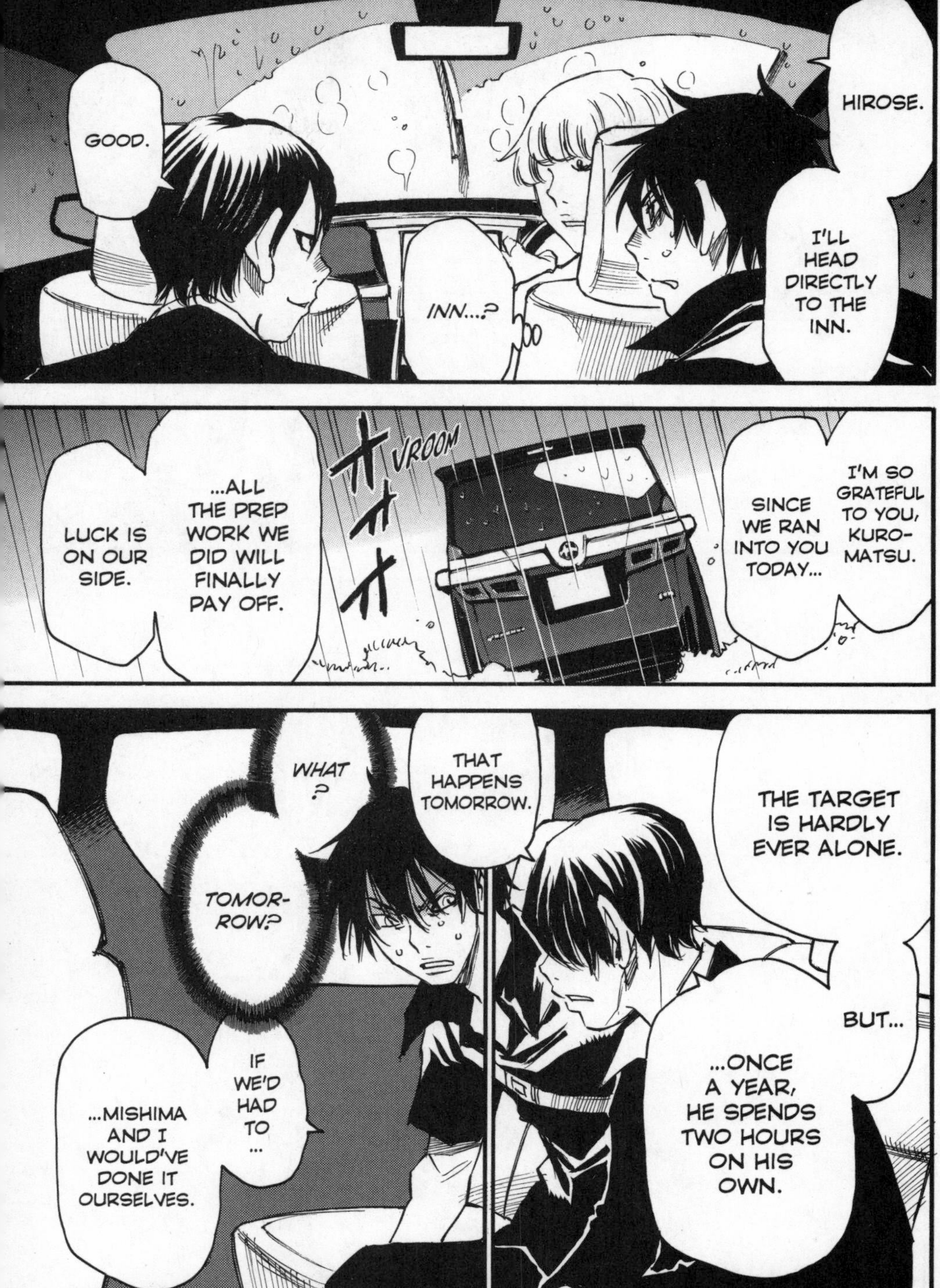
HIROSE.
I'LL HEAD DIRECTLY TO THE INN.
INN...?
GOOD.
I'M SO GRATEFUL TO YOU, KUROMATSU.
SINCE WE RAN INTO YOU TODAY...
VROOM
...ALL THE PREP WORK WE DID WILL FINALLY PAY OFF.
LUCK IS ON OUR SIDE.
THE TARGET IS HARDLY EVER ALONE.
BUT...
...ONCE A YEAR, HE SPENDS TWO HOURS ON HIS OWN.
THAT HAPPENS TOMORROW.
WHAT?
TOMORROW?
IF WE'D HAD TO...
...MISHIMA AND I WOULD'VE DONE IT OURSELVES.

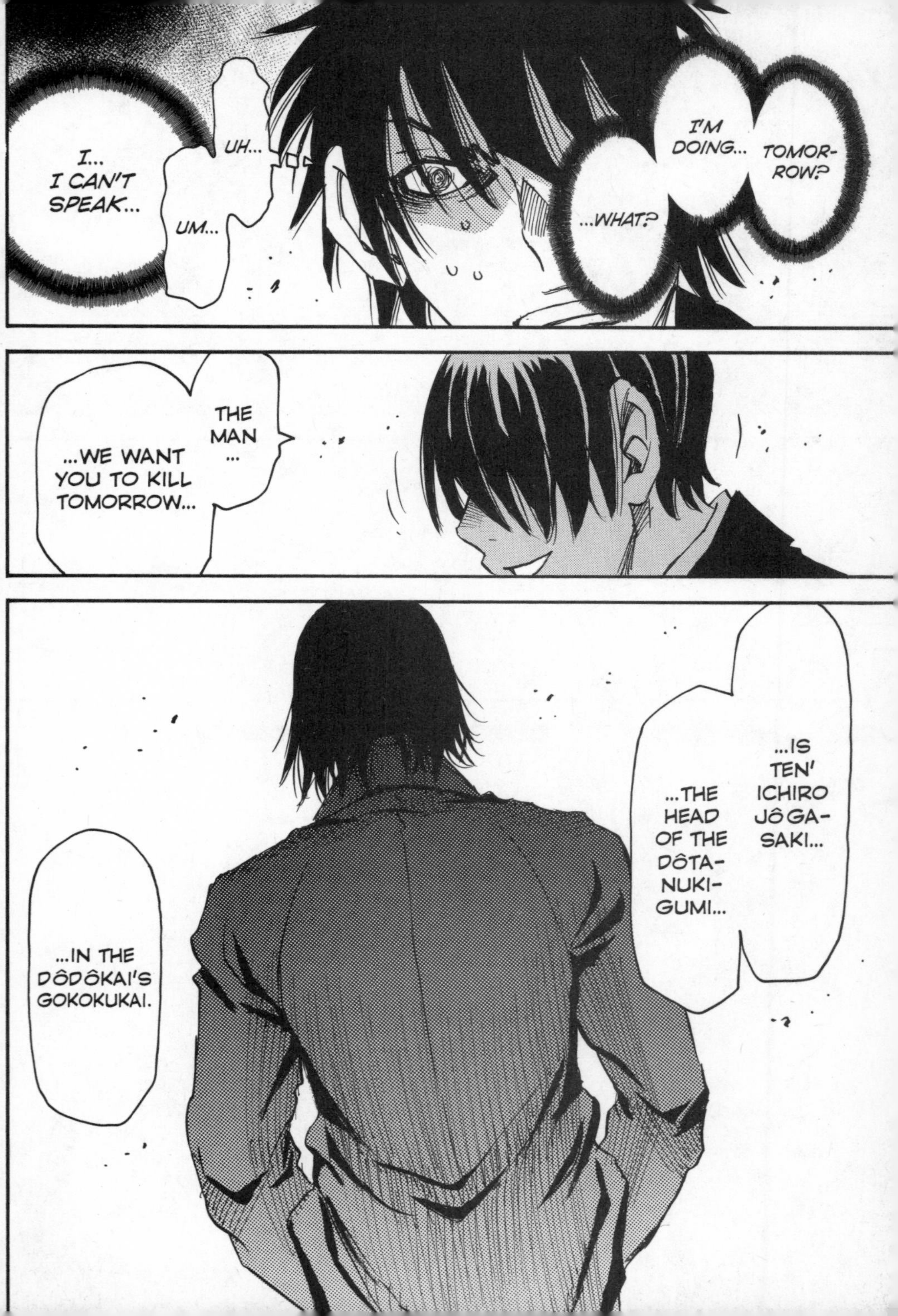
TOMOR-
ROW?
I'M
DOING...
...WHAT?
UH...
I...
I CAN'T
SPEAK...
UM...
THE
MAN
...
...WE WANT
YOU TO KILL
TOMORROW...
...IS
TEN'
ICHIRO
JÔGA-
SAKI...
...THE
HEAD
OF THE
DÔTA-
NUKI-
GUMI...
...IN THE
DÔDÔKAI'S
GOKOKUKAI.

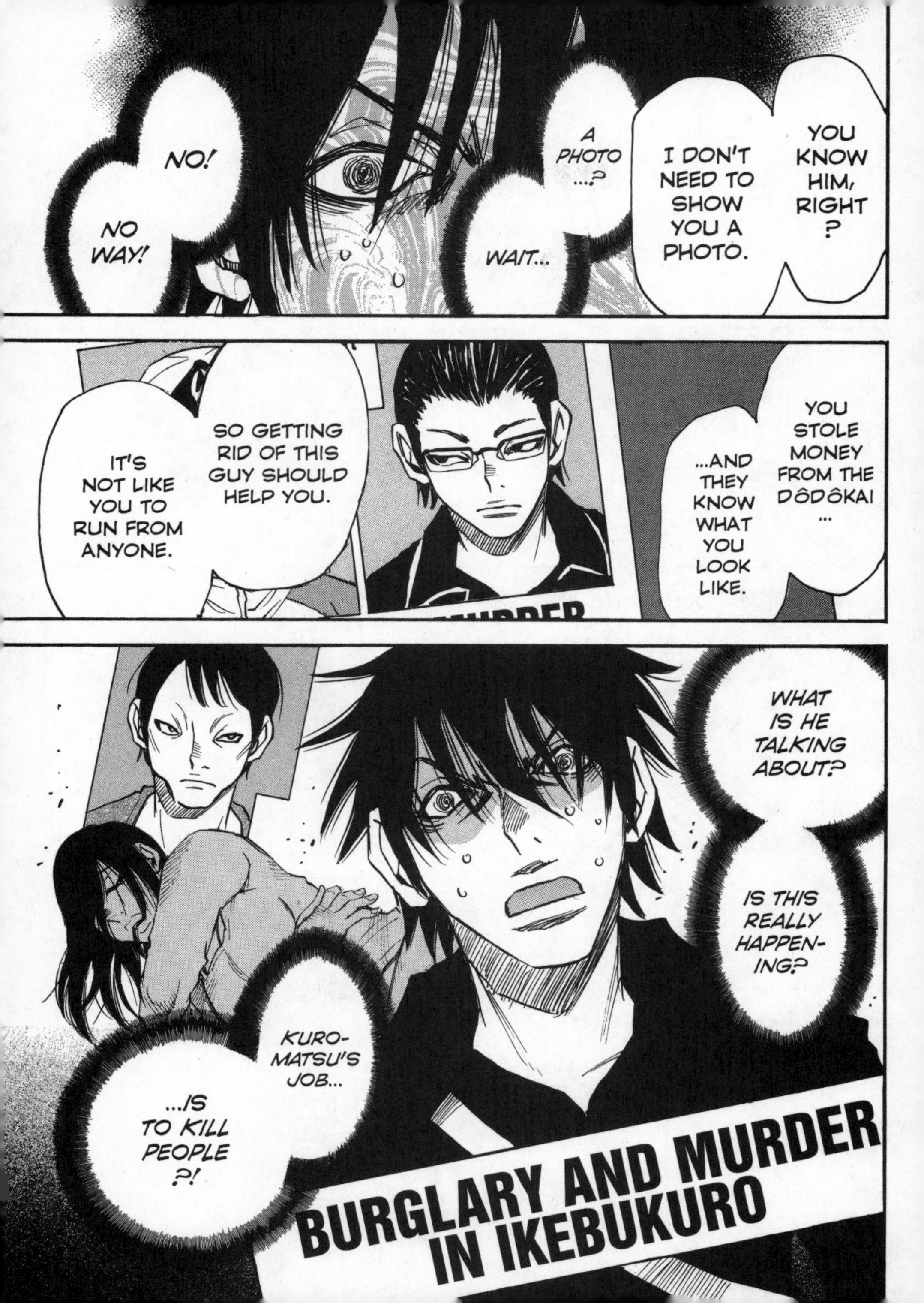
YOU KNOW HIM, RIGHT?
I DON'T NEED TO SHOW YOU A PHOTO.
A PHOTO ....?
WAIT...
NO!
NO WAY!
YOU STOLE MONEY FROM THE DÔDÔKAI ...
...AND THEY KNOW WHAT YOU LOOK LIKE.
SO GETTING RID OF THIS GUY SHOULD HELP YOU.
IT'S NOT LIKE YOU TO RUN FROM ANYONE.
WHAT IS HE TALKING ABOUT?
IS THIS REALLY HAPPENING?
KURO-MATSU'S JOB...
...IS TO KILL PEOPLE ?!
BURGLARY AND MURDER IN IKEBUKURO

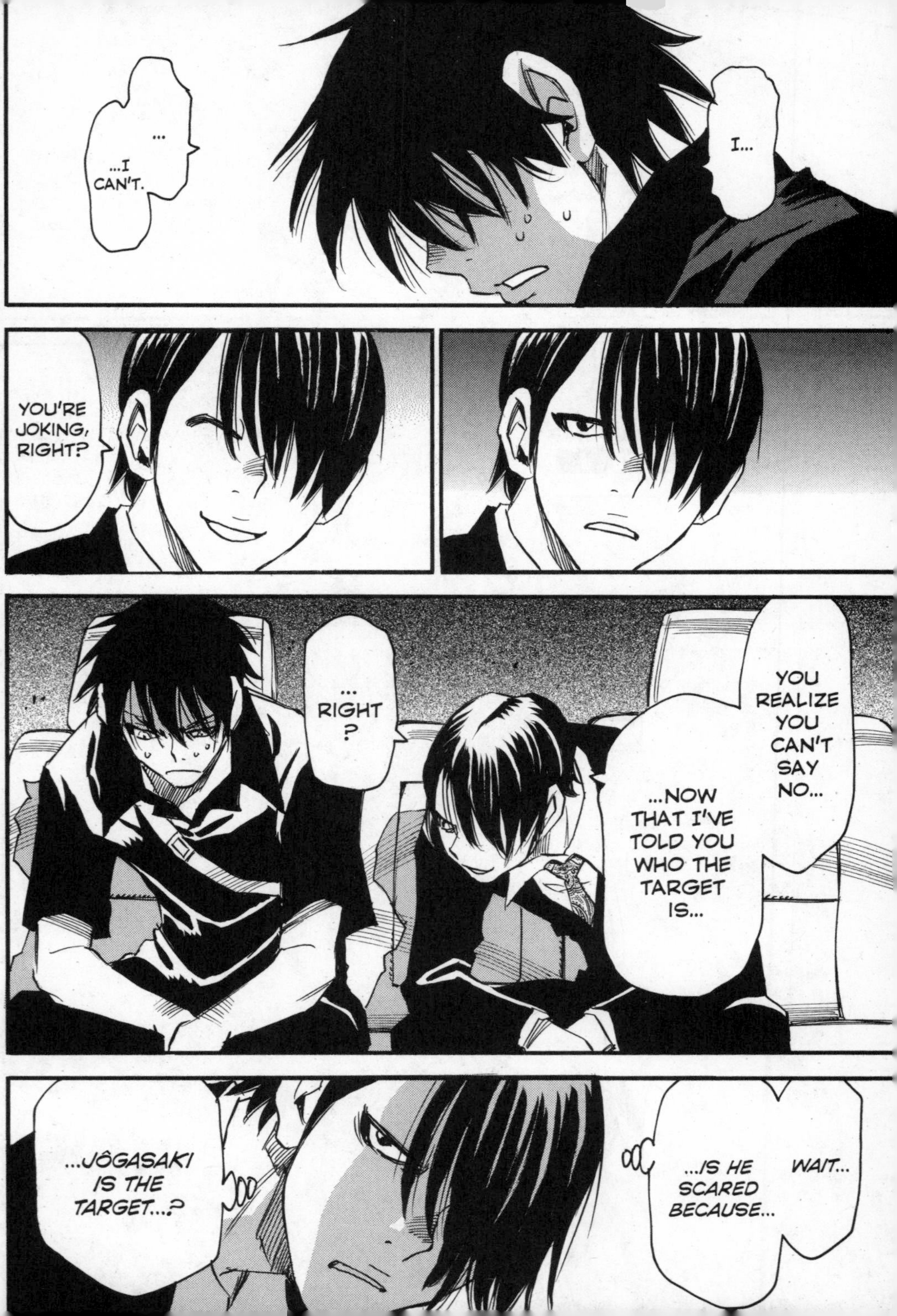
I...
... ...I CAN'T.
YOU'RE JOKING, RIGHT?
YOU REALIZE YOU CAN'T SAY NO...
...NOW THAT I'VE TOLD YOU WHO THE TARGET IS...
... RIGHT?
WAIT...
...IS HE SCARED BECAUSE...
...JÔGASAKI IS THE TARGET...?

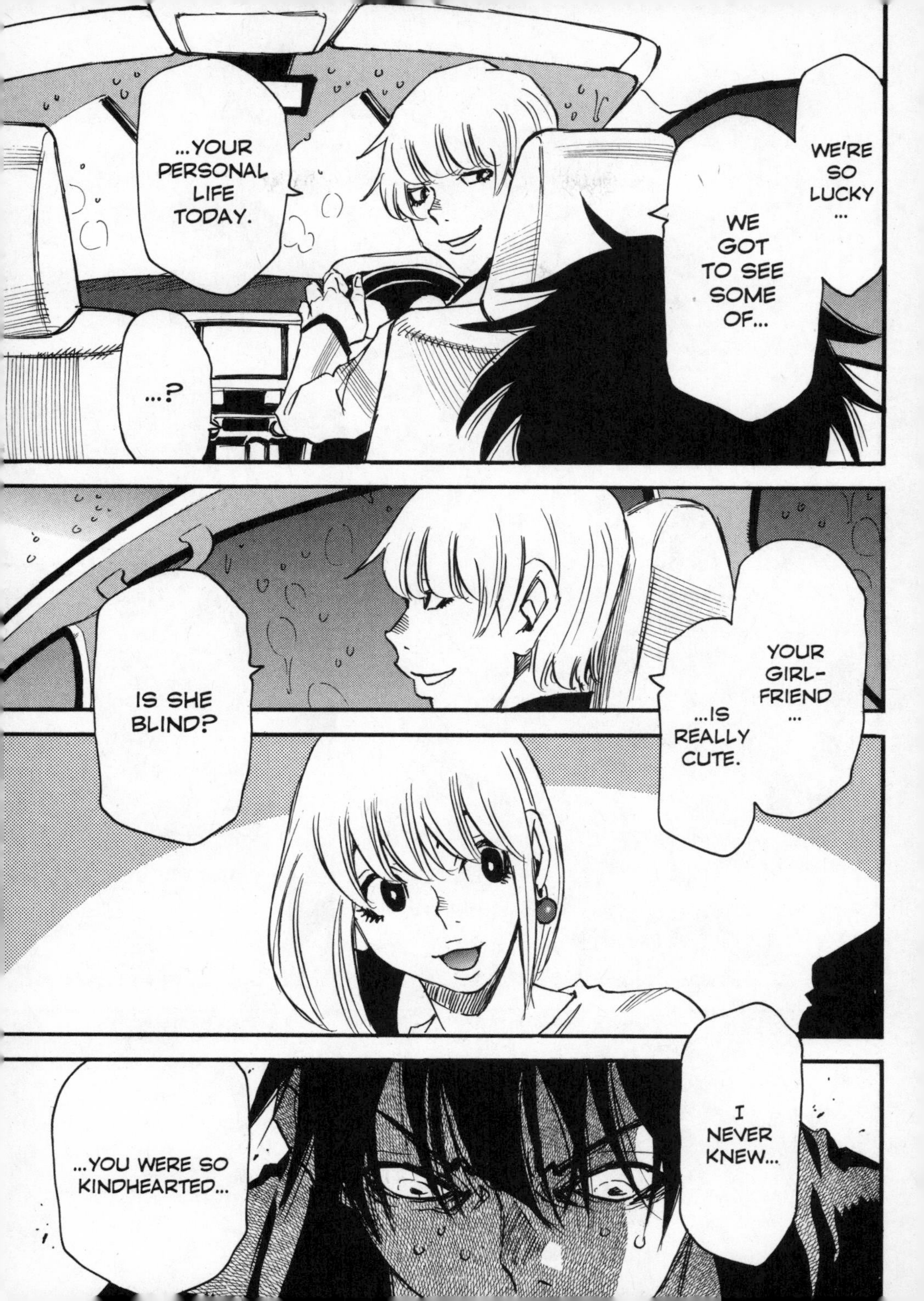
WE'RE SO LUCKY ...
WE GOT TO SEE SOME OF...
...YOUR PERSONAL LIFE TODAY.
...?
YOUR GIRL-FRIEND ...
...IS REALLY CUTE.
IS SHE BLIND?
I NEVER KNEW...
...YOU WERE SO KINDHEARTED...

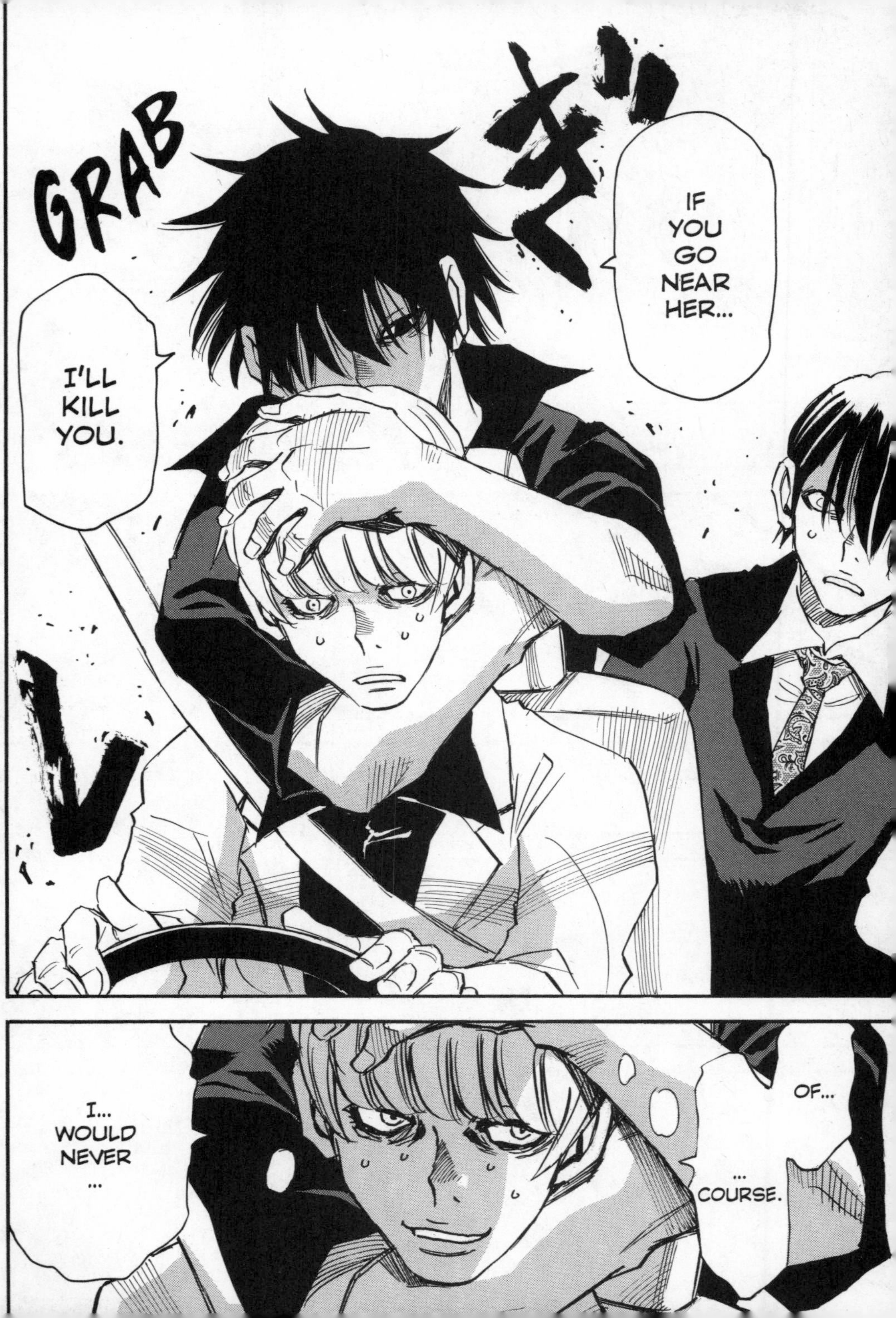
GRAB
IF YOU GO NEAR HER...
I'LL KILL YOU.
OF... ...COURSE.
I... WOULD NEVER ...

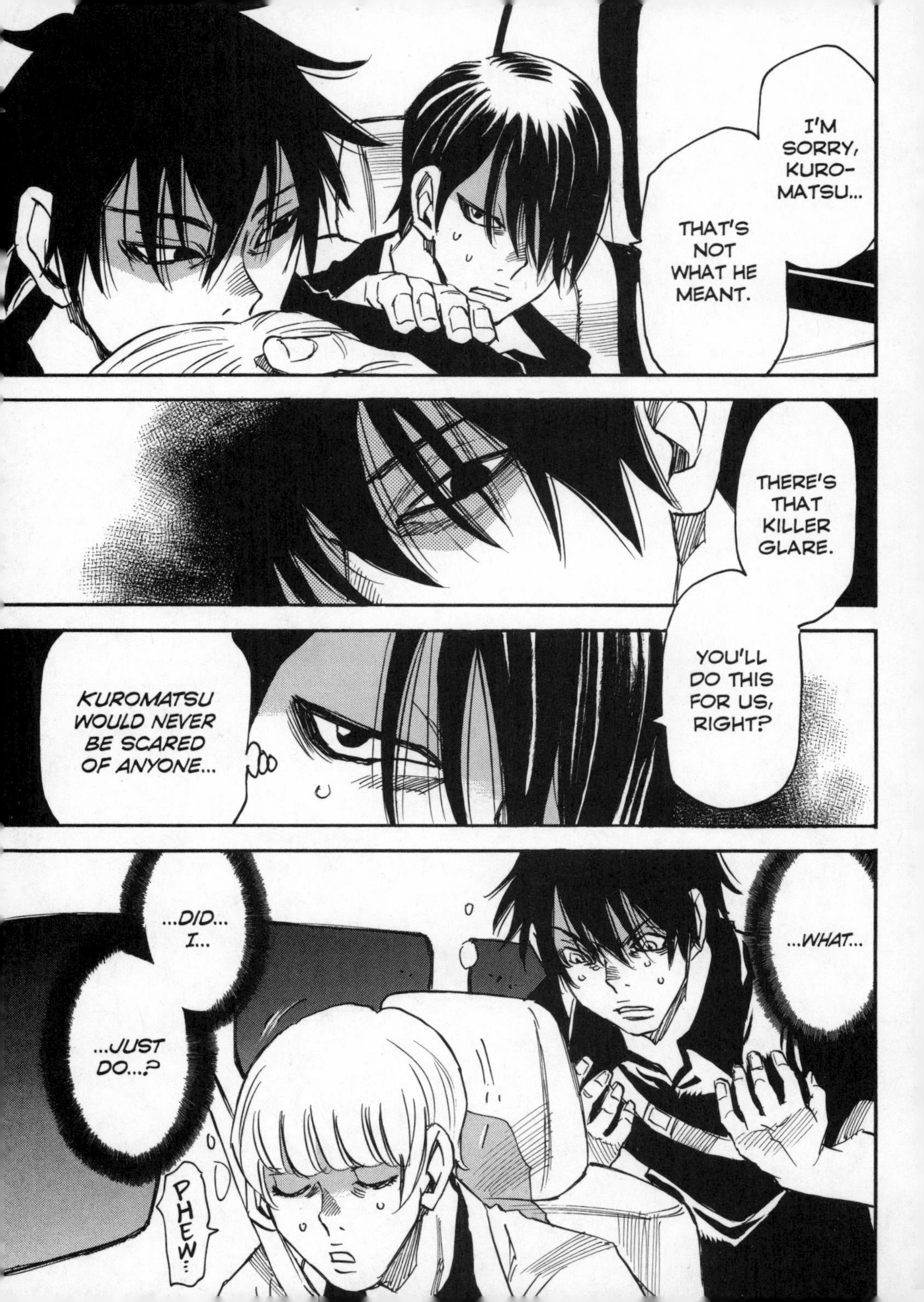
I'M SORRY, KURO-MATSU...
THAT'S NOT WHAT HE MEANT.
THERE'S THAT KILLER GLARE.
YOU'LL DO THIS FOR US, RIGHT?
KUROMATSU WOULD NEVER BE SCARED OF ANYONE...
...WHAT...
...DID... I...
...JUST DO...?
PHEW...

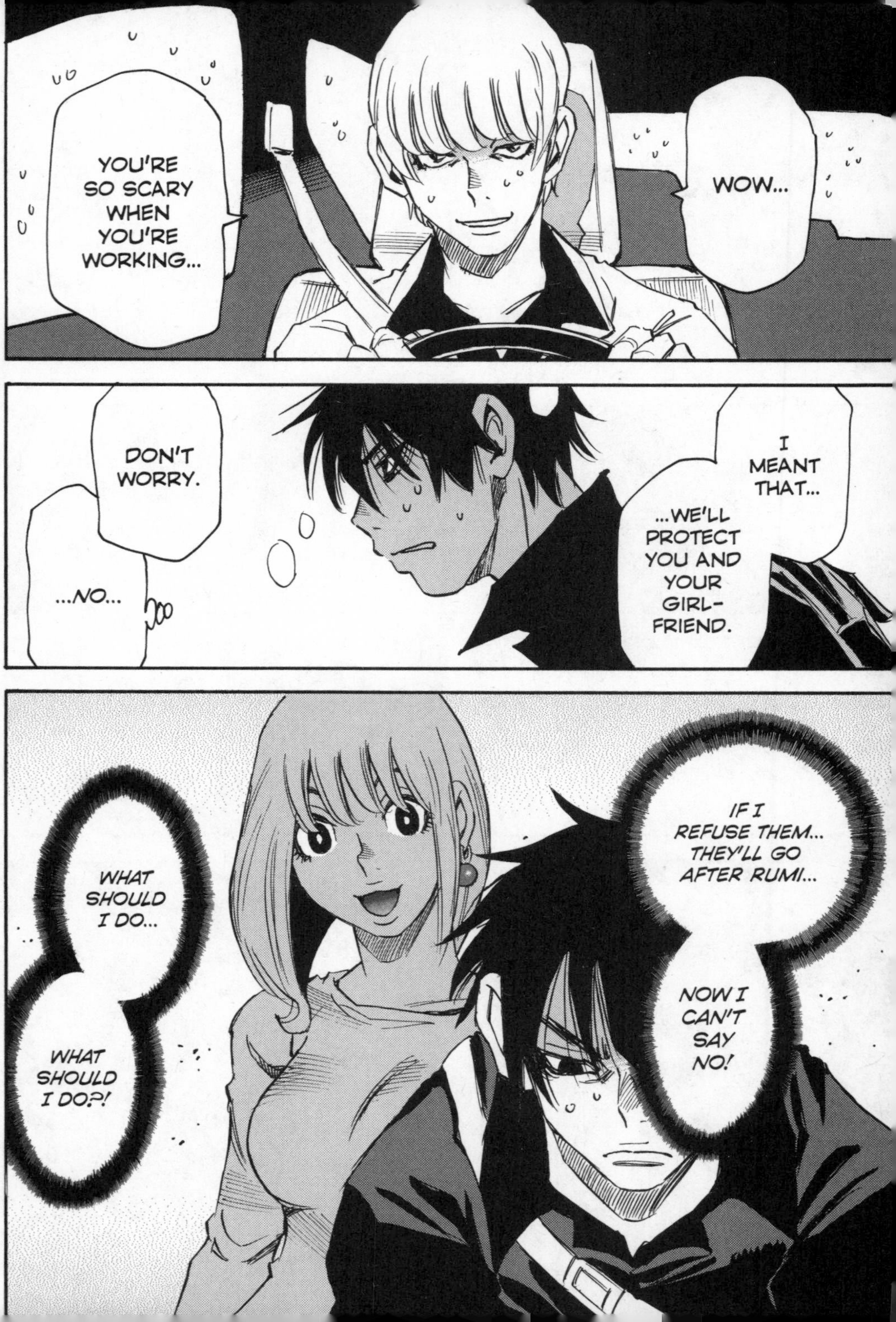
WOW...
YOU'RE SO SCARY WHEN YOU'RE WORKING...
I MEANT THAT...
...WE'LL PROTECT YOU AND YOUR GIRL-FRIEND.
DON'T WORRY.
...NO...
IF I REFUSE THEM... THEY'LL GO AFTER RUMI...
NOW I CAN'T SAY NO!
WHAT SHOULD I DO...
WHAT SHOULD I DO?!

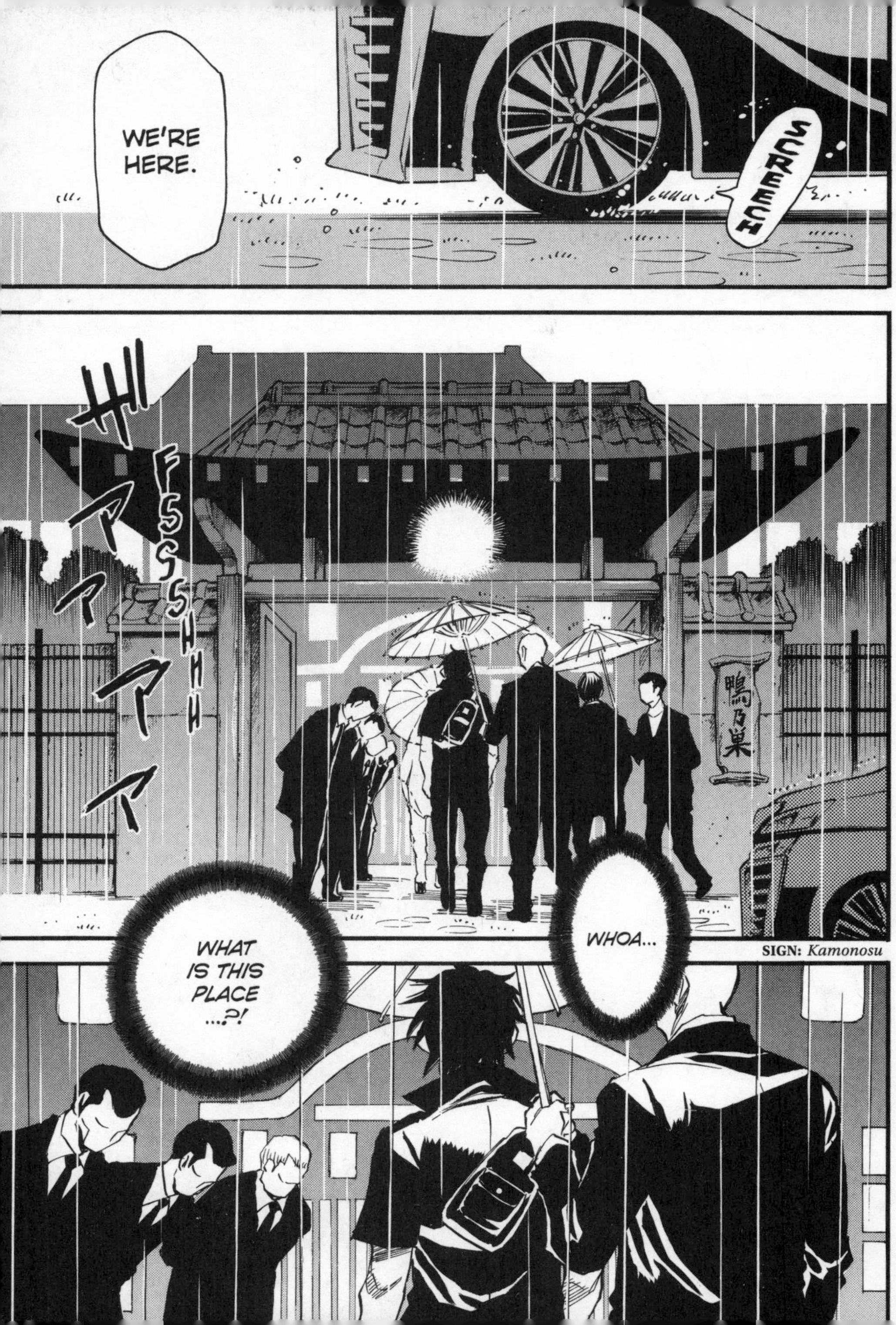
SCREECH
WE'RE HERE.
ザァァァァ
FSSHHH
鴨乃巣
WHOA...
WHAT IS THIS PLACE ...?!

SIGN: *Kamonosu*

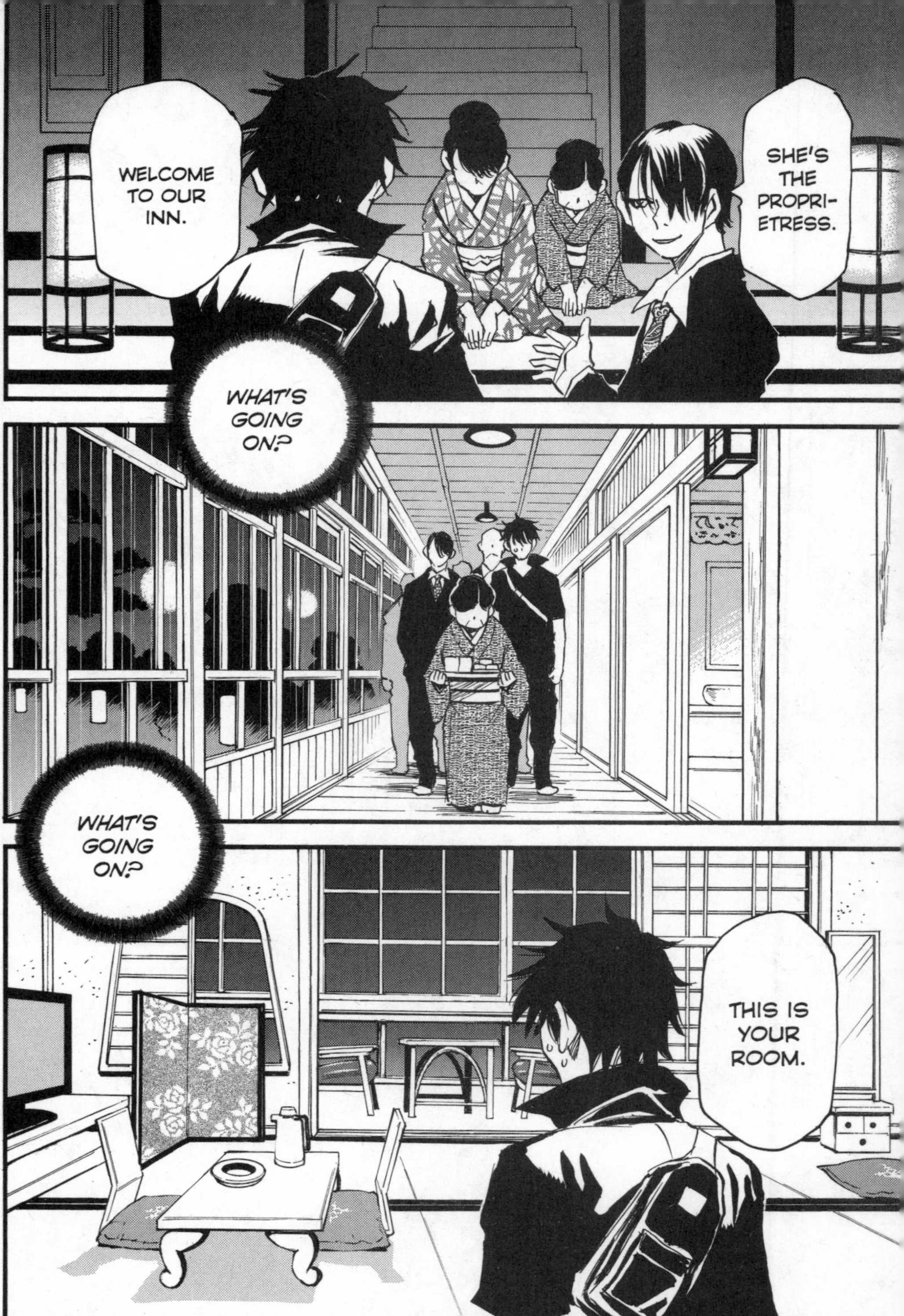
SHE'S THE PROPRI-ETRESS.
WELCOME TO OUR INN.
WHAT'S GOING ON?
WHAT'S GOING ON?
THIS IS YOUR ROOM.

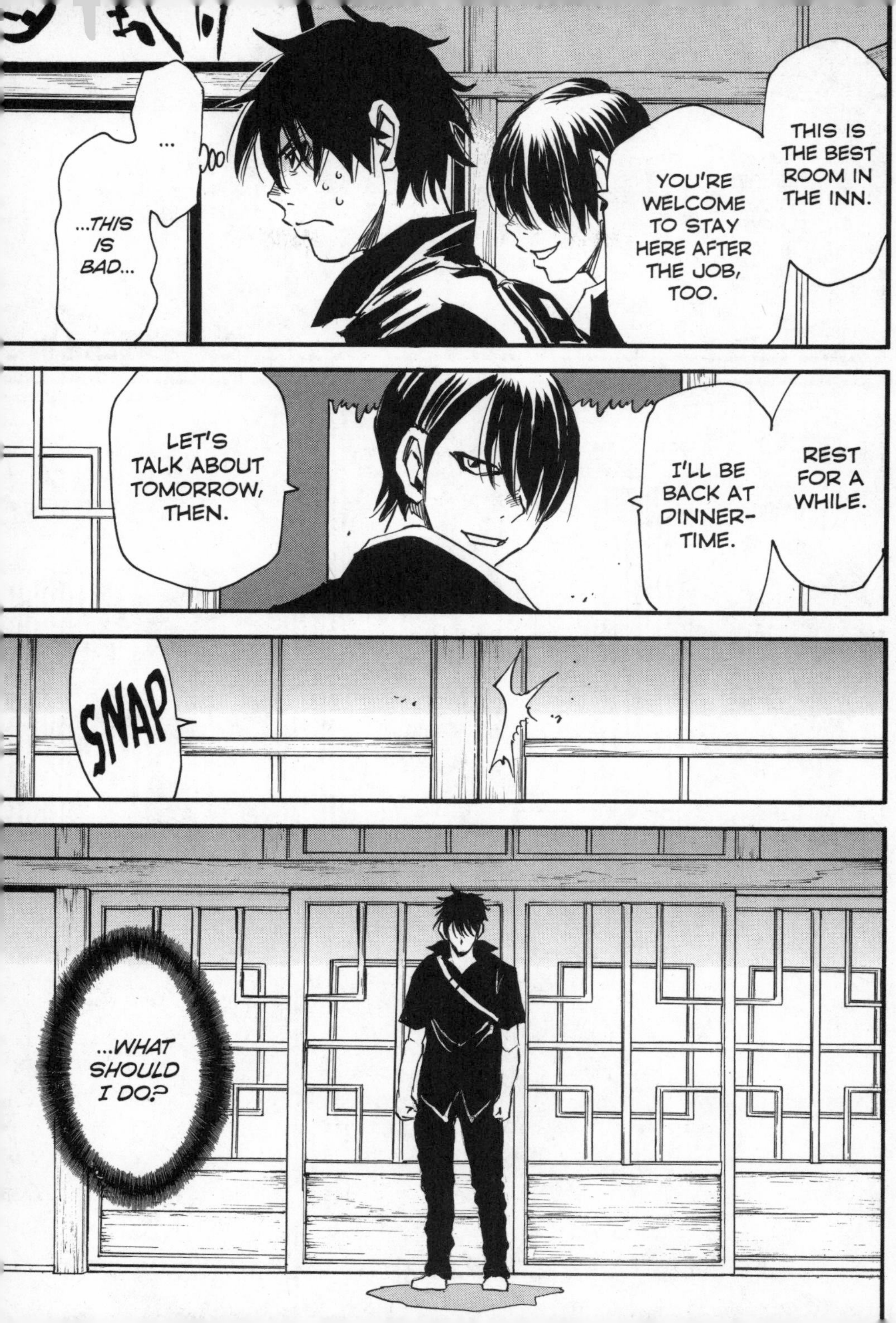
THIS IS THE BEST ROOM IN THE INN.
YOU'RE WELCOME TO STAY HERE AFTER THE JOB, TOO.
...
...THIS IS BAD...
REST FOR A WHILE.
I'LL BE BACK AT DINNER-TIME.
LET'S TALK ABOUT TOMORROW, THEN.
SNAP
...WHAT SHOULD I DO?

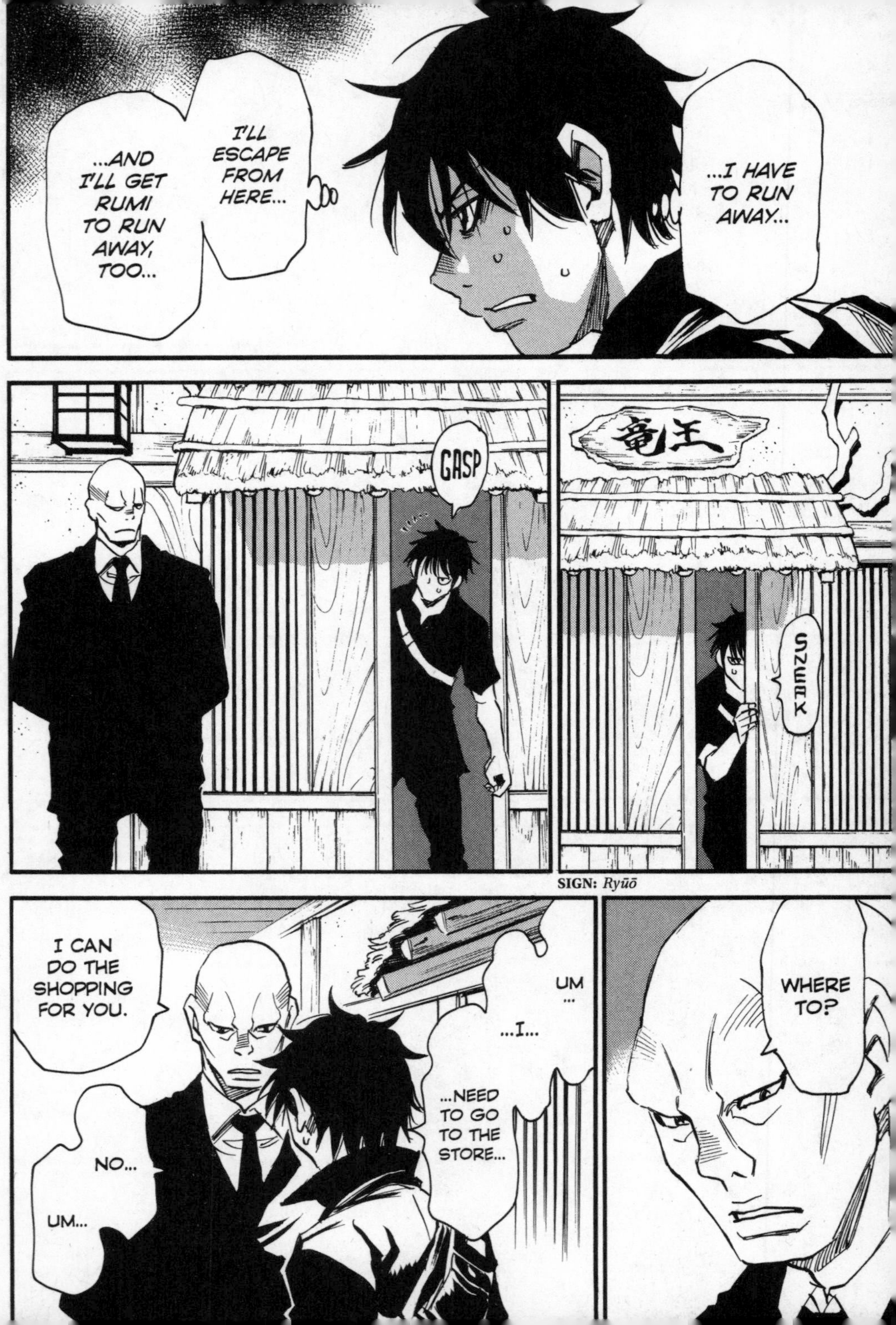
...I HAVE TO RUN AWAY...
I'LL ESCAPE FROM HERE...
...AND I'LL GET RUMI TO RUN AWAY, TOO...
竜王
SNEAK
GASP
WHERE TO?
UM ...
...I...
...NEED TO GO TO THE STORE...
I CAN DO THE SHOPPING FOR YOU.
NO...
UM...

SIGN: *Ryūō*

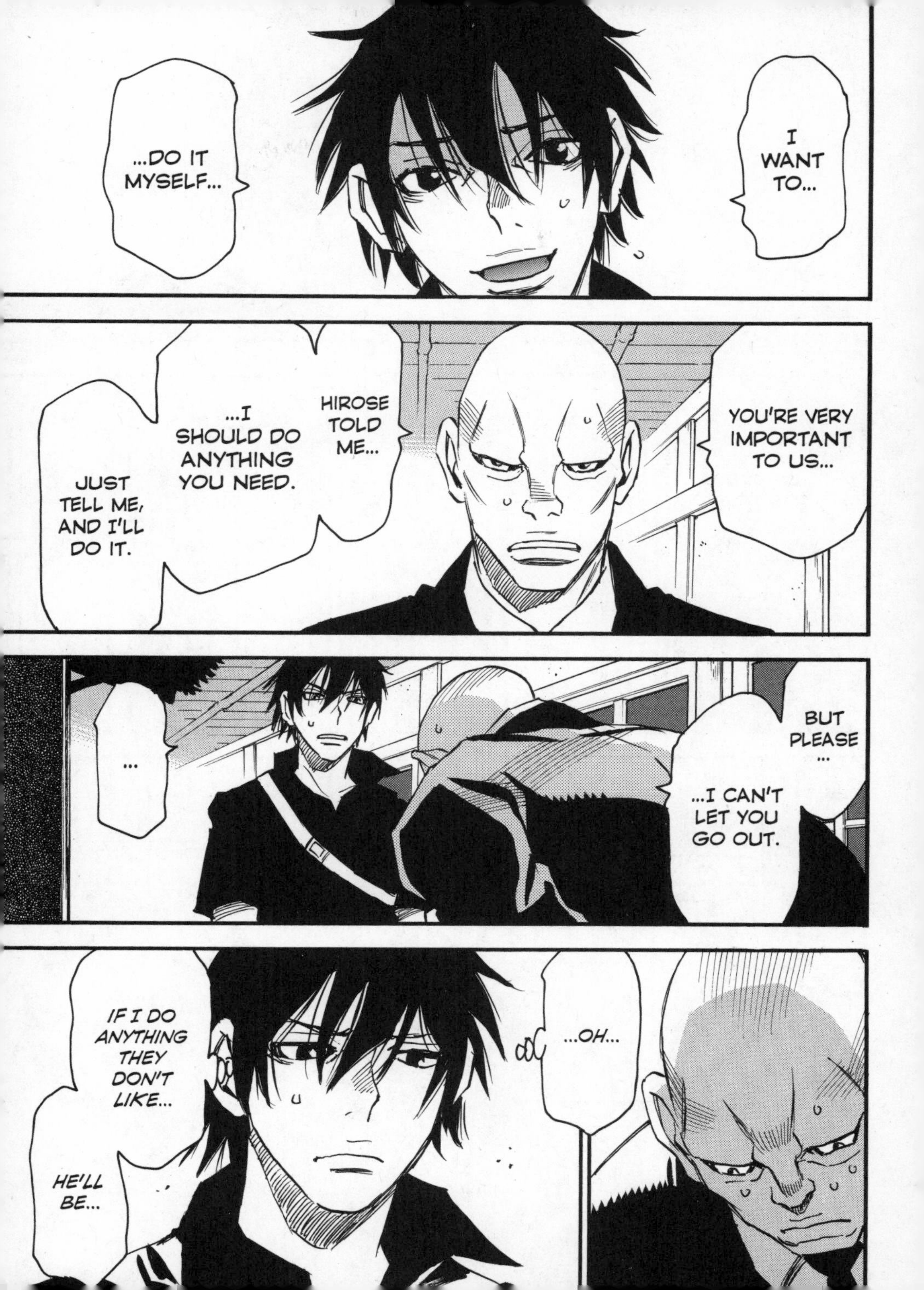
I WANT TO...
...DO IT MYSELF...
YOU'RE VERY IMPORTANT TO US...
HIROSE TOLD ME...
...I SHOULD DO ANYTHING YOU NEED.
JUST TELL ME, AND I'LL DO IT.
BUT PLEASE ...
...I CAN'T LET YOU GO OUT.
...
...OH...
IF I DO ANYTHING THEY DON'T LIKE...
HE'LL BE...

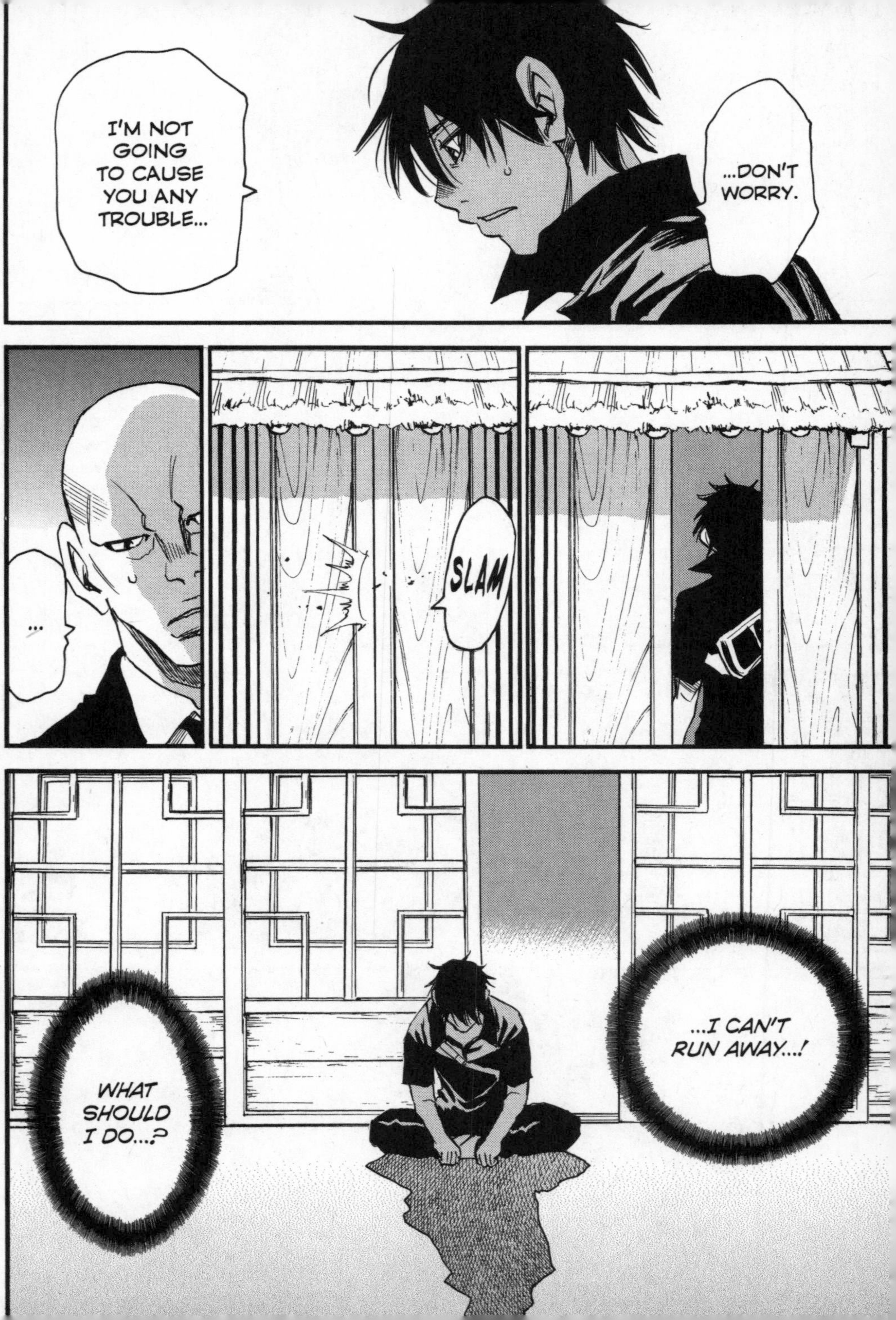
...DON'T WORRY.
I'M NOT GOING TO CAUSE YOU ANY TROUBLE...
SLAM
...
...I CAN'T RUN AWAY...!
WHAT SHOULD I DO...?

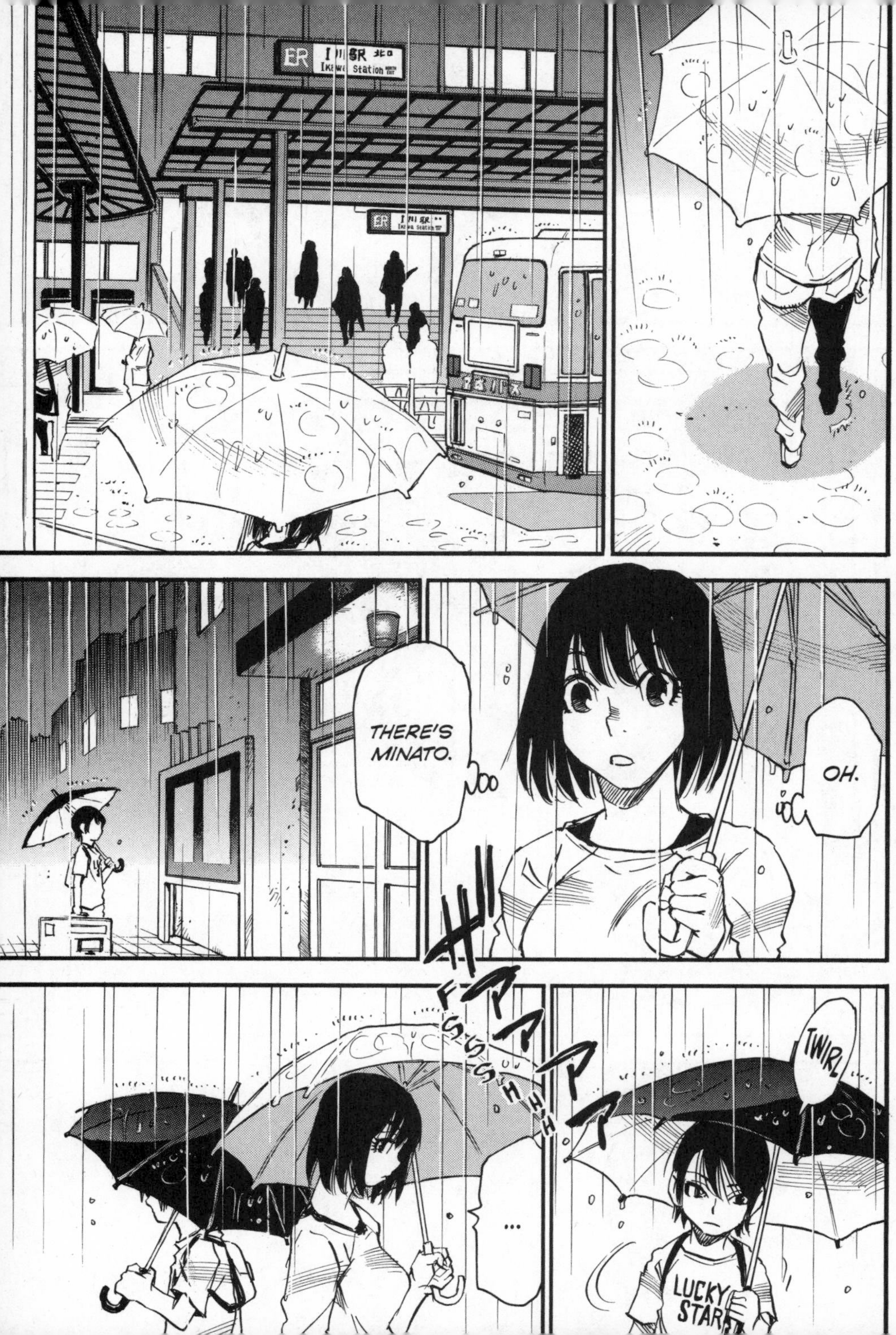

Ikawa Station
OH.
THERE'S MINATO.
FSSSSHHH
TWIRL
LUCKY STAR
...

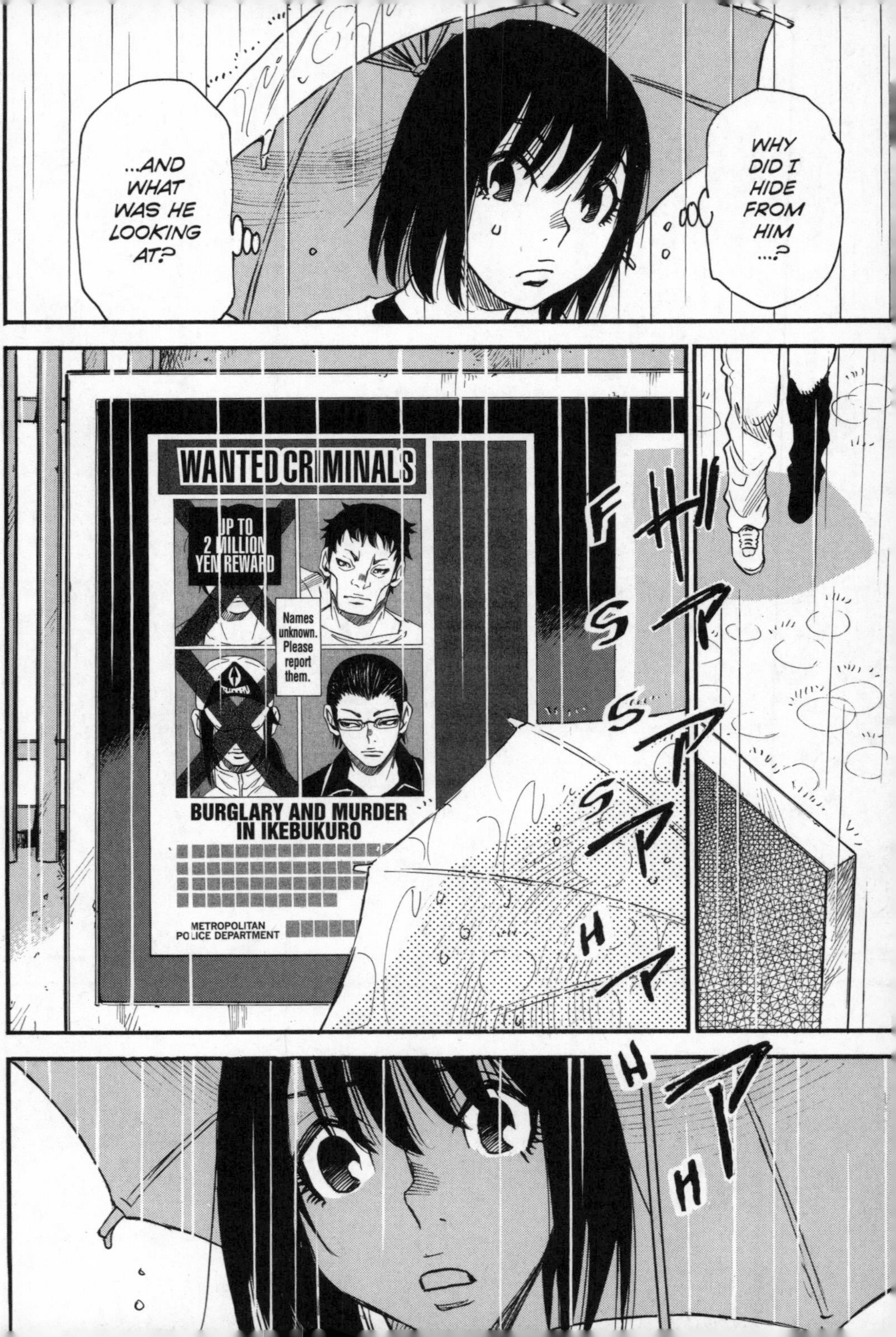
WHY DID I HIDE FROM HIM ...?
...AND WHAT WAS HE LOOKING AT?
WANTED CRIMINALS
UP TO 2 MILLION YEN REWARD
Names unknown. Please report them.
BURGLARY AND MURDER IN IKEBUKURO
METROPOLITAN POLICE DEPARTMENT
FSSSHHH

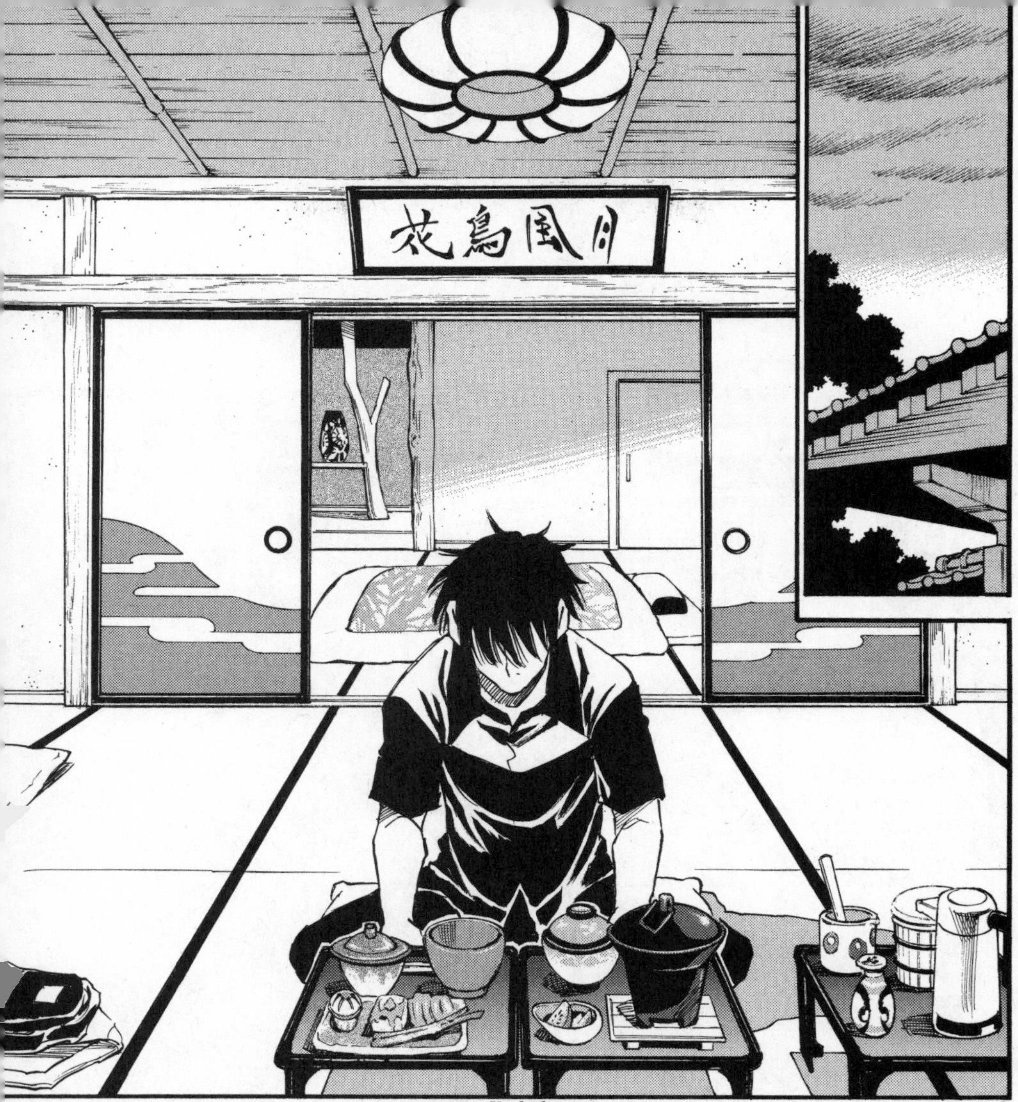
花鳥風月

SIGN: *Kachōfugetsu*

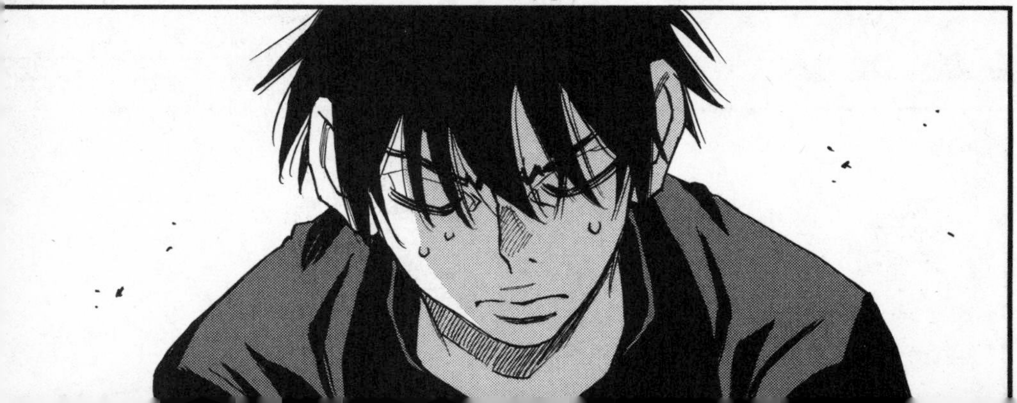

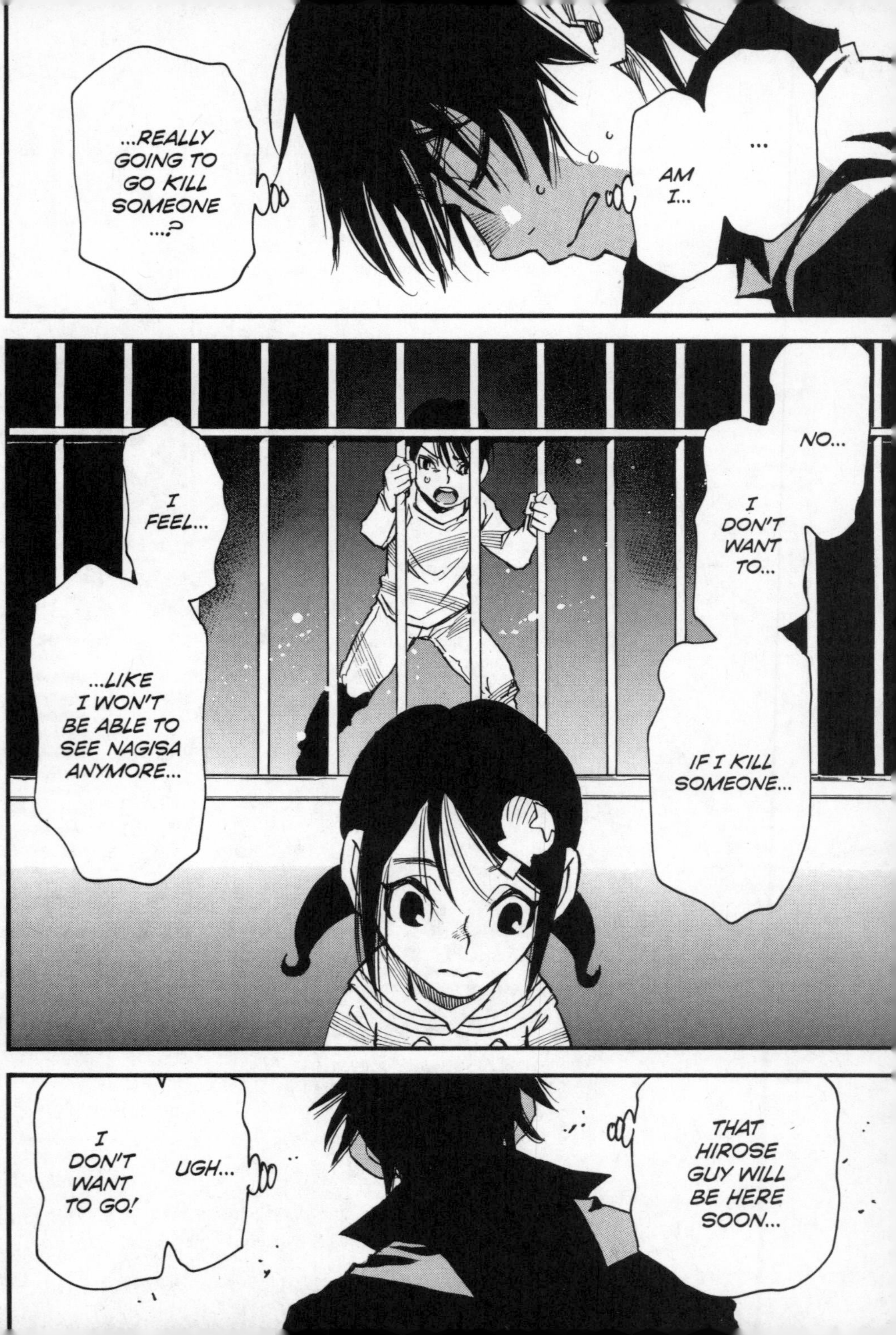
... AM I...
...REALLY GOING TO GO KILL SOMEONE ...?
NO...
I DON'T WANT TO...
IF I KILL SOMEONE...
I FEEL...
...LIKE I WON'T BE ABLE TO SEE NAGISA ANYMORE...
THAT HIROSE GUY WILL BE HERE SOON...
UGH...
I DON'T WANT TO GO!

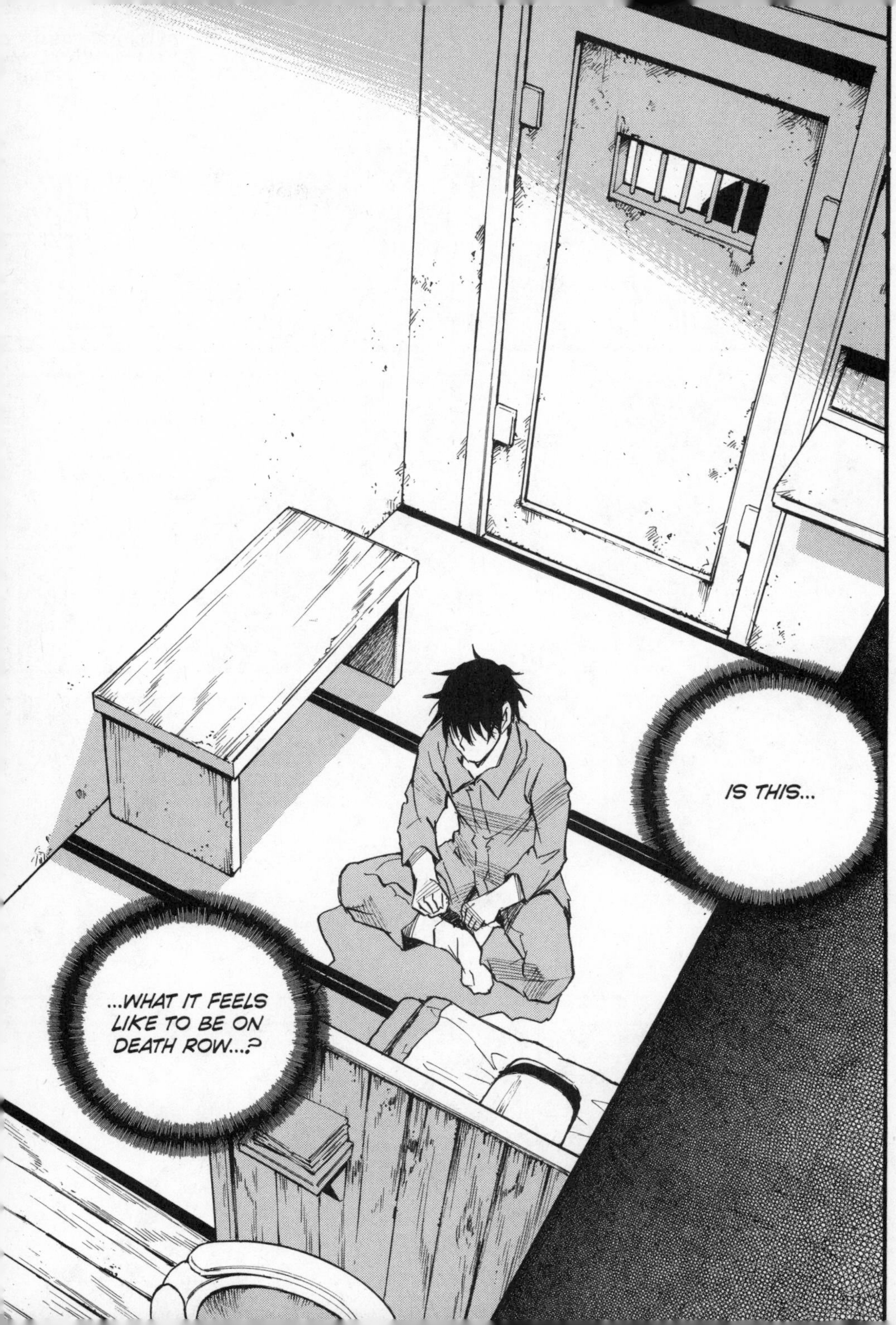
IS THIS...
...WHAT IT FEELS LIKE TO BE ON DEATH ROW...?

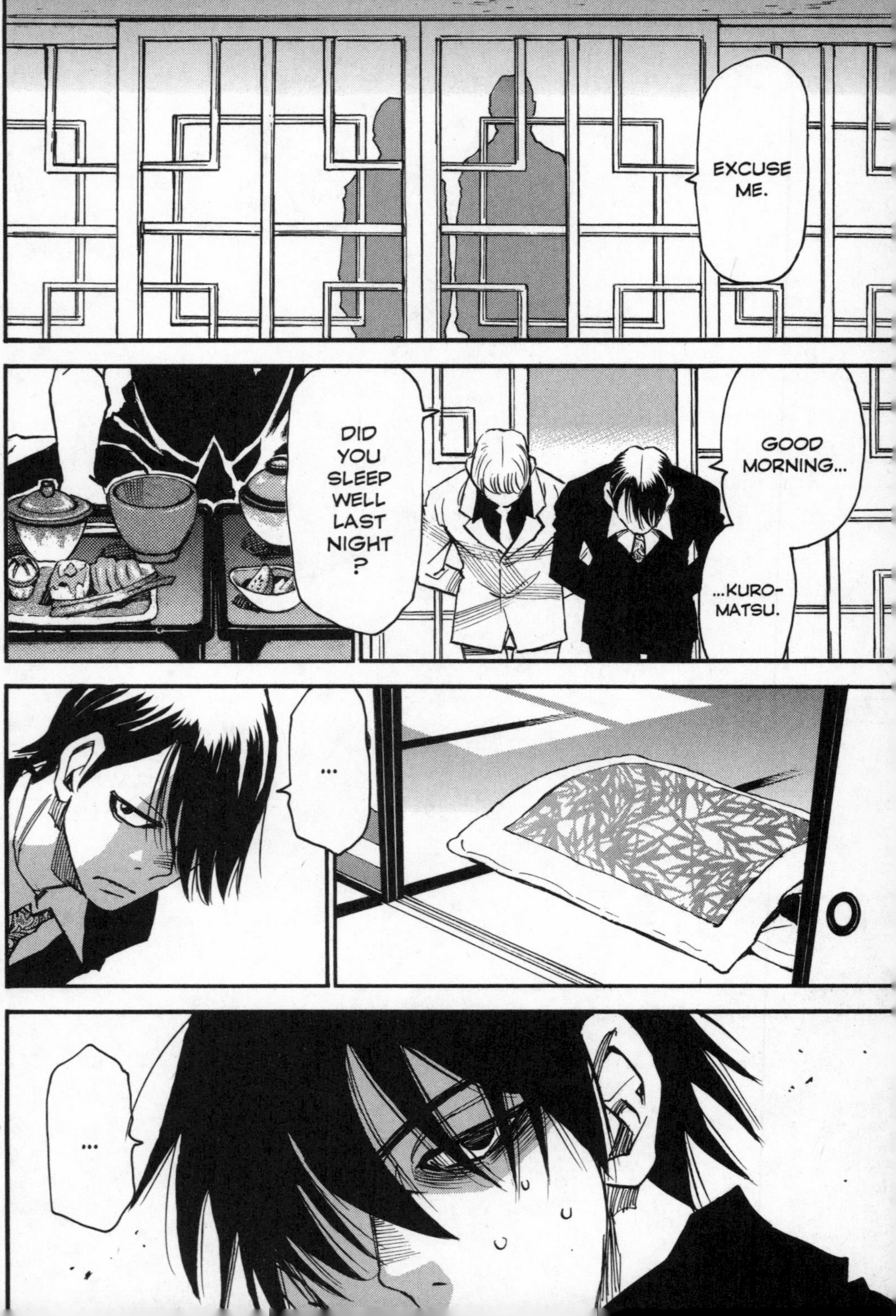
EXCUSE ME.
GOOD MORNING...
...KURO-MATSU.
DID YOU SLEEP WELL LAST NIGHT?
...
...

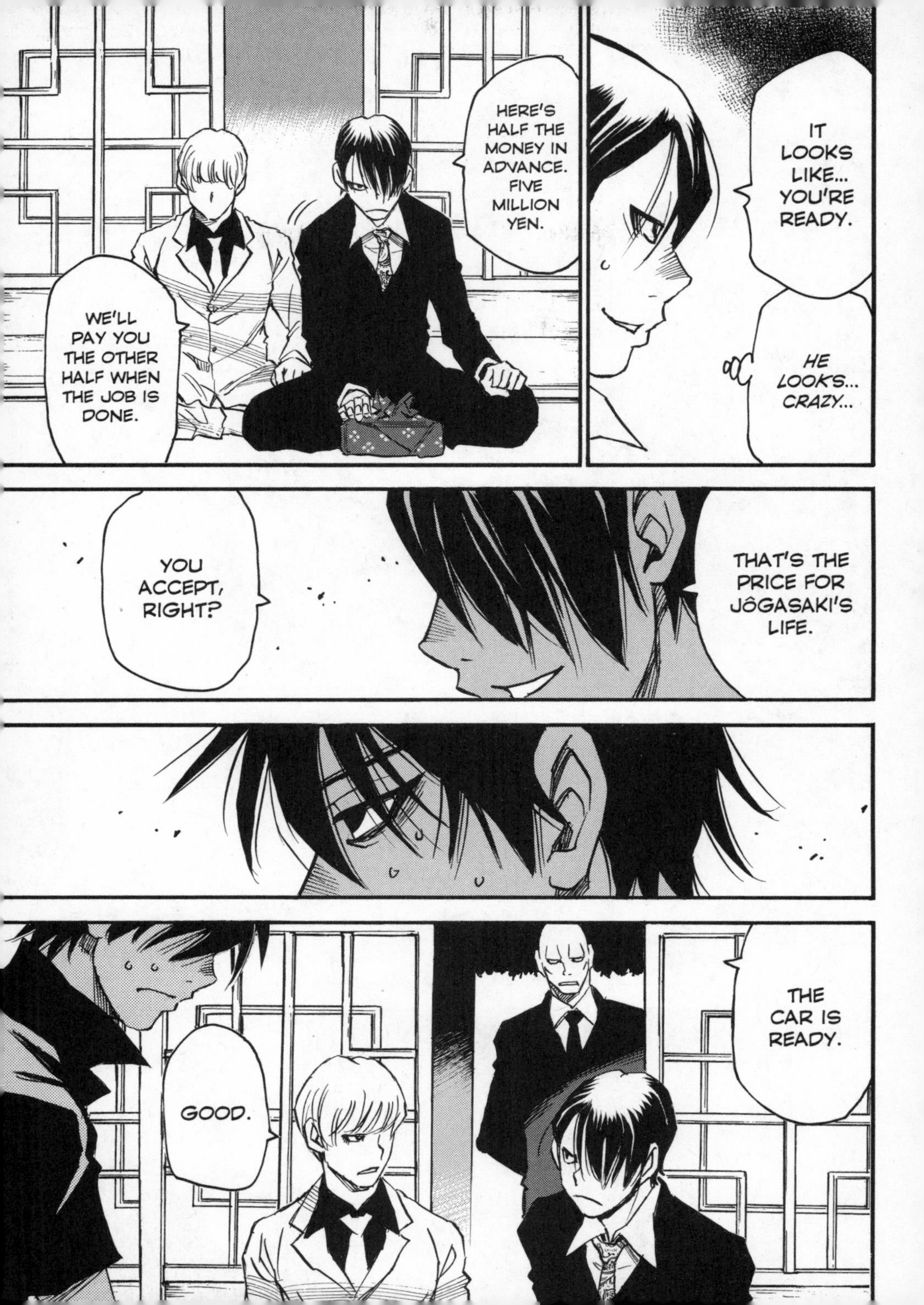
IT LOOKS LIKE... YOU'RE READY.
HE LOOKS... CRAZY...
HERE'S HALF THE MONEY IN ADVANCE. FIVE MILLION YEN.
WE'LL PAY YOU THE OTHER HALF WHEN THE JOB IS DONE.
THAT'S THE PRICE FOR JÔGASAKI'S LIFE.
YOU ACCEPT, RIGHT?
THE CAR IS READY.
GOOD.

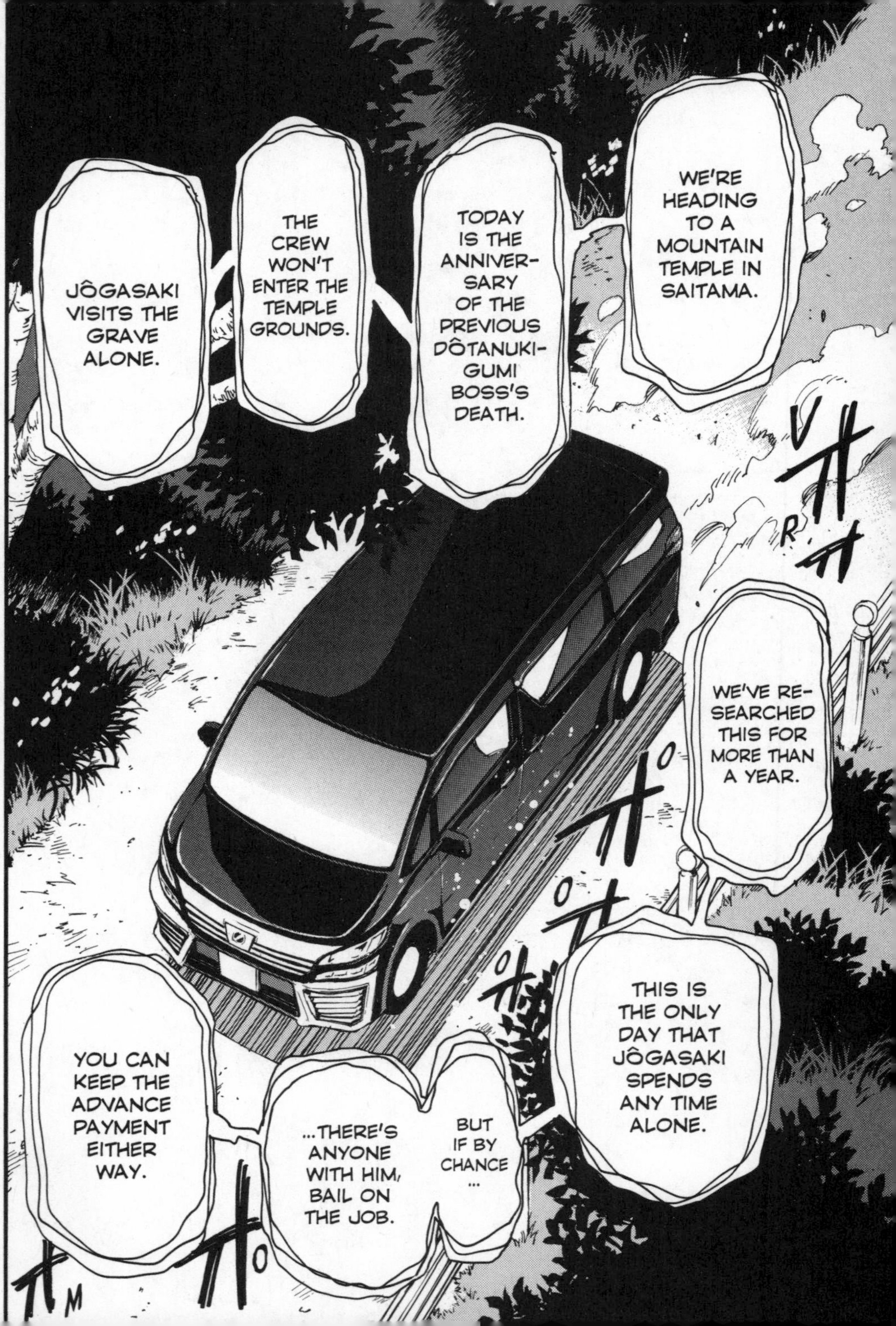

WE'RE HEADING TO A MOUNTAIN TEMPLE IN SAITAMA.
TODAY IS THE ANNIVERSARY OF THE PREVIOUS DÔTANUKI-GUMI BOSS'S DEATH.
THE CREW WON'T ENTER THE TEMPLE GROUNDS.
JÔGASAKI VISITS THE GRAVE ALONE.
WE'VE RESEARCHED THIS FOR MORE THAN A YEAR.
THIS IS THE ONLY DAY THAT JÔGASAKI SPENDS ANY TIME ALONE.
BUT IF BY CHANCE...
...THERE'S ANYONE WITH HIM, BAIL ON THE JOB.
YOU CAN KEEP THE ADVANCE PAYMENT EITHER WAY.

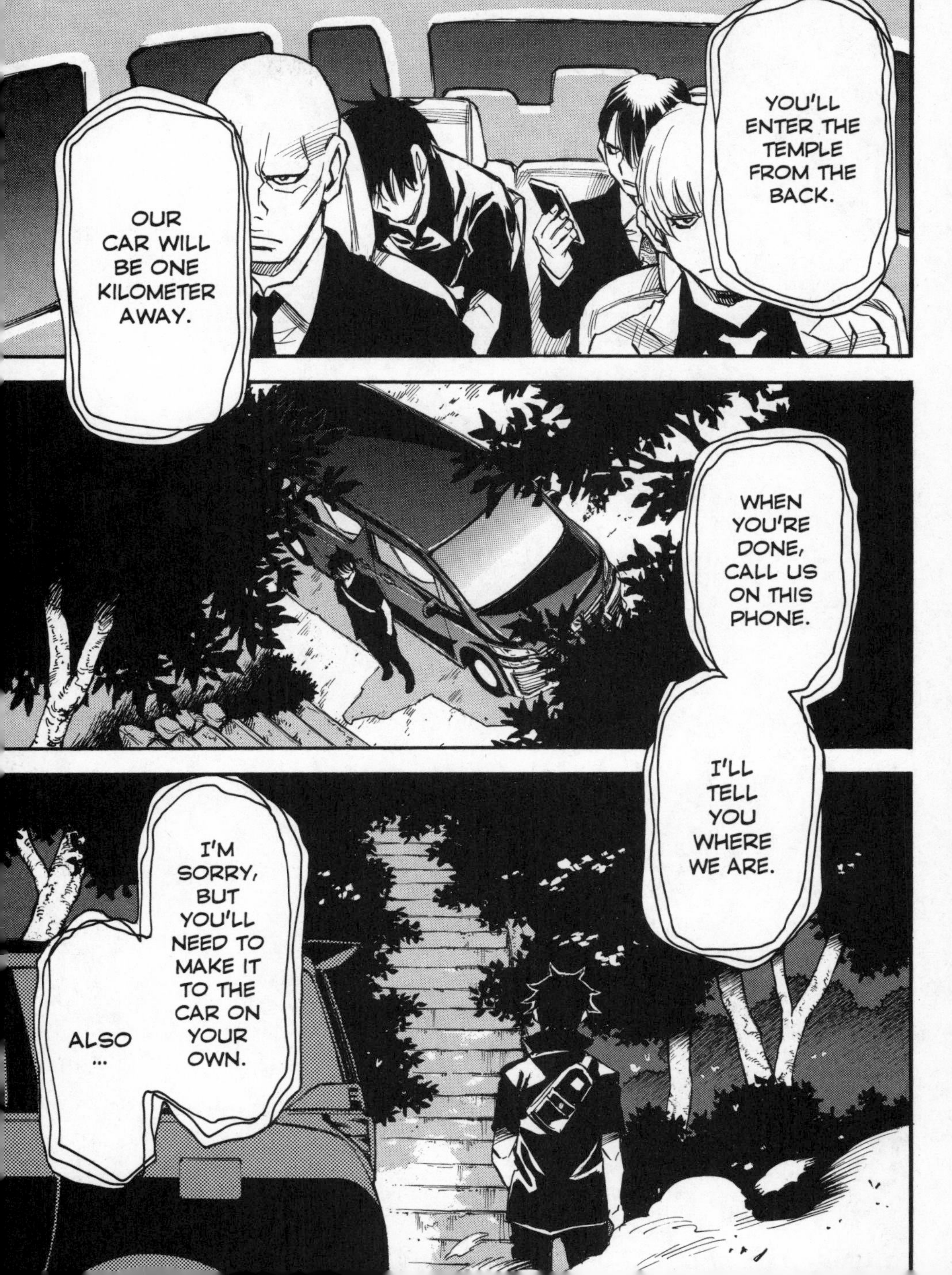
YOU'LL ENTER THE TEMPLE FROM THE BACK.
OUR CAR WILL BE ONE KILOMETER AWAY.
WHEN YOU'RE DONE, CALL US ON THIS PHONE.
I'LL TELL YOU WHERE WE ARE.
I'M SORRY, BUT YOU'LL NEED TO MAKE IT TO THE CAR ON YOUR OWN.
ALSO ...

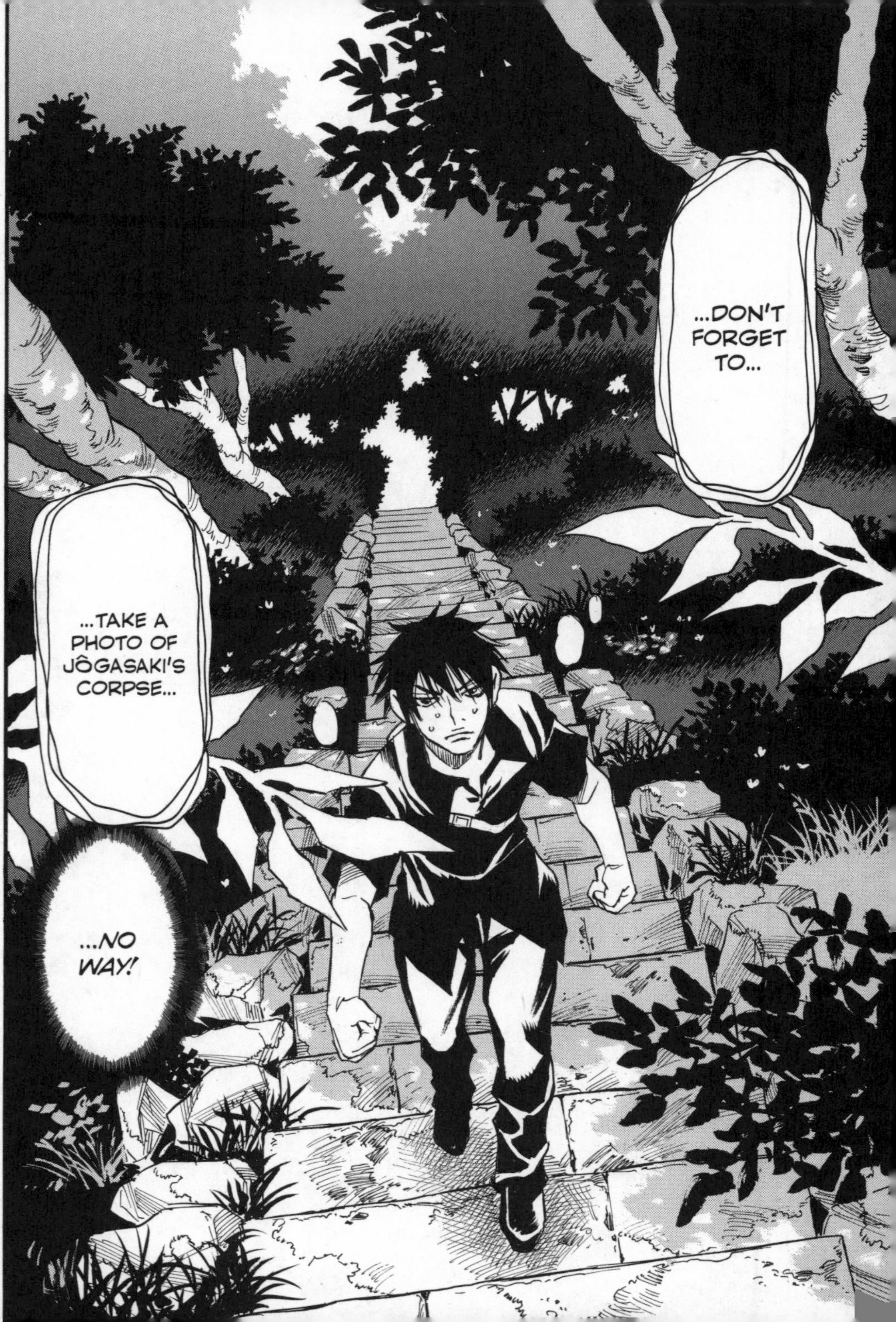
...DON'T FORGET TO...
...TAKE A PHOTO OF JÔGASAKI'S CORPSE...
...NO WAY!

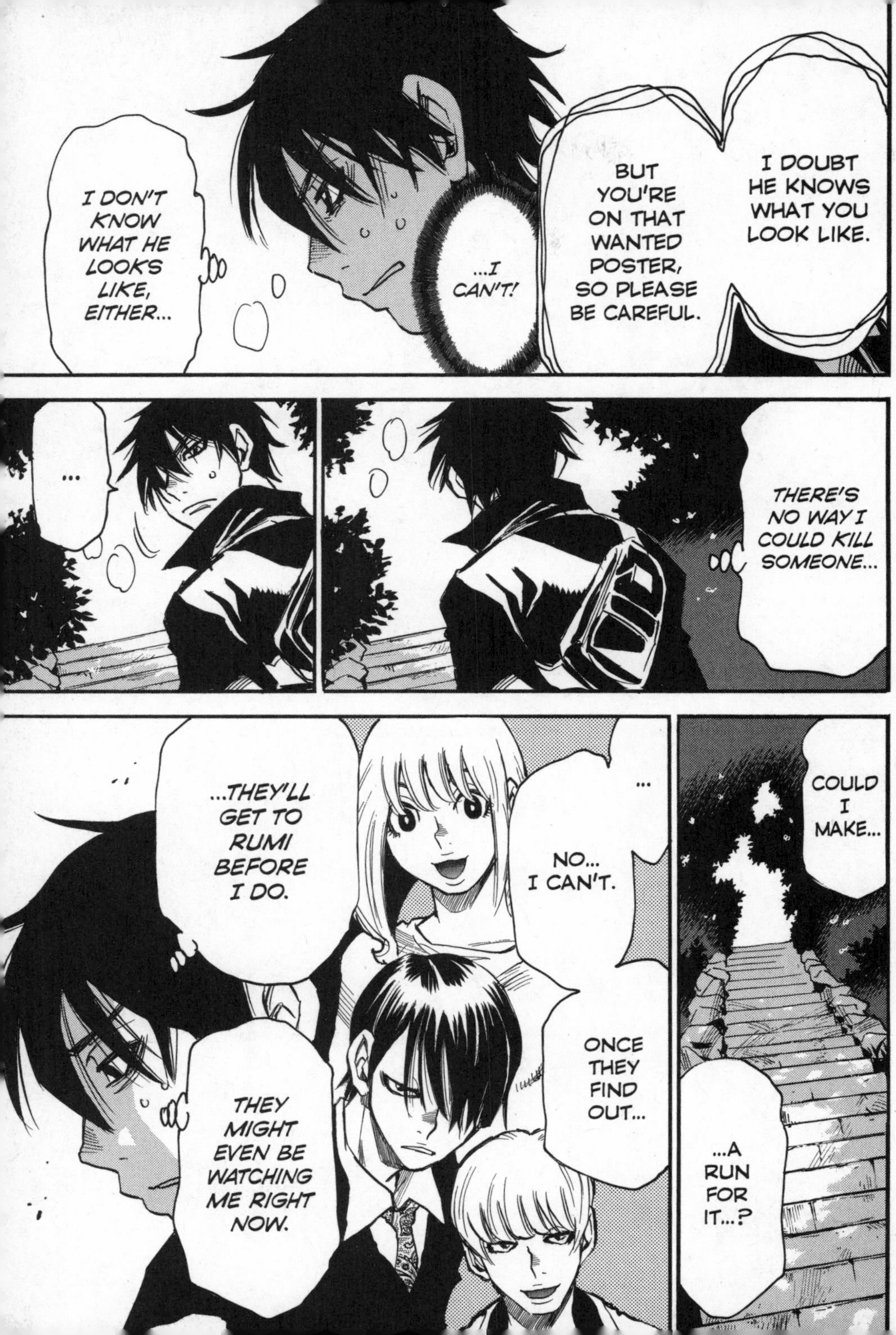
I DOUBT HE KNOWS WHAT YOU LOOK LIKE.
BUT YOU'RE ON THAT WANTED POSTER, SO PLEASE BE CAREFUL.
...I CAN'T!
I DON'T KNOW WHAT HE LOOKS LIKE, EITHER...
THERE'S NO WAY I COULD KILL SOMEONE...
...
COULD I MAKE...
...A RUN FOR IT...?
...
NO... I CAN'T.
ONCE THEY FIND OUT...
...THEY'LL GET TO RUMI BEFORE I DO.
THEY MIGHT EVEN BE WATCHING ME RIGHT NOW.

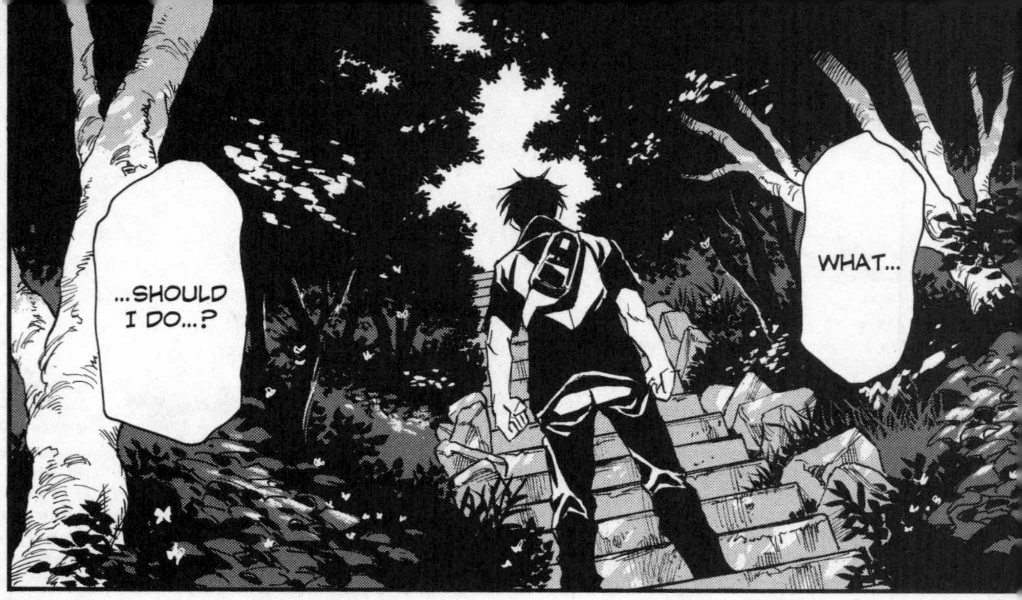

WHAT...
...SHOULD I DO...?

MONK: Heart Sutra **SIGN:** *Jikyōji*

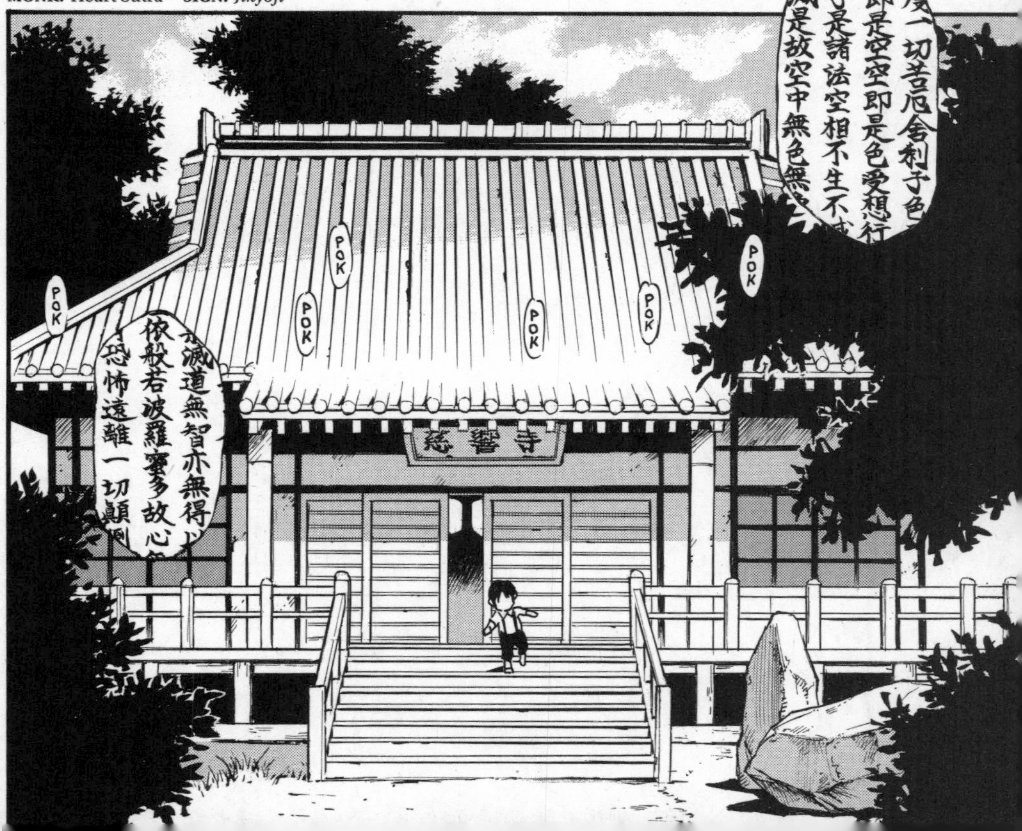

度一切苦厄舍利子色
色即是空空即是色受想行
利子是諸法空相不生不
減是故空中無色無
POK
POK
POK
POK
POK
POK
POK
慈響寺
滅道無智亦無得
依般若波羅蜜多故心
恐怖遠離一切顛倒

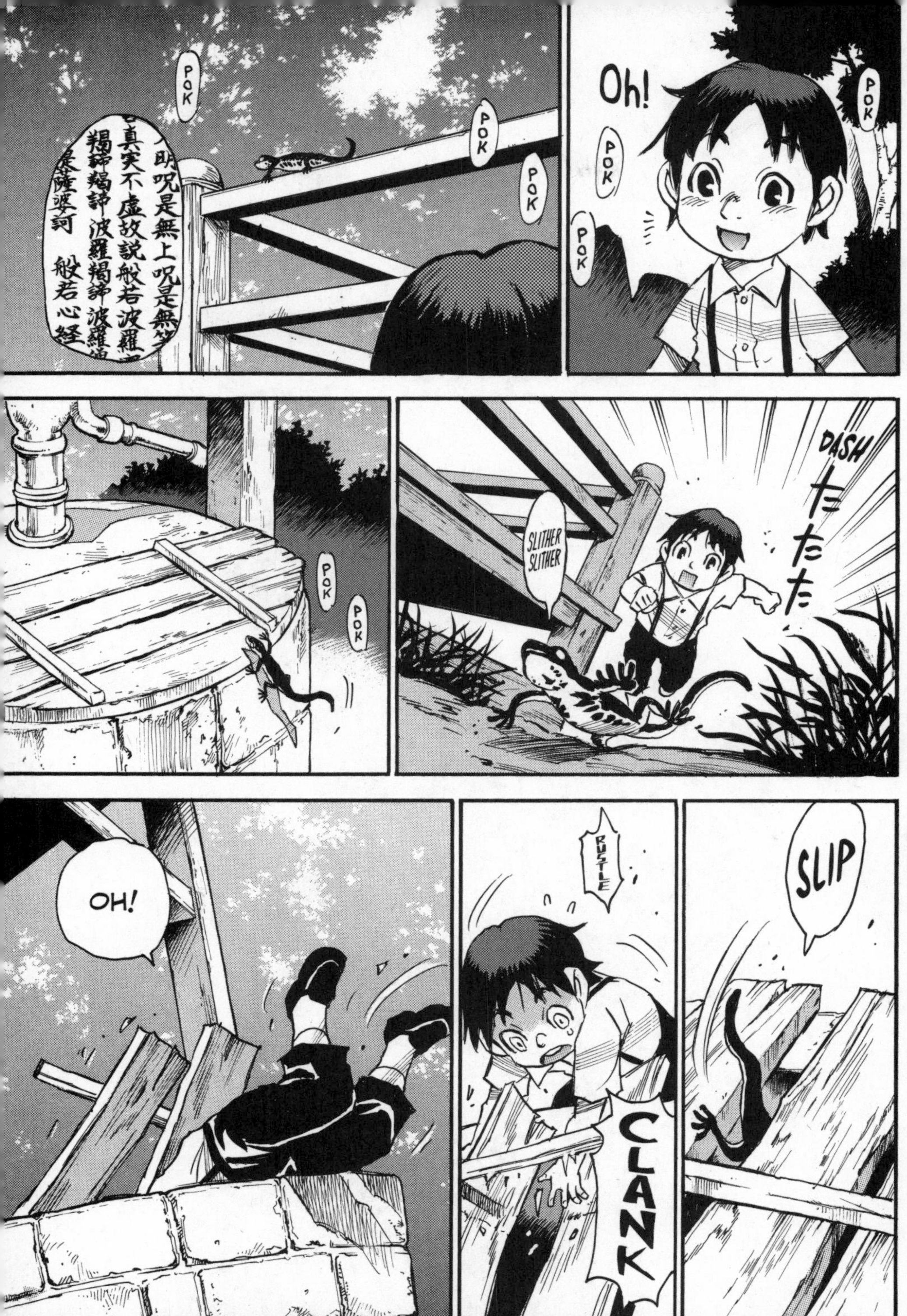

Oh!
POK
POK
POK
POK
POK
POK
POK
呪是無上呪是無
真実不虚故説般若波羅
羯諦羯諦 波羅羯諦 波羅僧
菩薩婆訶 般若心経
DASH
たたた
SLITHER SLITHER
POK
POK
SLIP
RUSTLE
CLANK
OH!

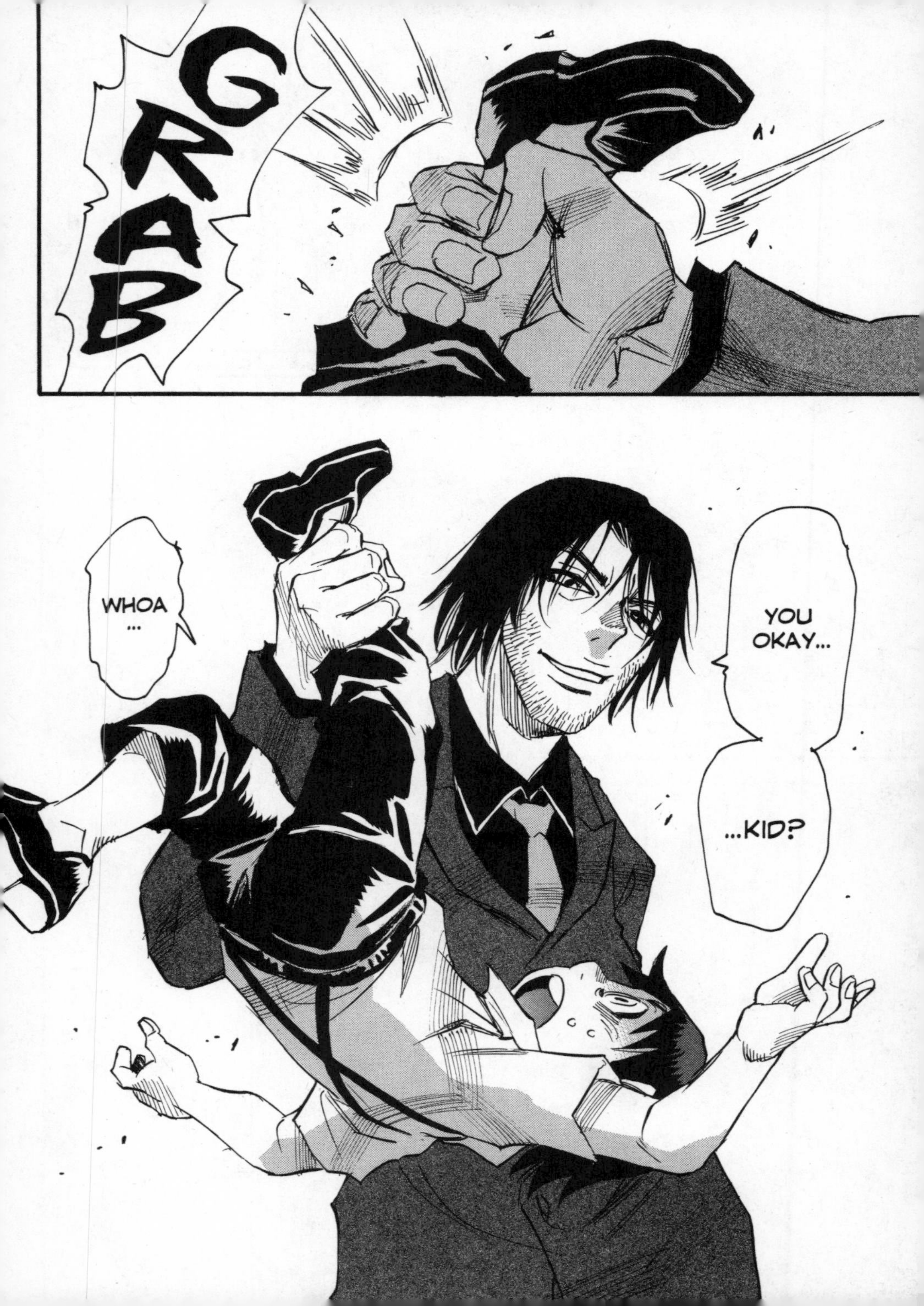
GRAB
YOU OKAY...
...KID?
WHOA ...

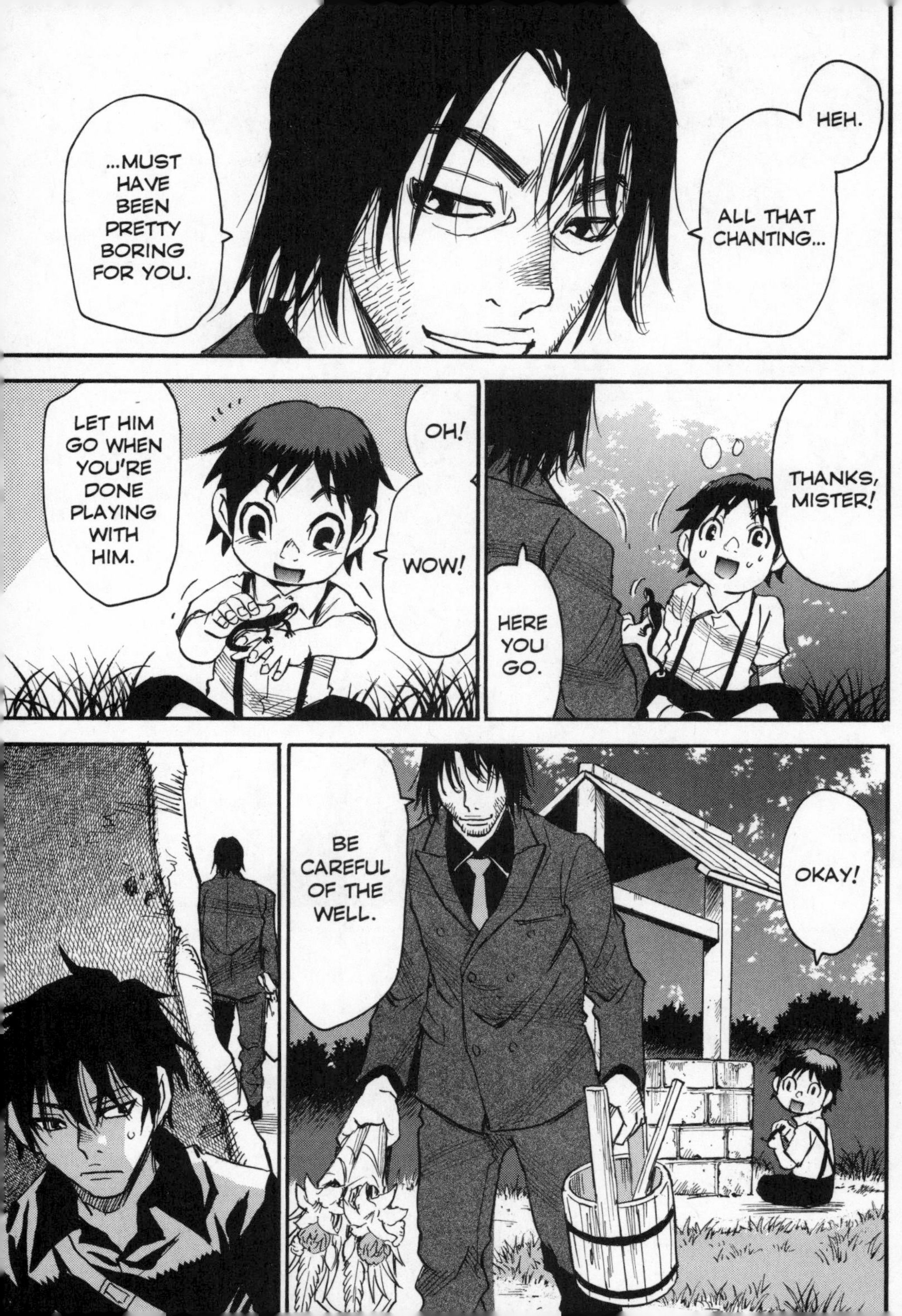
HEH.
ALL THAT CHANTING...
...MUST HAVE BEEN PRETTY BORING FOR YOU.
THANKS, MISTER!
HERE YOU GO.
OH!
WOW!
LET HIM GO WHEN YOU'RE DONE PLAYING WITH HIM.
BE CAREFUL OF THE WELL.
OKAY!

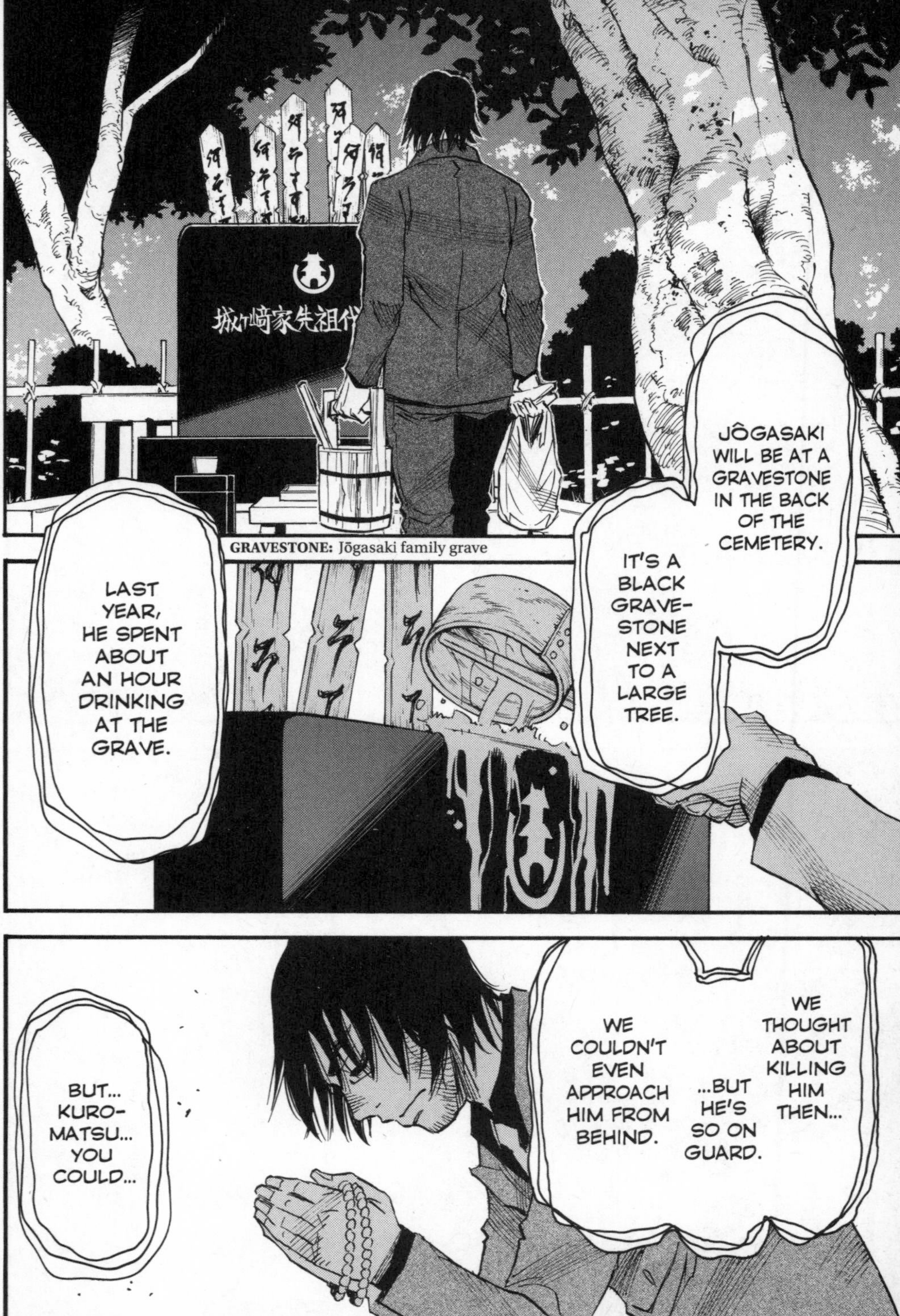
城ヶ崎家先祖代
JÔGASAKI WILL BE AT A GRAVESTONE IN THE BACK OF THE CEMETERY.
GRAVESTONE: Jōgasaki family grave
IT'S A BLACK GRAVE-STONE NEXT TO A LARGE TREE.
LAST YEAR, HE SPENT ABOUT AN HOUR DRINKING AT THE GRAVE.
WE THOUGHT ABOUT KILLING HIM THEN...
...BUT HE'S SO ON GUARD.
WE COULDN'T EVEN APPROACH HIM FROM BEHIND.
BUT... KURO-MATSU... YOU COULD...

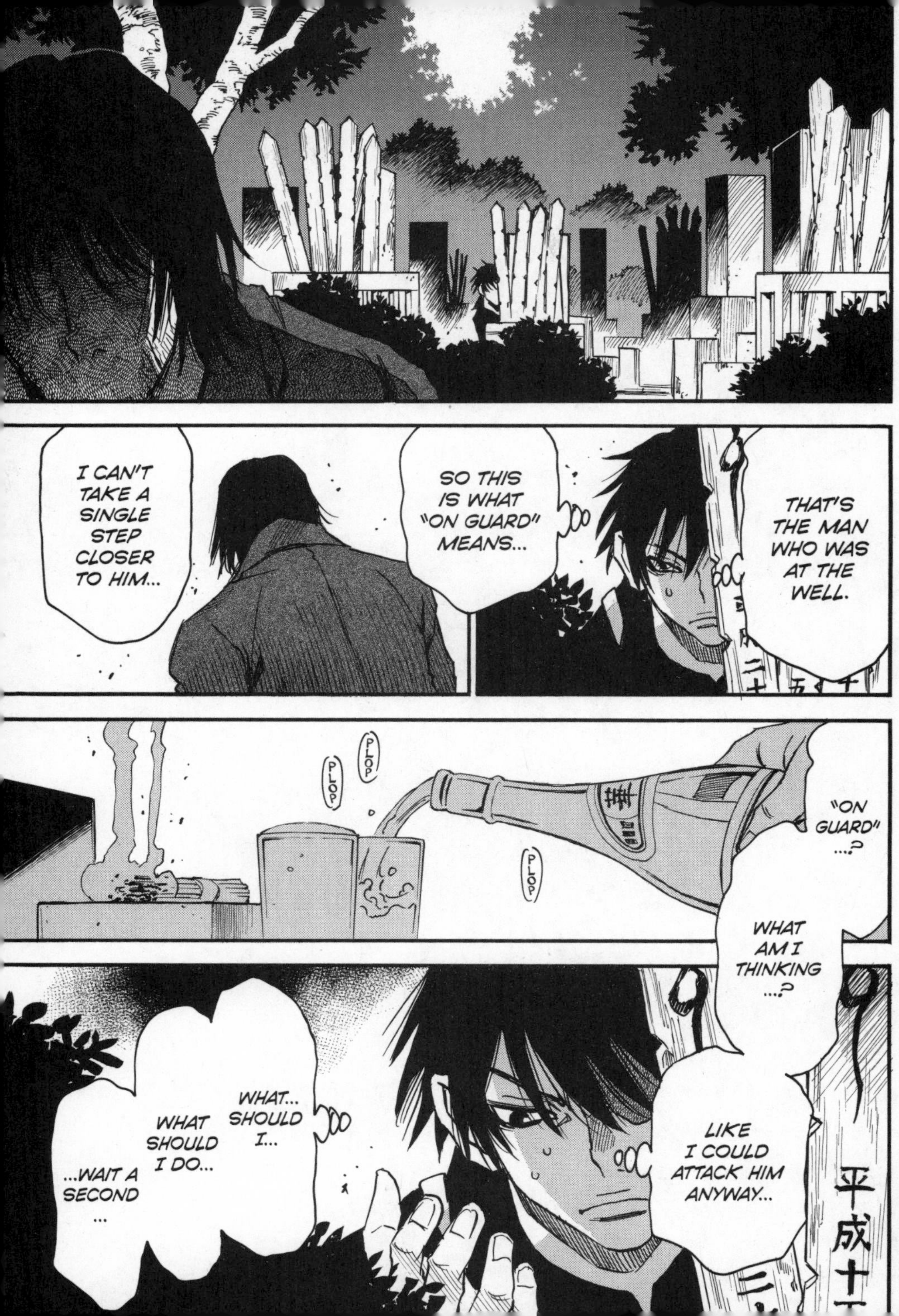
THAT'S THE MAN WHO WAS AT THE WELL.
SO THIS IS WHAT "ON GUARD" MEANS...
I CAN'T TAKE A SINGLE STEP CLOSER TO HIM...
"ON GUARD" ...?
PLOP
PLOP
PLOP
WHAT AM I THINKING ...?
平成十
LIKE I COULD ATTACK HIM ANYWAY...
WHAT... SHOULD I...
WHAT SHOULD I DO...
...WAIT A SECOND ...

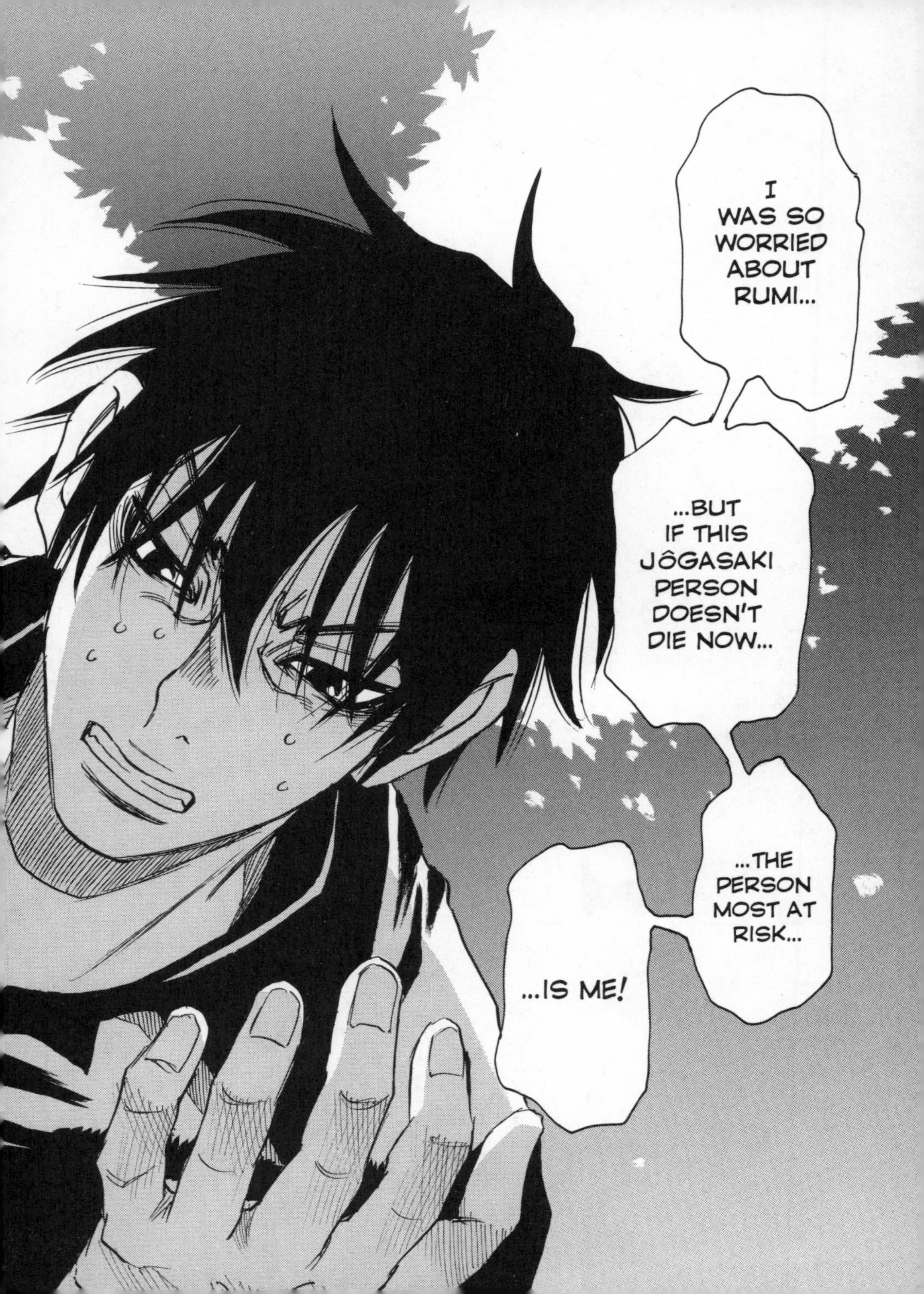
I WAS SO WORRIED ABOUT RUMI...
...BUT IF THIS JÔGASAKI PERSON DOESN'T DIE NOW...
...THE PERSON MOST AT RISK...
...IS ME!

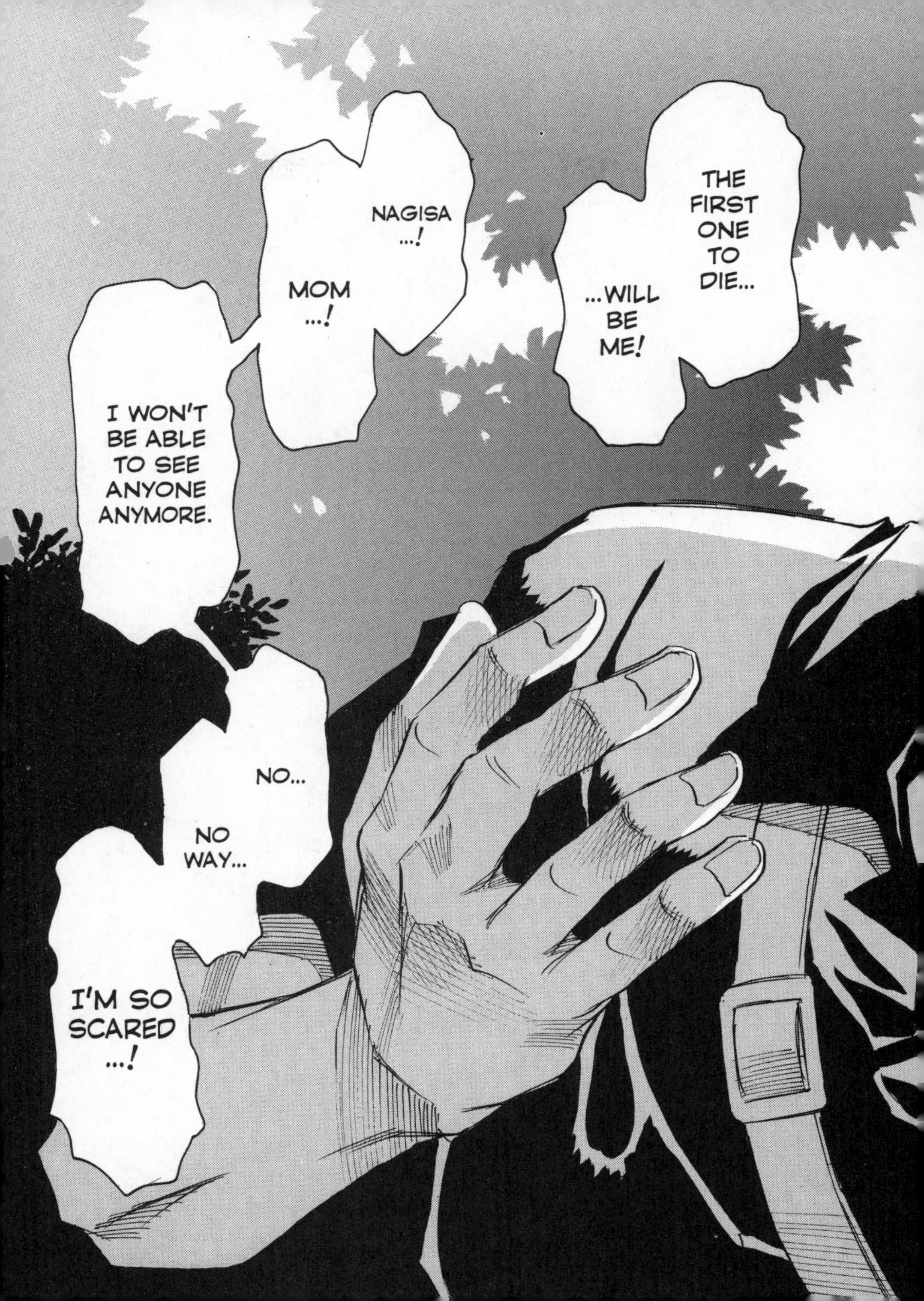
THE FIRST ONE TO DIE... ...WILL BE ME!
NAGISA ...! MOM ...!
I WON'T BE ABLE TO SEE ANYONE ANYMORE.
NO... NO WAY... I'M SO SCARED ...!

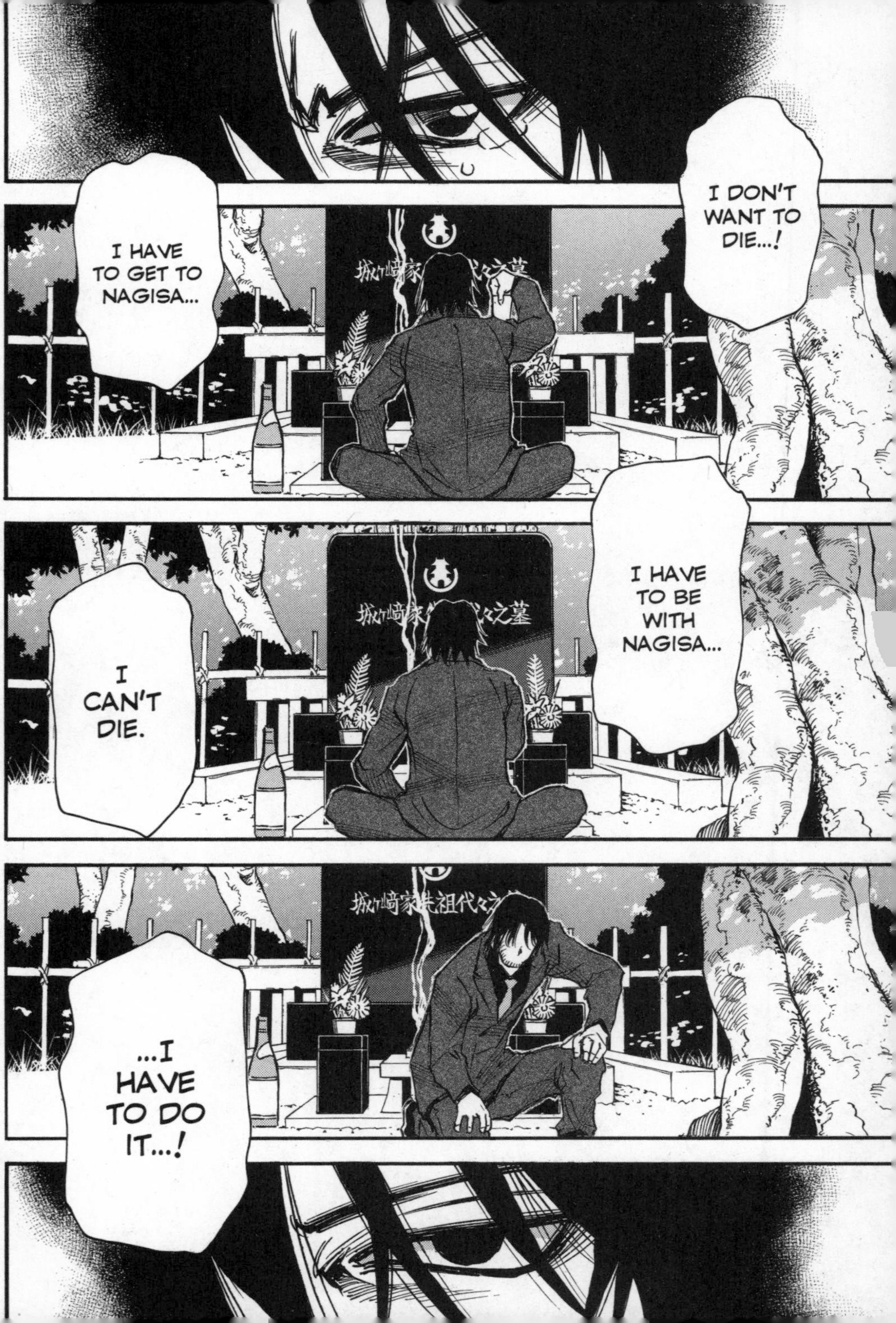
I DON'T WANT TO DIE...!
I HAVE TO GET TO NAGISA...
I HAVE TO BE WITH NAGISA...
I CAN'T DIE.
...I HAVE TO DO IT...!

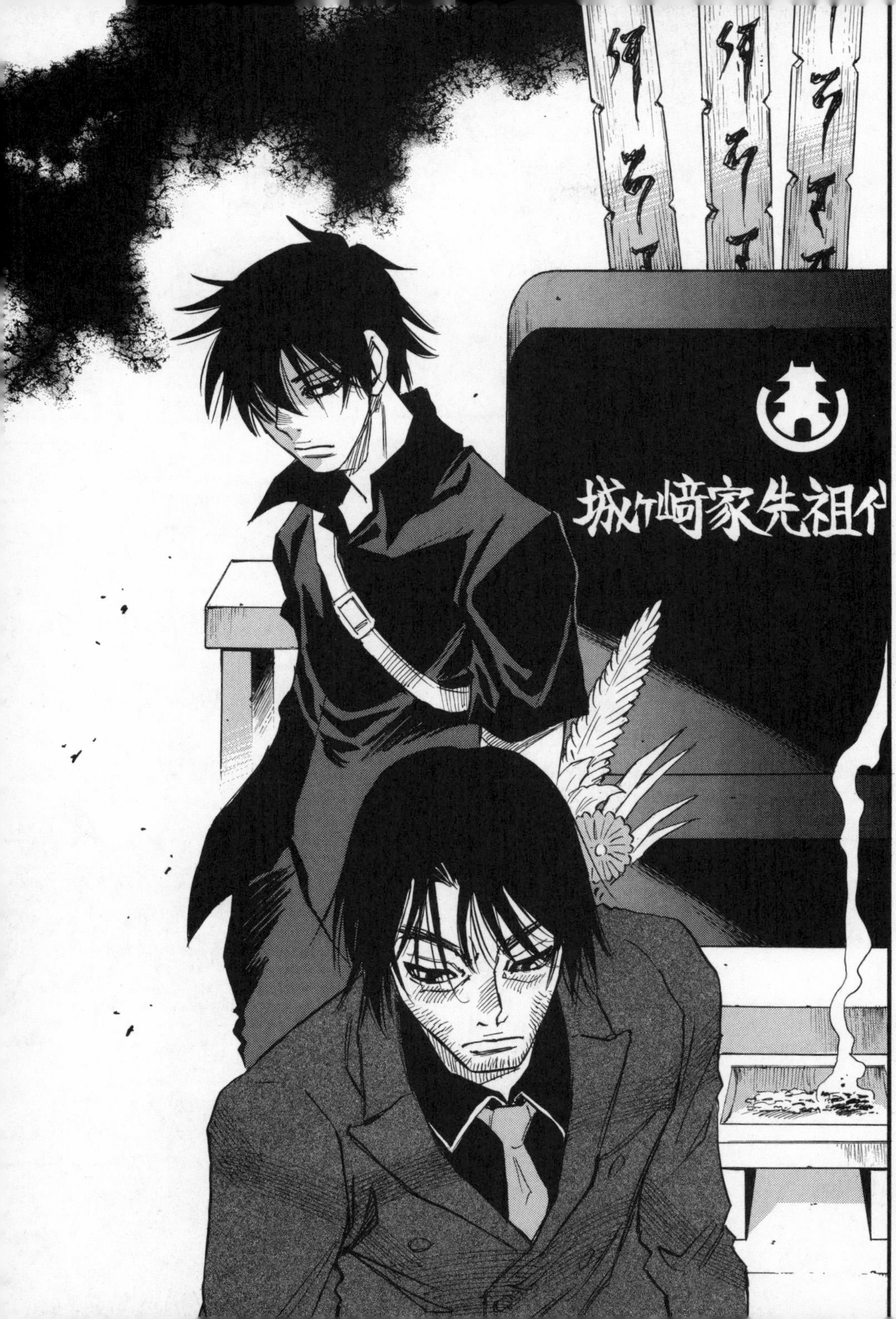
城ケ崎家先祖代

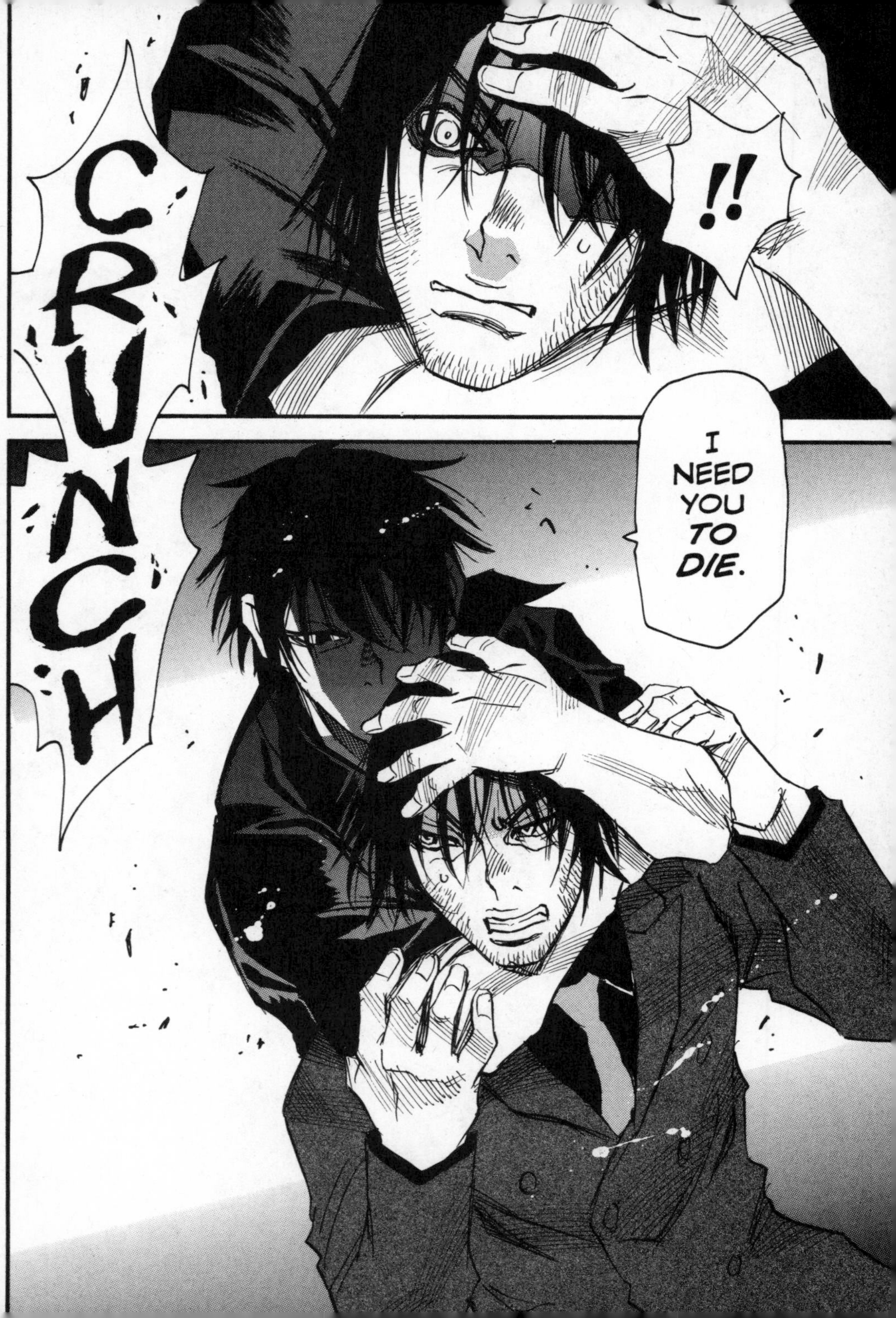
!!
CRUNCH
I NEED YOU TO DIE.

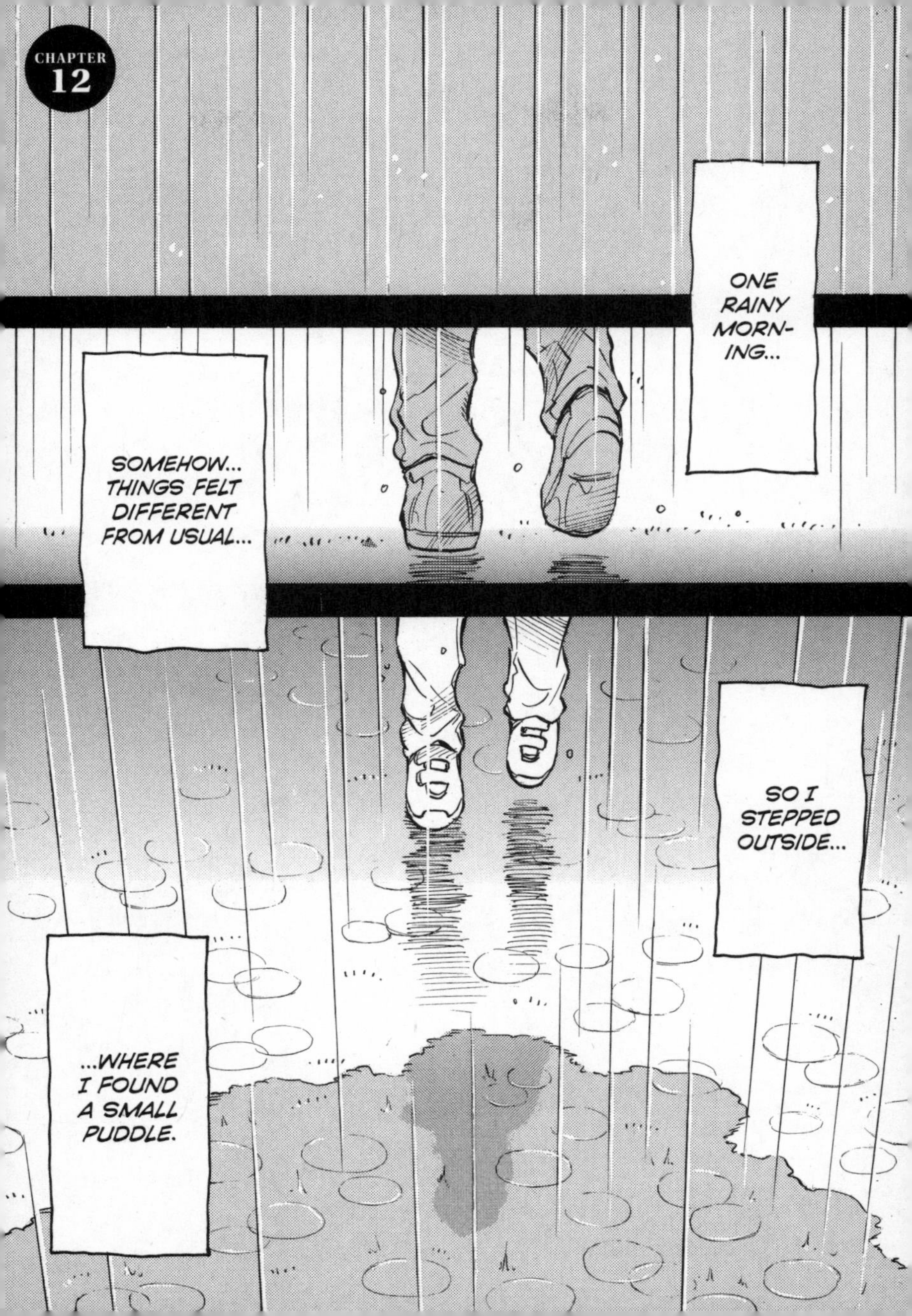
CHAPTER 12
ONE RAINY MORNING...
SOMEHOW... THINGS FELT DIFFERENT FROM USUAL...
SO I STEPPED OUTSIDE...
...WHERE I FOUND A SMALL PUDDLE.

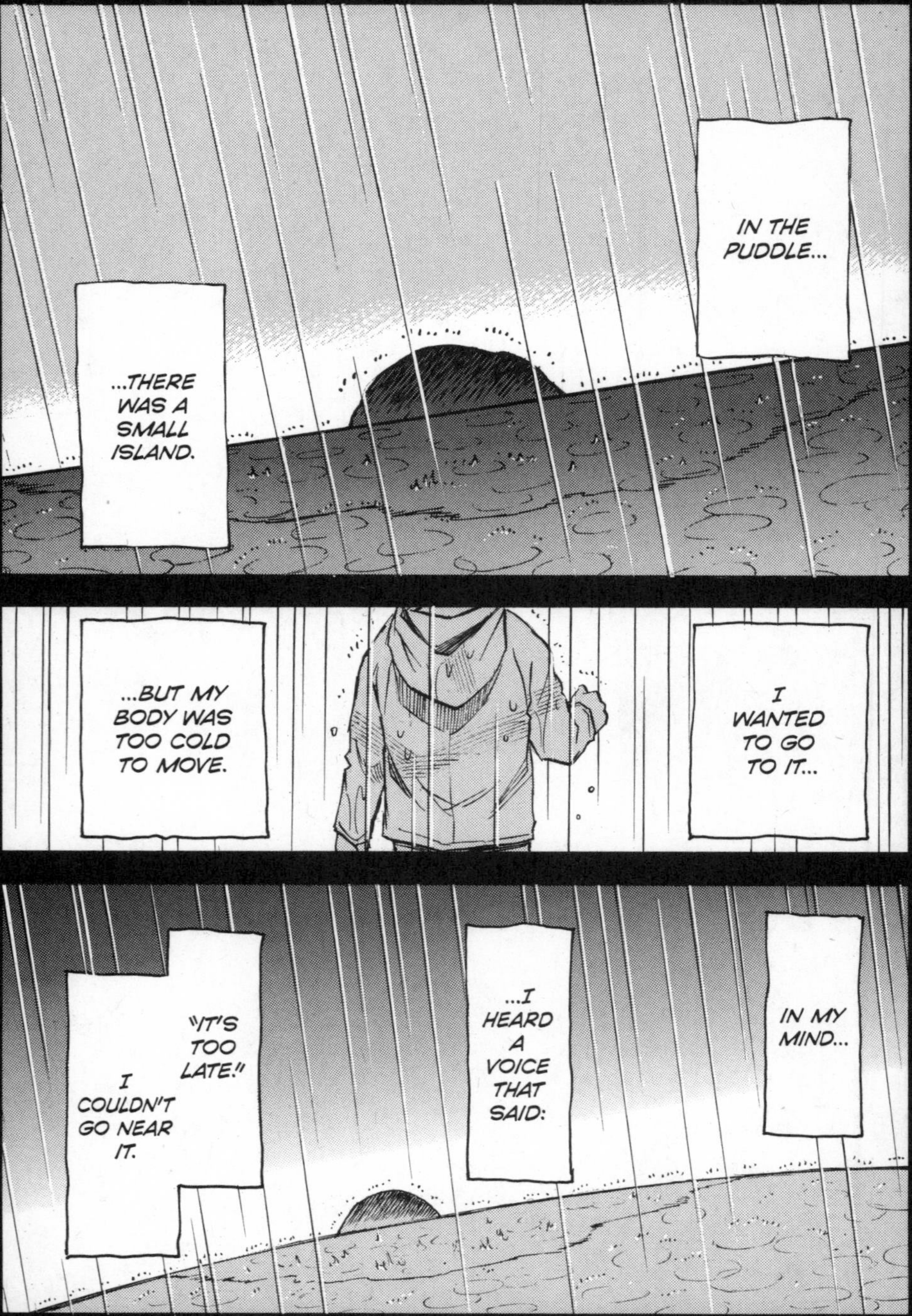

IN THE PUDDLE...
...THERE WAS A SMALL ISLAND.
I WANTED TO GO TO IT...
...BUT MY BODY WAS TOO COLD TO MOVE.
IN MY MIND...
...I HEARD A VOICE THAT SAID:
"IT'S TOO LATE."
I COULDN'T GO NEAR IT.

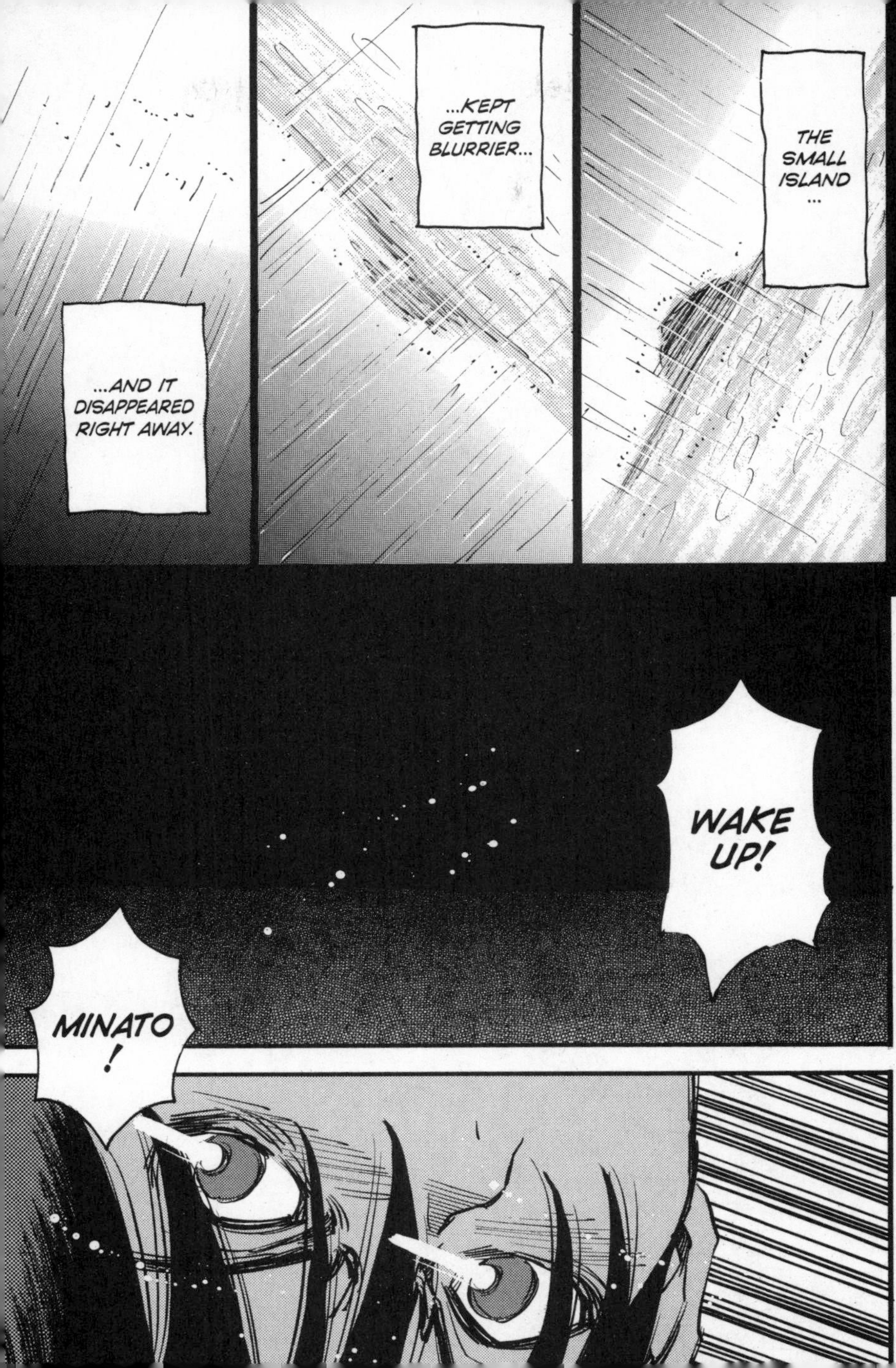
THE SMALL ISLAND ...
...KEPT GETTING BLURRIER...
...AND IT DISAPPEARED RIGHT AWAY.
WAKE UP!
MINATO!

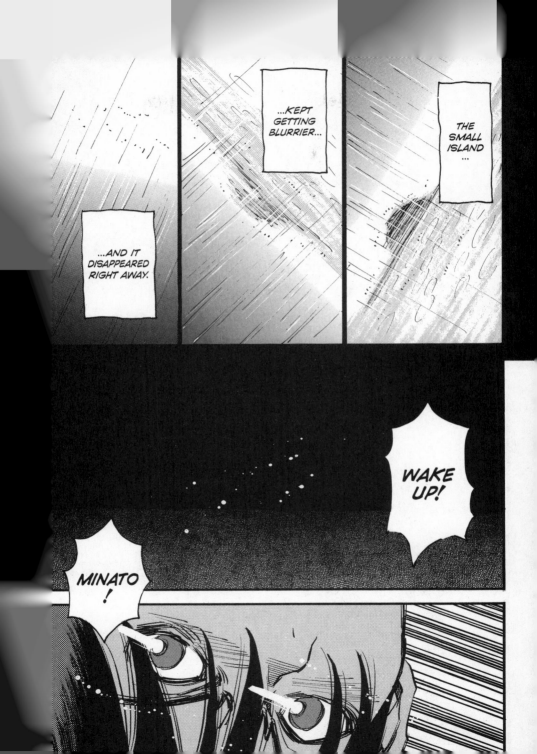

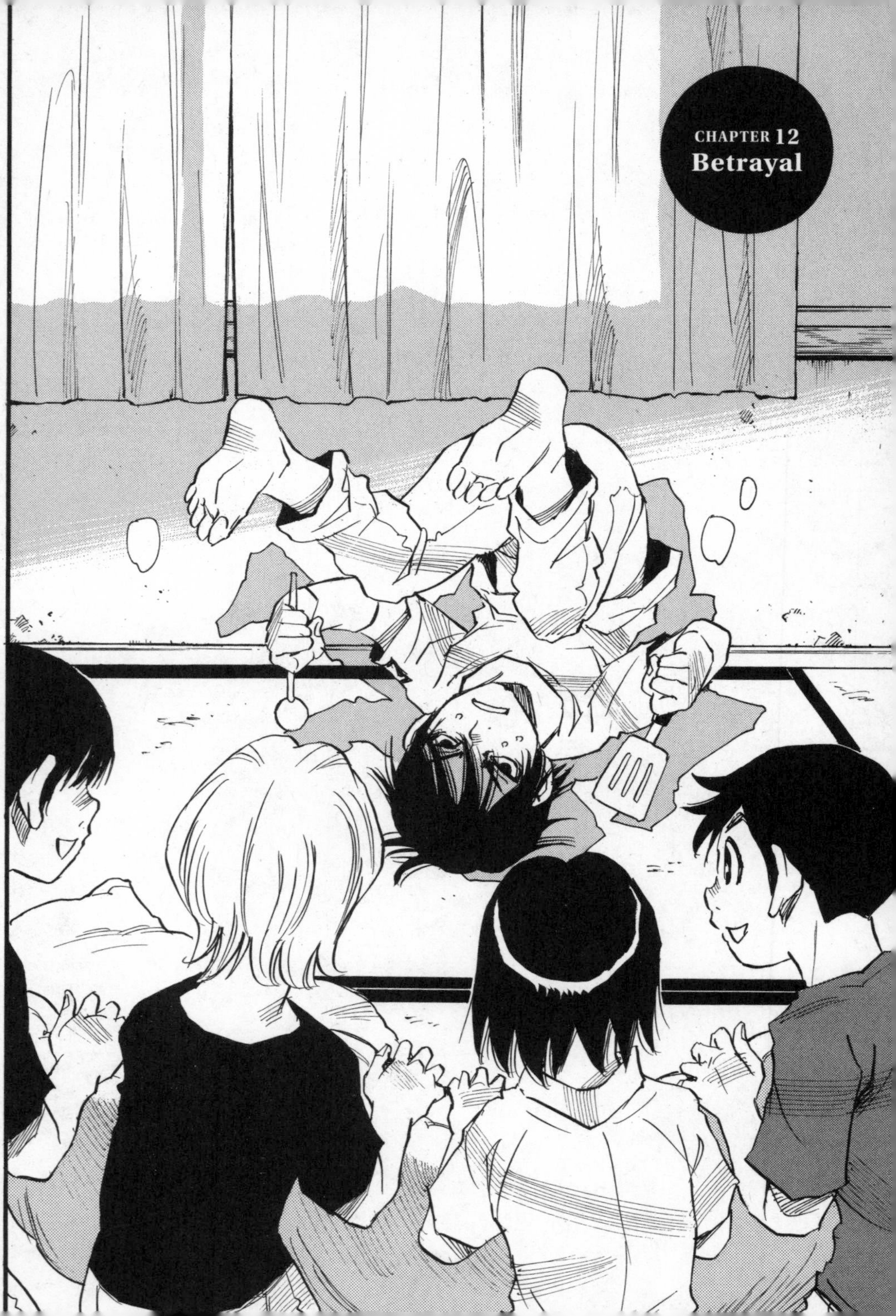
CHAPTER 12
Betrayal

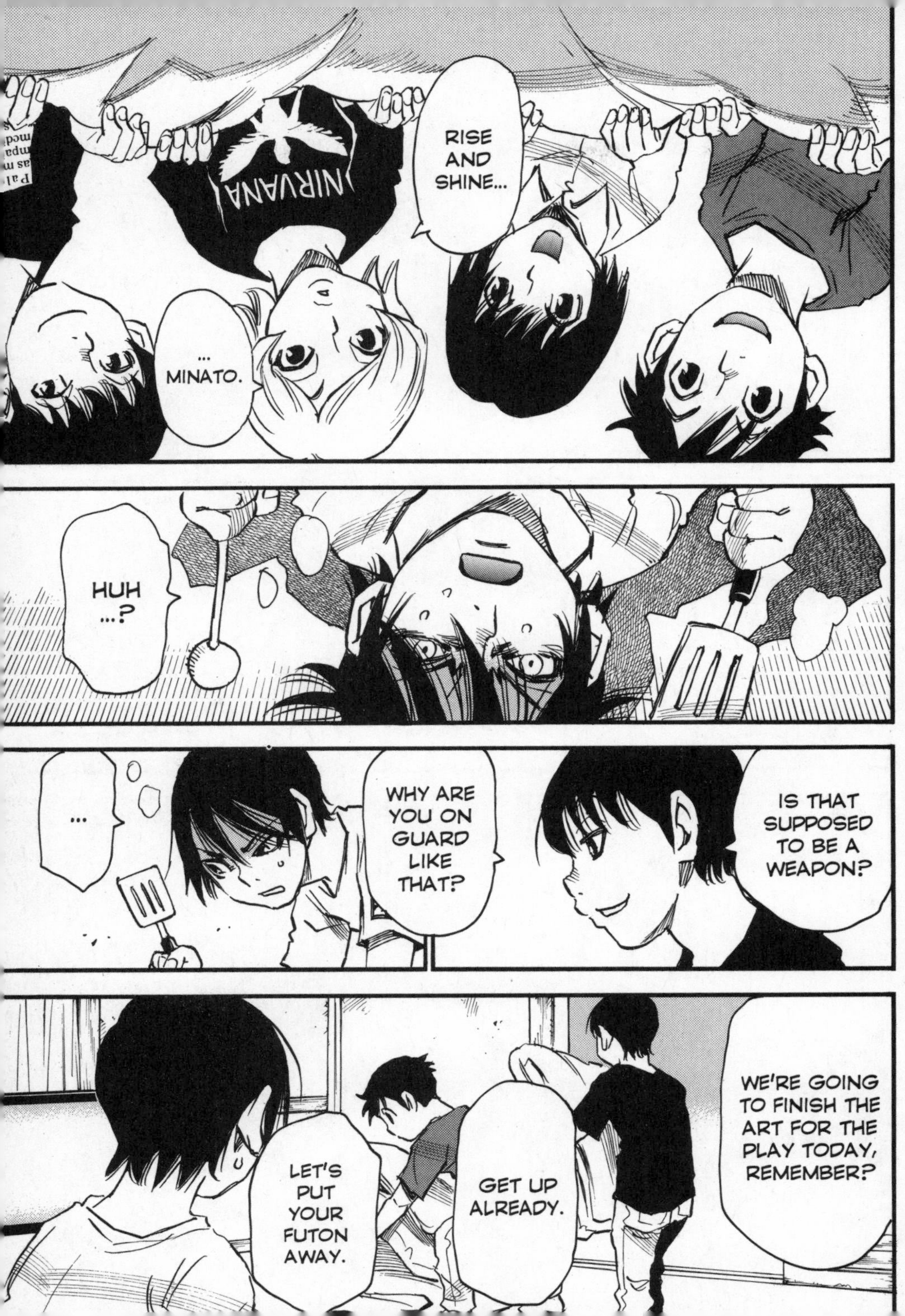
RISE AND SHINE...
... MINATO.
HUH ...?
IS THAT SUPPOSED TO BE A WEAPON?
WHY ARE YOU ON GUARD LIKE THAT?
...
WE'RE GOING TO FINISH THE ART FOR THE PLAY TODAY, REMEMBER?
GET UP ALREADY.
LET'S PUT YOUR FUTON AWAY.

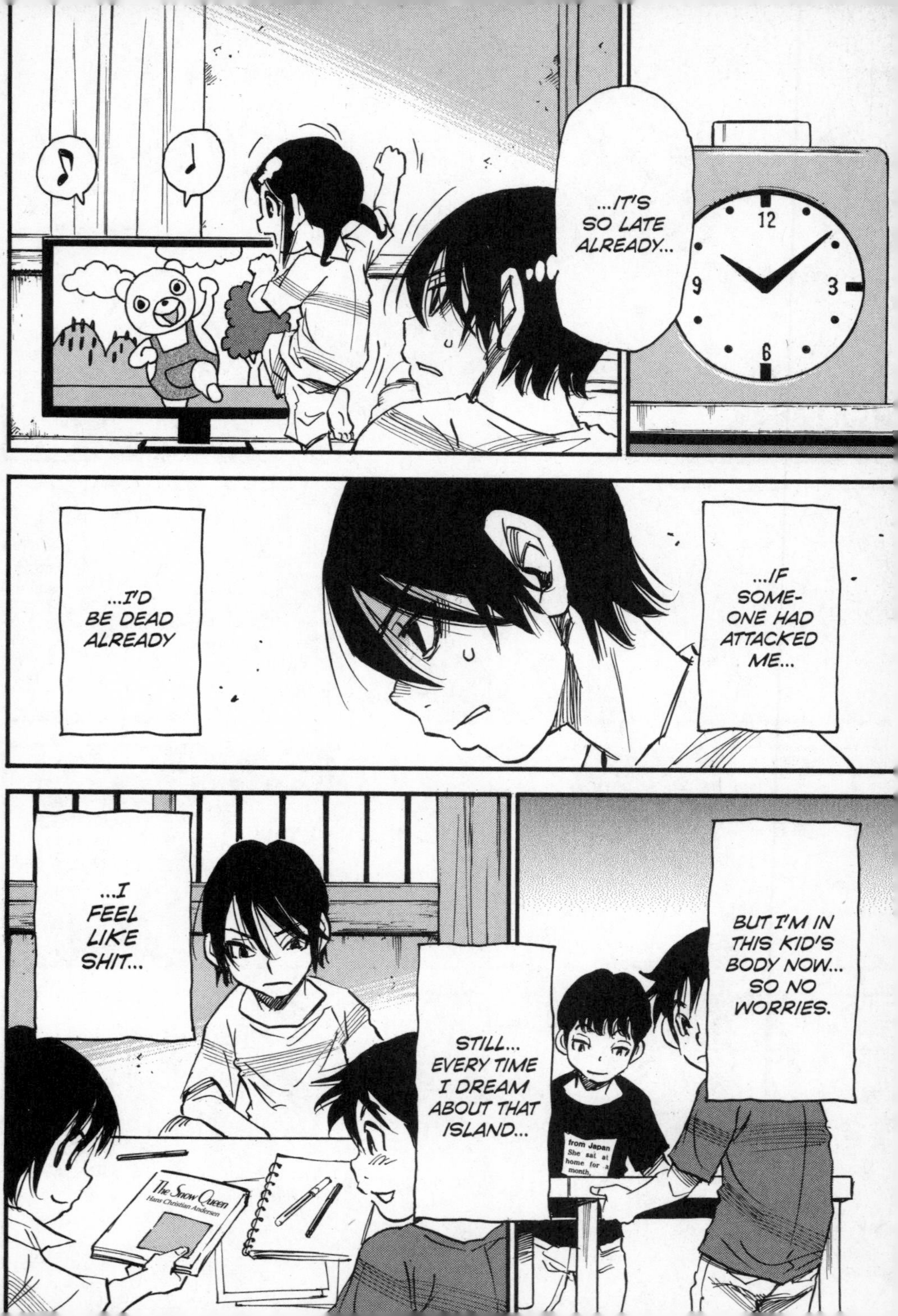
...IT'S SO LATE ALREADY...
...IF SOMEONE HAD ATTACKED ME...
...I'D BE DEAD ALREADY
BUT I'M IN THIS KID'S BODY NOW... SO NO WORRIES.
from Japan She sat at home for a month.
STILL... EVERY TIME I DREAM ABOUT THAT ISLAND...
...I FEEL LIKE SHIT...
The Snow Queen Hans Christian Andersen

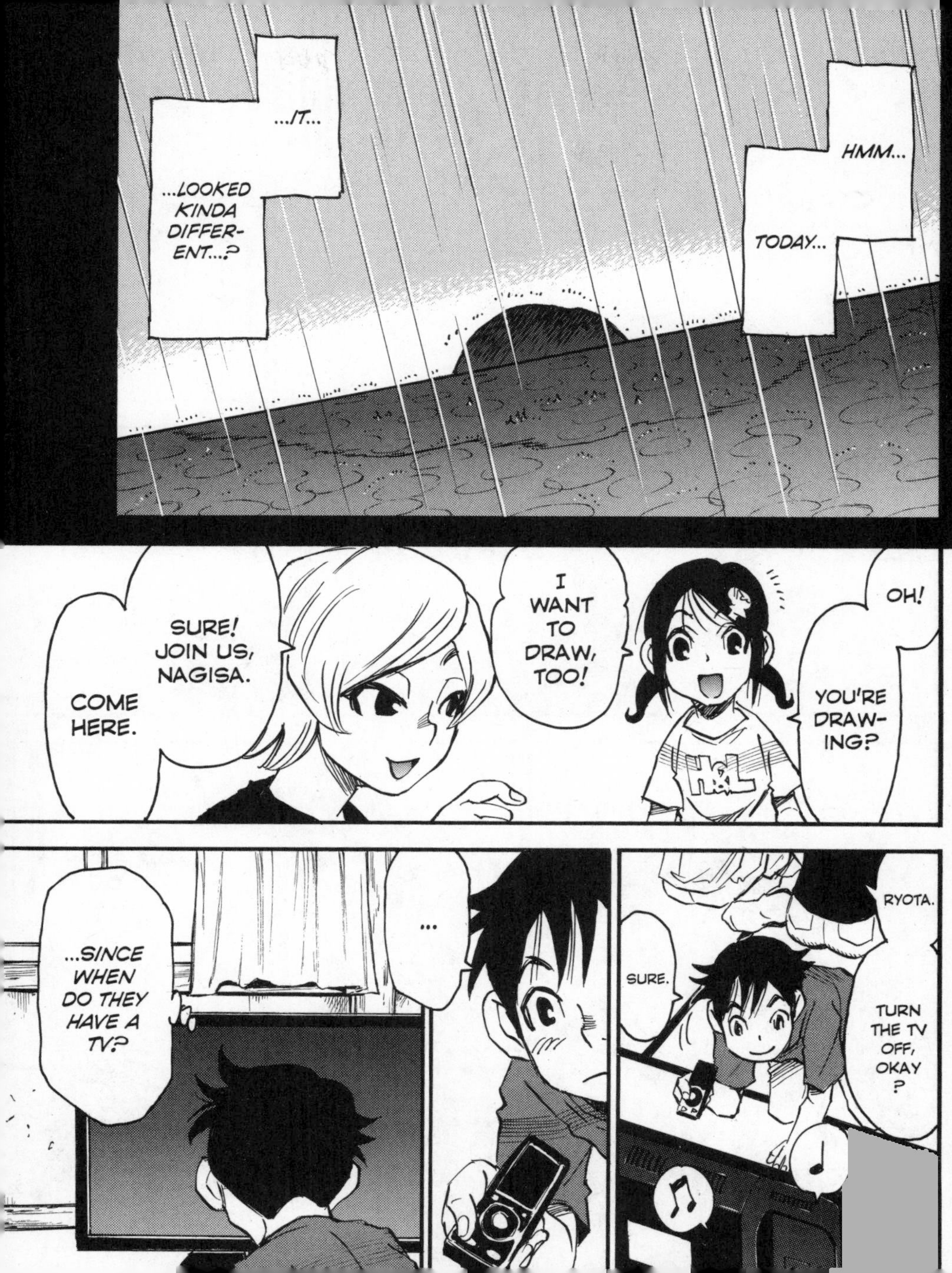
HMM...
TODAY...
...IT...
...LOOKED KINDA DIFFERENT...?
OH!
YOU'RE DRAWING?
I WANT TO DRAW, TOO!
SURE! JOIN US, NAGISA.
COME HERE.
RYOTA.
TURN THE TV OFF, OKAY?
SURE.
...
...SINCE WHEN DO THEY HAVE A TV?

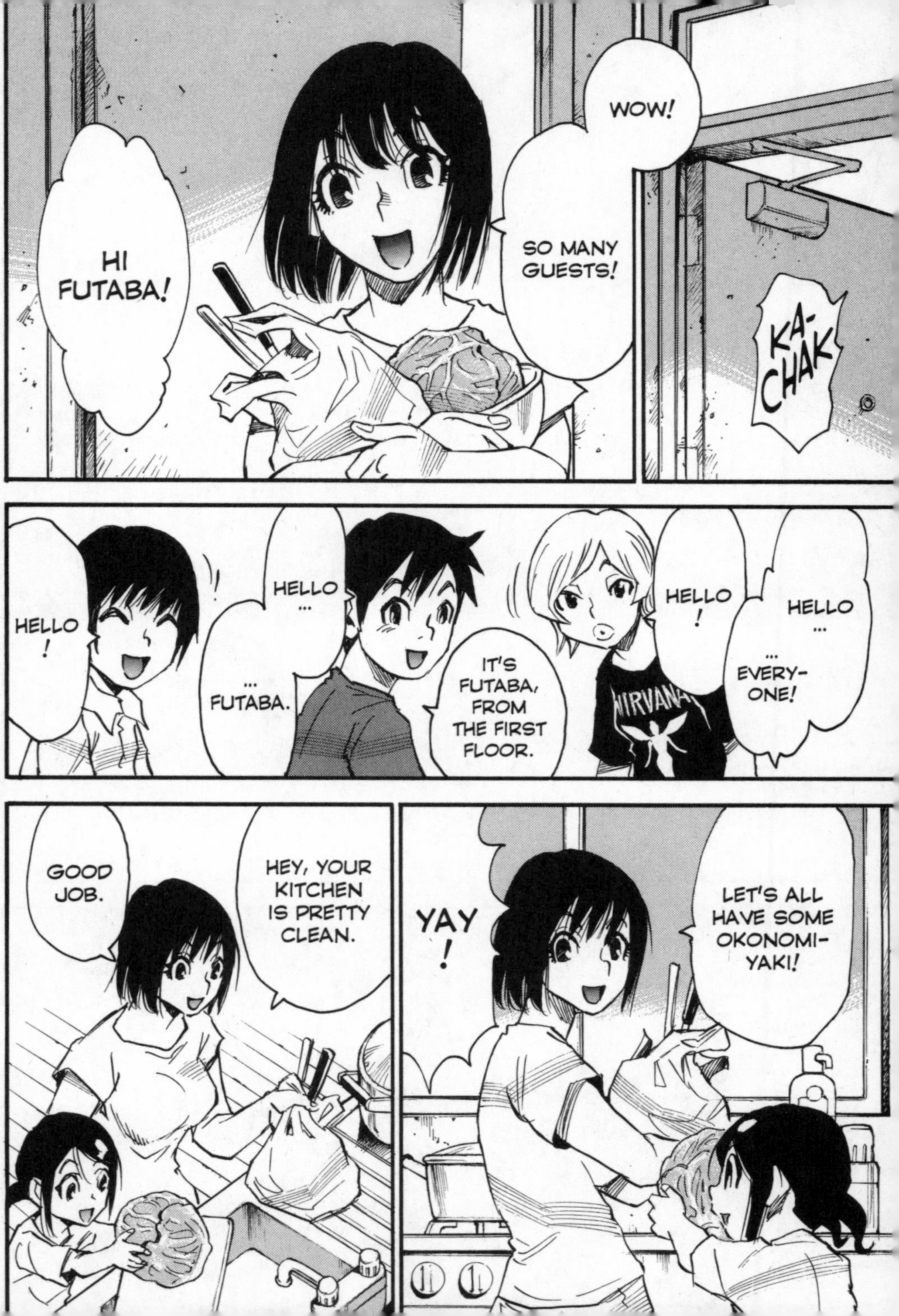
KA-CHAK
WOW!
SO MANY GUESTS!
HI FUTABA!
HELLO ... ... EVERY-ONE!
HELLO !
IT'S FUTABA, FROM THE FIRST FLOOR.
HELLO ... ... FUTABA.
HELLO !
LET'S ALL HAVE SOME OKONOMI-YAKI!
YAY !
HEY, YOUR KITCHEN IS PRETTY CLEAN.
GOOD JOB.

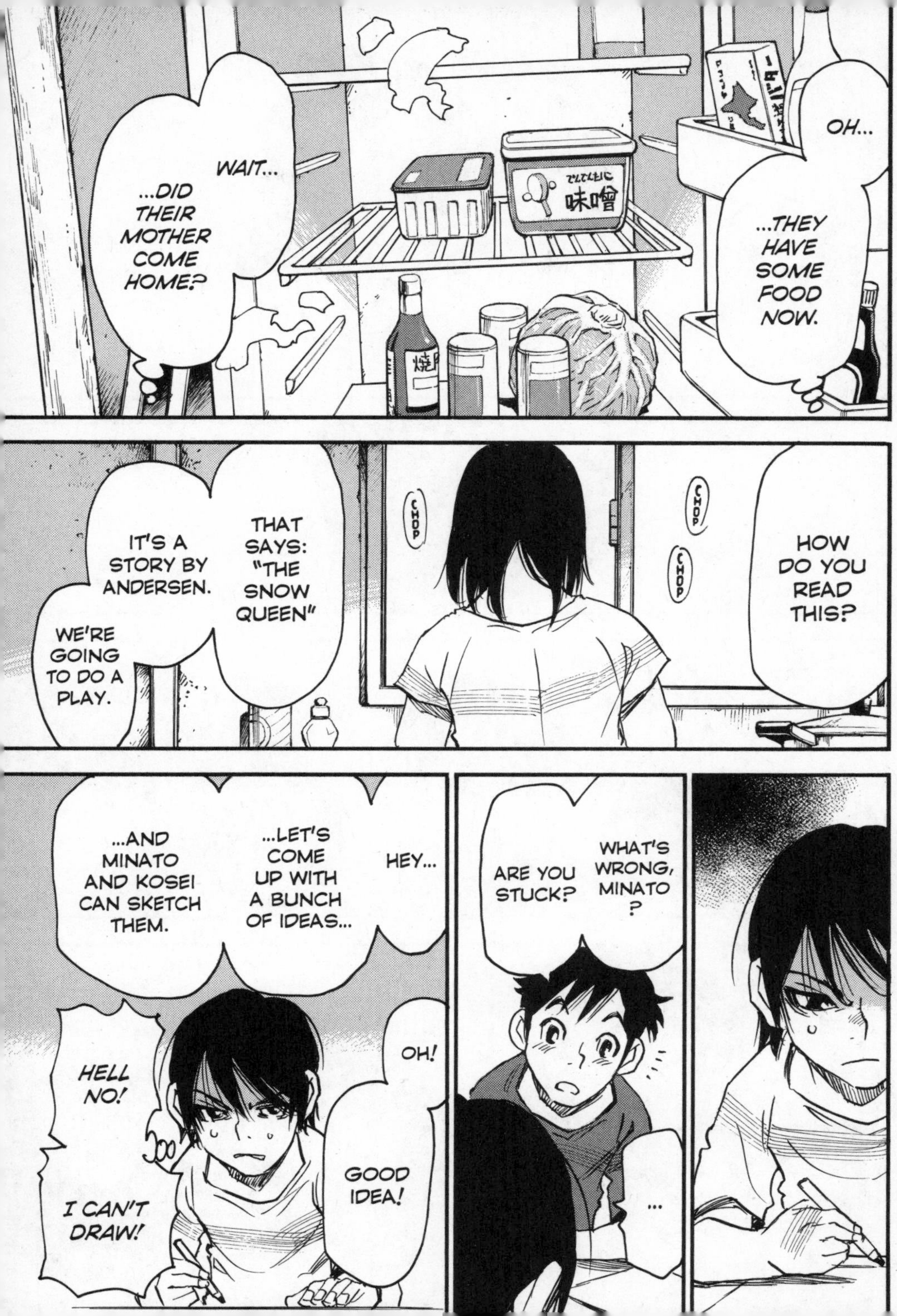
OH...
...THEY HAVE SOME FOOD NOW.
WAIT...
...DID THEIR MOTHER COME HOME?
味噌
HOW DO YOU READ THIS?
CHOP
CHOP
CHOP
THAT SAYS: "THE SNOW QUEEN"
IT'S A STORY BY ANDERSEN.
WE'RE GOING TO DO A PLAY.
WHAT'S WRONG, MINATO?
ARE YOU STUCK?
...
HEY...
...LET'S COME UP WITH A BUNCH OF IDEAS...
...AND MINATO AND KOSEI CAN SKETCH THEM.
OH!
GOOD IDEA!
HELL NO!
I CAN'T DRAW!

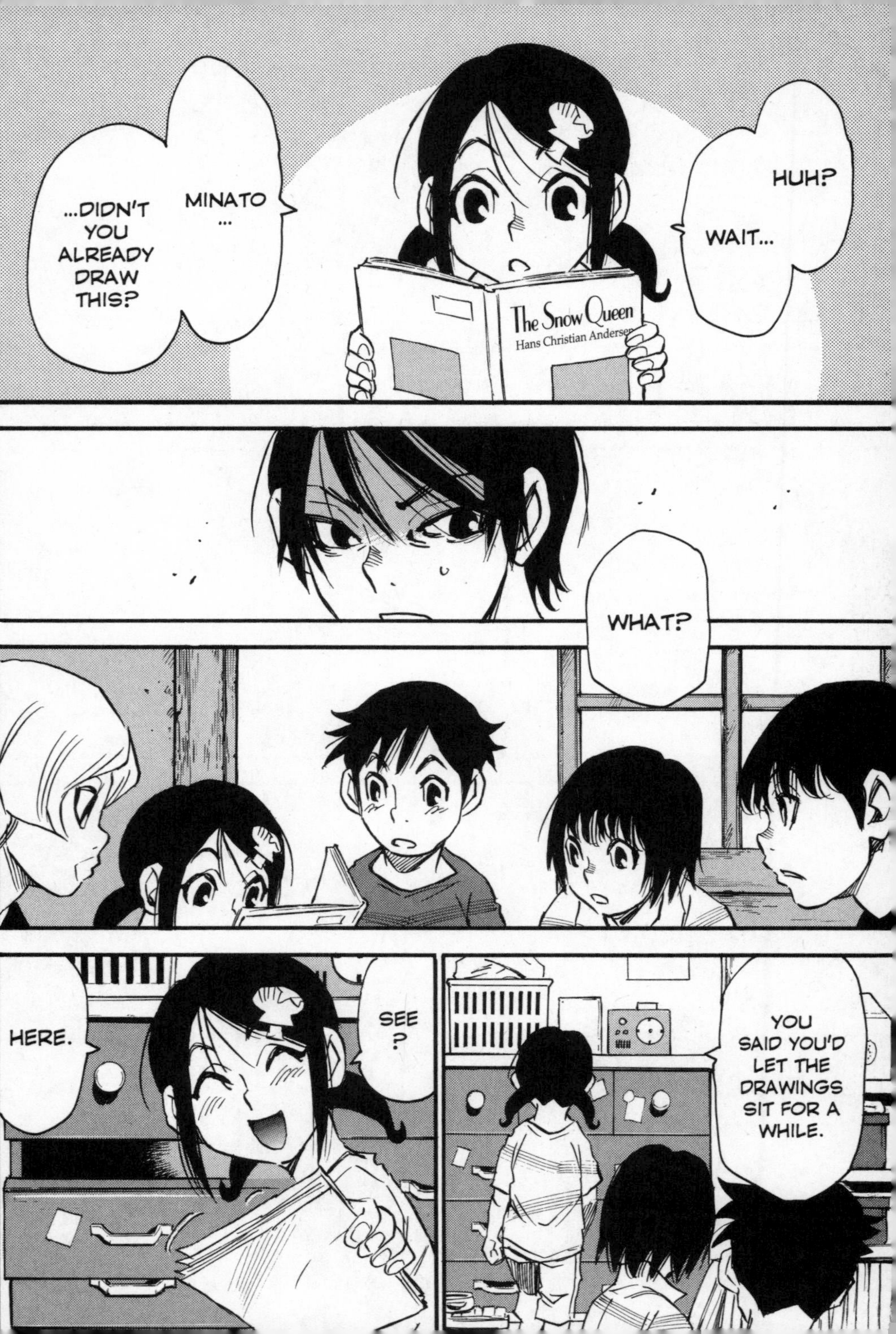

HUH? WAIT...
MINATO ...
...DIDN'T YOU ALREADY DRAW THIS?
The Snow Queen
Hans Christian Anderse
WHAT?
YOU SAID YOU'D LET THE DRAWINGS SIT FOR A WHILE.
SEE?
HERE.

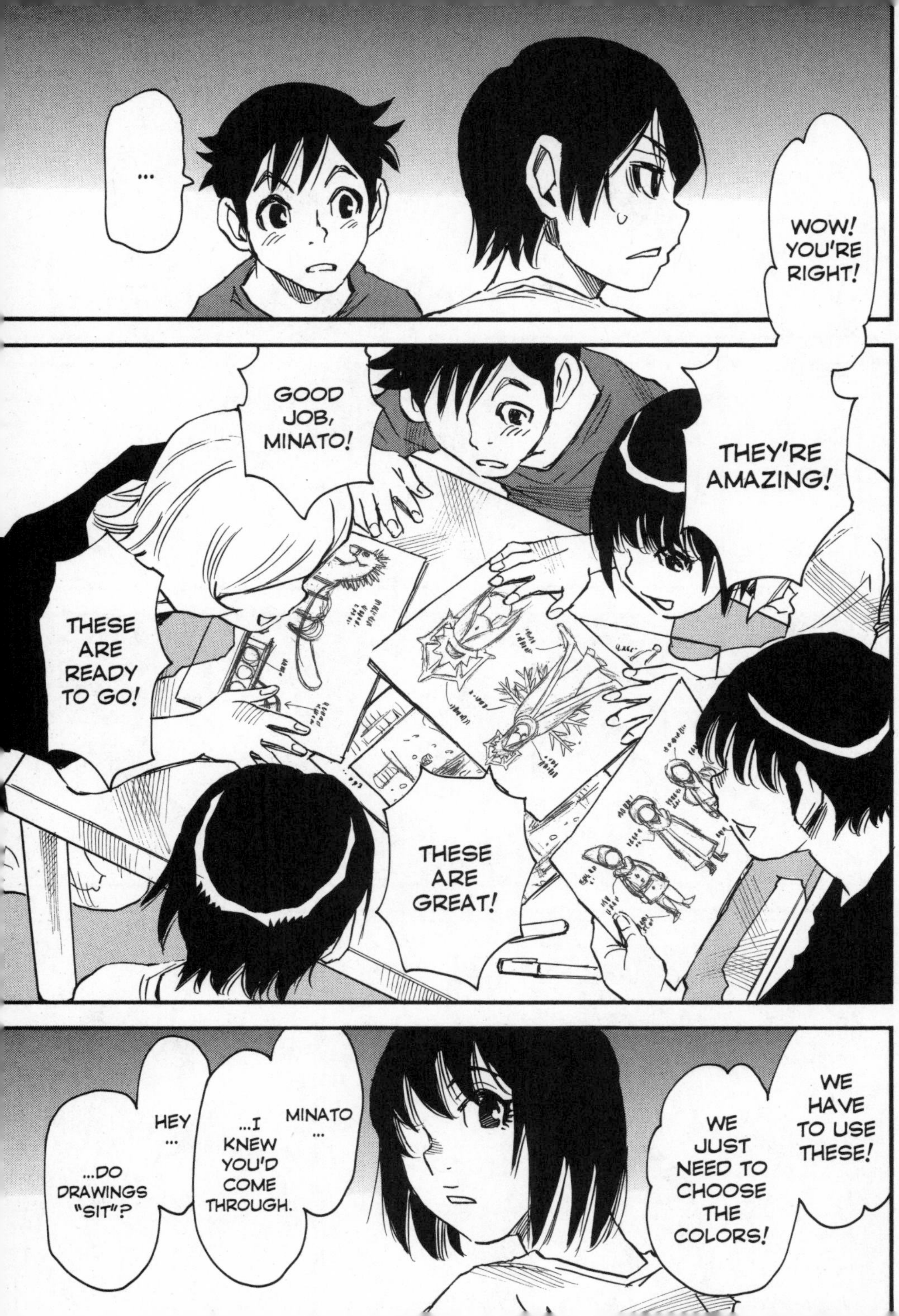
WOW! YOU'RE RIGHT!
...
THEY'RE AMAZING!
GOOD JOB, MINATO!
THESE ARE READY TO GO!
THESE ARE GREAT!
WE HAVE TO USE THESE!
WE JUST NEED TO CHOOSE THE COLORS!
MINATO ...
...I KNEW YOU'D COME THROUGH.
HEY ...
...DO DRAWINGS "SIT"?

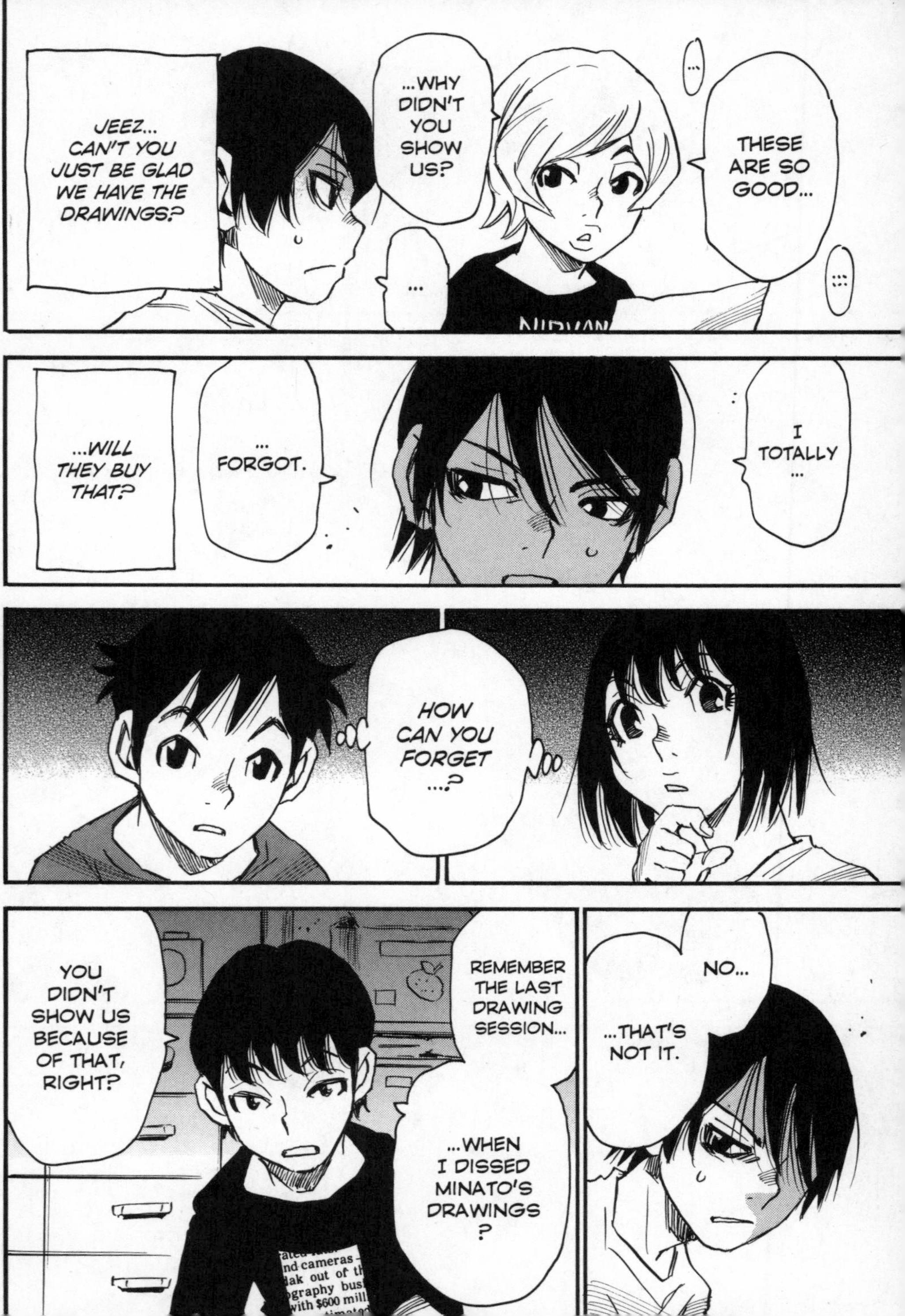
...
THESE ARE SO GOOD...
...WHY DIDN'T YOU SHOW US?
...
JEEZ... CAN'T YOU JUST BE GLAD WE HAVE THE DRAWINGS?
I TOTALLY ...
... FORGOT.
...WILL THEY BUY THAT?
HOW CAN YOU FORGET ...?
NO...
...THAT'S NOT IT.
REMEMBER THE LAST DRAWING SESSION...
YOU DIDN'T SHOW US BECAUSE OF THAT, RIGHT?
...WHEN I DISSED MINATO'S DRAWINGS?

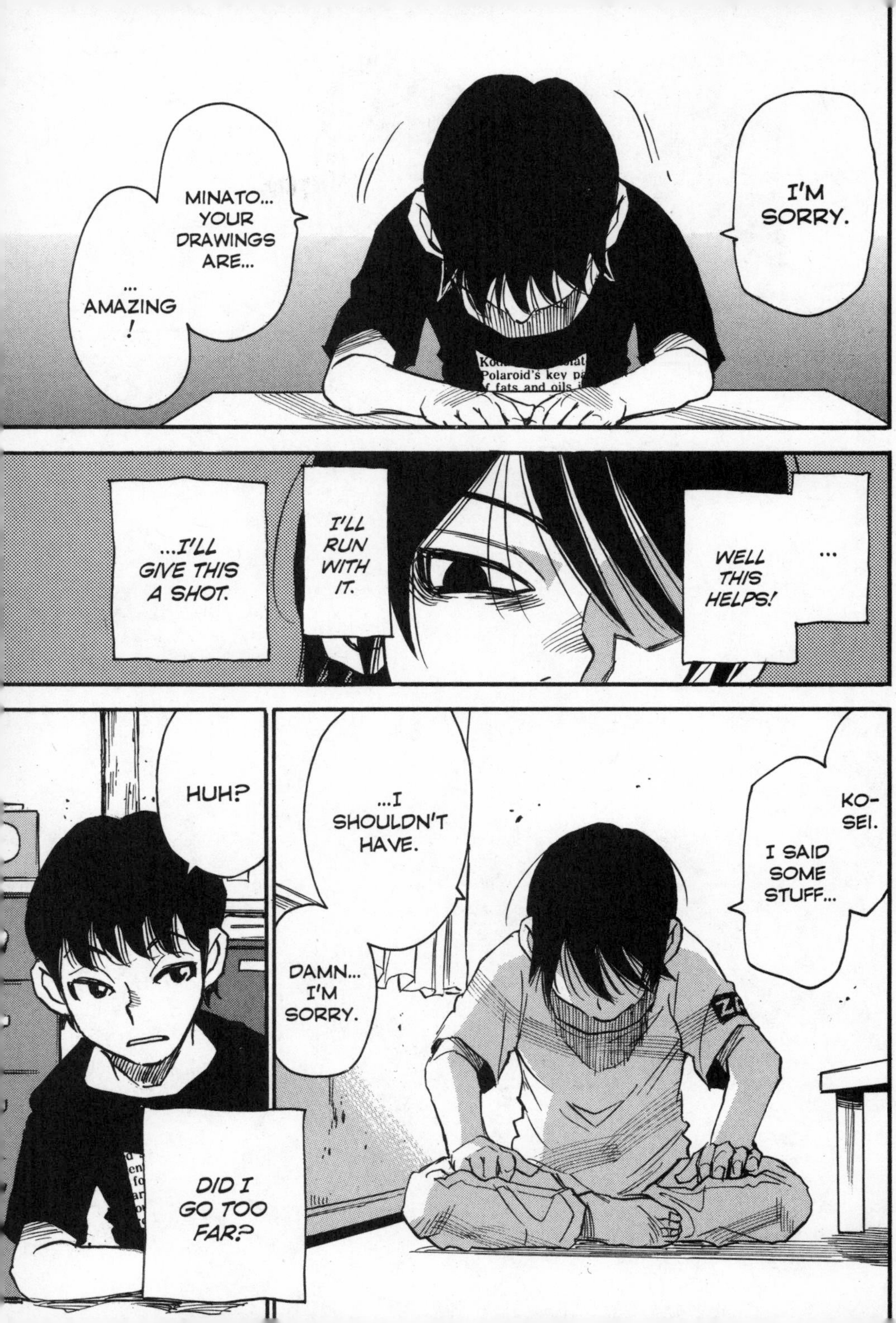
I'M SORRY.
MINATO... YOUR DRAWINGS ARE...
... AMAZING!
... WELL THIS HELPS!
I'LL RUN WITH IT.
...I'LL GIVE THIS A SHOT.
KO-SEI.
I SAID SOME STUFF...
...I SHOULDN'T HAVE.
DAMN... I'M SORRY.
HUH?
DID I GO TOO FAR?

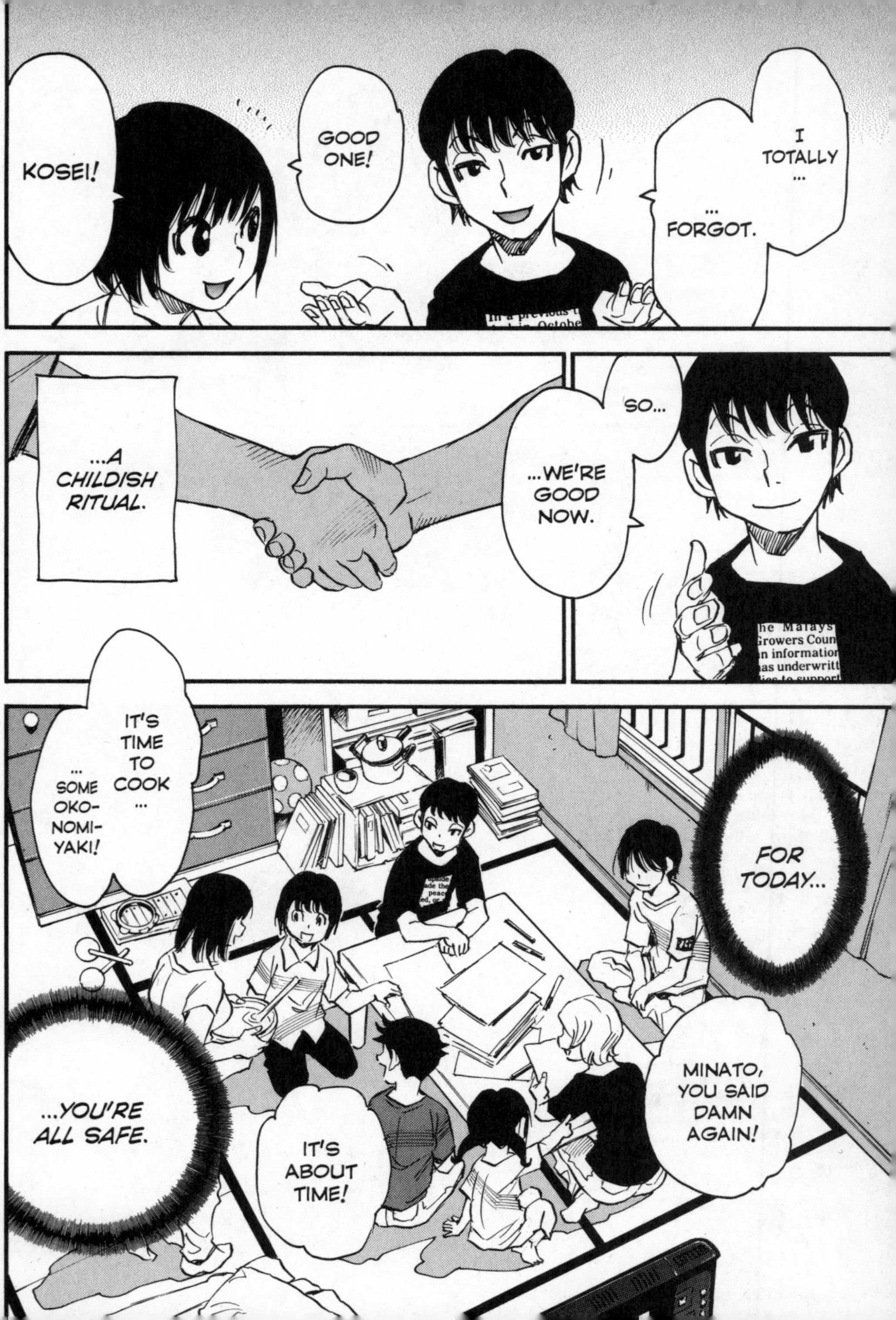
I TOTALLY ...
... FORGOT.
GOOD ONE!
KOSEI!
SO...
...WE'RE GOOD NOW.
...A CHILDISH RITUAL.
FOR TODAY...
IT'S TIME TO COOK ...
... SOME OKONOMIYAKI!
MINATO, YOU SAID DAMN AGAIN!
IT'S ABOUT TIME!
...YOU'RE ALL SAFE.

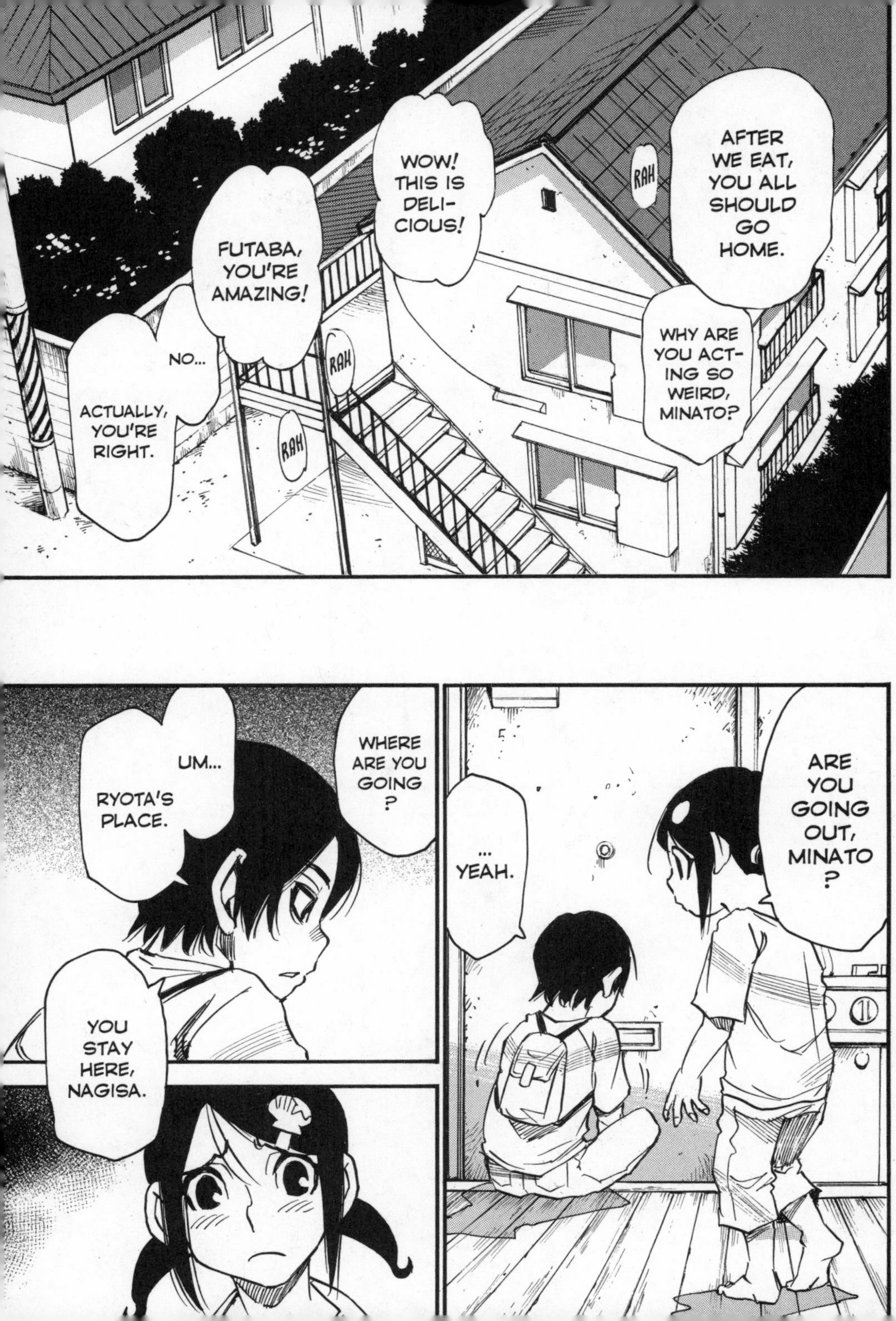
AFTER WE EAT, YOU ALL SHOULD GO HOME.
RAH
WHY ARE YOU ACTING SO WEIRD, MINATO?
WOW! THIS IS DELICIOUS!
FUTABA, YOU'RE AMAZING!
RAH
NO... ACTUALLY, YOU'RE RIGHT.
RAH
ARE YOU GOING OUT, MINATO?
... YEAH.
WHERE ARE YOU GOING?
UM... RYOTA'S PLACE.
YOU STAY HERE, NAGISA.

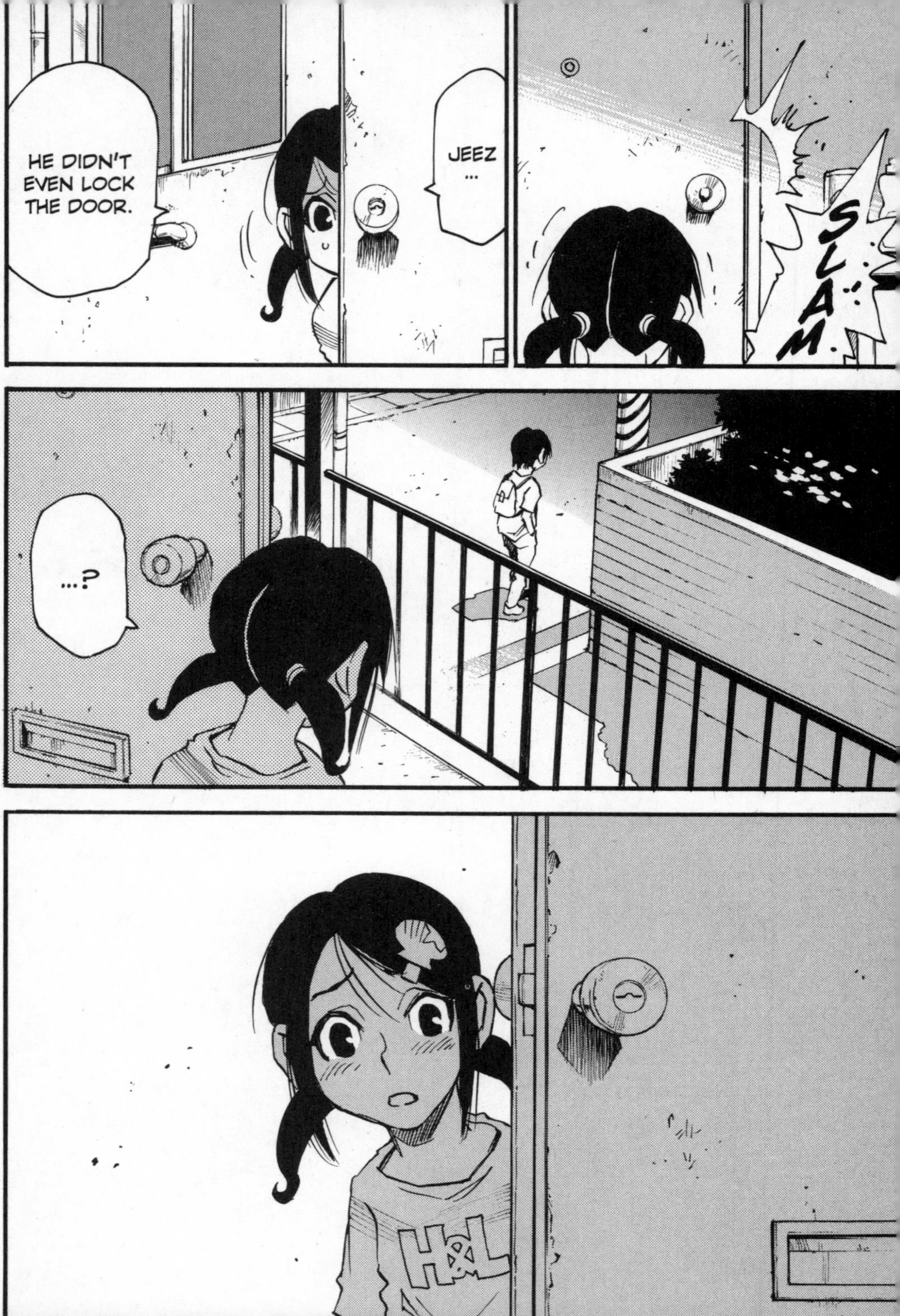
SLAM.
JEEZ ...
HE DIDN'T EVEN LOCK THE DOOR.
...?

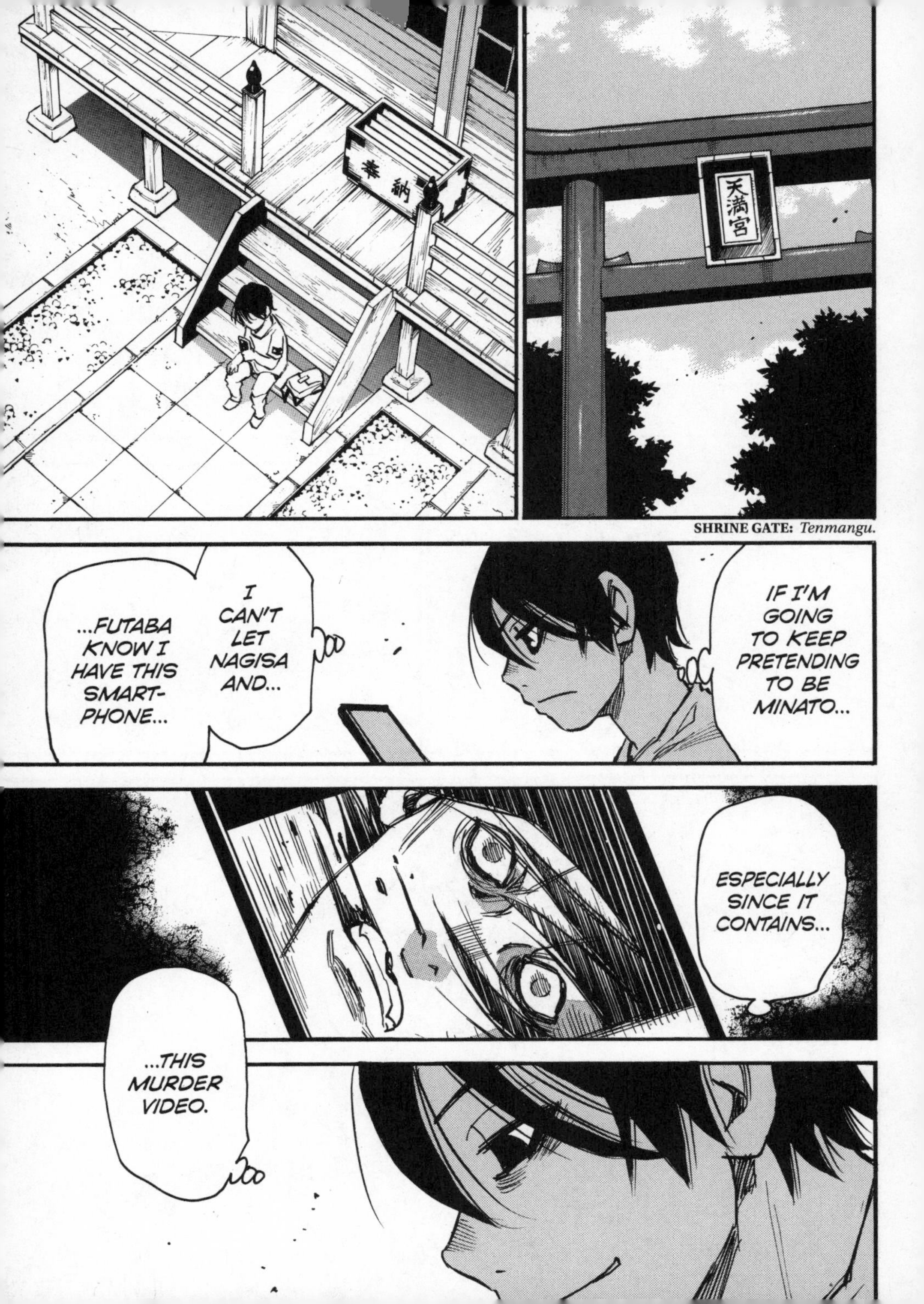
天満宮
奉納
SHRINE GATE: Tenmangu.
IF I'M GOING TO KEEP PRETENDING TO BE MINATO...
I CAN'T LET NAGISA AND...
...FUTABA KNOW I HAVE THIS SMARTPHONE...
ESPECIALLY SINCE IT CONTAINS...
...THIS MURDER VIDEO.

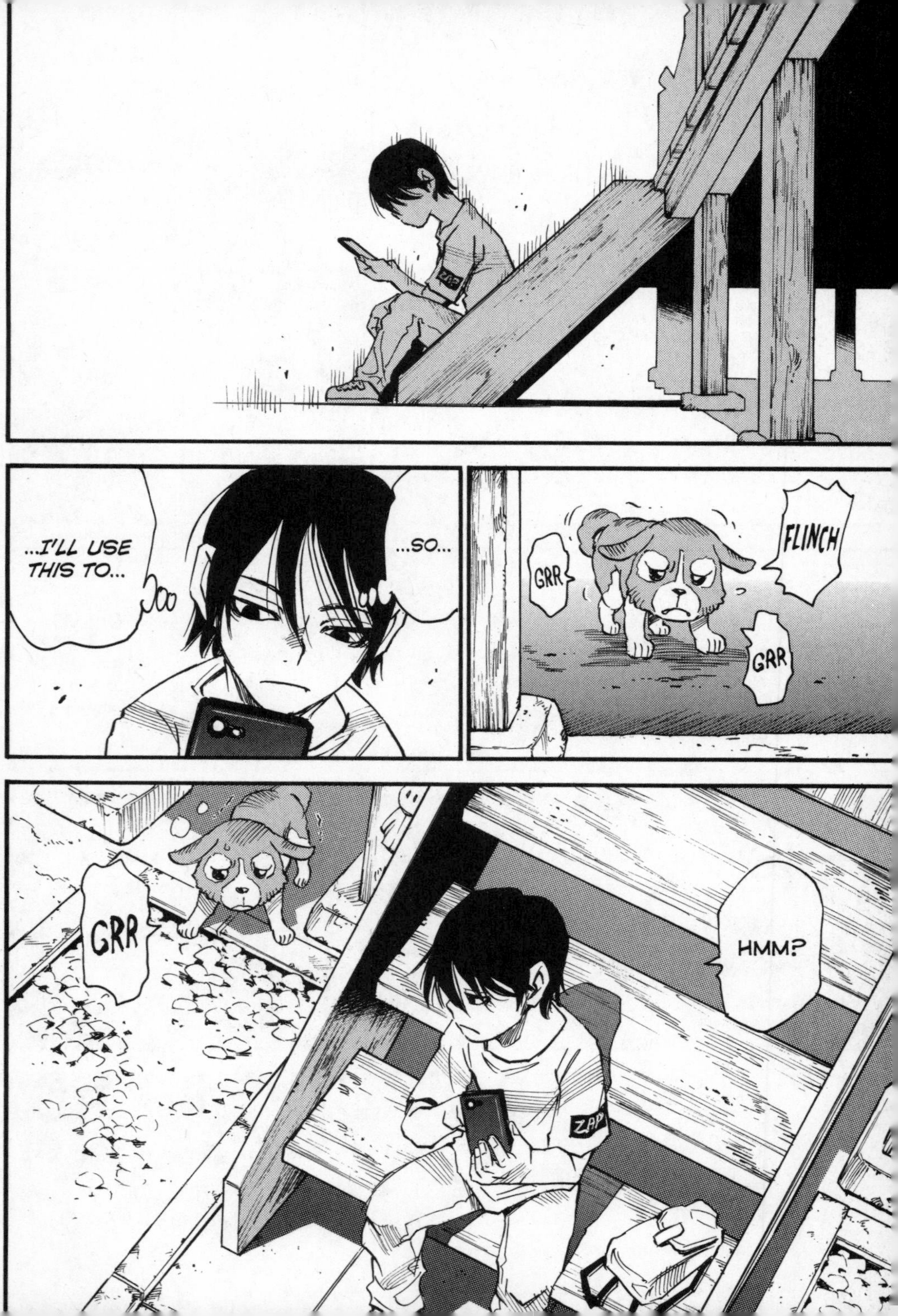
FLINCH
GRR
GRR
...SO...
...I'LL USE THIS TO...
HMM?
GRR

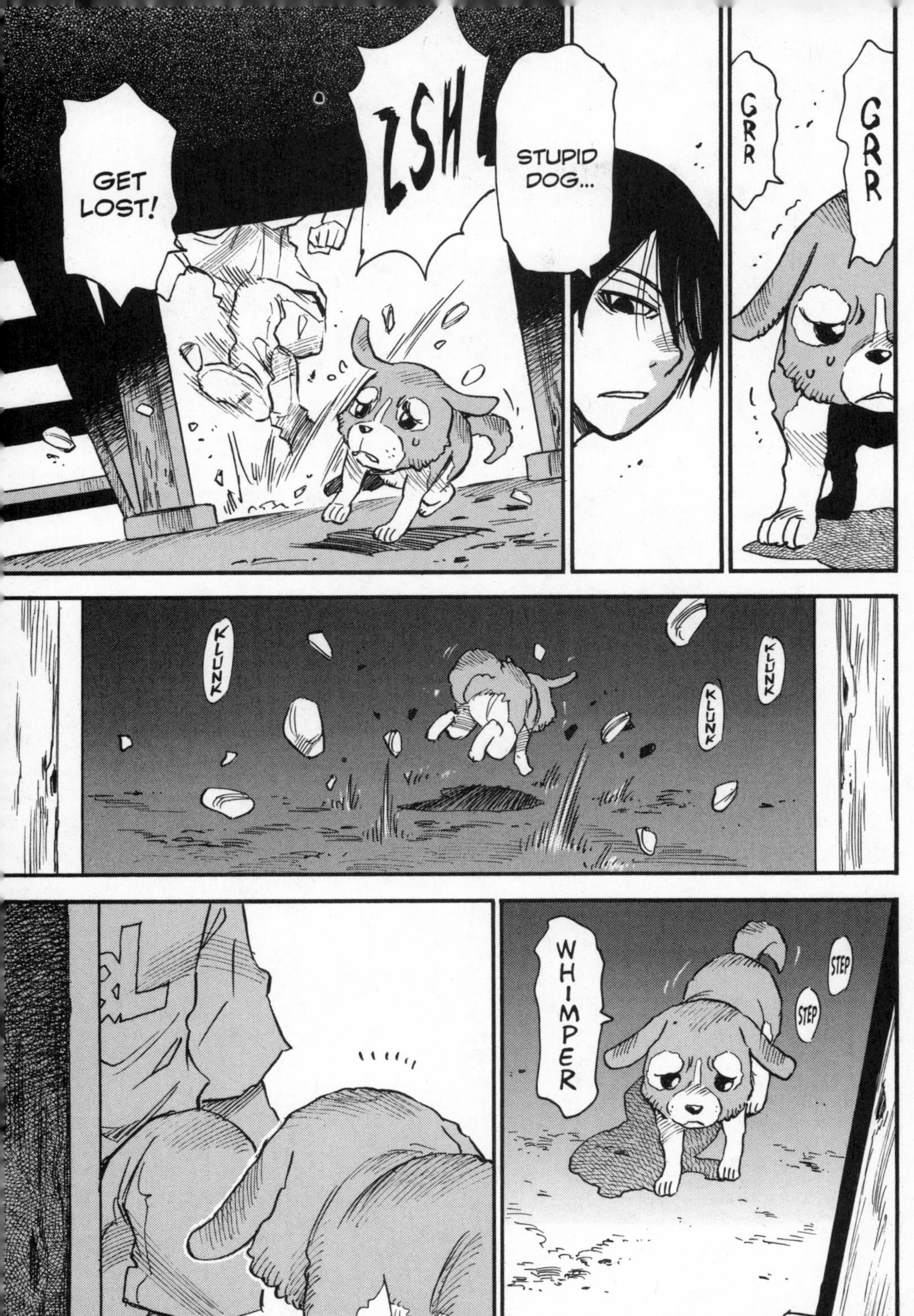
GRR
GRR
STUPID DOG...
ZSH
GET LOST!
KLUNK
KLUNK
KLUNK
STEP
STEP
WHIMPER

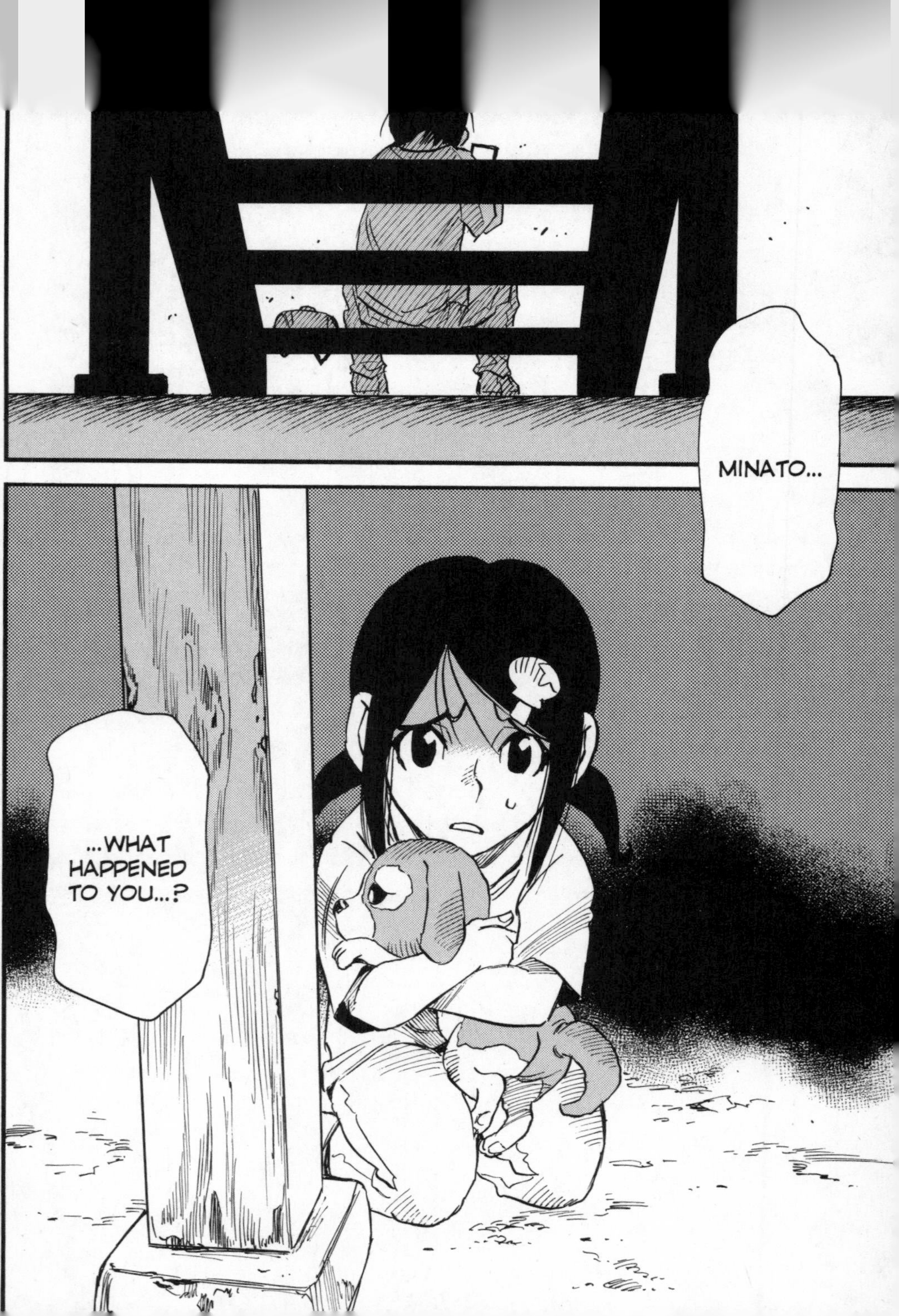
MINATO...
...WHAT HAPPENED TO YOU...?

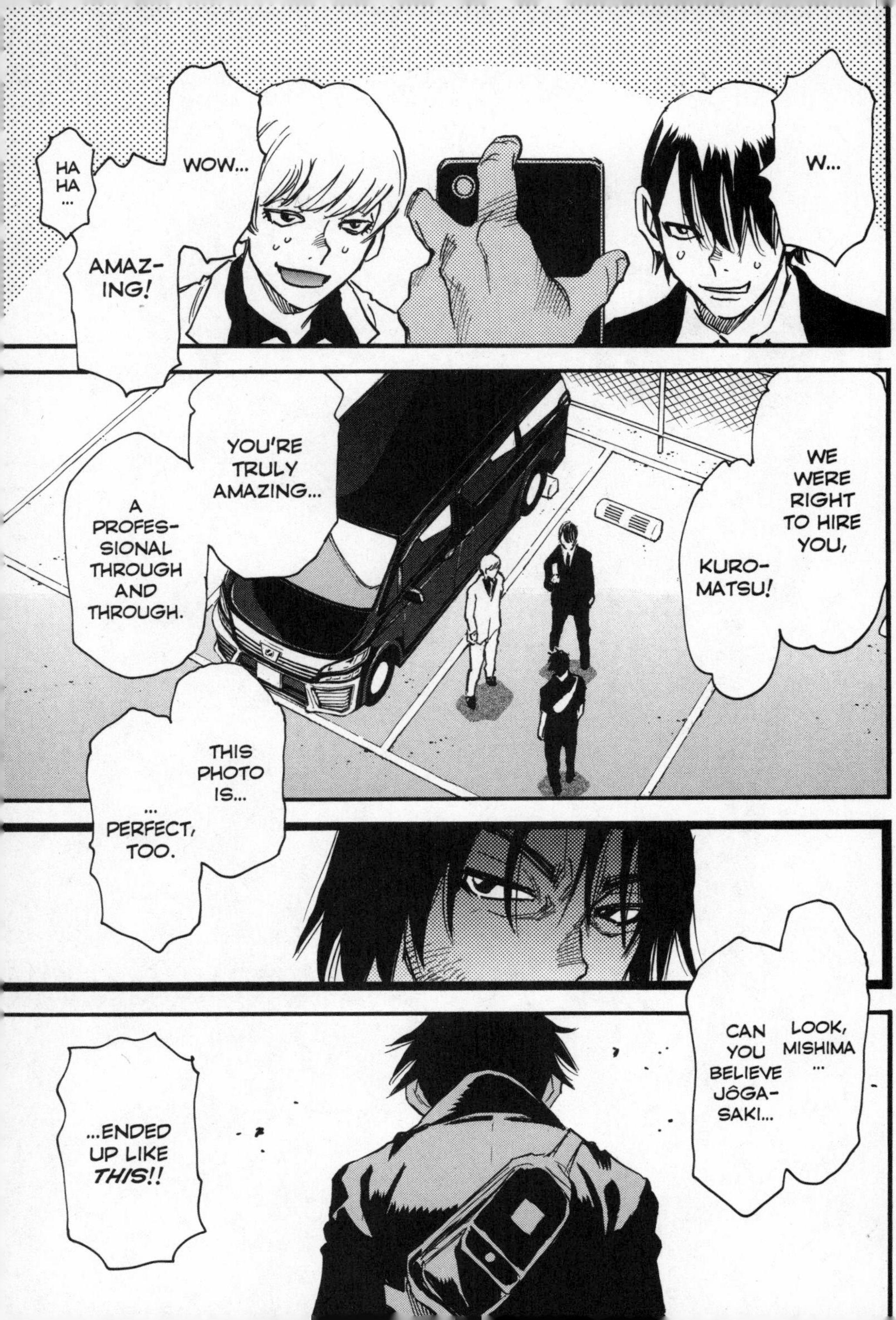

W...
WOW...
HA HA ...
AMAZ-ING!
WE WERE RIGHT TO HIRE YOU, KURO-MATSU!
YOU'RE TRULY AMAZING...
A PROFES-SIONAL THROUGH AND THROUGH.
THIS PHOTO IS...
... PERFECT, TOO.
LOOK, MISHIMA ...
CAN YOU BELIEVE JÔGA-SAKI...
...ENDED UP LIKE *THIS*!!

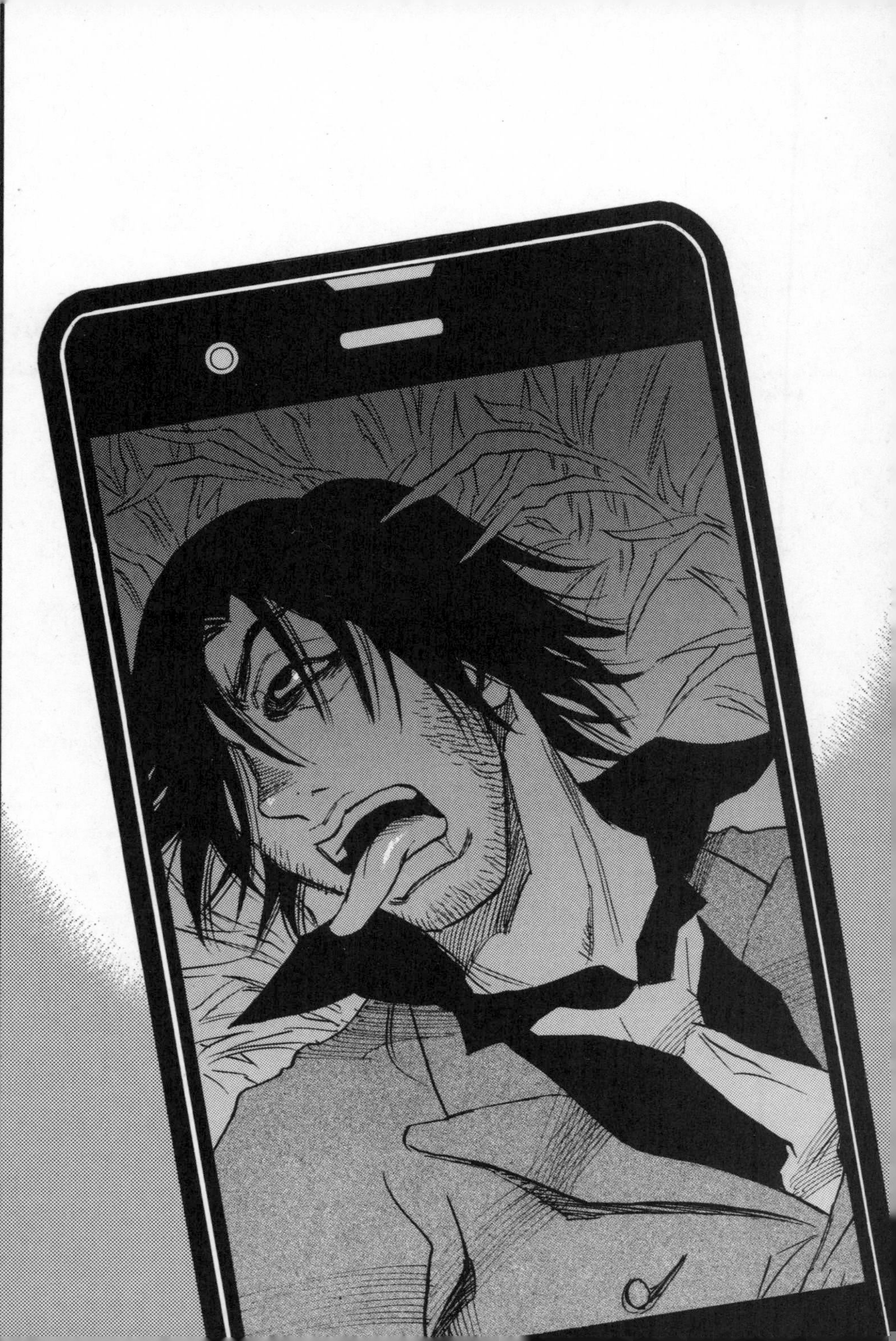

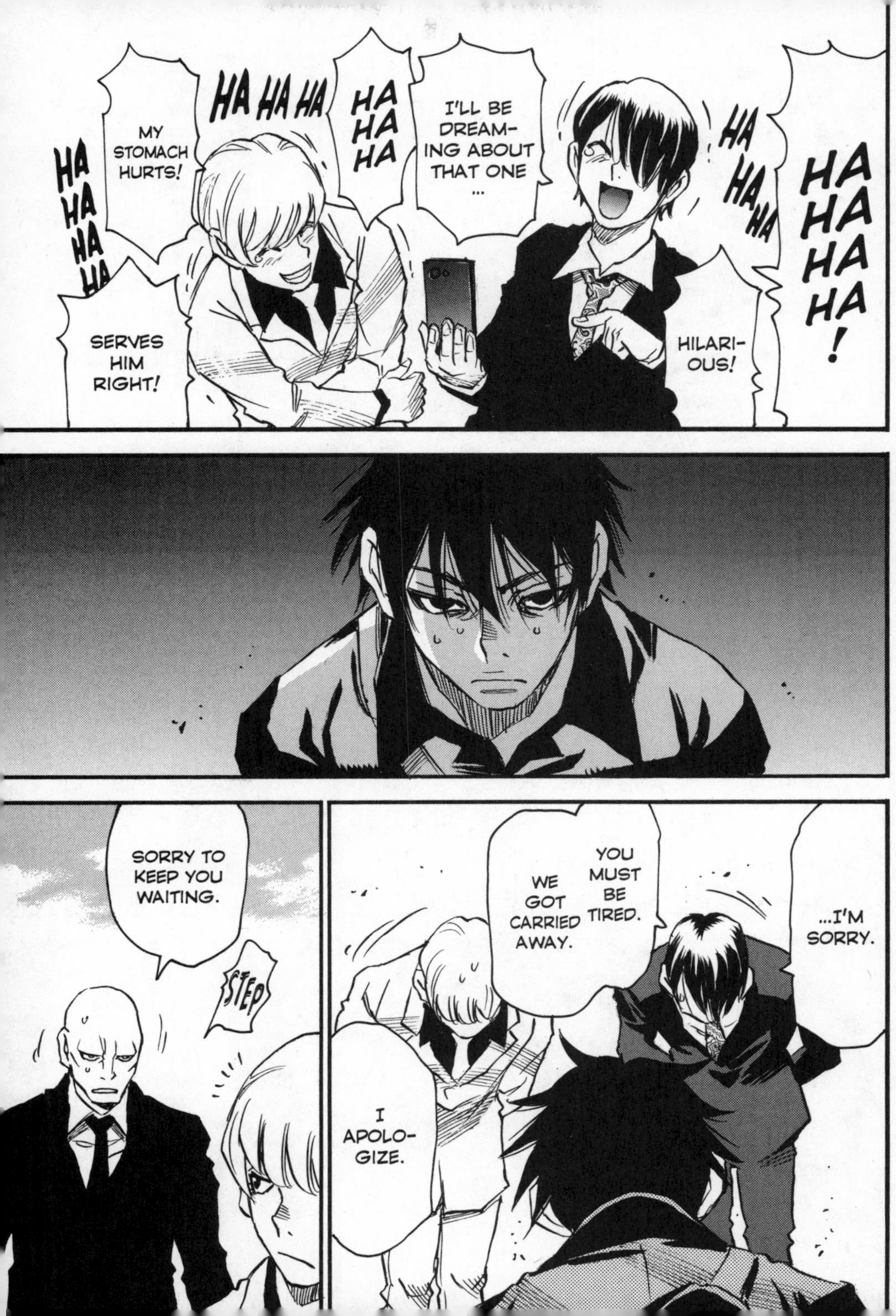

HA HA HA HA HA!
HA HA HA
HILARI-OUS!
I'LL BE DREAMING-ING ABOUT THAT ONE ...
HA HA HA
HA HA HA
MY STOMACH HURTS!
HA HA HA HA HA
SERVES HIM RIGHT!
...I'M SORRY.
YOU MUST BE TIRED.
WE GOT CARRIED AWAY.
I APOLO-GIZE.
SORRY TO KEEP YOU WAITING.
STEP

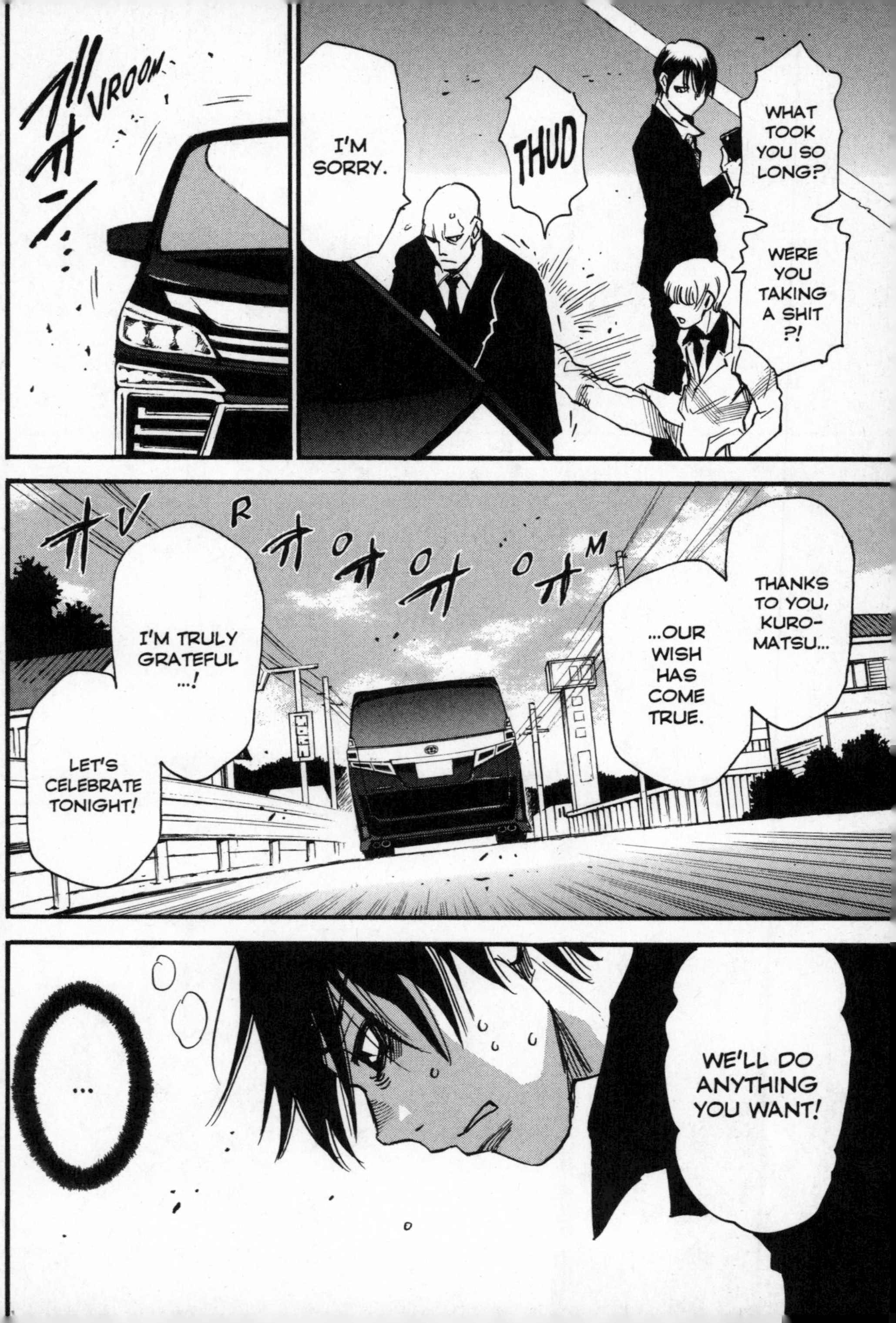
WHAT TOOK YOU SO LONG?
WERE YOU TAKING A SHIT ?!
THUD
I'M SORRY.
VROOM
VROOOM
THANKS TO YOU, KURO-MATSU...
...OUR WISH HAS COME TRUE.
I'M TRULY GRATEFUL ...!
LET'S CELEBRATE TONIGHT!
WE'LL DO ANYTHING YOU WANT!
...

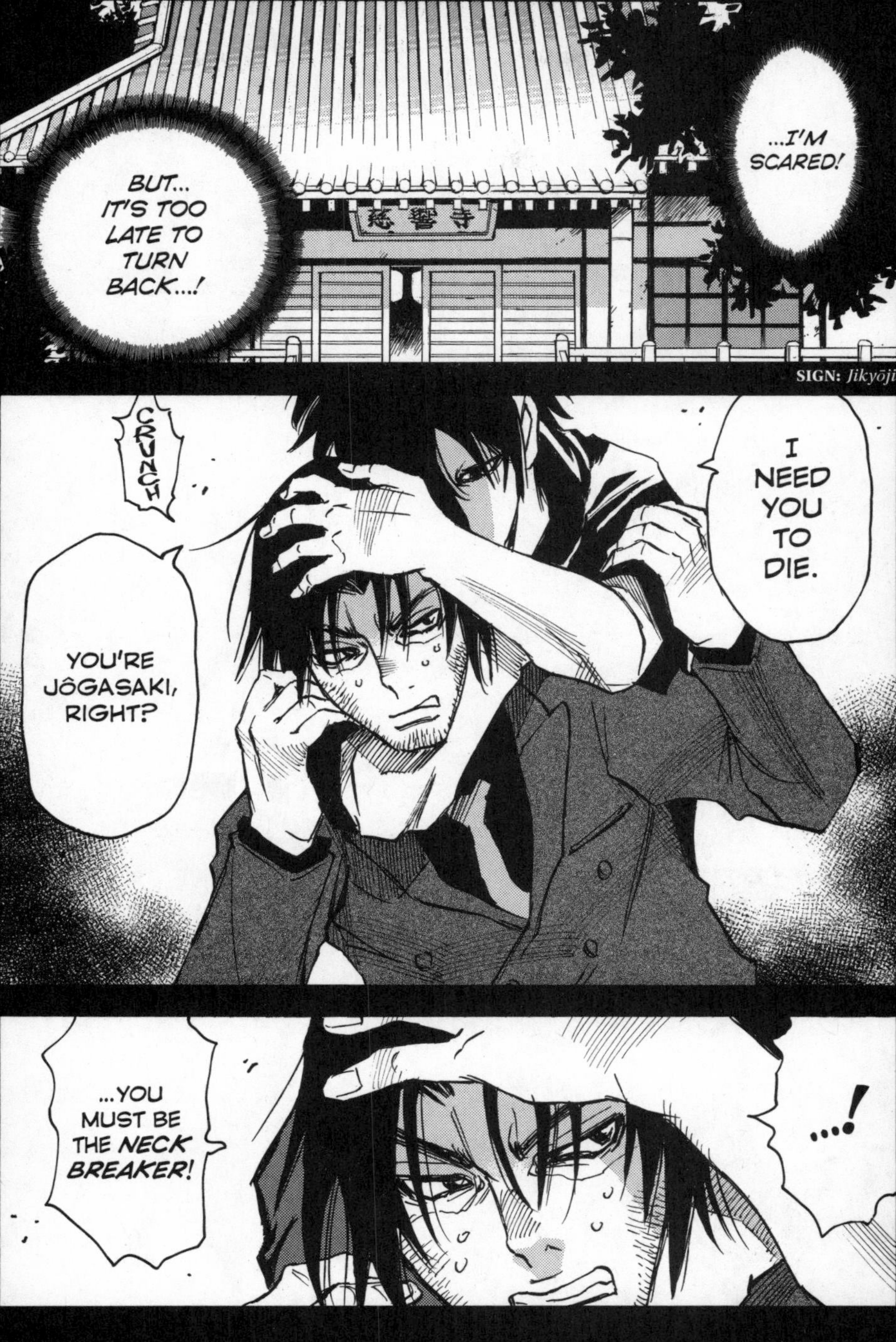
...I'M SCARED!
BUT... IT'S TOO LATE TO TURN BACK...!
I NEED YOU TO DIE.
CRUNCH
YOU'RE JÔGASAKI, RIGHT?
...!
...YOU MUST BE THE *NECK BREAKER*!

SIGN: *Jikyōji*

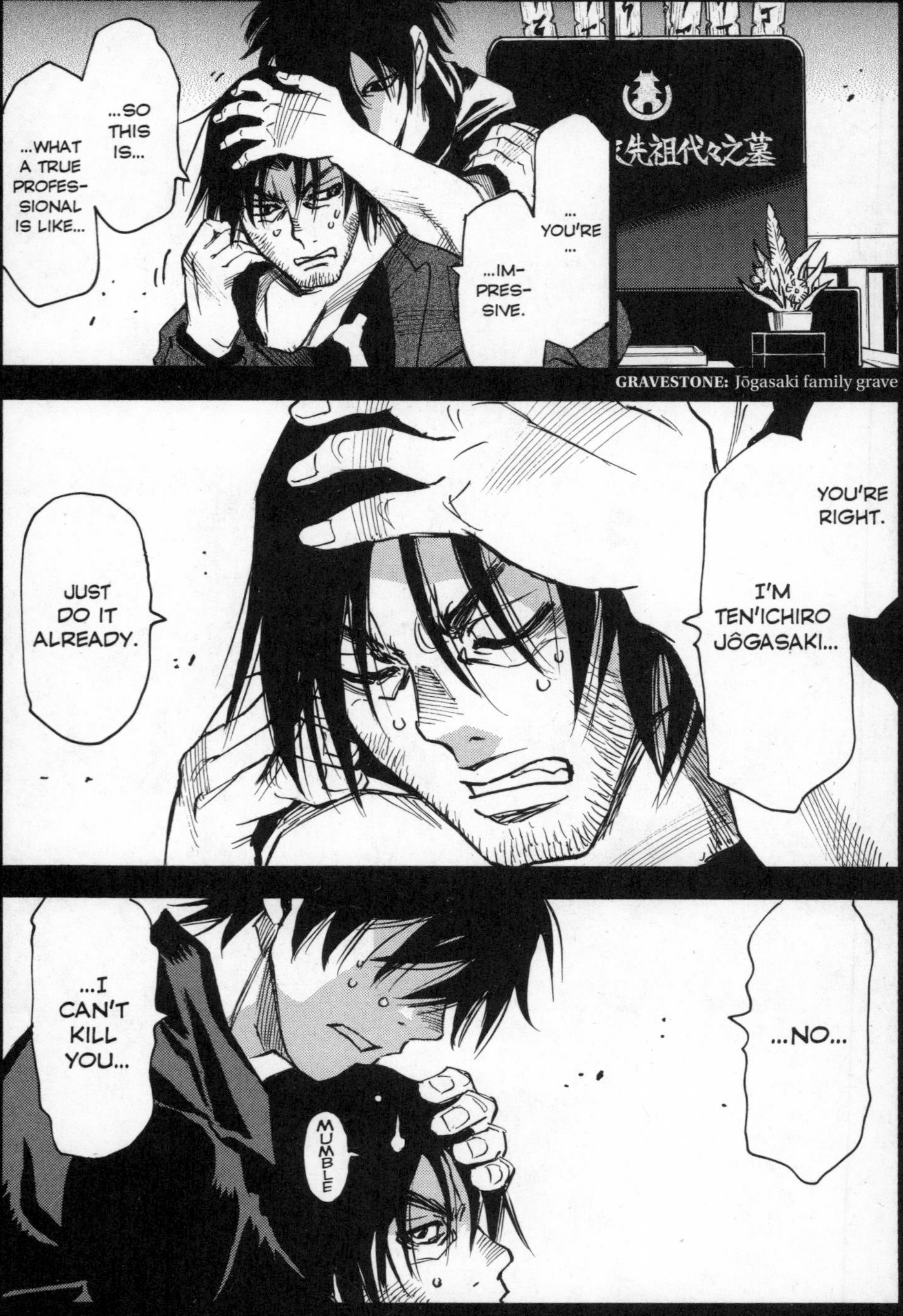
... YOU'RE ...
...IMPRESSIVE.
先祖代々之墓
...SO THIS IS...
...WHAT A TRUE PROFESSIONAL IS LIKE...
YOU'RE RIGHT.
I'M TEN'ICHIRO JÔGASAKI...
JUST DO IT ALREADY.
...NO...
MUMBLE
...I CAN'T KILL YOU...

GRAVESTONE: Jōgasaki family grave

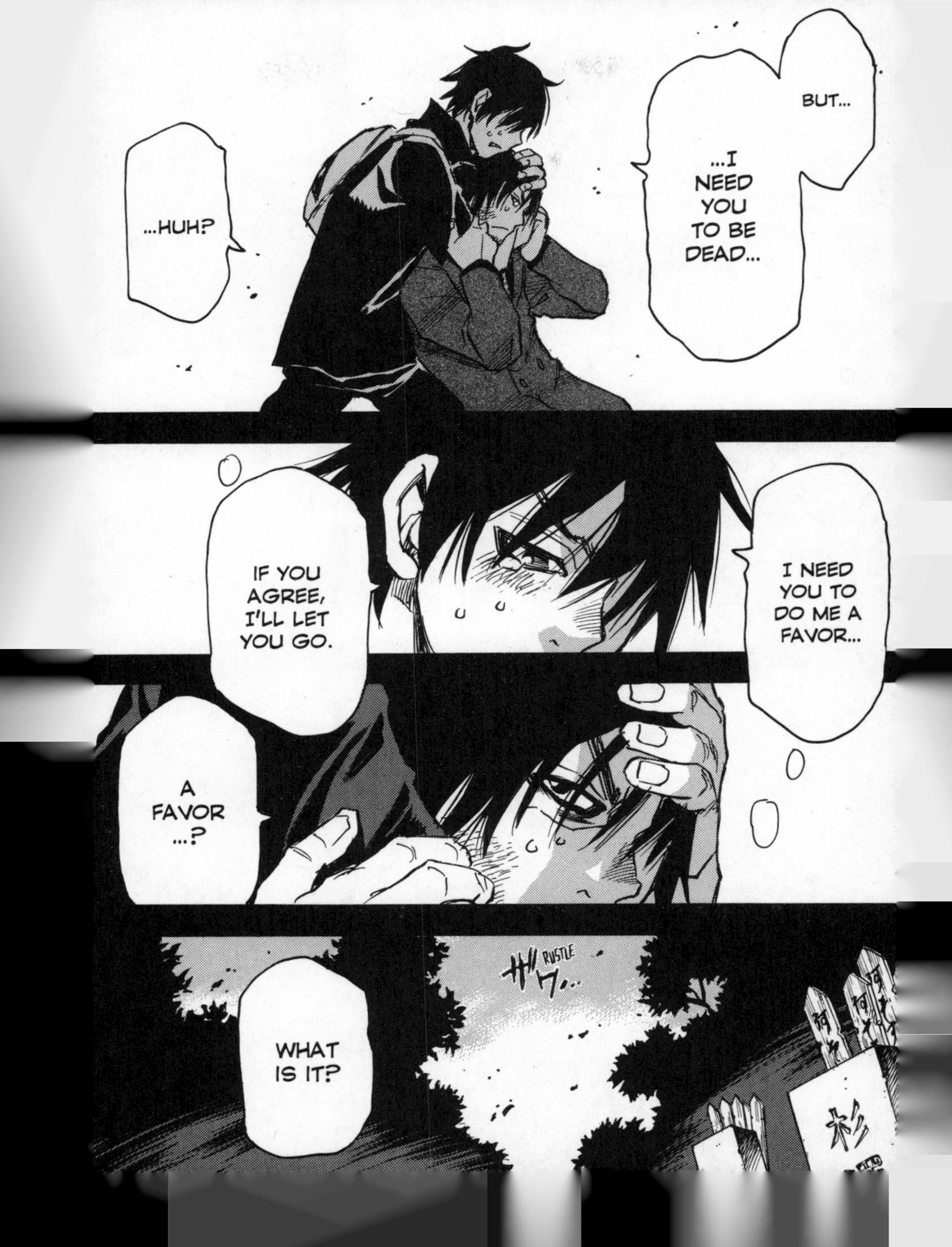
BUT...
...I NEED YOU TO BE DEAD...
...HUH?
I NEED YOU TO DO ME A FAVOR...
IF YOU AGREE, I'LL LET YOU GO.
A FAVOR ...?
RUSTLE
WHAT IS IT?

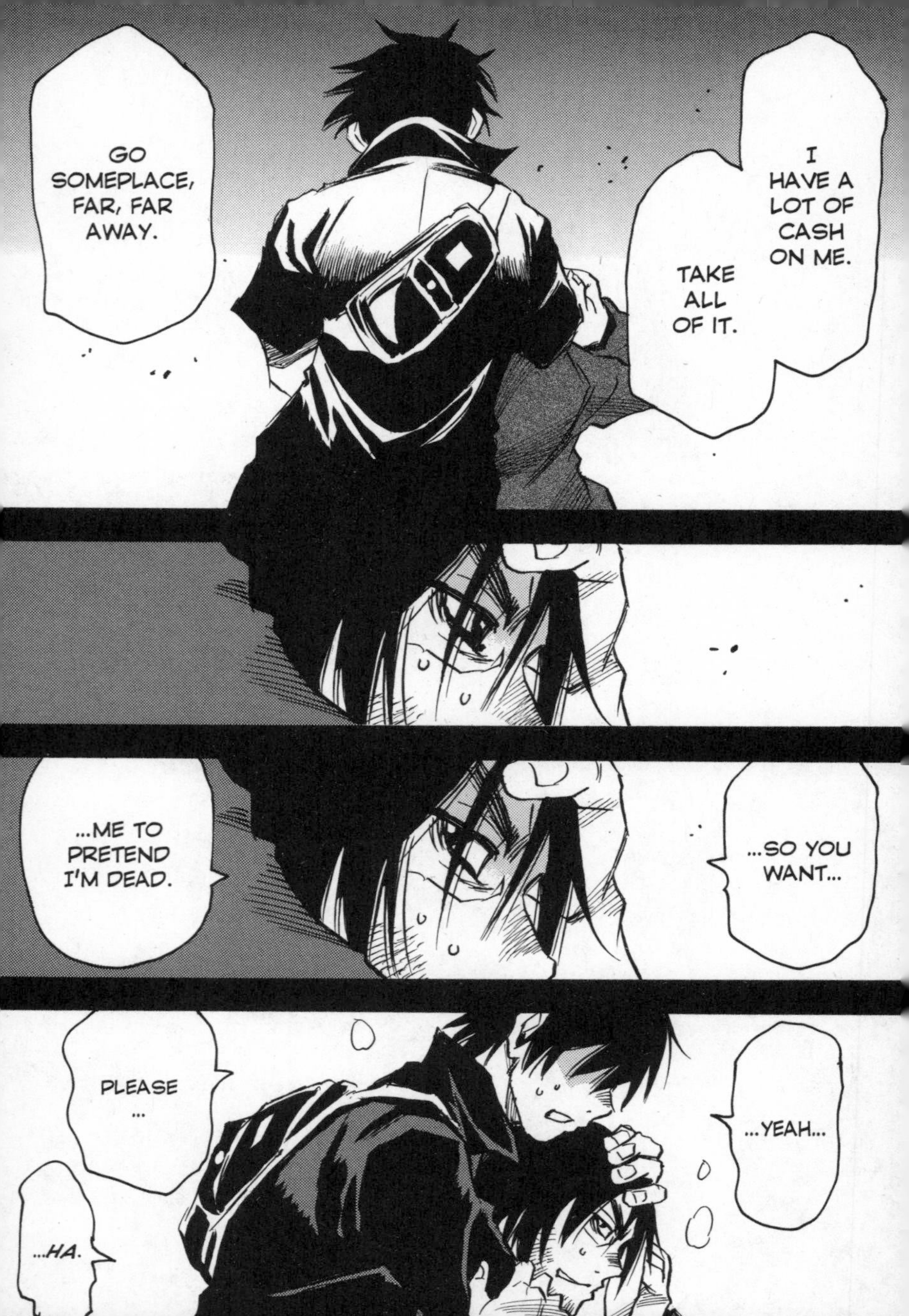
I HAVE A LOT OF CASH ON ME.
TAKE ALL OF IT.
GO SOMEPLACE, FAR, FAR AWAY.
...SO YOU WANT...
...ME TO PRETEND I'M DEAD.
...YEAH...
PLEASE ...
...HA.

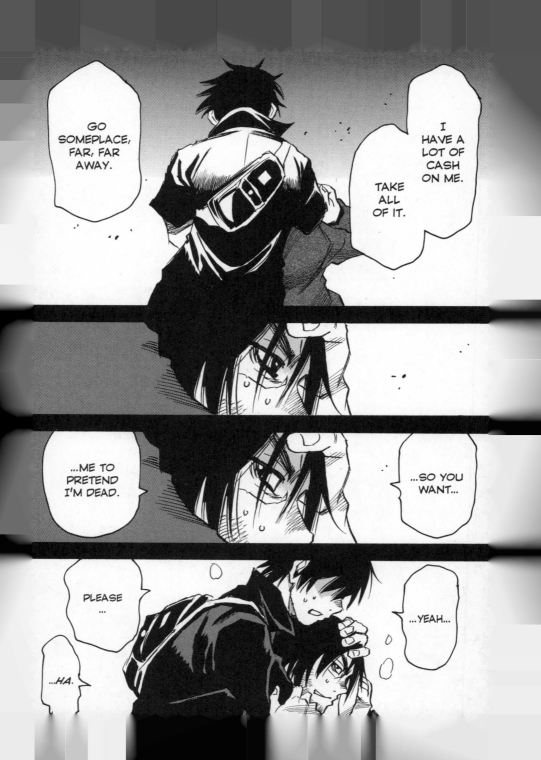

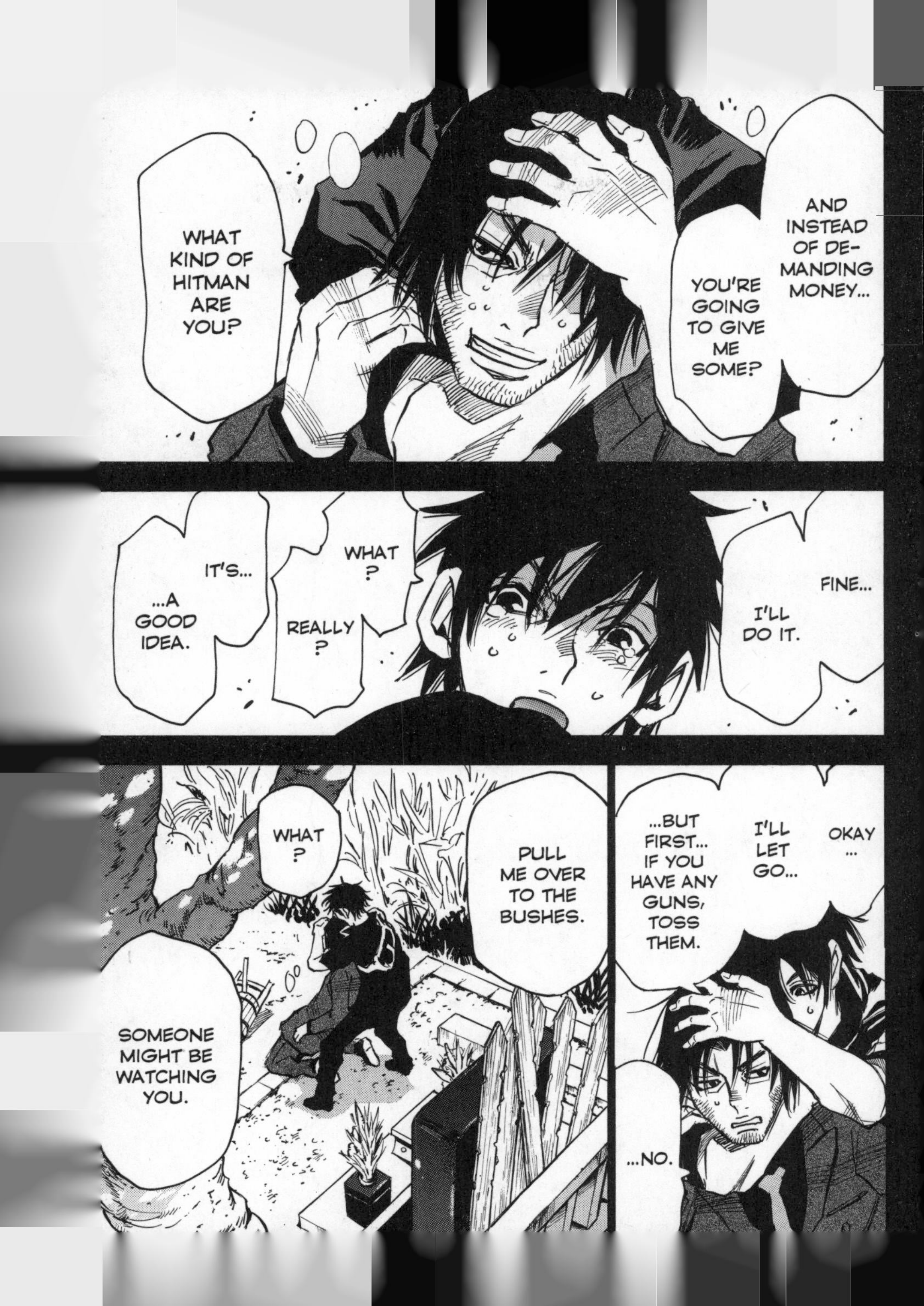
AND INSTEAD OF DE-MANDING MONEY...
YOU'RE GOING TO GIVE ME SOME?
WHAT KIND OF HITMAN ARE YOU?
FINE...
I'LL DO IT.
WHAT?
REALLY?
IT'S...
...A GOOD IDEA.
OKAY...
I'LL LET GO...
...BUT FIRST... IF YOU HAVE ANY GUNS, TOSS THEM.
...NO.
PULL ME OVER TO THE BUSHES.
WHAT?
SOMEONE MIGHT BE WATCHING YOU.

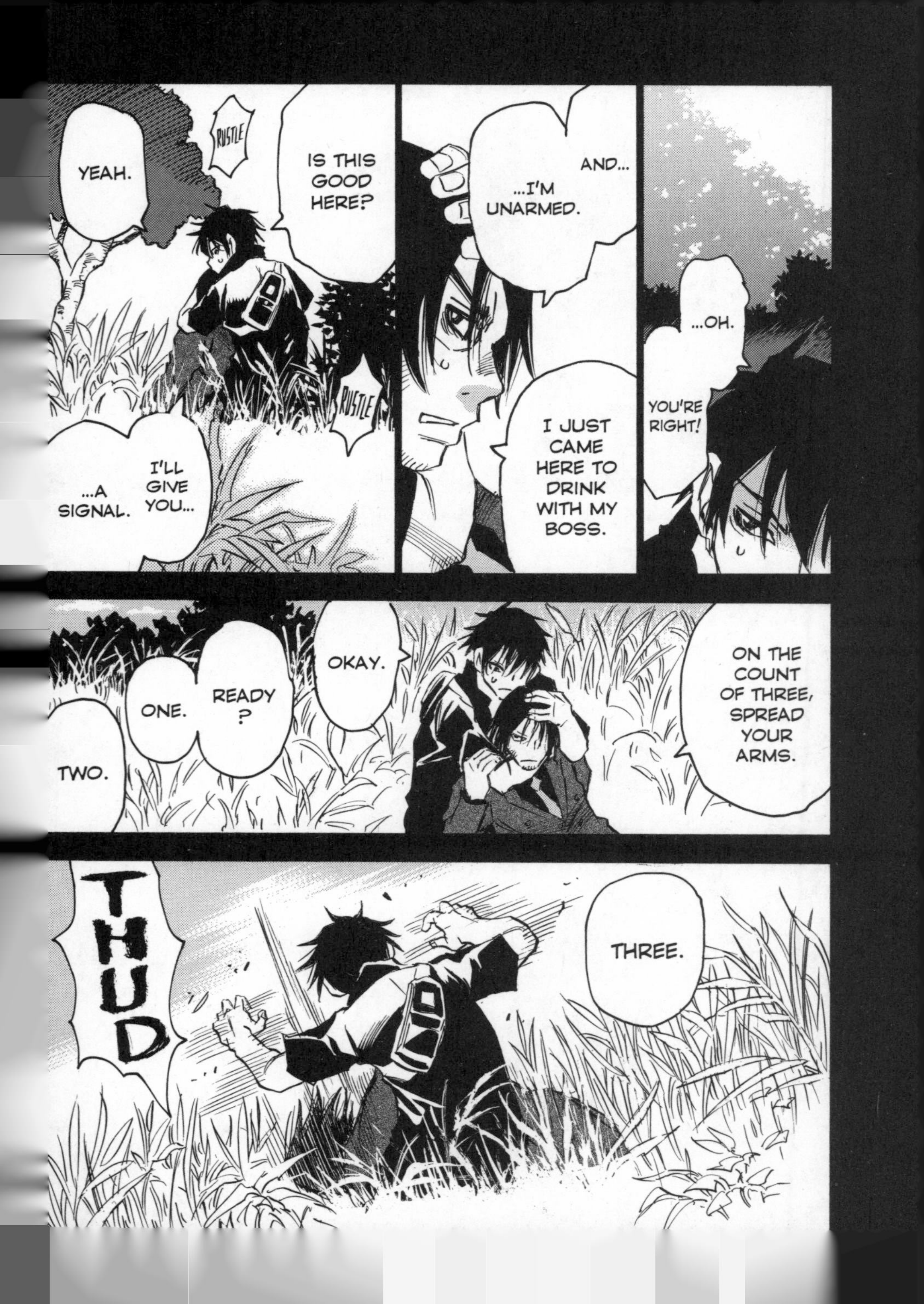
...OH.
YOU'RE RIGHT!
AND...
...I'M UNARMED.
I JUST CAME HERE TO DRINK WITH MY BOSS.
IS THIS GOOD HERE?
RUSTLE
YEAH.
RUSTLE
I'LL GIVE YOU...
...A SIGNAL.
ON THE COUNT OF THREE, SPREAD YOUR ARMS.
OKAY.
READY?
ONE.
TWO.
THREE.
THUD

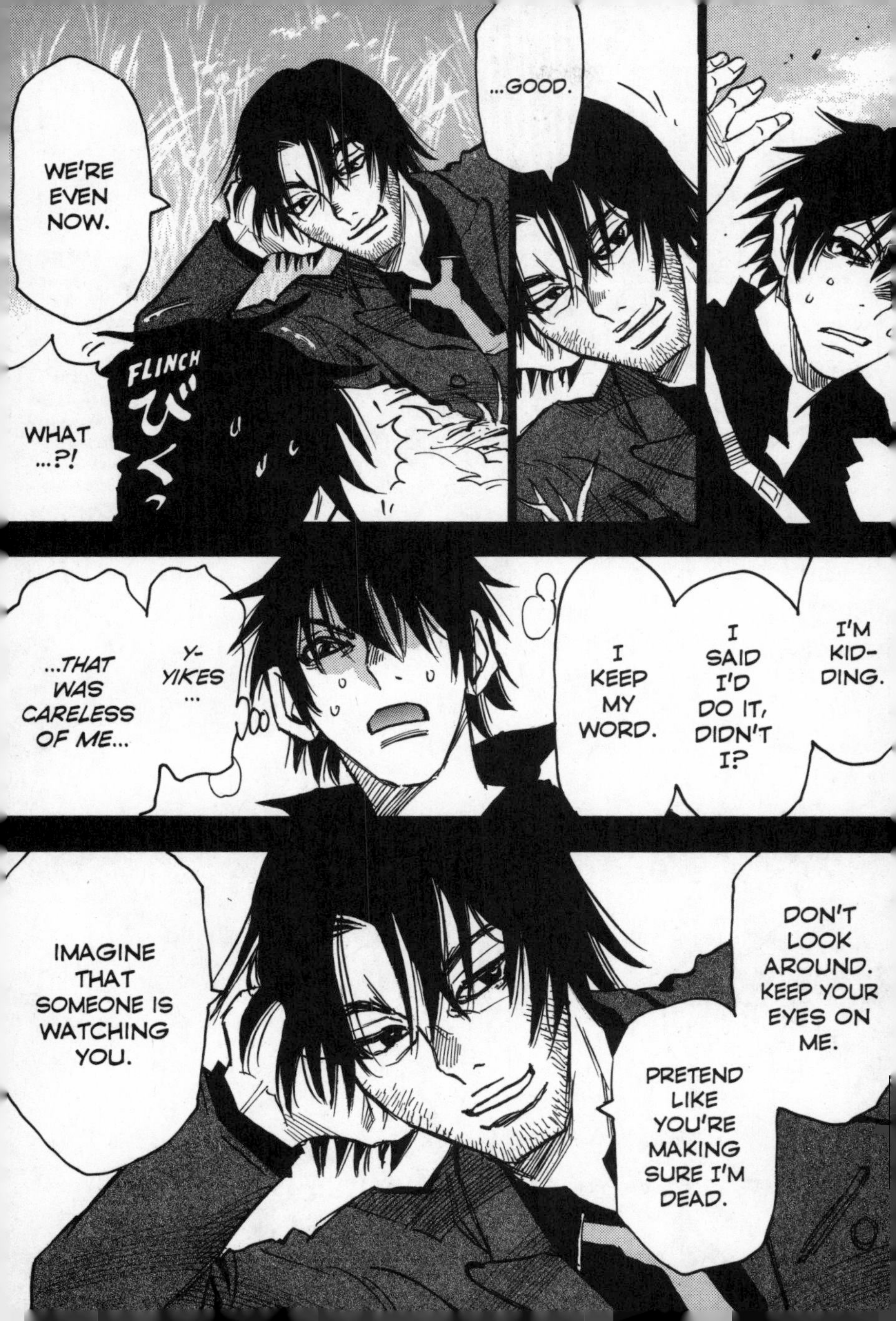
...GOOD.
WE'RE EVEN NOW.
FLINCH
WHAT ...?!
I'M KIDDING.
I SAID I'D DO IT, DIDN'T I?
I KEEP MY WORD.
Y-YIKES ...
...THAT WAS CARELESS OF ME...
DON'T LOOK AROUND. KEEP YOUR EYES ON ME.
PRETEND LIKE YOU'RE MAKING SURE I'M DEAD.
IMAGINE THAT SOMEONE IS WATCHING YOU.

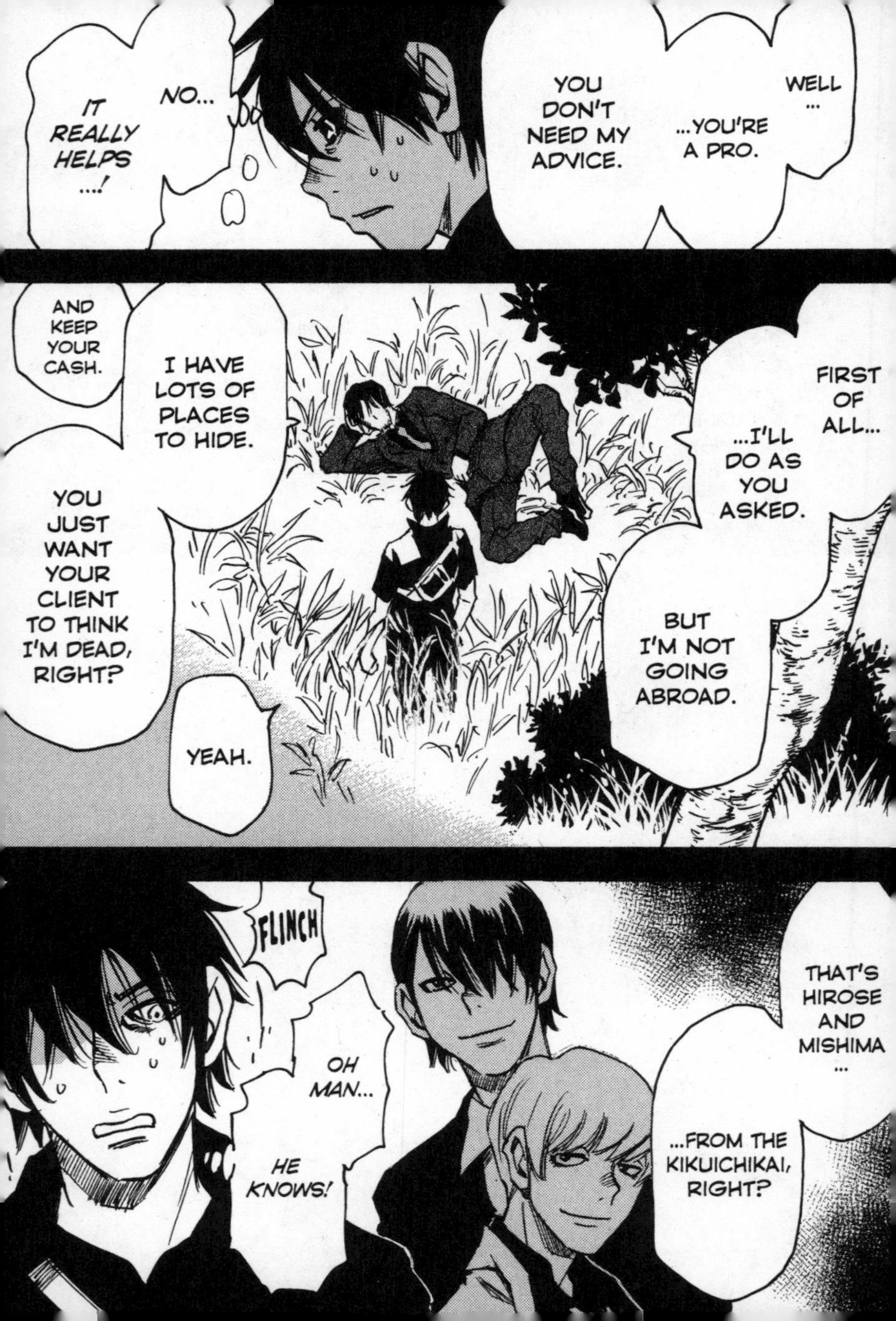
WELL ...
...YOU'RE A PRO.
YOU DON'T NEED MY ADVICE.
NO...
IT REALLY HELPS ...!
FIRST OF ALL...
...I'LL DO AS YOU ASKED.
BUT I'M NOT GOING ABROAD.
I HAVE LOTS OF PLACES TO HIDE.
AND KEEP YOUR CASH.
YOU JUST WANT YOUR CLIENT TO THINK I'M DEAD, RIGHT?
YEAH.
THAT'S HIROSE AND MISHIMA ...
...FROM THE KIKUICHIKAI, RIGHT?
FLINCH
OH MAN...
HE KNOWS!

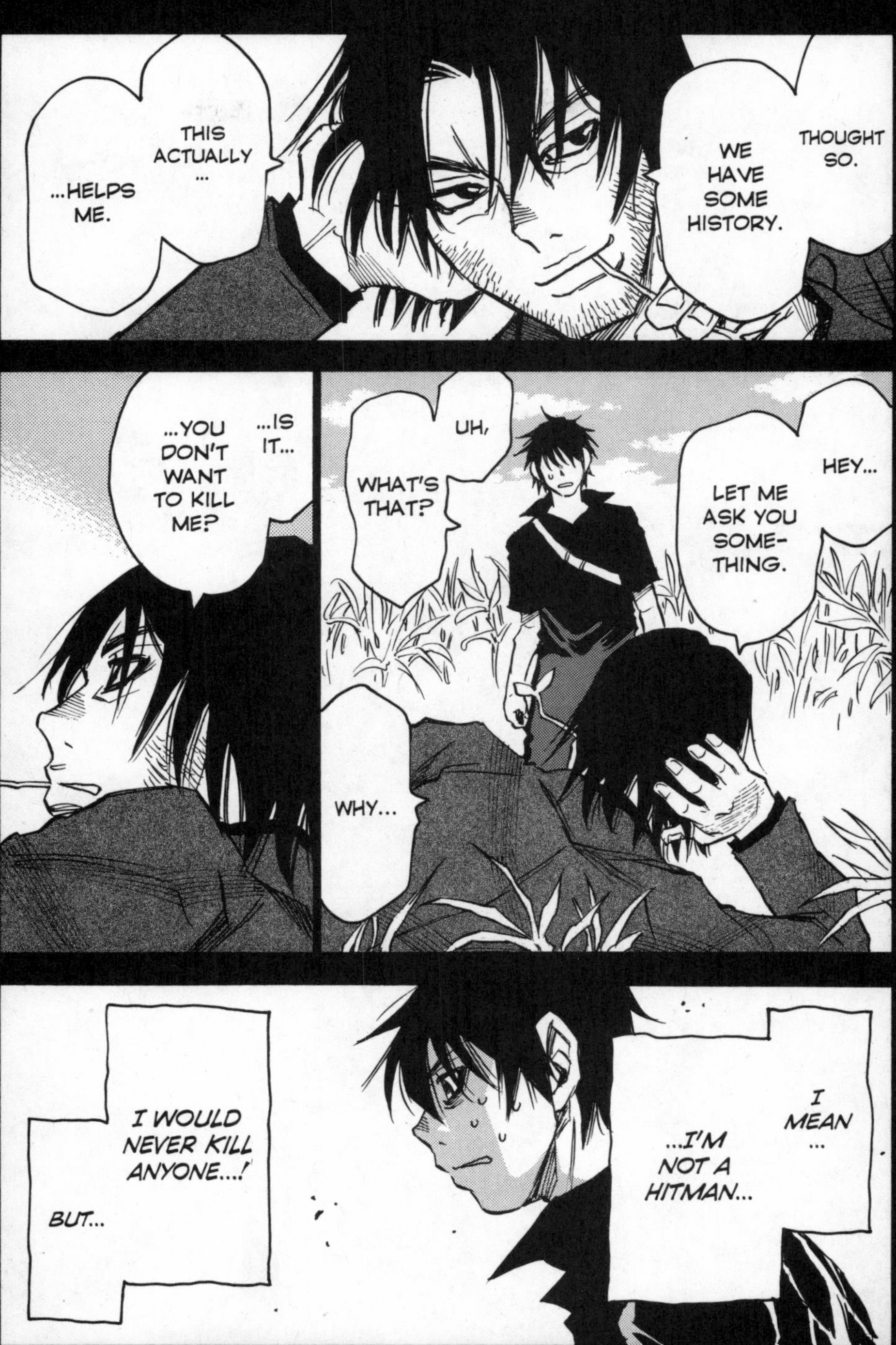
THOUGHT SO.
WE HAVE SOME HISTORY.
THIS ACTUALLY...
...HELPS ME.
HEY...
LET ME ASK YOU SOME-THING.
UH,
WHAT'S THAT?
WHY...
...IS IT...
...YOU DON'T WANT TO KILL ME?
I MEAN...
...I'M NOT A HITMAN...
I WOULD NEVER KILL ANYONE...!
BUT...

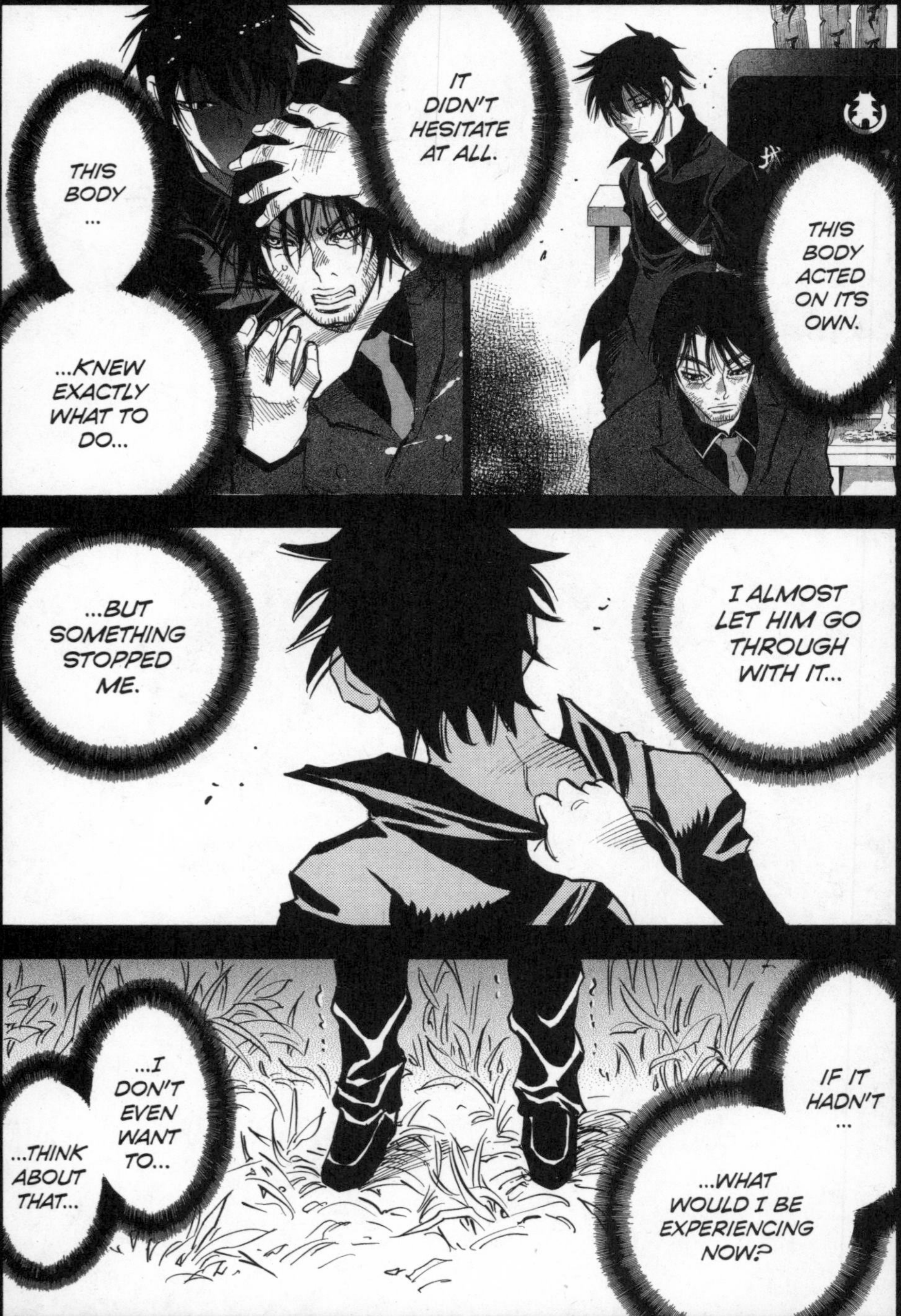
THIS BODY ACTED ON ITS OWN.
IT DIDN'T HESITATE AT ALL.
THIS BODY ...
...KNEW EXACTLY WHAT TO DO...
I ALMOST LET HIM GO THROUGH WITH IT...
...BUT SOMETHING STOPPED ME.
IF IT HADN'T ...
...WHAT WOULD I BE EXPERIENCING NOW?
...I DON'T EVEN WANT TO...
...THINK ABOUT THAT...

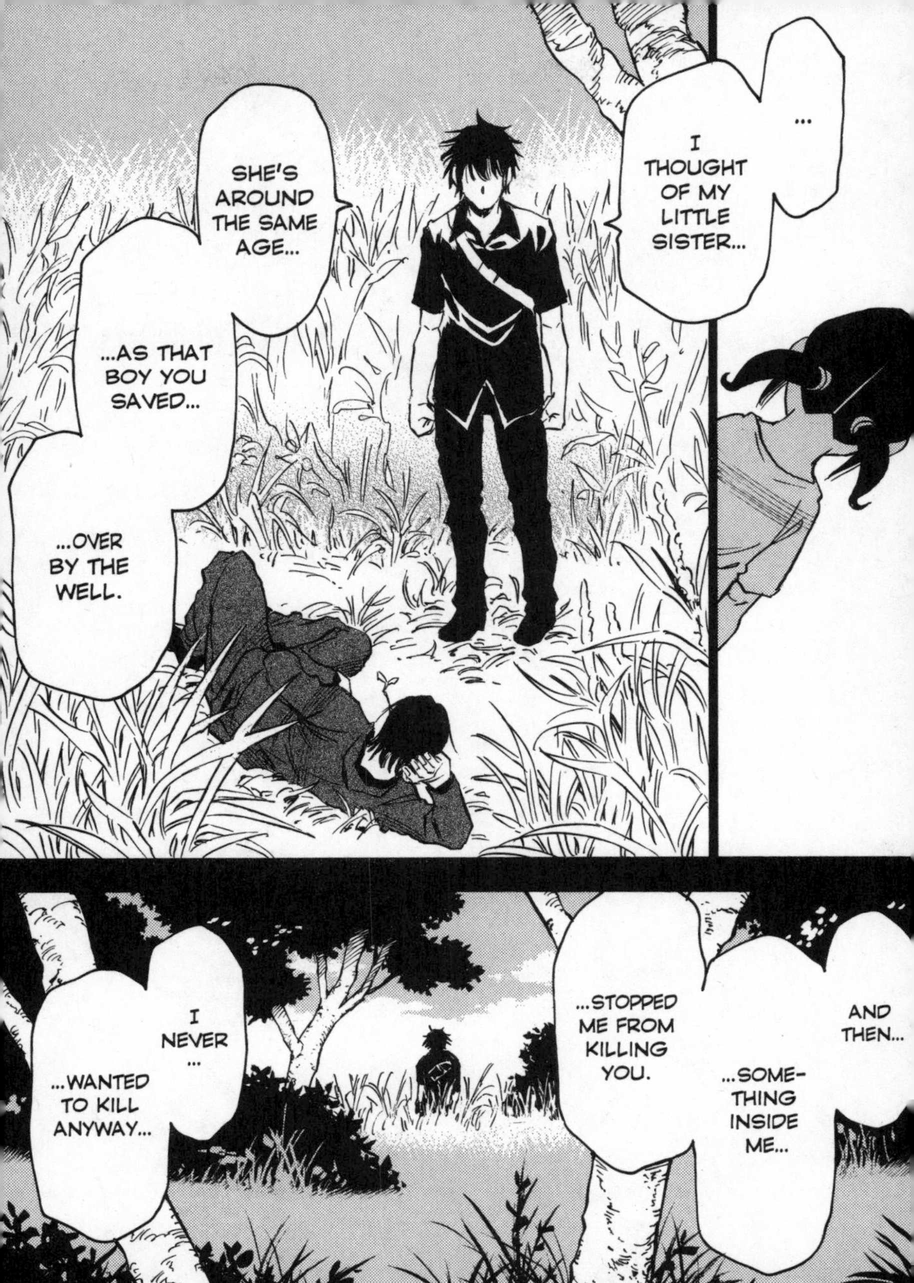
... I THOUGHT OF MY LITTLE SISTER...
SHE'S AROUND THE SAME AGE...
...AS THAT BOY YOU SAVED...
...OVER BY THE WELL.
AND THEN...
...SOME-THING INSIDE ME...
...STOPPED ME FROM KILLING YOU.
I NEVER ...
...WANTED TO KILL ANYWAY...

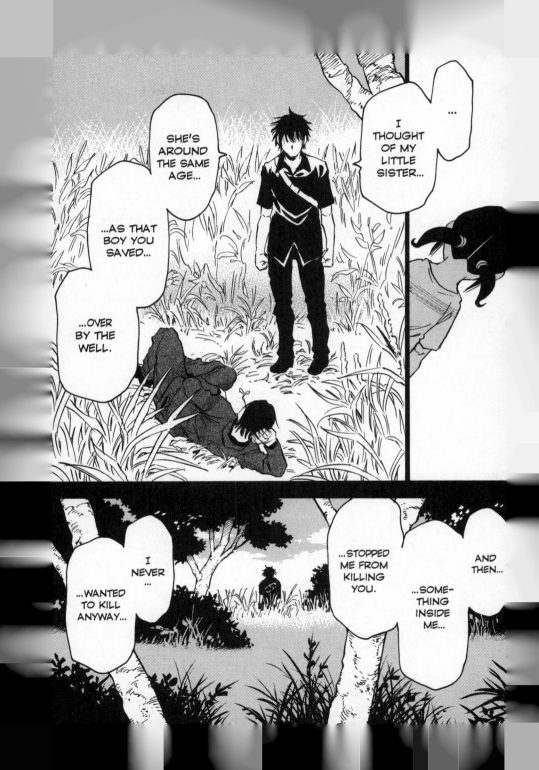

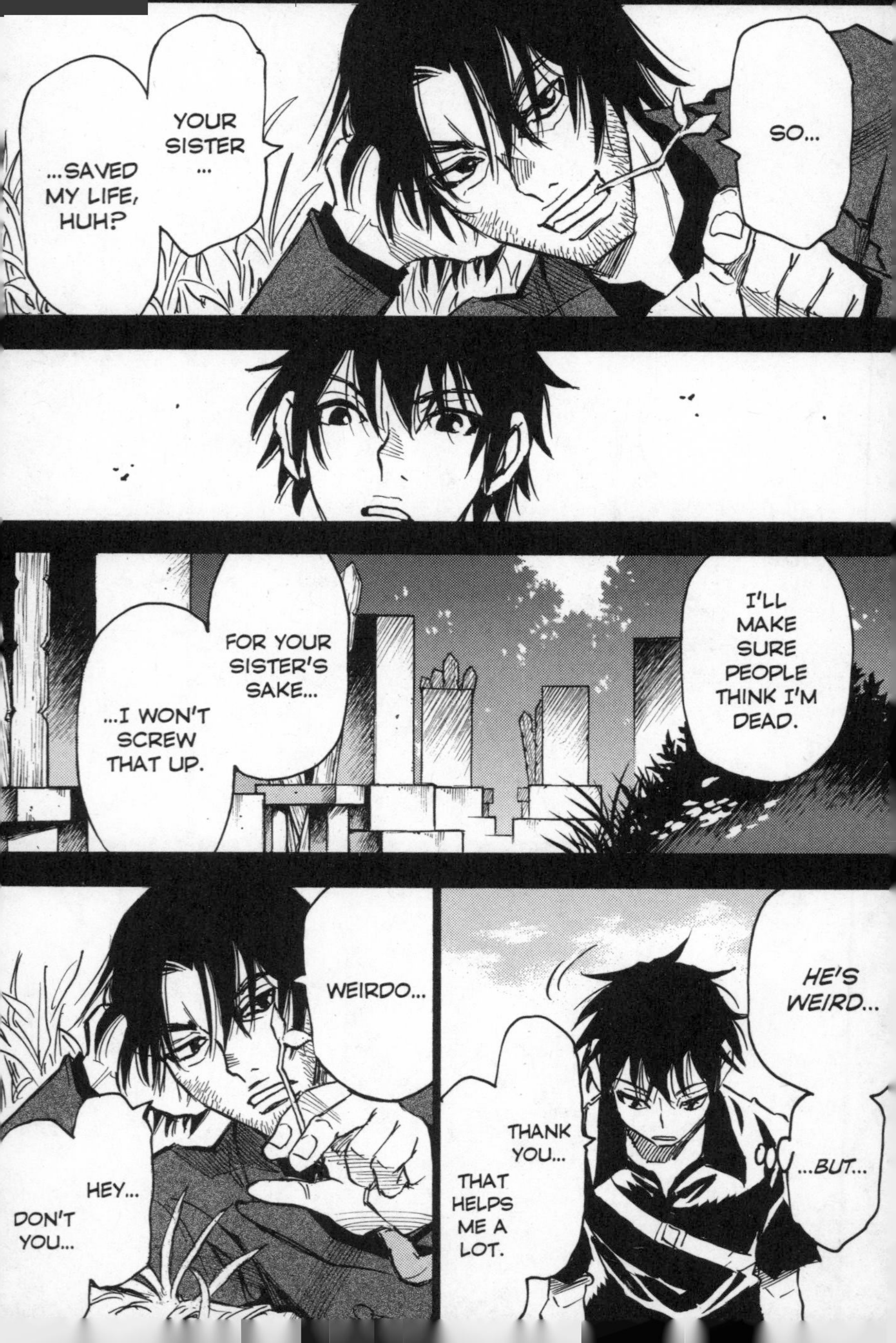
SO...
YOUR SISTER ...
...SAVED MY LIFE, HUH?
I'LL MAKE SURE PEOPLE THINK I'M DEAD.
FOR YOUR SISTER'S SAKE...
...I WON'T SCREW THAT UP.
HE'S WEIRD...
...BUT...
THANK YOU...
THAT HELPS ME A LOT.
WEIRDO...
HEY...
DON'T YOU...

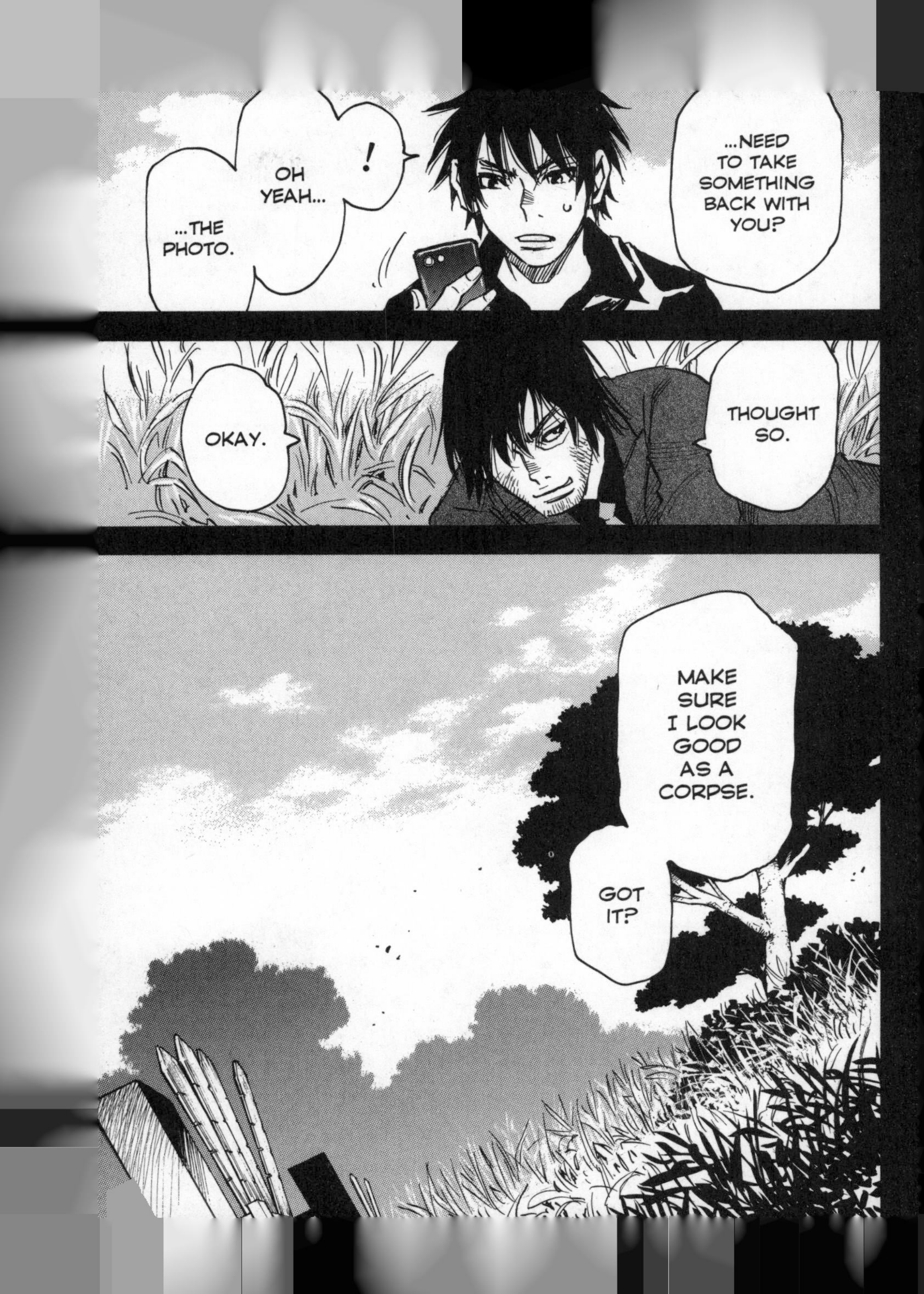
...NEED TO TAKE SOMETHING BACK WITH YOU?
!
OH YEAH...
...THE PHOTO.
THOUGHT SO.
OKAY.
MAKE SURE I LOOK GOOD AS A CORPSE.
GOT IT?

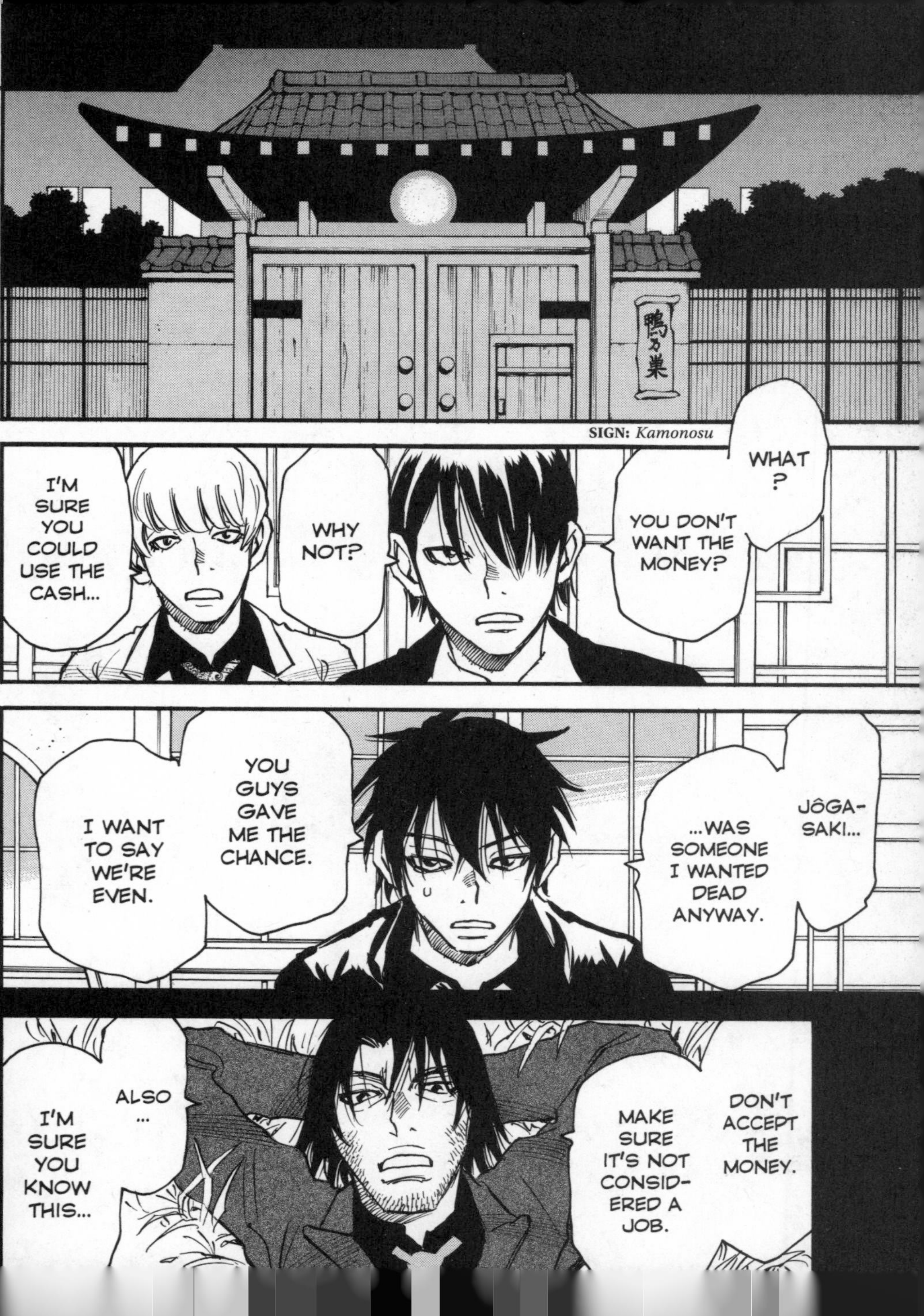

鴨乃巣
SIGN: *Kamonosu*
WHAT?
YOU DON'T WANT THE MONEY?
WHY NOT?
I'M SURE YOU COULD USE THE CASH...
JÔGA-SAKI...
...WAS SOMEONE I WANTED DEAD ANYWAY.
YOU GUYS GAVE ME THE CHANCE.
I WANT TO SAY WE'RE EVEN.
DON'T ACCEPT THE MONEY.
MAKE SURE IT'S NOT CONSIDERED A JOB.
ALSO...
I'M SURE YOU KNOW THIS...

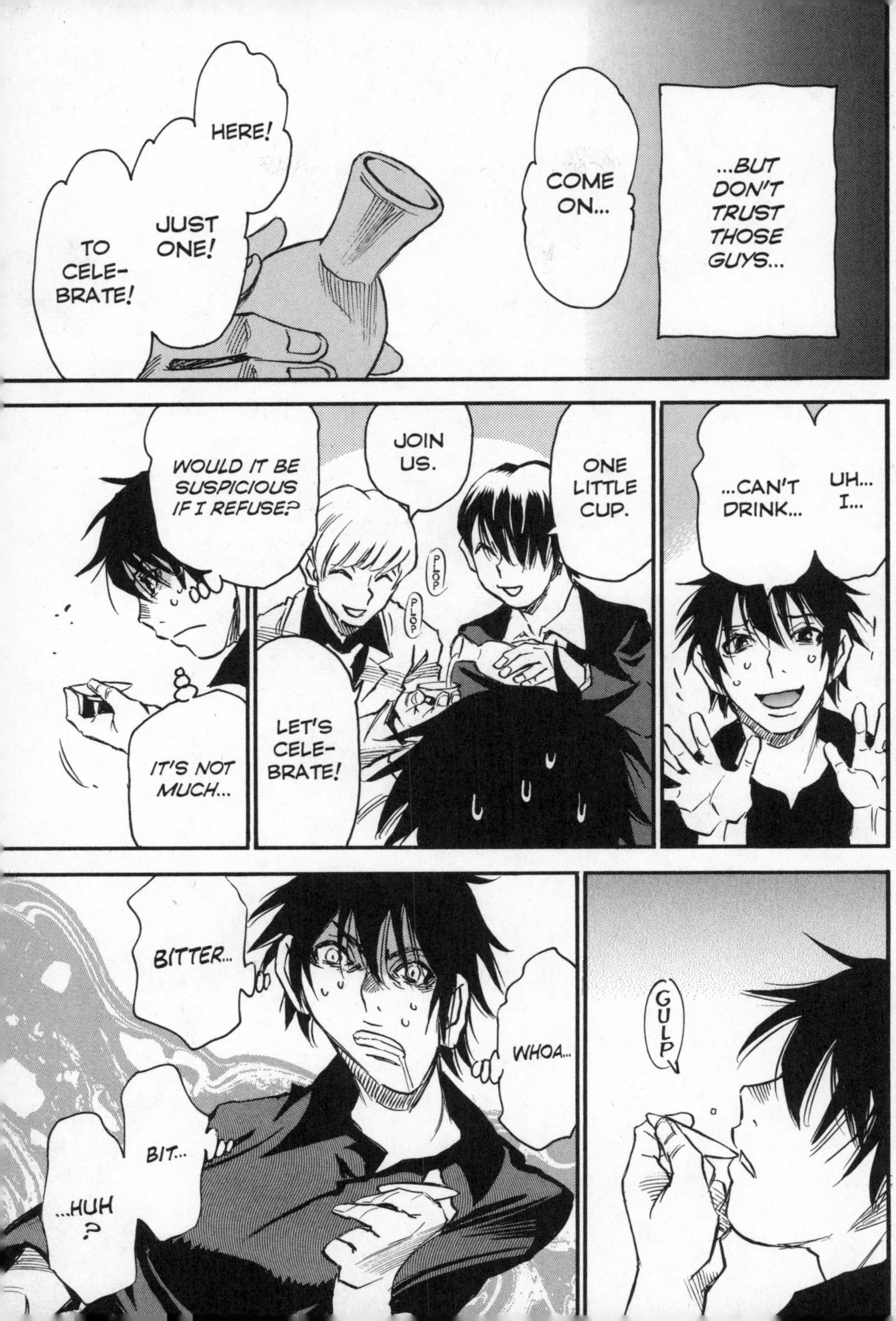
...BUT DON'T TRUST THOSE GUYS...
COME ON...
HERE!
JUST ONE!
TO CELE-BRATE!
UH... I...
...CAN'T DRINK...
ONE LITTLE CUP.
JOIN US.
PLOP
PLOP
LET'S CELE-BRATE!
WOULD IT BE SUSPICIOUS IF I REFUSE?
IT'S NOT MUCH...
GULP
WHOA...
BITTER...
BIT...
...HUH?

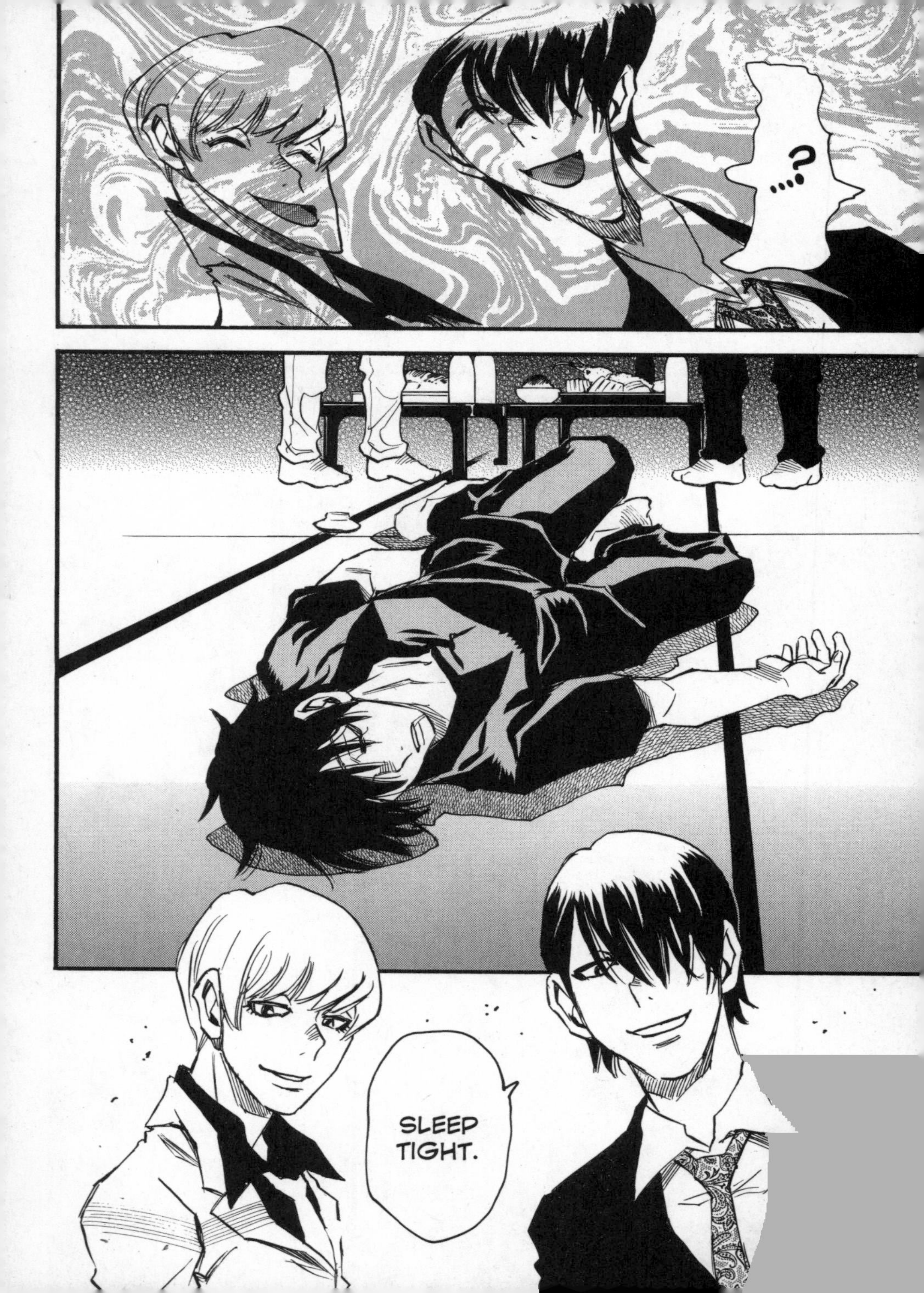
...?
SLEEP TIGHT.

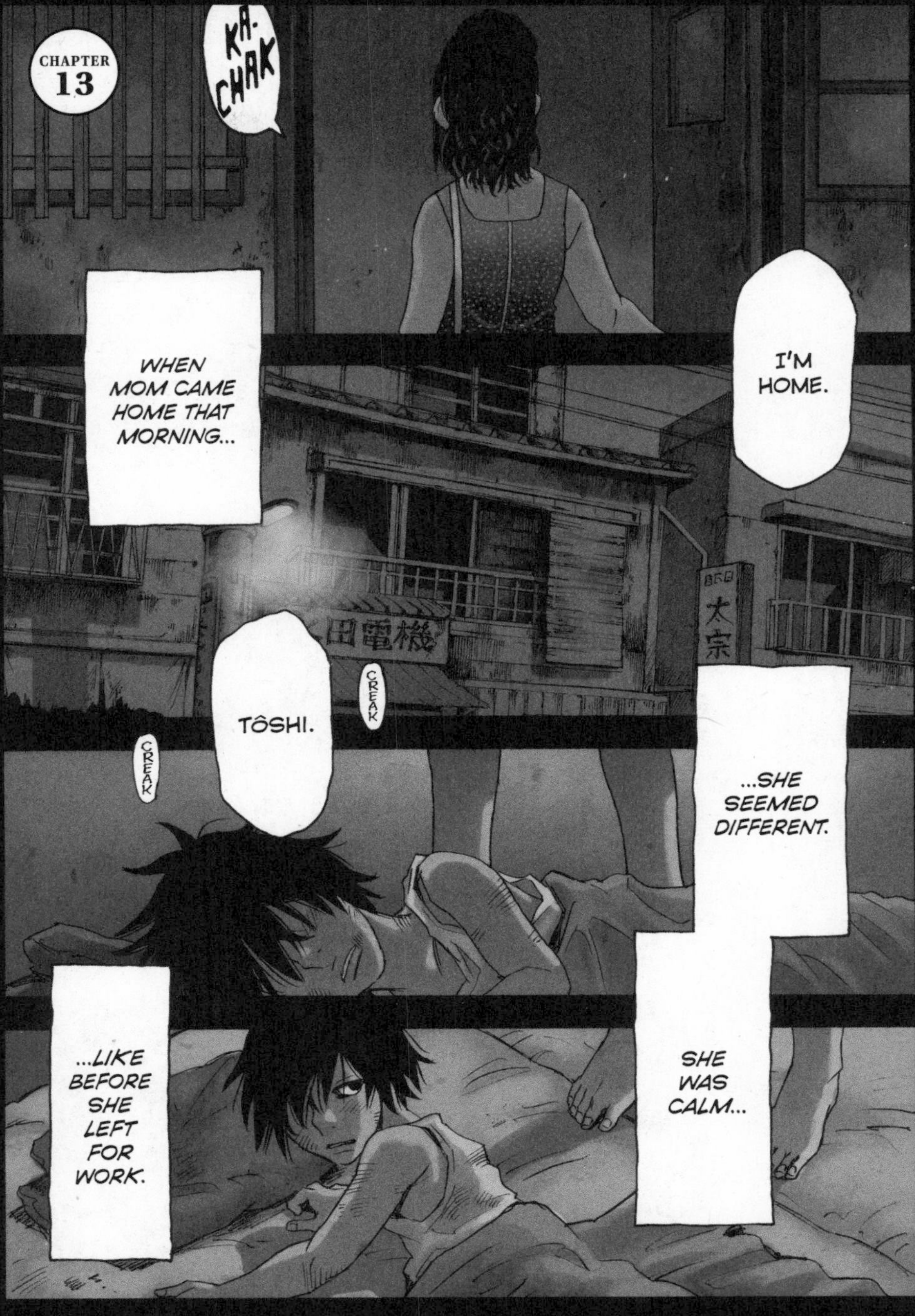
CHAPTER 13
KA-CHAK
I'M HOME.
WHEN MOM CAME HOME THAT MORNING...
太宗
田電機
...SHE SEEMED DIFFERENT.
CREAK
TÔSHI.
CREAK
SHE WAS CALM...
...LIKE BEFORE SHE LEFT FOR WORK.

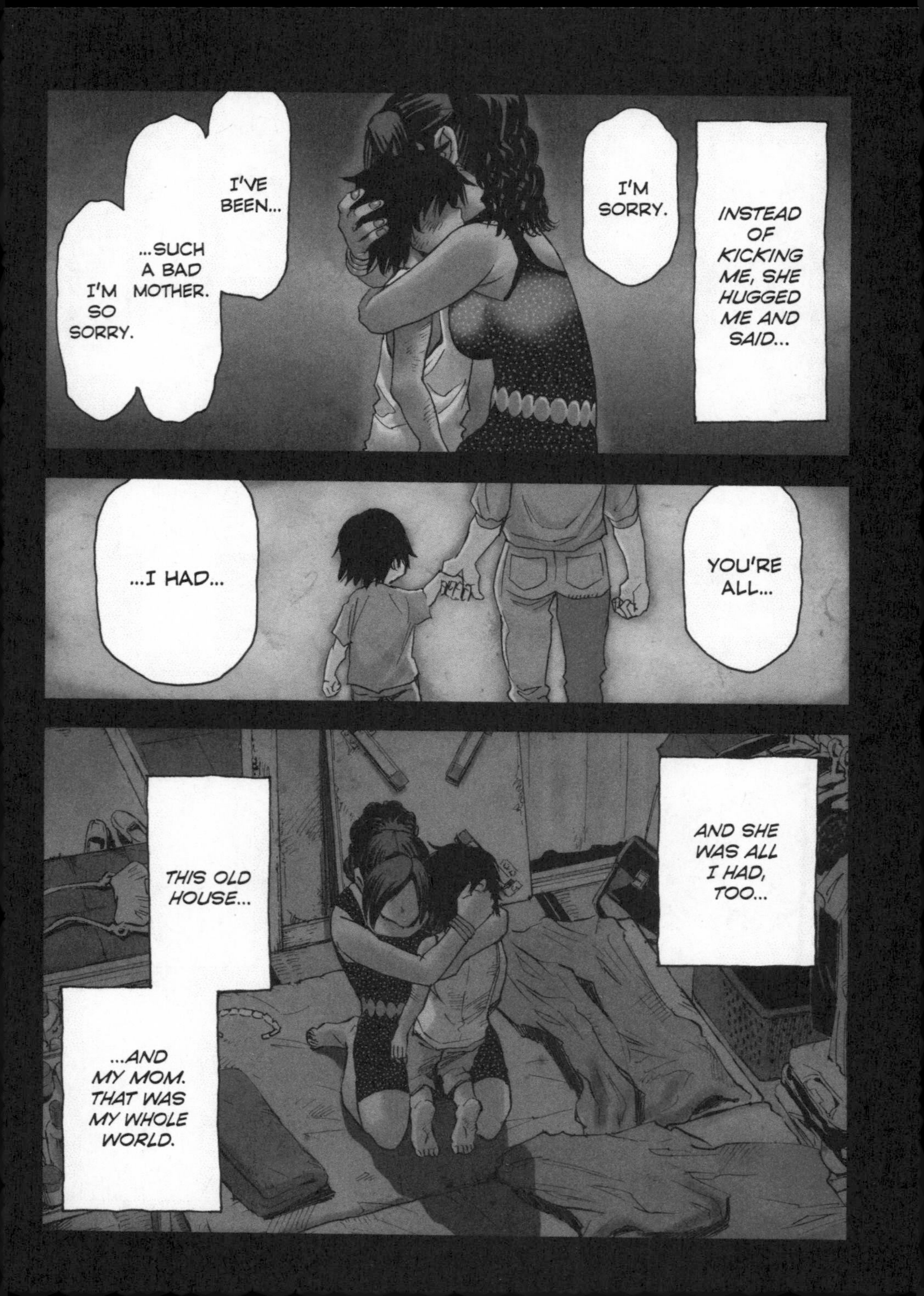
INSTEAD OF KICKING ME, SHE HUGGED ME AND SAID...
I'M SORRY.
I'VE BEEN...
...SUCH A BAD MOTHER.
I'M SO SORRY.
YOU'RE ALL...
...I HAD...
AND SHE WAS ALL I HAD, TOO...
THIS OLD HOUSE...
...AND MY MOM. THAT WAS MY WHOLE WORLD.

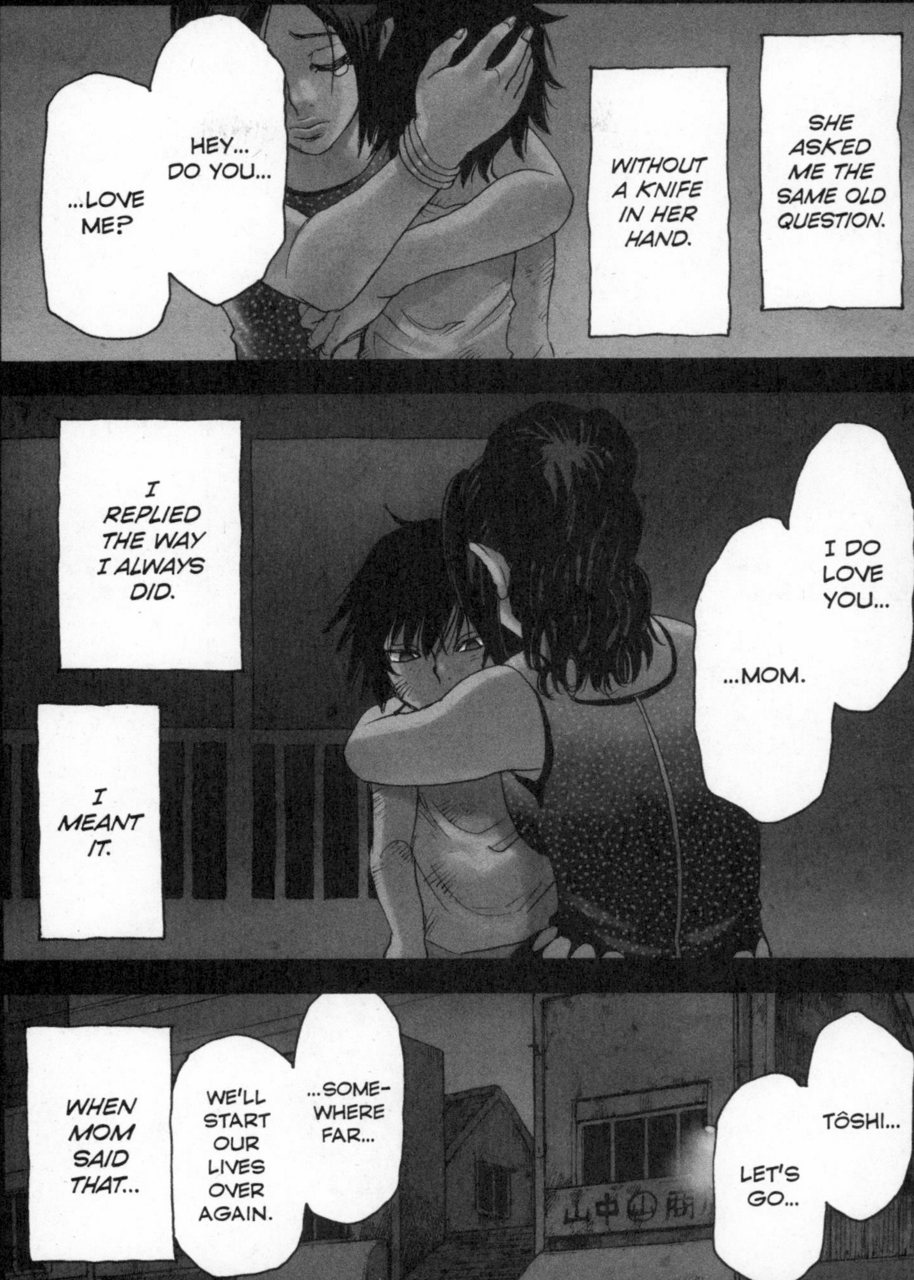
SHE ASKED ME THE SAME OLD QUESTION.
WITHOUT A KNIFE IN HER HAND.
HEY... DO YOU...
...LOVE ME?
I DO LOVE YOU...
...MOM.
I REPLIED THE WAY I ALWAYS DID.
I MEANT IT.
TÔSHI...
LET'S GO...
...SOME-WHERE FAR...
WE'LL START OUR LIVES OVER AGAIN.
WHEN MOM SAID THAT...

CHAPTER 13
Footsteps of Revenge

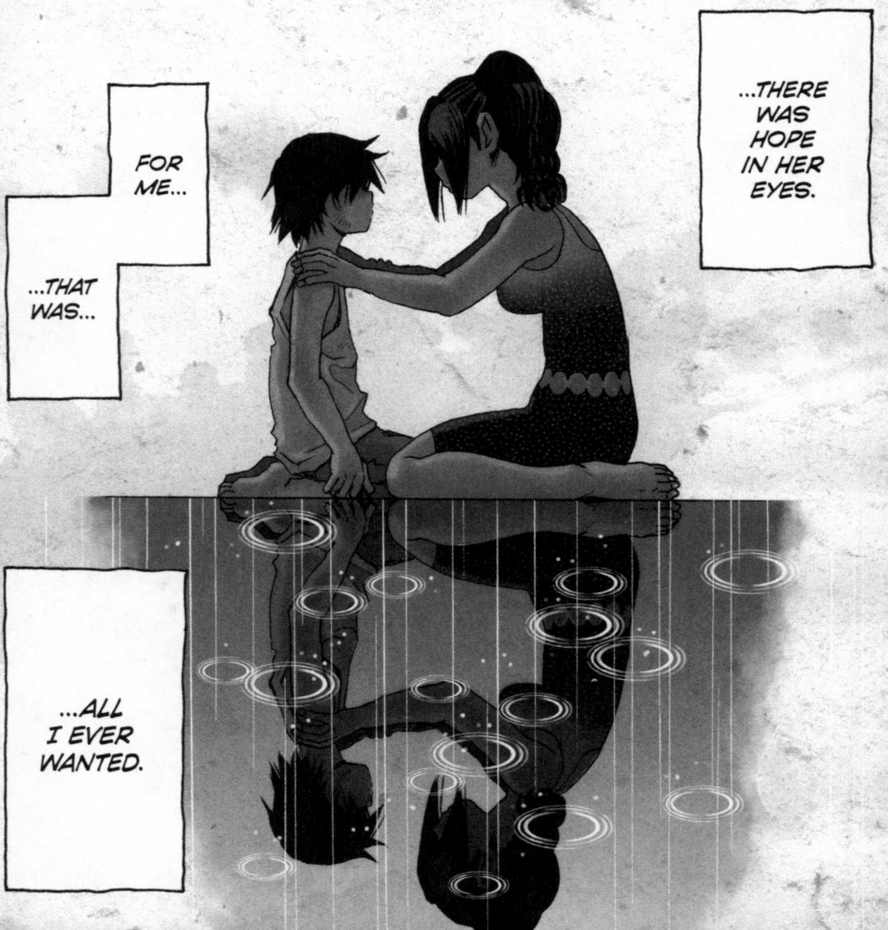
...THERE WAS HOPE IN HER EYES.
FOR ME...
...THAT WAS...
...ALL I EVER WANTED.

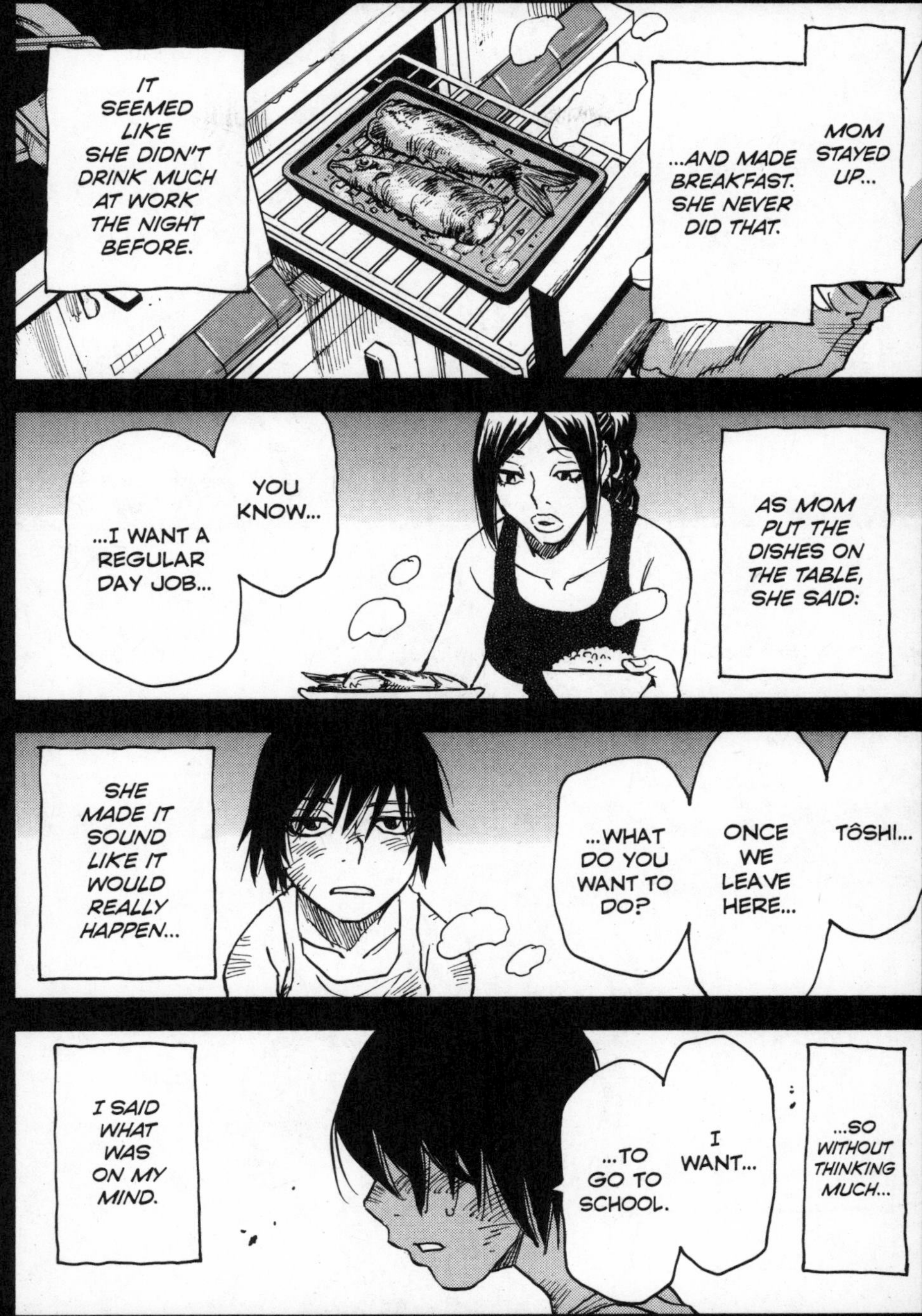

MOM STAYED UP...
...AND MADE BREAKFAST. SHE NEVER DID THAT.
IT SEEMED LIKE SHE DIDN'T DRINK MUCH AT WORK THE NIGHT BEFORE.
AS MOM PUT THE DISHES ON THE TABLE, SHE SAID:
YOU KNOW... ...I WANT A REGULAR DAY JOB...
TÔSHI... ONCE WE LEAVE HERE... ...WHAT DO YOU WANT TO DO?
SHE MADE IT SOUND LIKE IT WOULD REALLY HAPPEN...
...SO WITHOUT THINKING MUCH...
I WANT... ...TO GO TO SCHOOL.
I SAID WHAT WAS ON MY MIND.

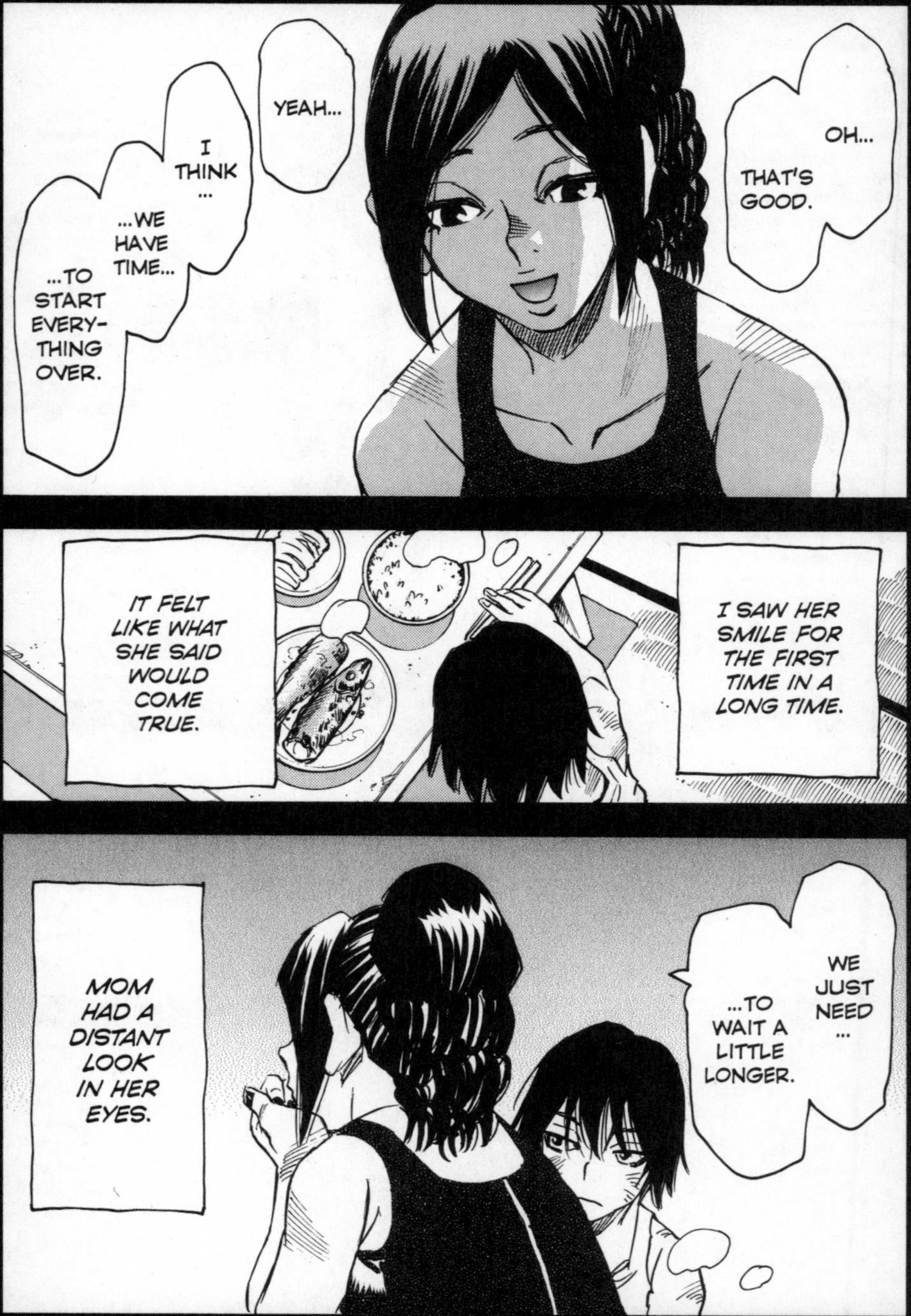
OH... THAT'S GOOD.
YEAH...
I THINK ...
...WE HAVE TIME...
...TO START EVERY-THING OVER.
I SAW HER SMILE FOR THE FIRST TIME IN A LONG TIME.
IT FELT LIKE WHAT SHE SAID WOULD COME TRUE.
WE JUST NEED ...
...TO WAIT A LITTLE LONGER.
MOM HAD A DISTANT LOOK IN HER EYES.

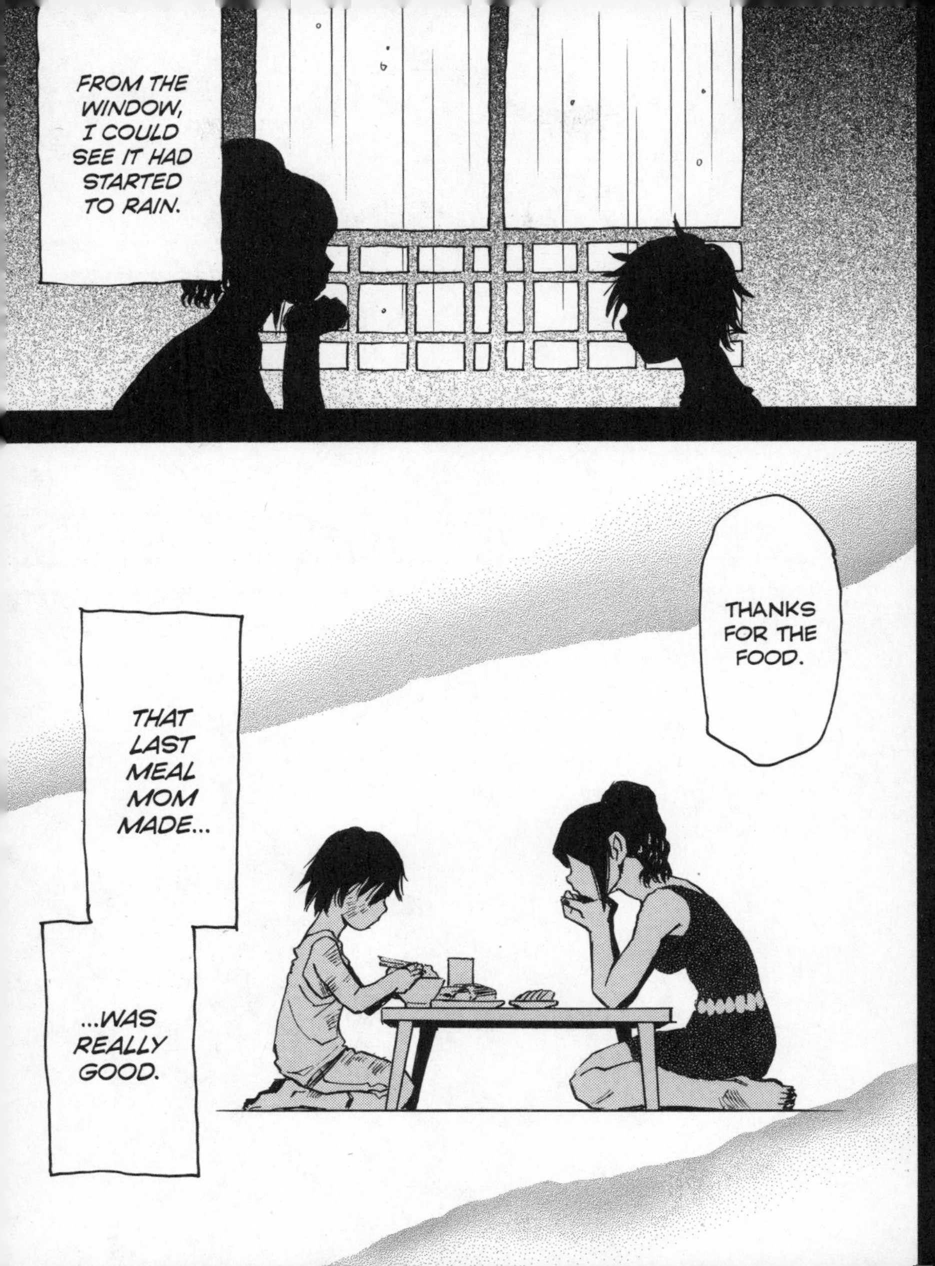
FROM THE WINDOW, I COULD SEE IT HAD STARTED TO RAIN.
THANKS FOR THE FOOD.
THAT LAST MEAL MOM MADE...
...WAS REALLY GOOD.

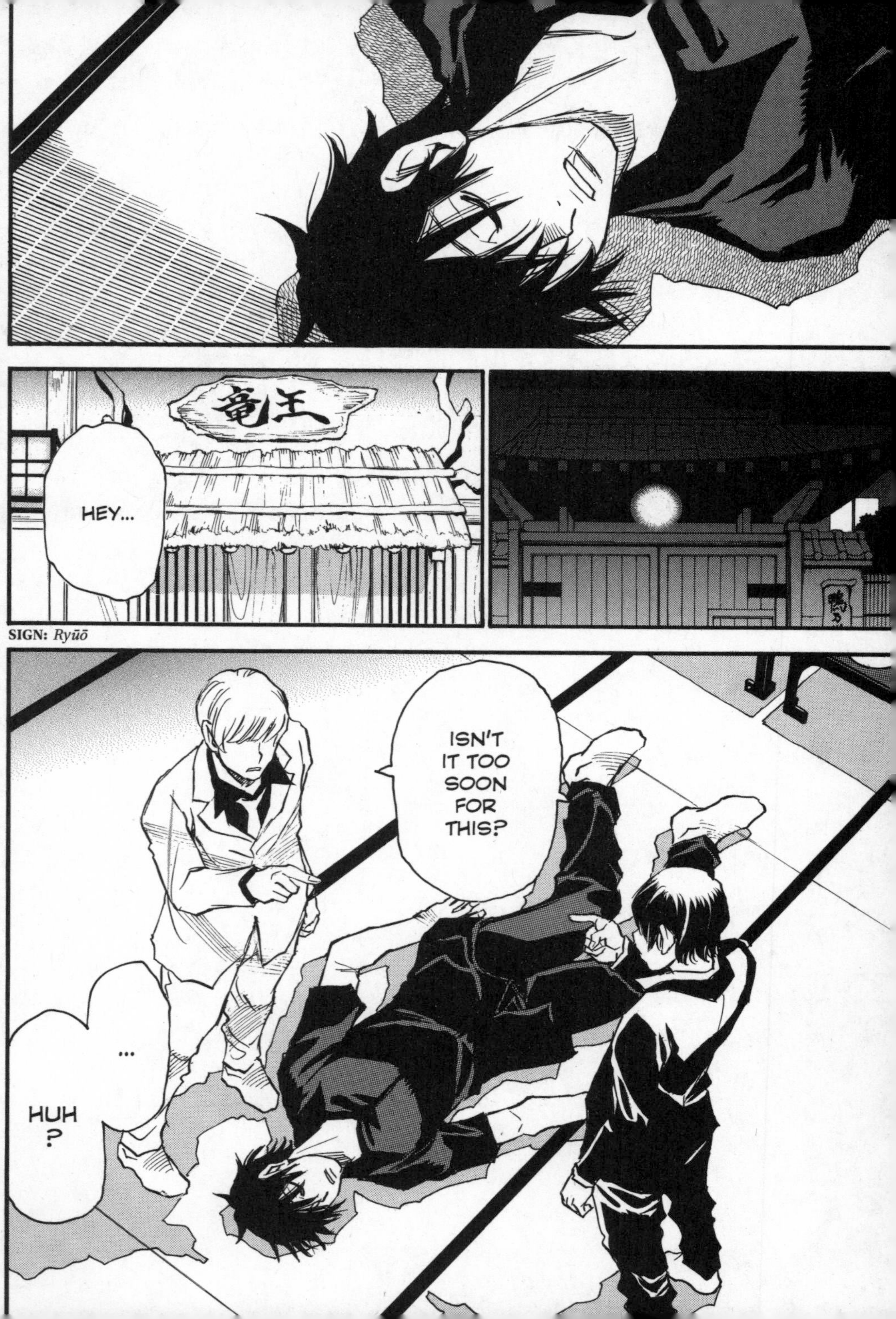
竜王
HEY...
ISN'T IT TOO SOON FOR THIS?
... HUH?
SIGN: *Ryūō*

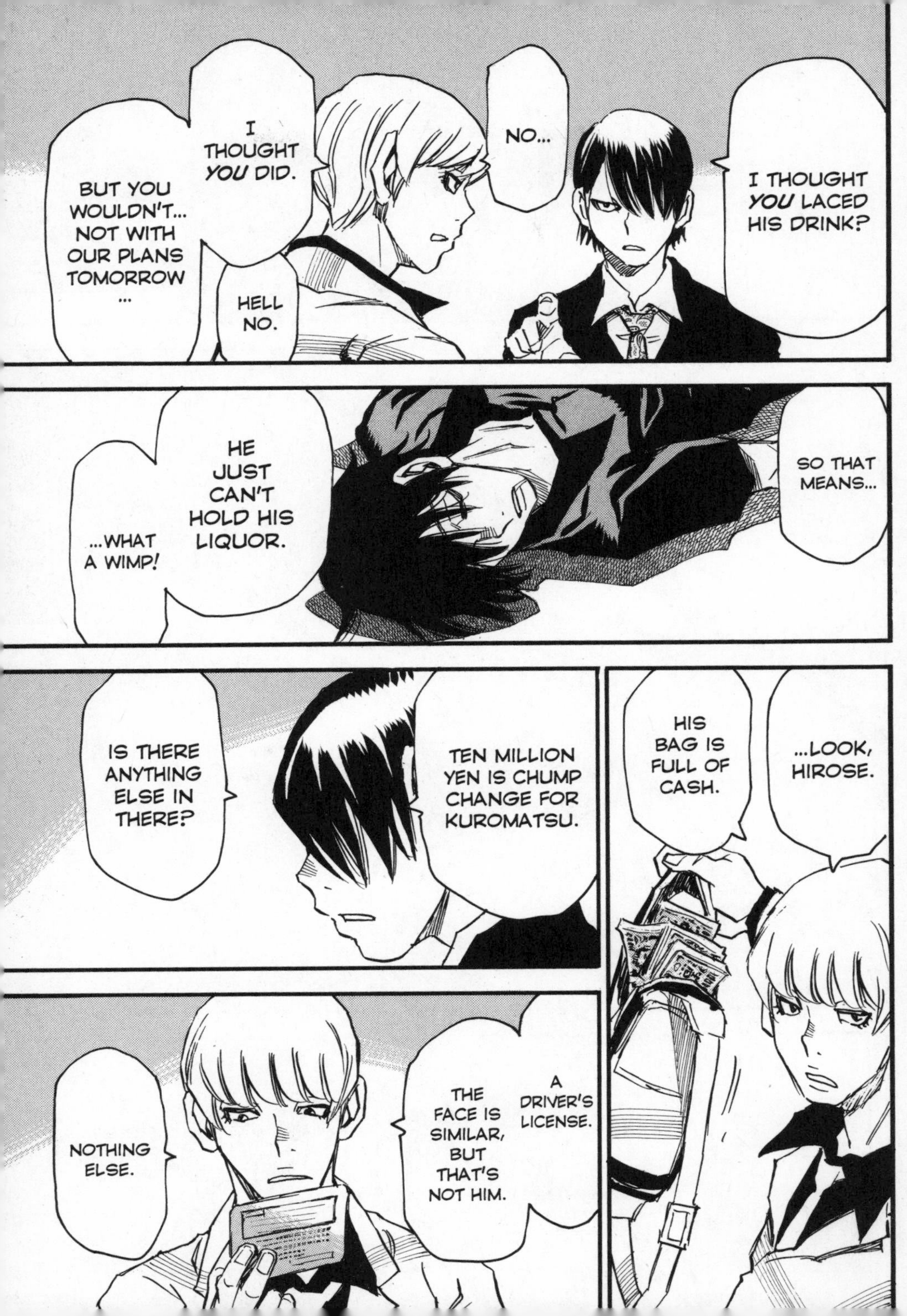
I THOUGHT *YOU* LACED HIS DRINK?
NO...
I THOUGHT *YOU* DID.
BUT YOU WOULDN'T... NOT WITH OUR PLANS TOMORROW ...
HELL NO.
SO THAT MEANS...
HE JUST CAN'T HOLD HIS LIQUOR.
...WHAT A WIMP!
...LOOK, HIROSE.
HIS BAG IS FULL OF CASH.
TEN MILLION YEN IS CHUMP CHANGE FOR KUROMATSU.
IS THERE ANYTHING ELSE IN THERE?
A DRIVER'S LICENSE.
THE FACE IS SIMILAR, BUT THAT'S NOT HIM.
NOTHING ELSE.

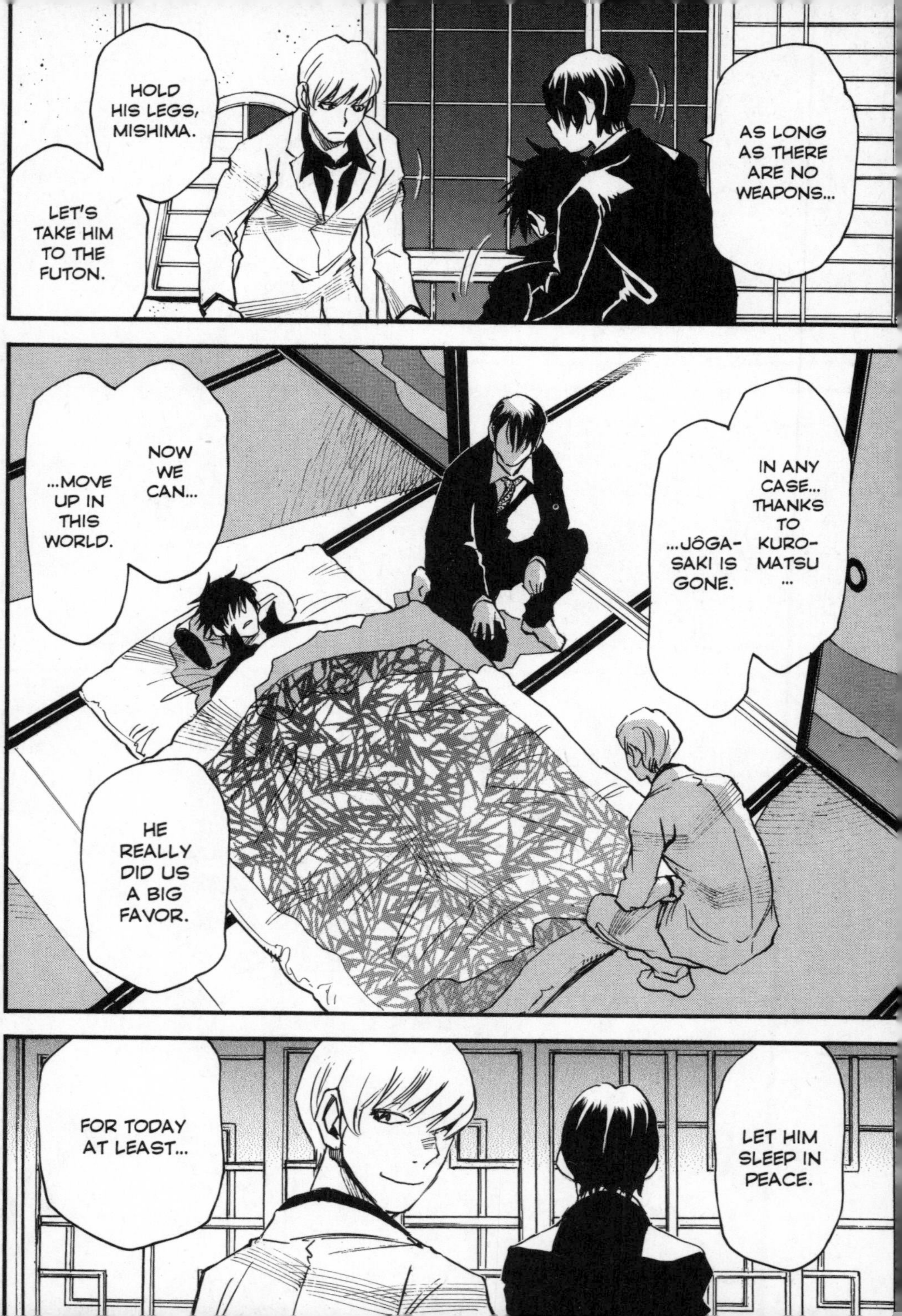
AS LONG AS THERE ARE NO WEAPONS...
HOLD HIS LEGS, MISHIMA.
LET'S TAKE HIM TO THE FUTON.
IN ANY CASE... THANKS TO KURO-MATSU...
...JÔGA-SAKI IS GONE.
NOW WE CAN...
...MOVE UP IN THIS WORLD.
HE REALLY DID US A BIG FAVOR.
LET HIM SLEEP IN PEACE.
FOR TODAY AT LEAST...

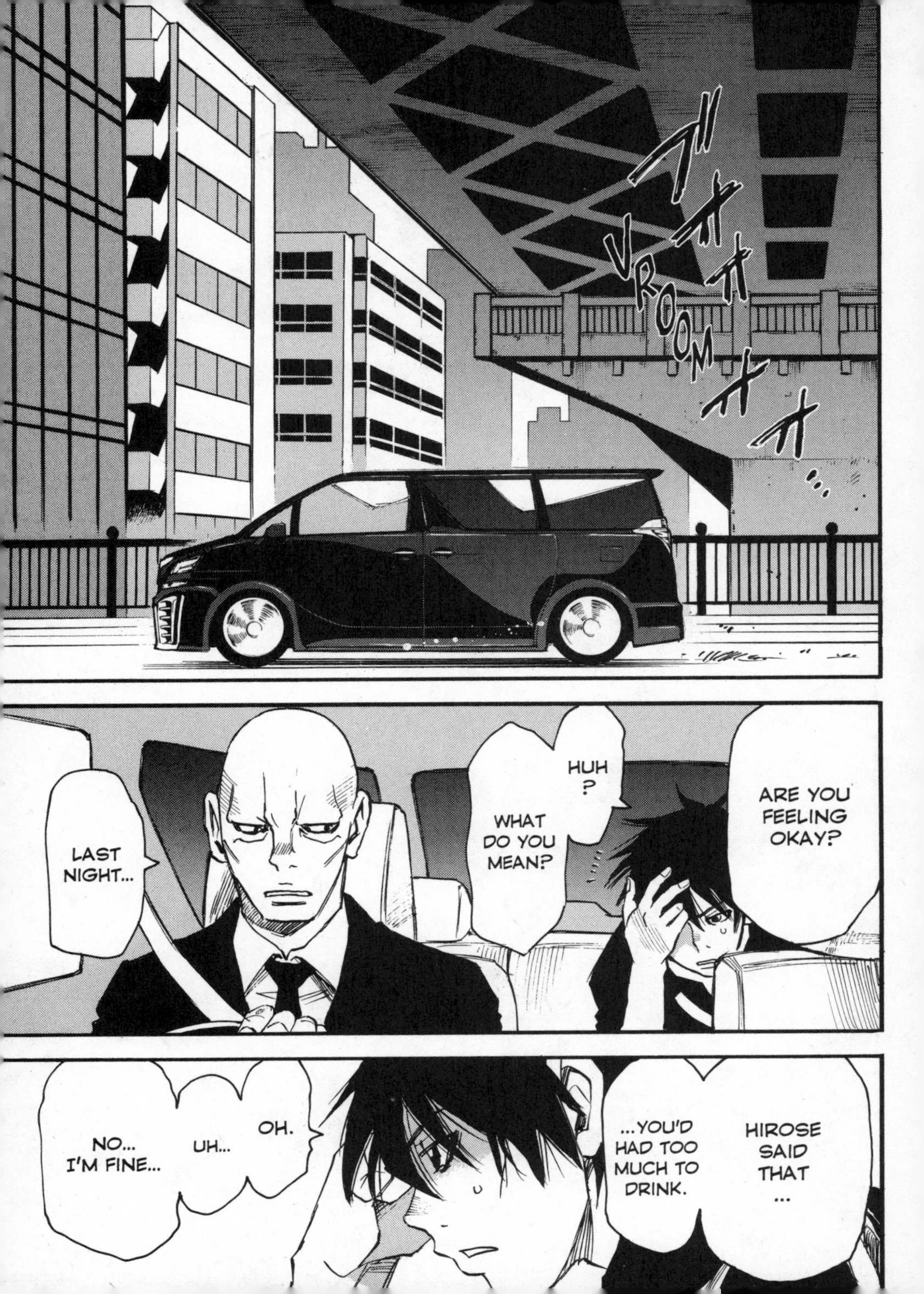
VROOM
ARE YOU FEELING OKAY?
HUH? WHAT DO YOU MEAN?
LAST NIGHT...
HIROSE SAID THAT...
...YOU'D HAD TOO MUCH TO DRINK.
OH.
UH...
NO... I'M FINE...

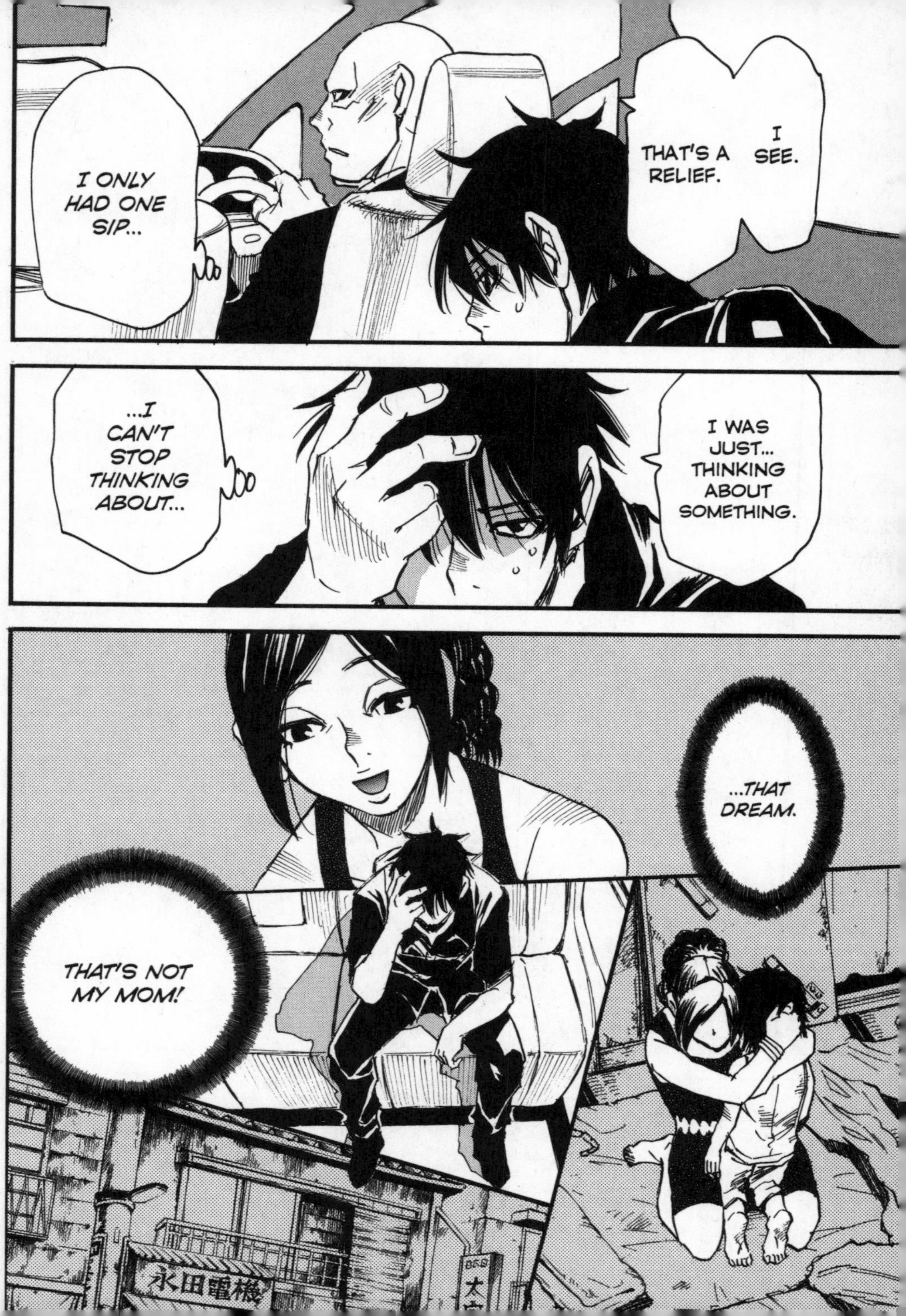
I SEE. THAT'S A RELIEF.
I ONLY HAD ONE SIP...
I WAS JUST... THINKING ABOUT SOMETHING.
...I CAN'T STOP THINKING ABOUT...
...THAT DREAM.
THAT'S NOT MY MOM!
永田電機

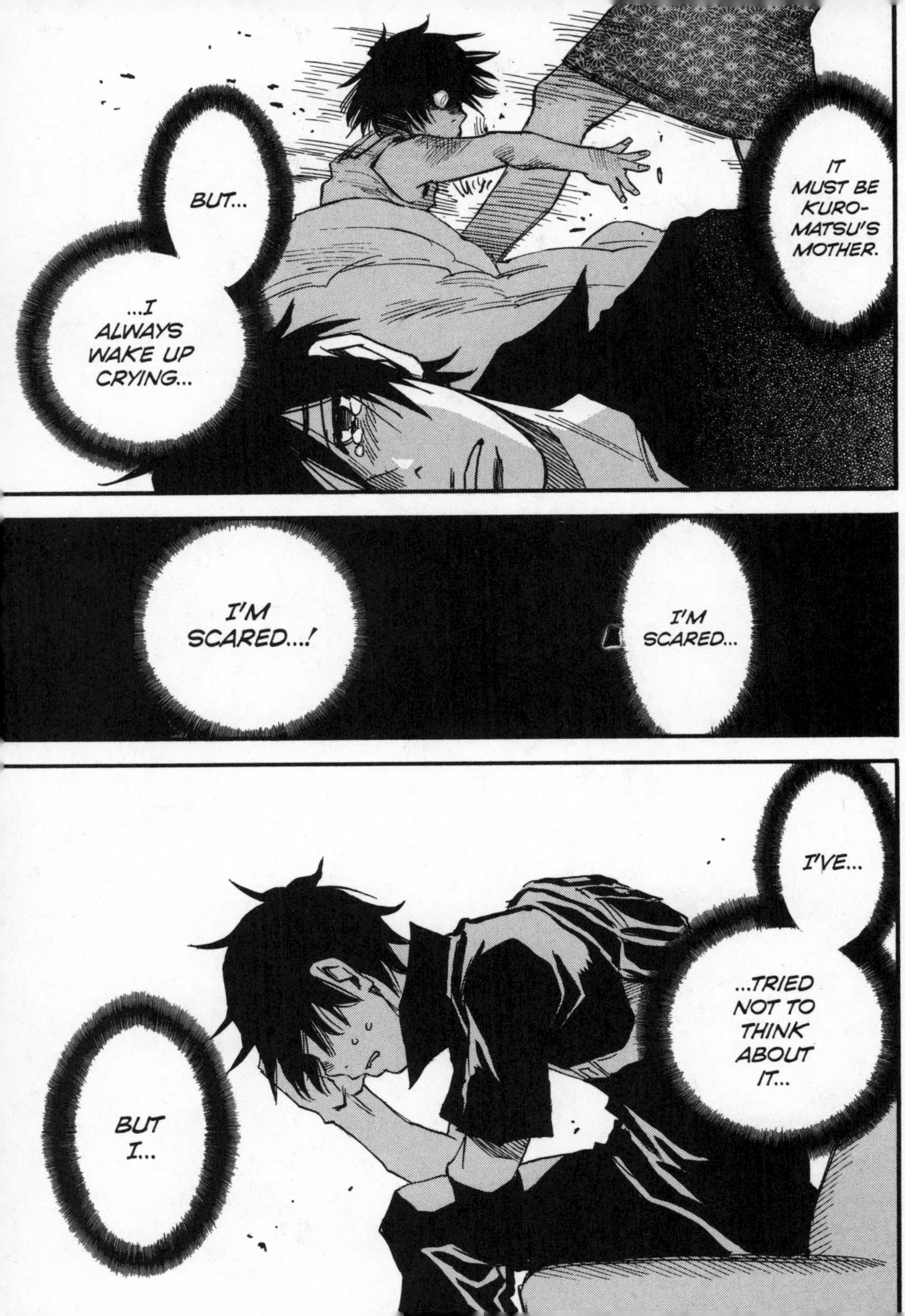
IT MUST BE KURO-MATSU'S MOTHER.
BUT...
...I ALWAYS WAKE UP CRYING...
I'M SCARED...
I'M SCARED...!
I'VE...
...TRIED NOT TO THINK ABOUT IT...
BUT I...

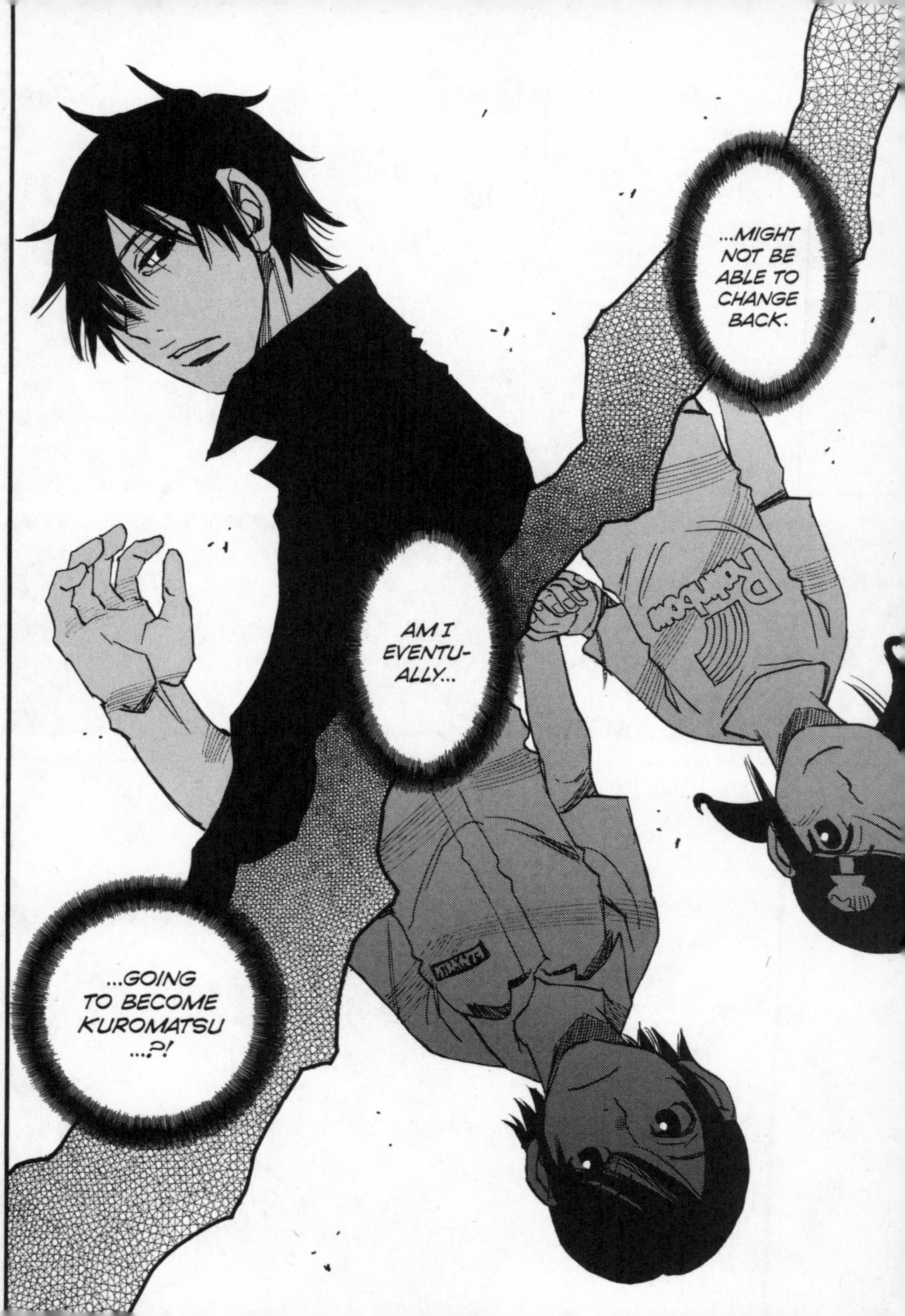
...MIGHT NOT BE ABLE TO CHANGE BACK.
AM I EVENTU-ALLY...
...GOING TO BECOME KUROMATSU ...?!

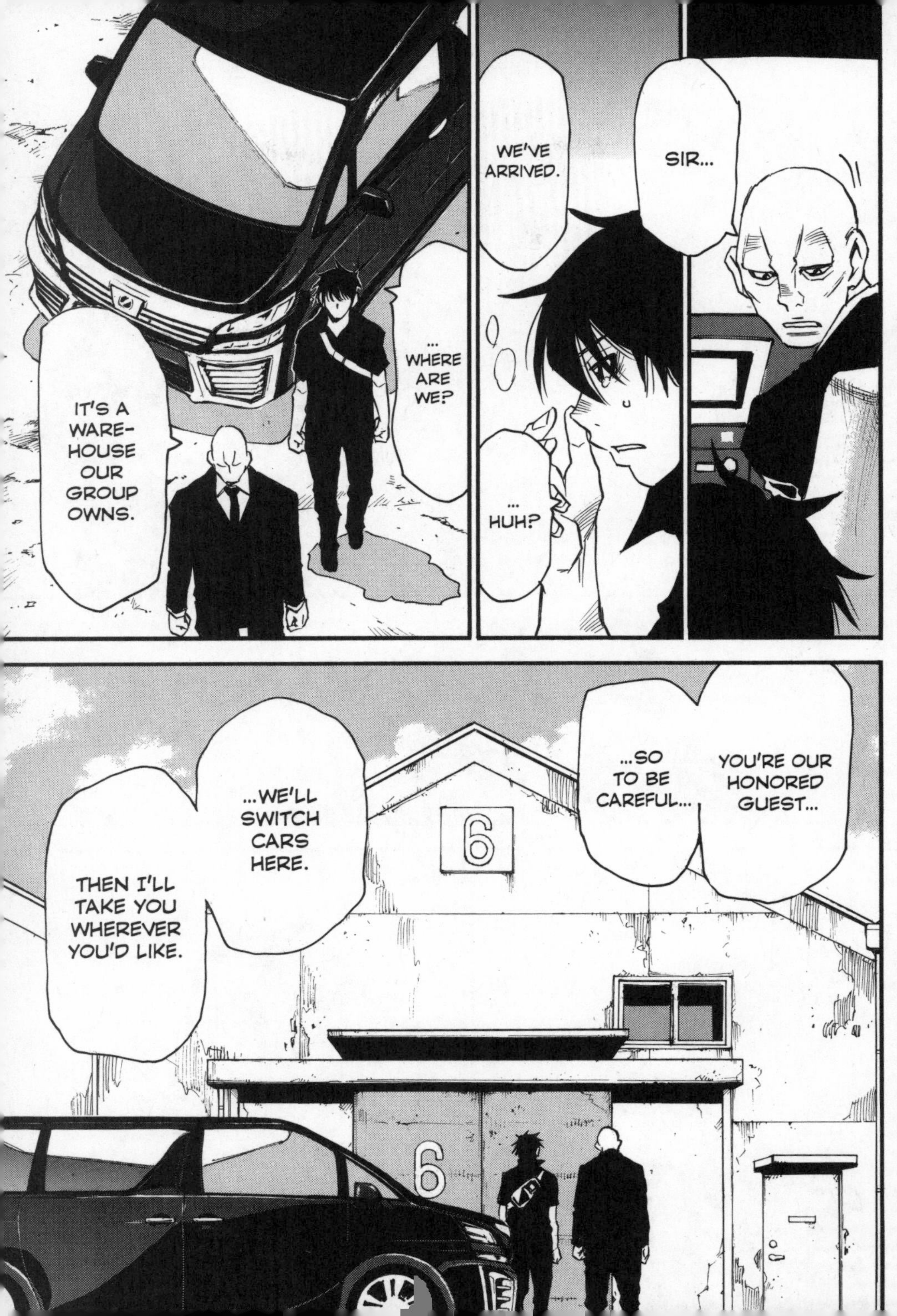
SIR...
WE'VE ARRIVED.
...HUH?
...WHERE ARE WE?
IT'S A WAREHOUSE OUR GROUP OWNS.
YOU'RE OUR HONORED GUEST...
...SO TO BE CAREFUL...
...WE'LL SWITCH CARS HERE.
THEN I'LL TAKE YOU WHEREVER YOU'D LIKE.

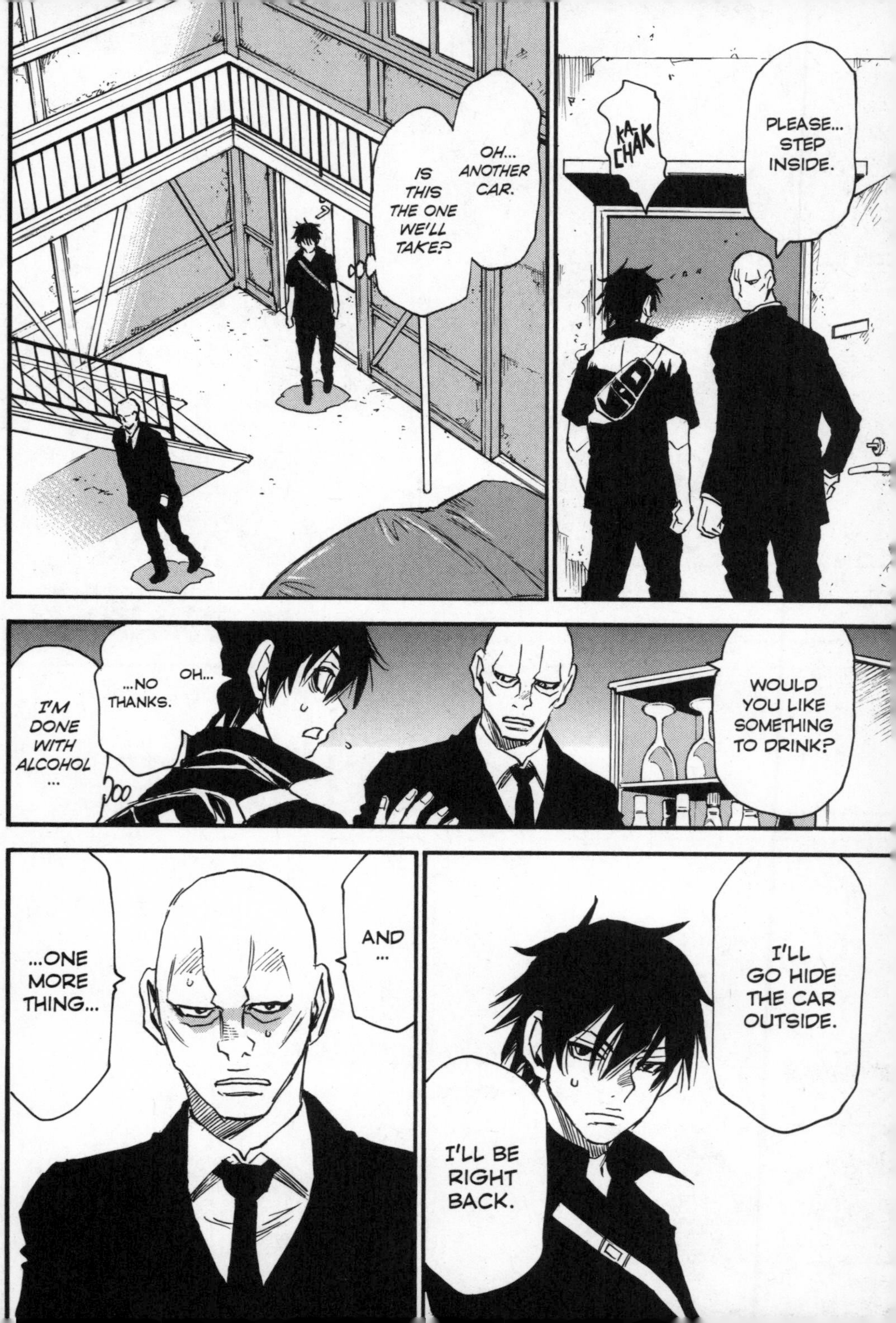
PLEASE... STEP INSIDE.
KA-CHAK
OH... ANOTHER CAR.
IS THIS THE ONE WE'LL TAKE?
WOULD YOU LIKE SOMETHING TO DRINK?
OH...
...NO THANKS.
I'M DONE WITH ALCOHOL...
I'LL GO HIDE THE CAR OUTSIDE.
I'LL BE RIGHT BACK.
AND...
...ONE MORE THING...

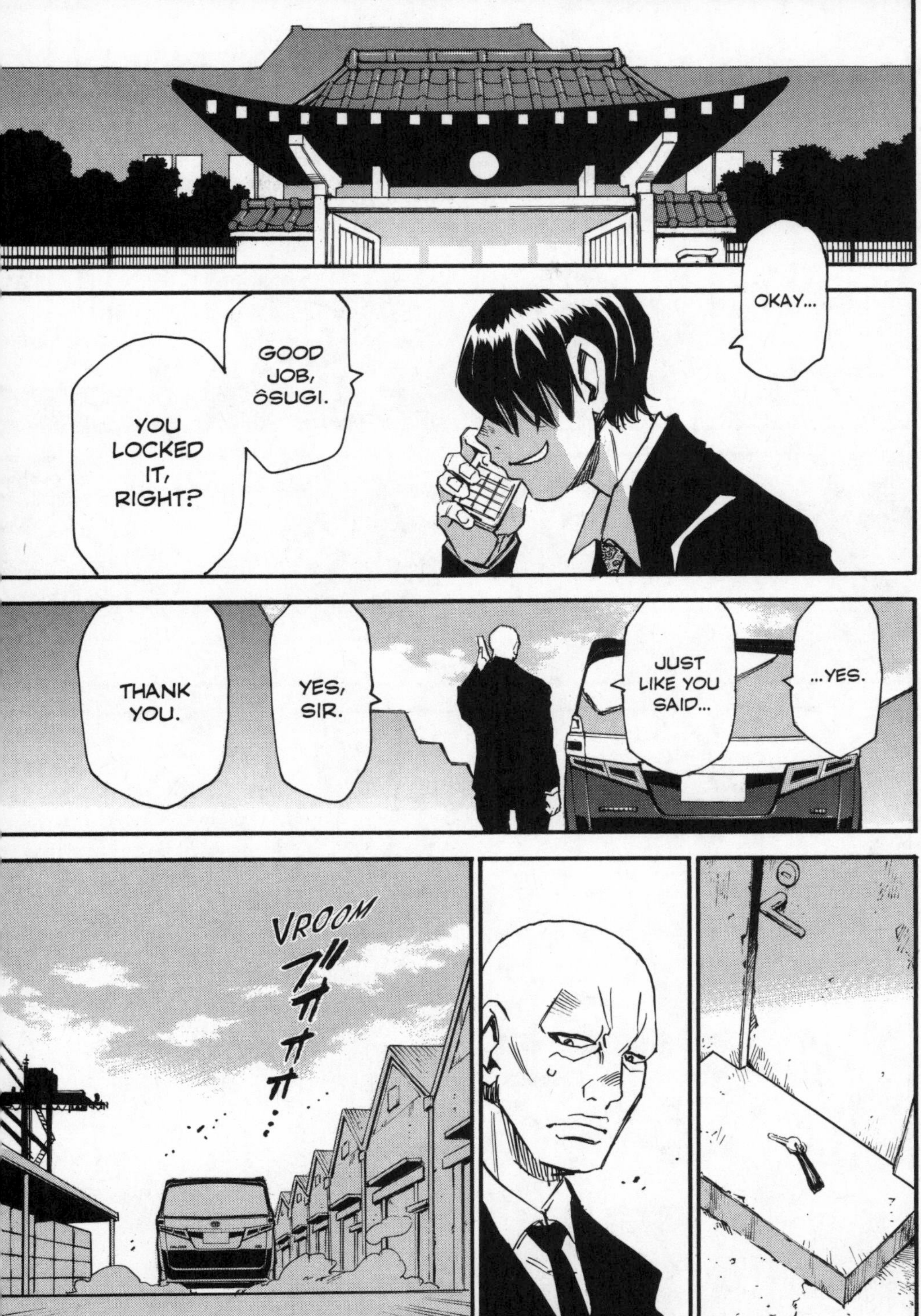
OKAY...
GOOD JOB, ÔSUGI.
YOU LOCKED IT, RIGHT?
...YES.
JUST LIKE YOU SAID...
YES, SIR.
THANK YOU.
VROOM

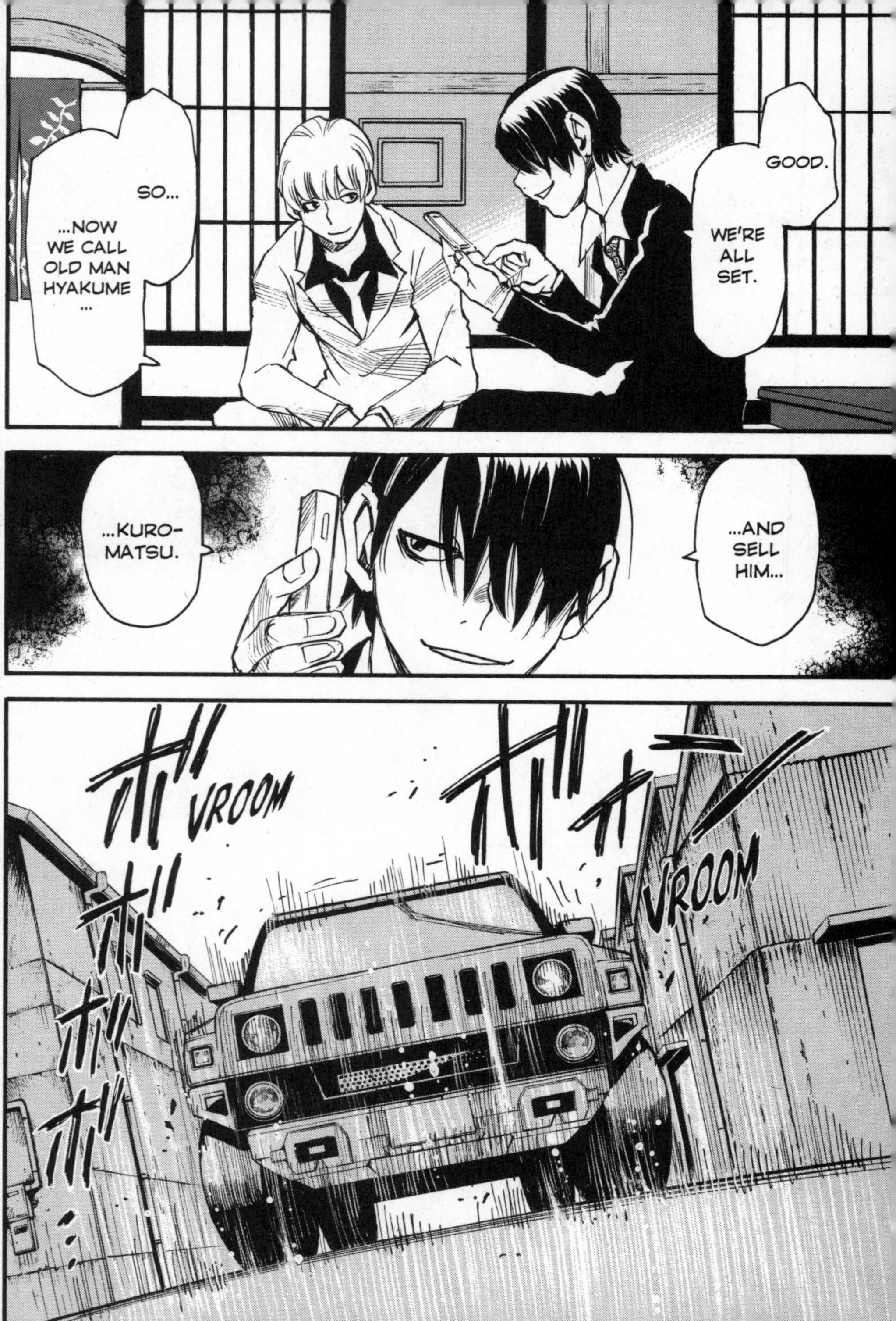
GOOD.
WE'RE ALL SET.
SO...
...NOW WE CALL OLD MAN HYAKUME ...
...AND SELL HIM...
...KURO-MATSU.
VROOM
VROOM

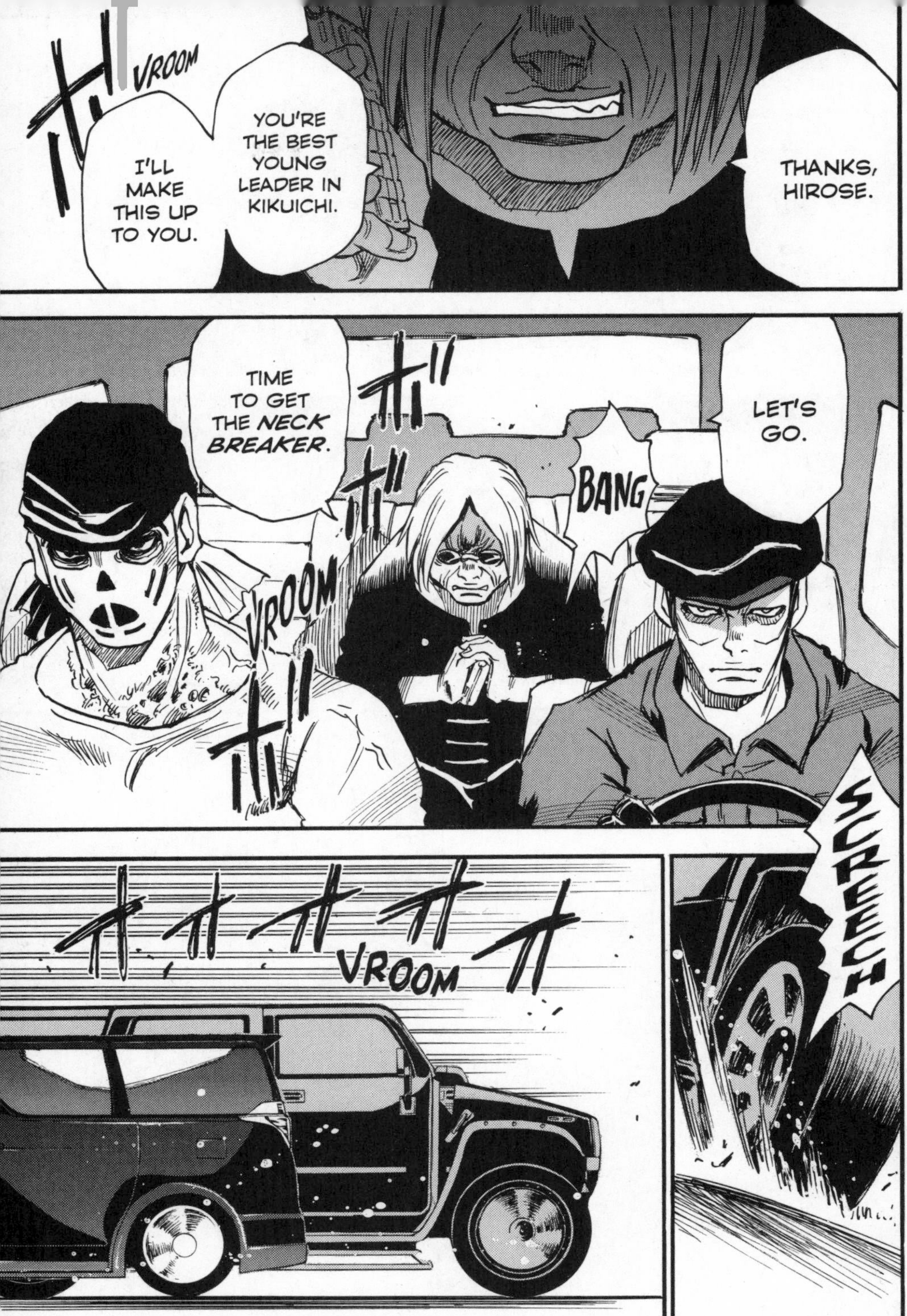
THANKS, HIROSE.
YOU'RE THE BEST YOUNG LEADER IN KIKUICHI.
I'LL MAKE THIS UP TO YOU.
VROOM
LET'S GO.
BANG
TIME TO GET THE *NECK BREAKER*.
VROOM
SCREECH
VROOM

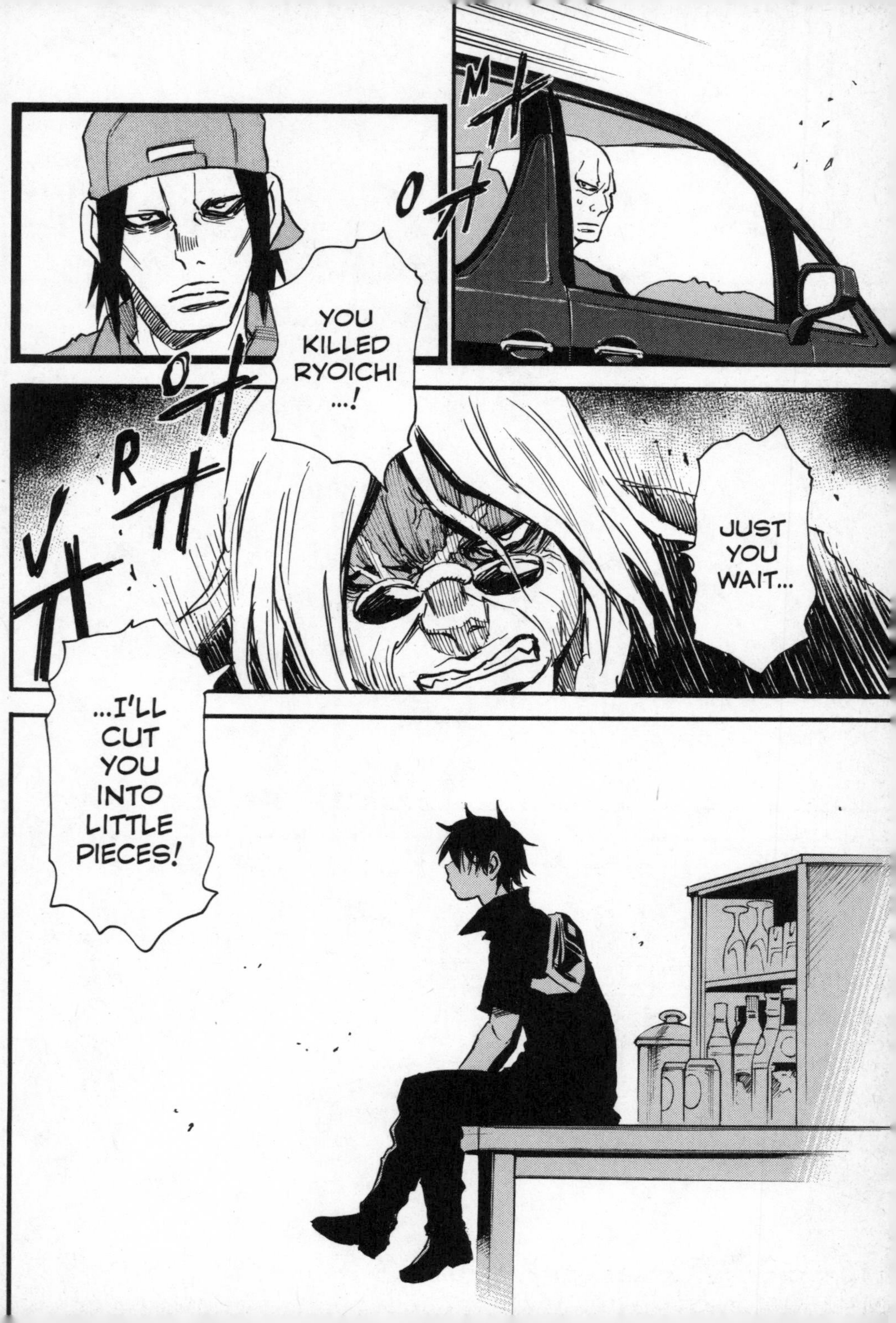
VROOM
YOU KILLED RYOICHI ...!
JUST YOU WAIT...
...I'LL CUT YOU INTO LITTLE PIECES!

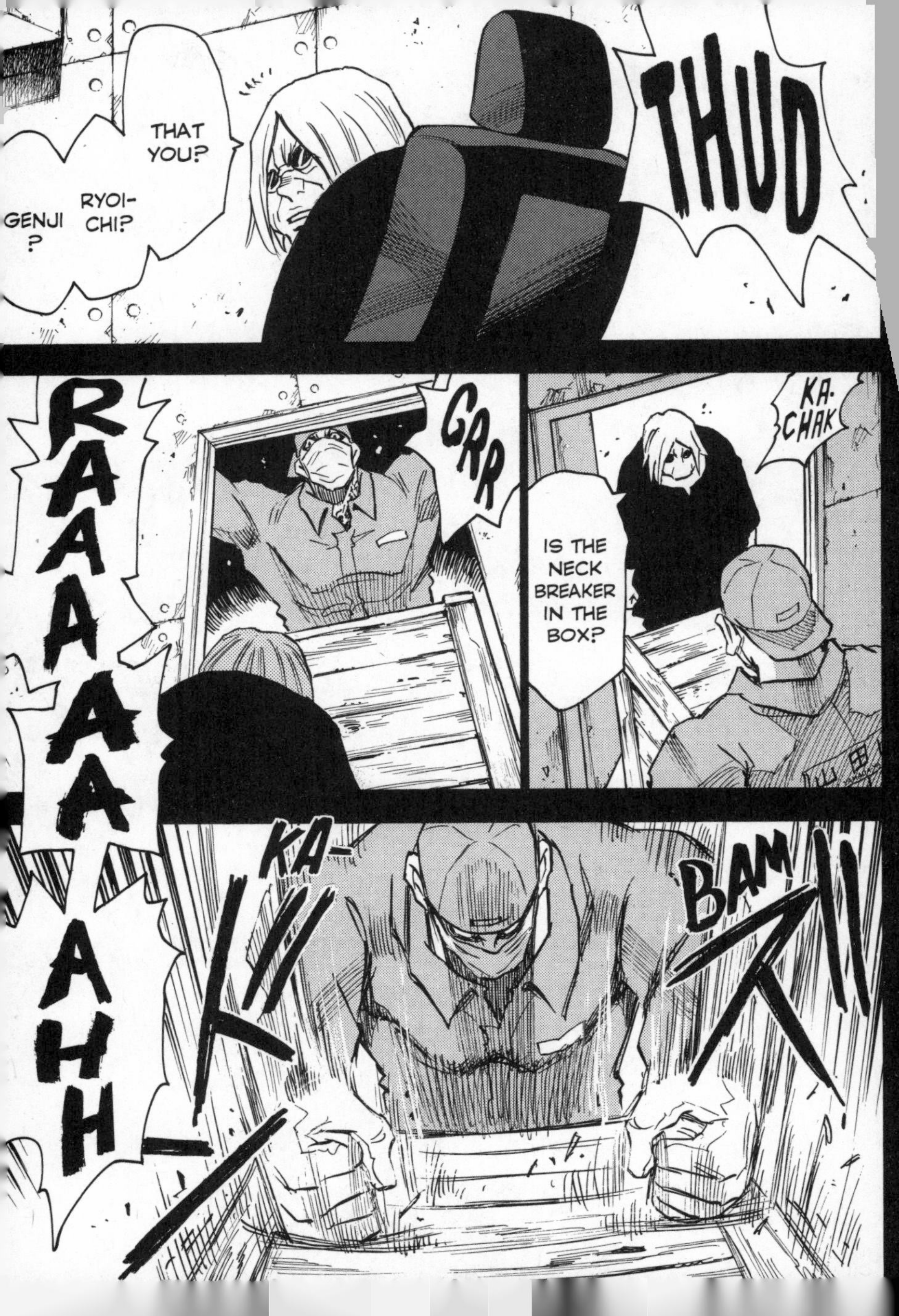

THUD
THAT YOU?
RYOI-CHI?
GENJI?
KA-CHAK
IS THE NECK BREAKER IN THE BOX?
GRR
RAAAAAAHH—
BAM
KA-

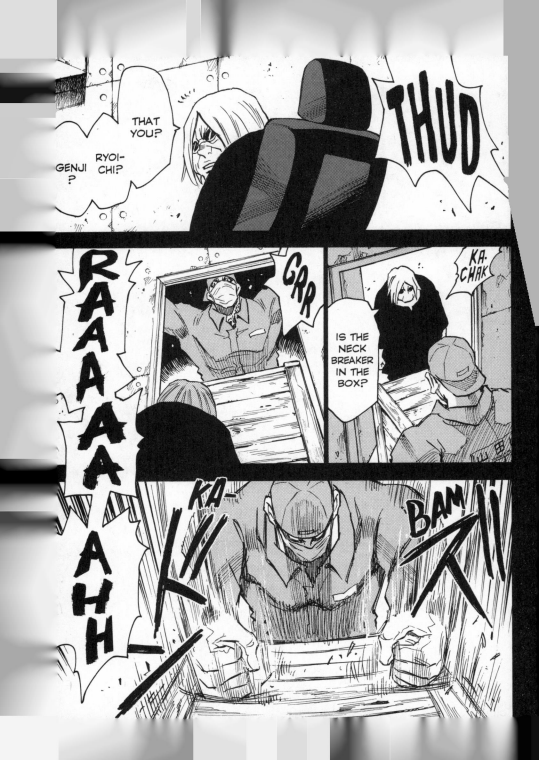

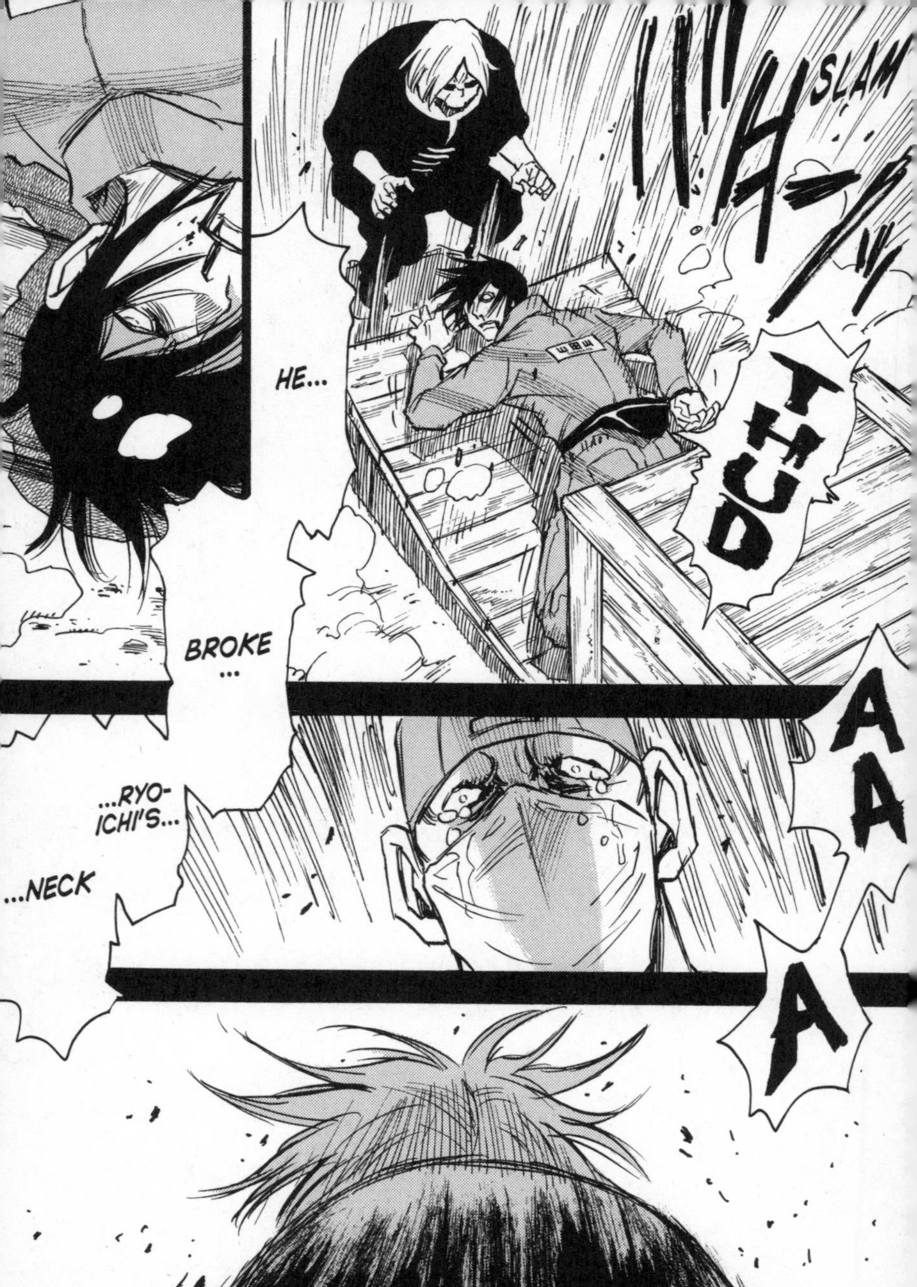
SLAM
THUD
HE...
BROKE ...
AAA
...RYO-ICHI'S...
...NECK

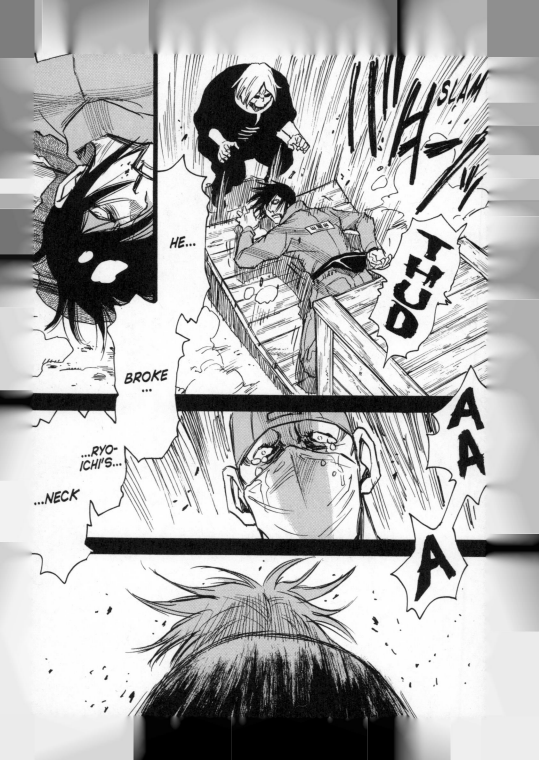

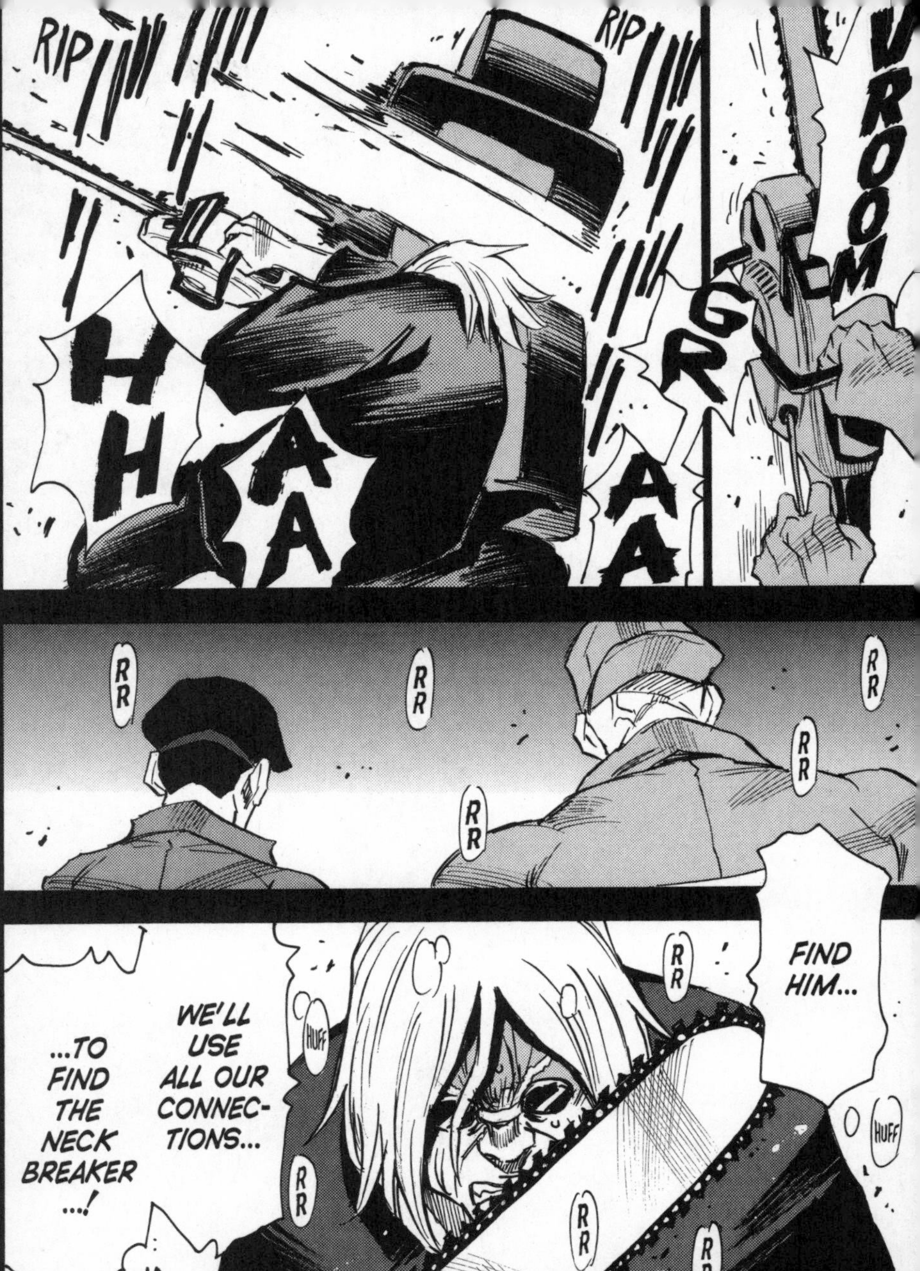
VROOM
GR
RIP
RIP
HHAA
AA
RR
RR
RR
RR
RR
FIND HIM...
RR
HUFF
HUFF
RR
RR
RR
WE'LL USE ALL OUR CONNEC-TIONS...
...TO FIND THE NECK BREAKER ...!
RR

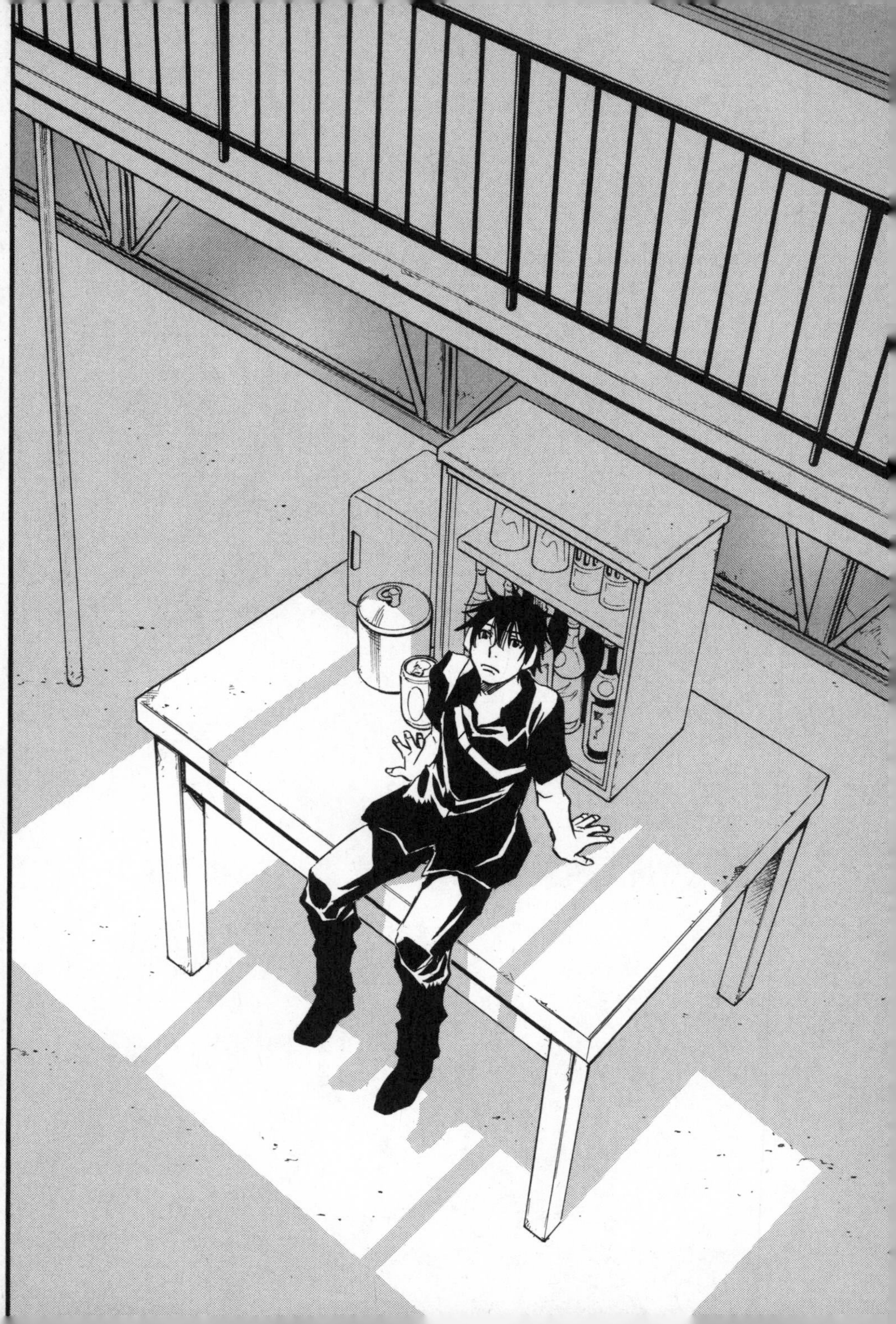

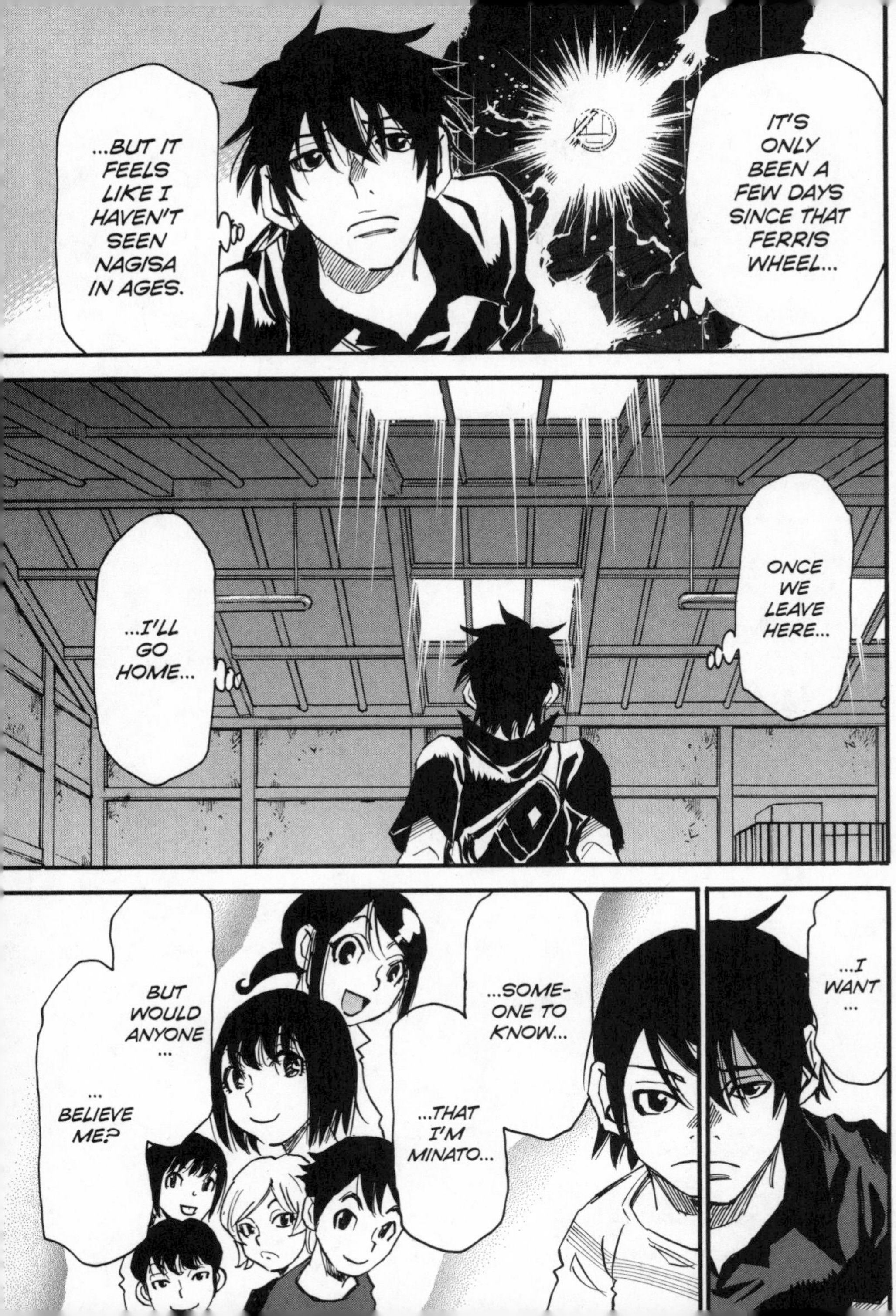
IT'S ONLY BEEN A FEW DAYS SINCE THAT FERRIS WHEEL...
...BUT IT FEELS LIKE I HAVEN'T SEEN NAGISA IN AGES.
ONCE WE LEAVE HERE...
...I'LL GO HOME...
...I WANT...
...SOME-ONE TO KNOW...
...THAT I'M MINATO...
BUT WOULD ANYONE...
...BELIEVE ME?

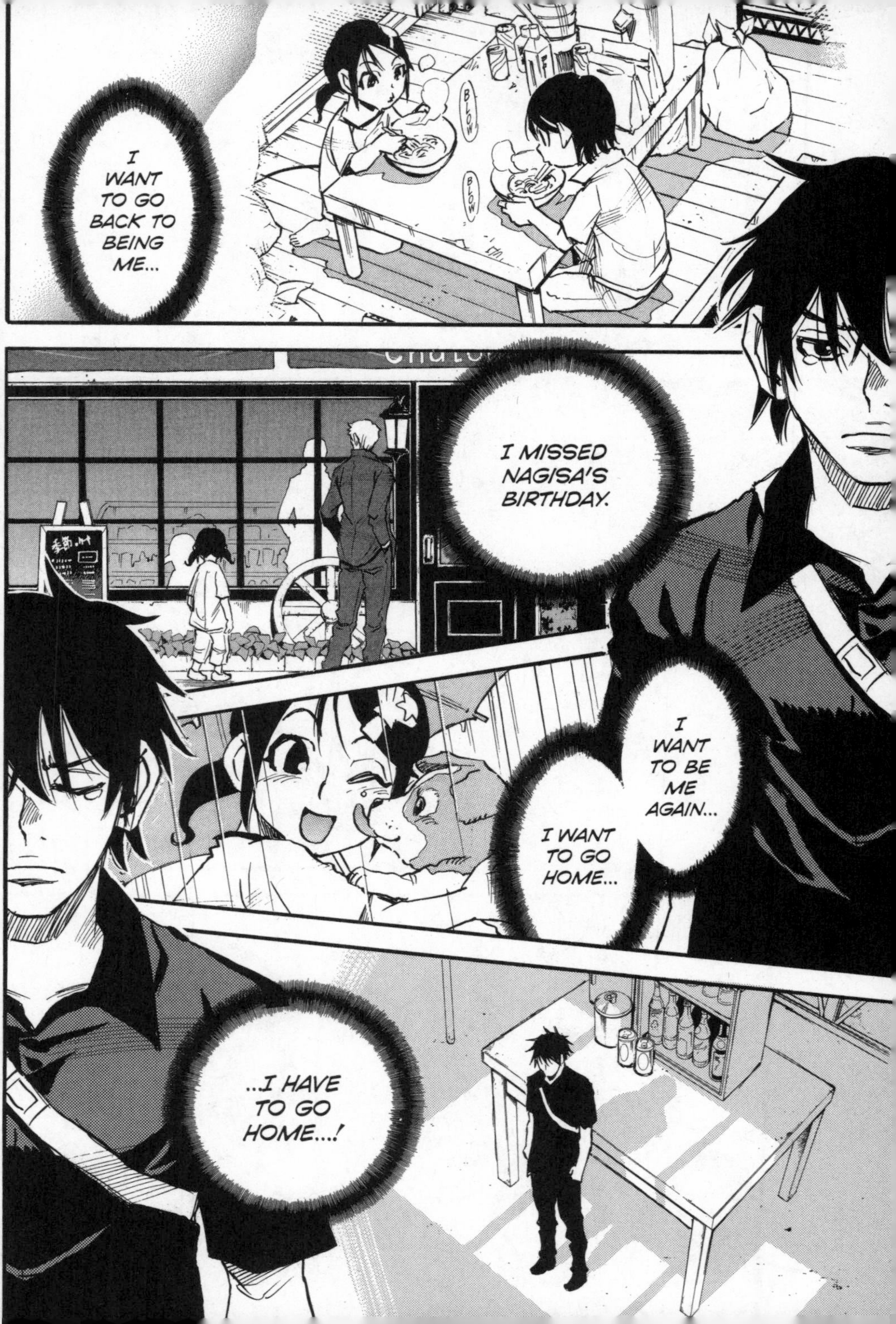
BLOW
BLOW
I WANT TO GO BACK TO BEING ME...
I MISSED NAGISA'S BIRTHDAY.
I WANT TO BE ME AGAIN...
I WANT TO GO HOME...
...I HAVE TO GO HOME...!

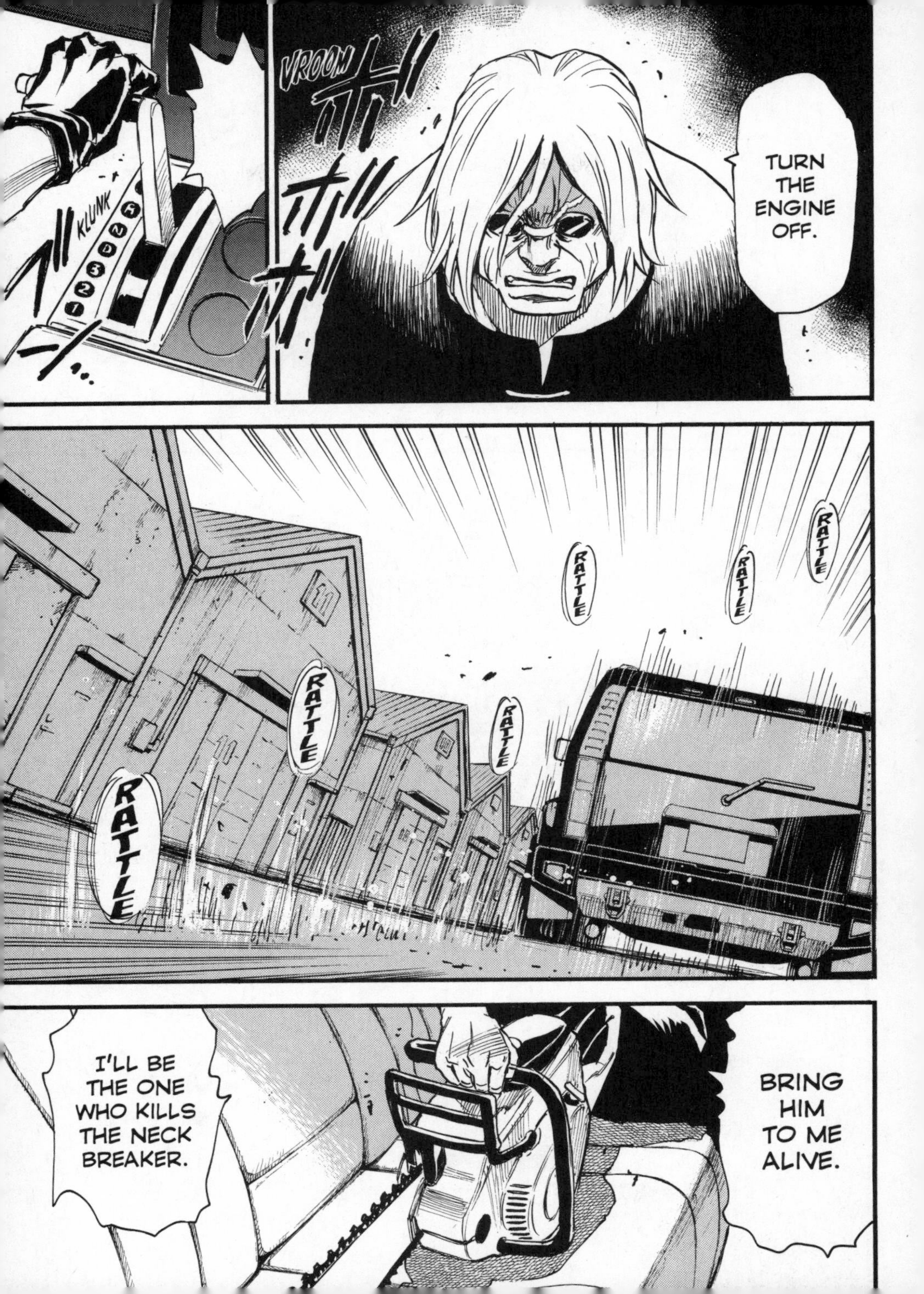
VROOM
TURN THE ENGINE OFF.
KLUNK
RATTLE
RATTLE
RATTLE
RATTLE
RATTLE
BRING HIM TO ME ALIVE.
I'LL BE THE ONE WHO KILLS THE NECK BREAKER.

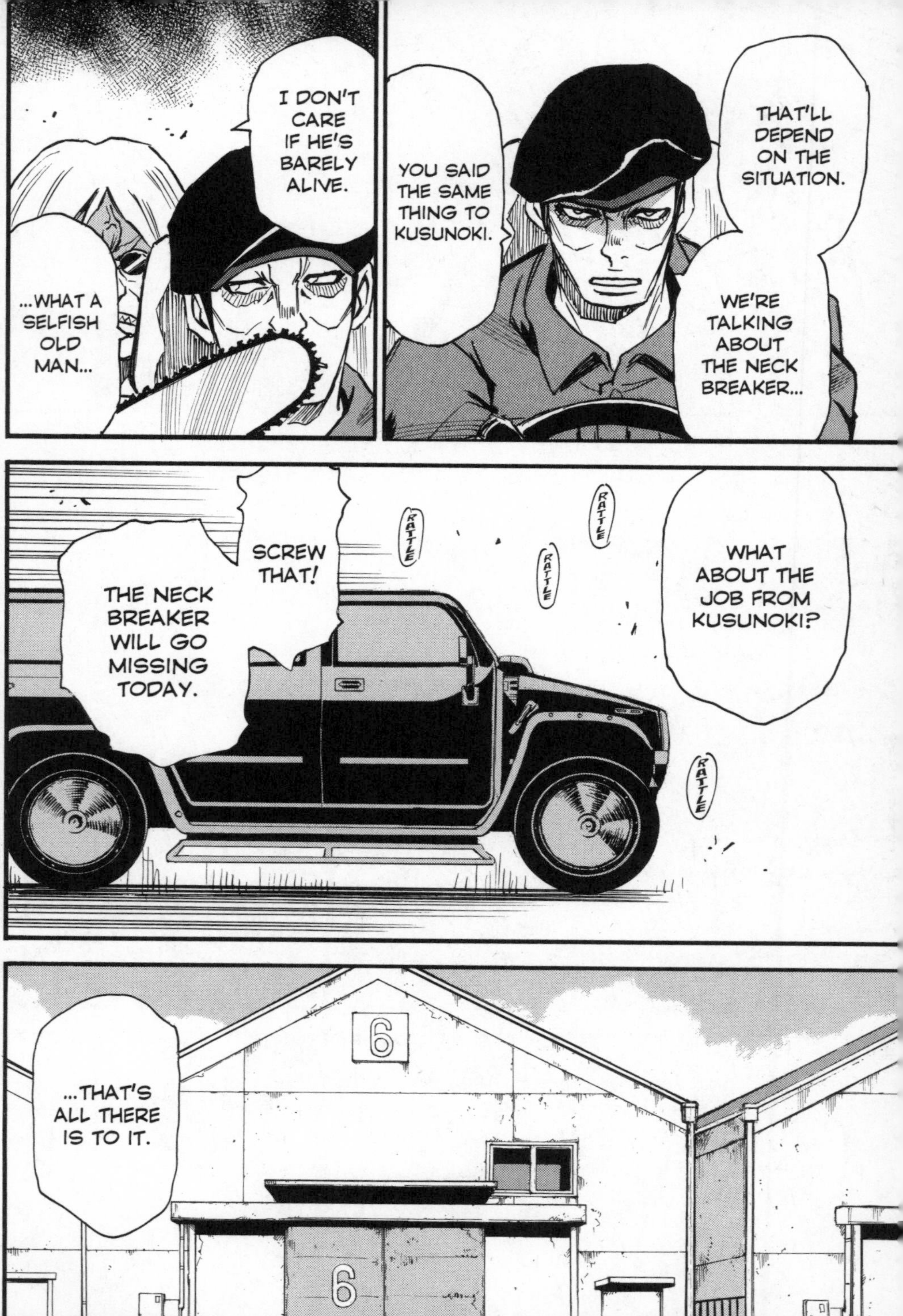
THAT'LL DEPEND ON THE SITUATION.
YOU SAID THE SAME THING TO KUSUNOKI.
WE'RE TALKING ABOUT THE NECK BREAKER...
I DON'T CARE IF HE'S BARELY ALIVE.
...WHAT A SELFISH OLD MAN...
WHAT ABOUT THE JOB FROM KUSUNOKI?
RATTLE
RATTLE
RATTLE
RATTLE
SCREW THAT!
THE NECK BREAKER WILL GO MISSING TODAY.
6
...THAT'S ALL THERE IS TO IT.
6

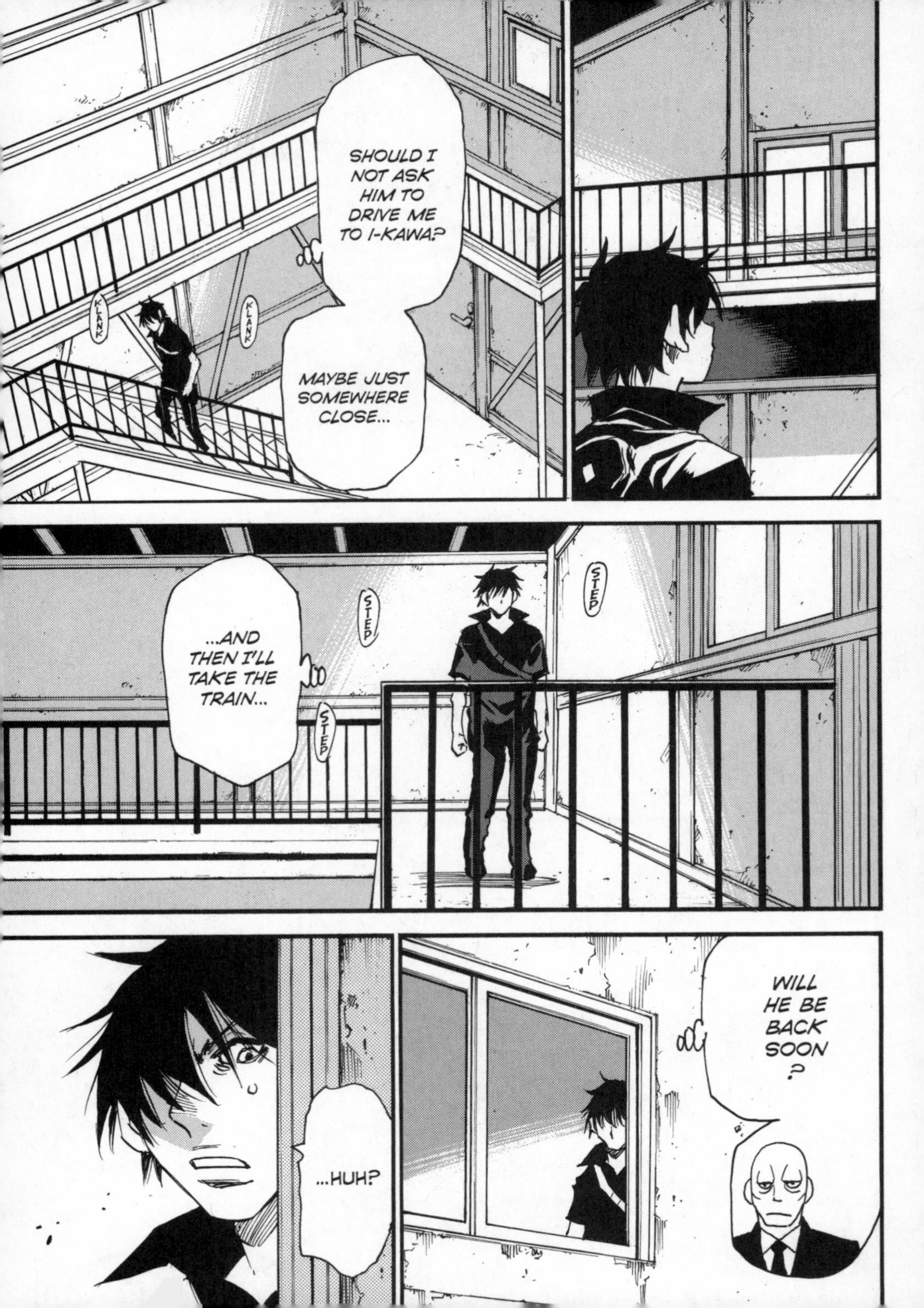

KLANK
KLANK
SHOULD I NOT ASK HIM TO DRIVE ME TO I-KAWA?
MAYBE JUST SOMEWHERE CLOSE...
STEP
STEP
...AND THEN I'LL TAKE THE TRAIN...
STEP
WILL HE BE BACK SOON?
...HUH?

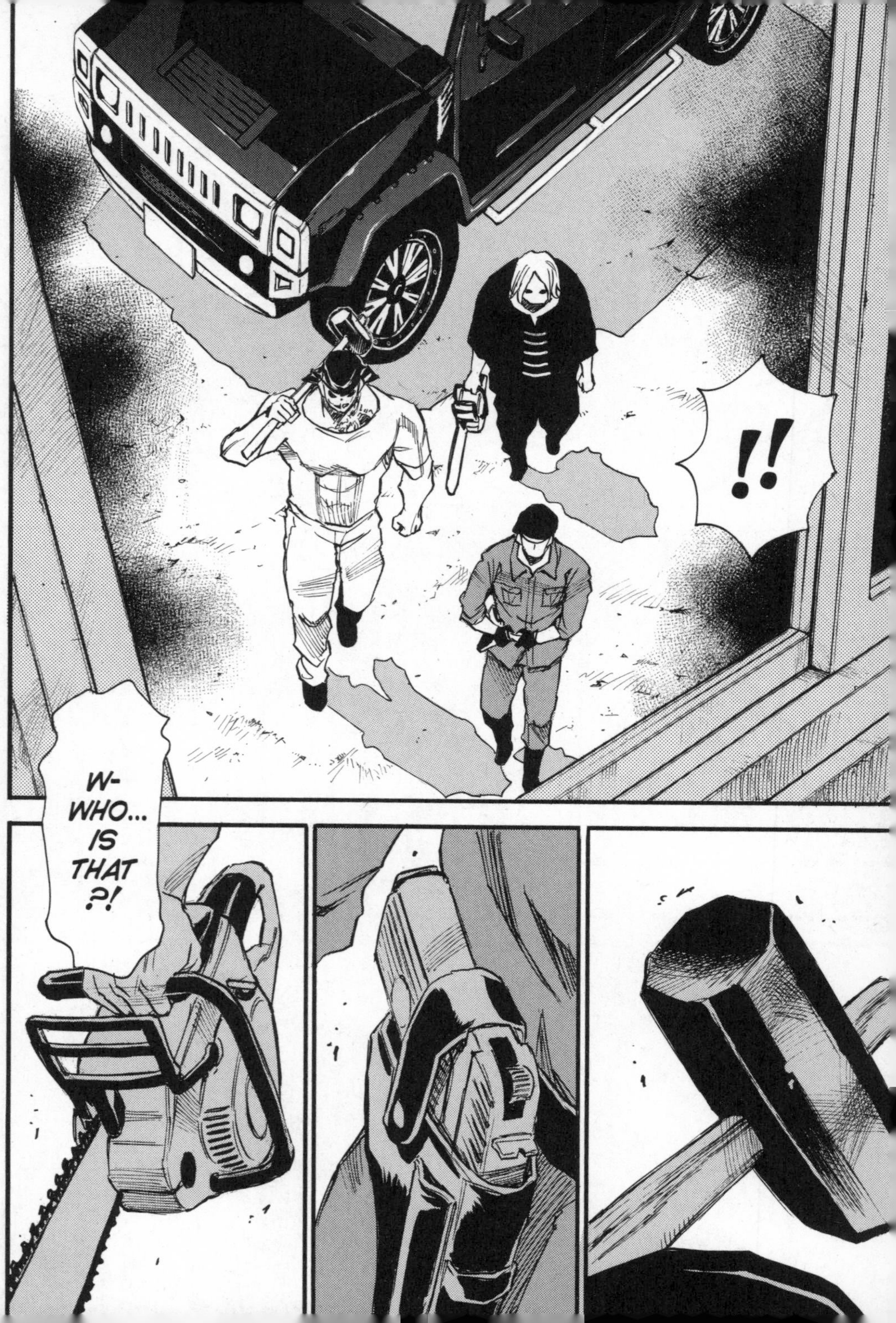
!!
W-WHO... IS THAT?!

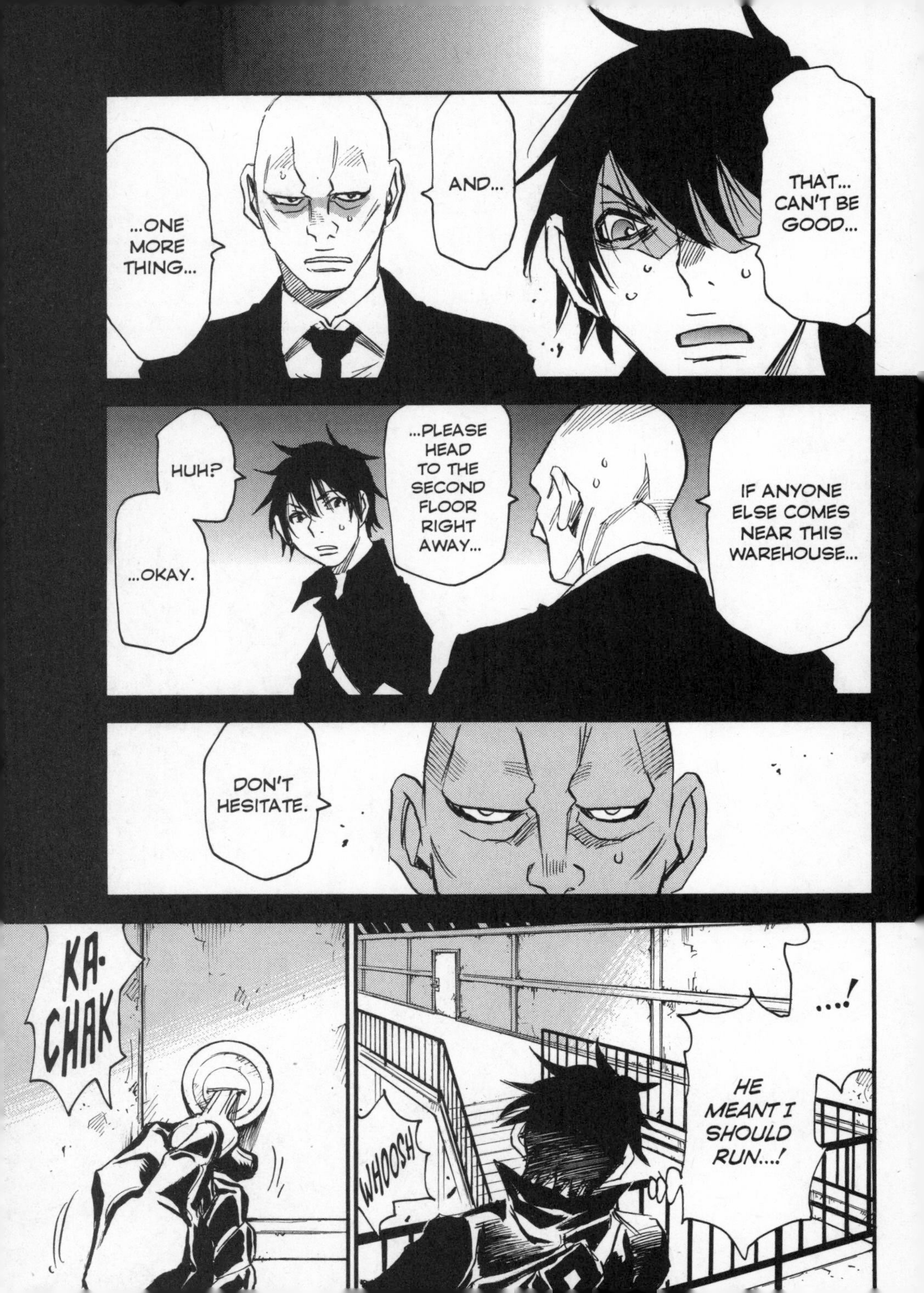
THAT... CAN'T BE GOOD...
AND...
...ONE MORE THING...
IF ANYONE ELSE COMES NEAR THIS WAREHOUSE...
...PLEASE HEAD TO THE SECOND FLOOR RIGHT AWAY...
HUH?
...OKAY.
DON'T HESITATE.
...!
HE MEANT I SHOULD RUN...!
WHOOSH
KA-CHAK

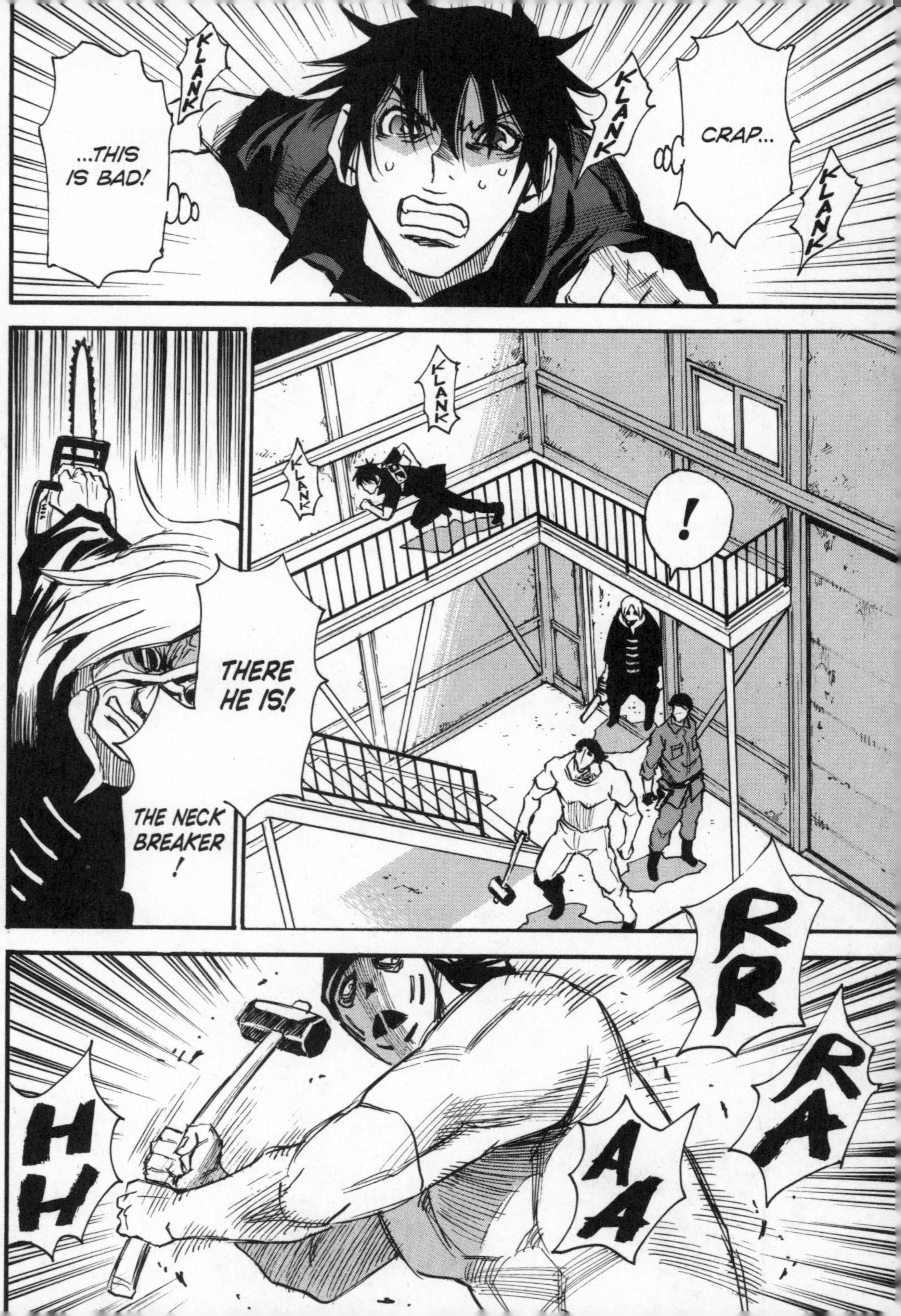
CRAP...
KLANK
KLANK
KLANK
...THIS IS BAD!
KLANK
KLANK
!
THERE HE IS!
THE NECK BREAKER !
RRRAAAHHH

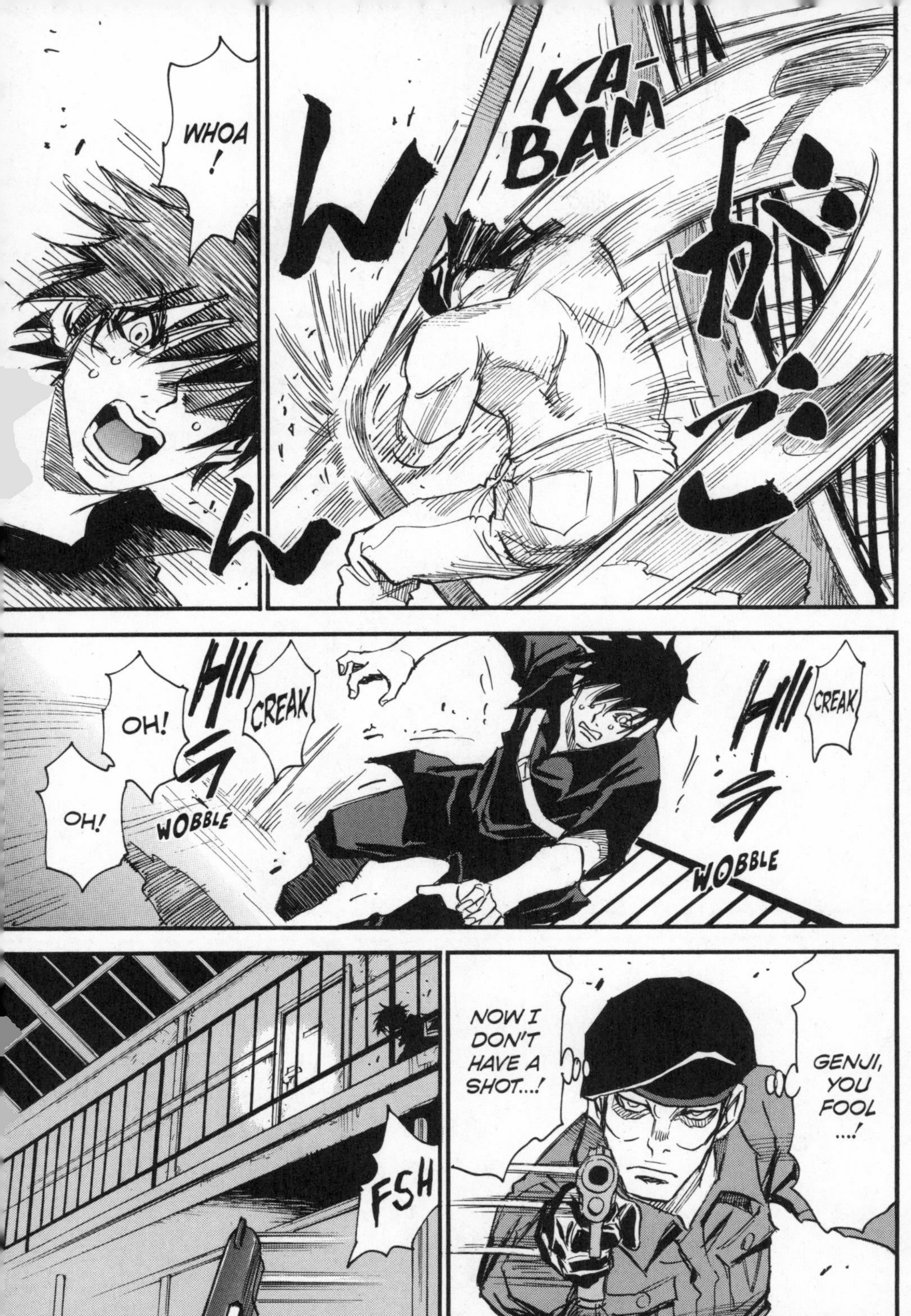
KA-BAM
WHOA!
CREAK
WOBBLE
CREAK
OH!
OH!
WOBBLE
GENJI, YOU FOOL...!
NOW I DON'T HAVE A SHOT...!
FSH

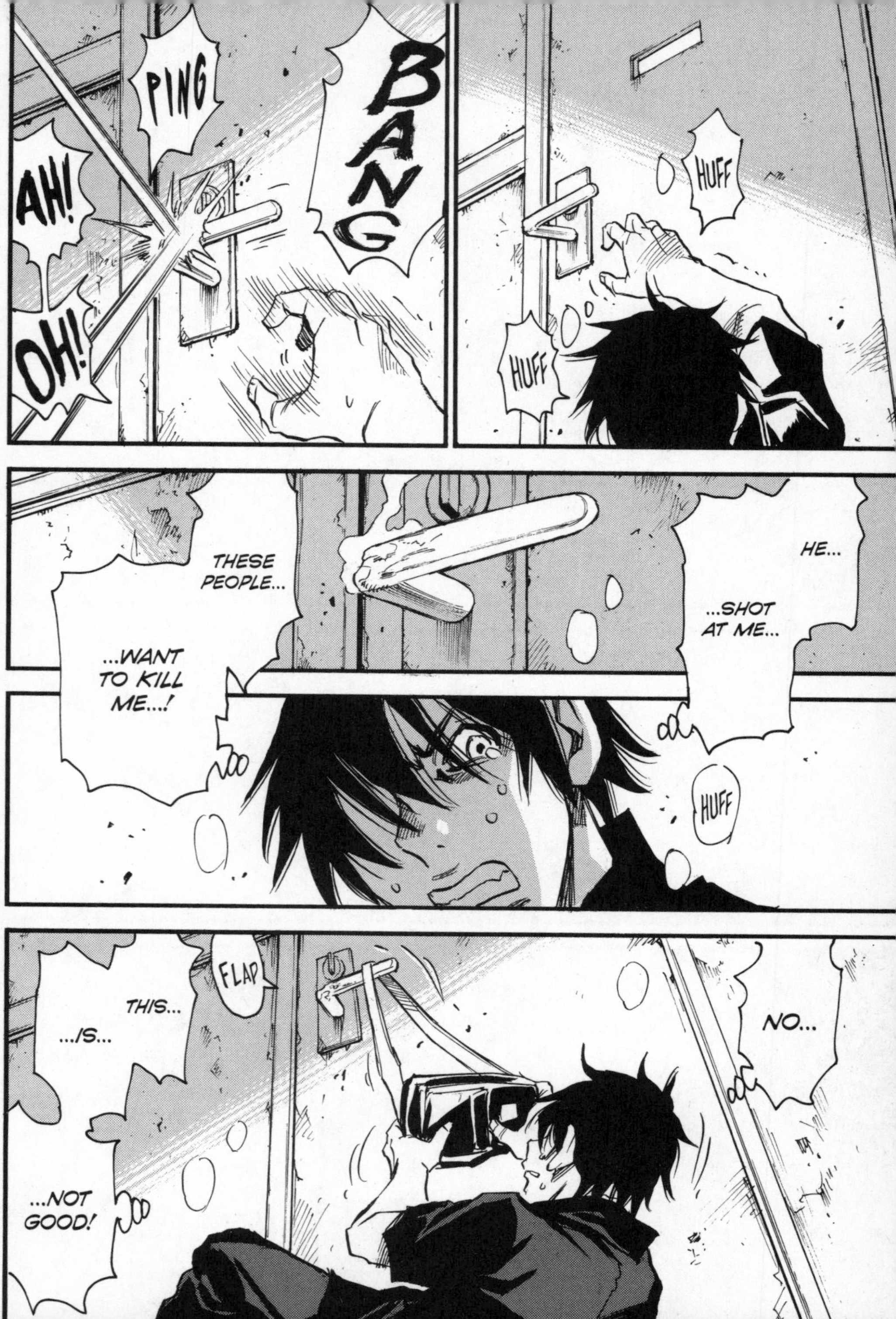
HUFF
HUFF
BANG
PING
AH!
OH!
HE...
...SHOT AT ME...
THESE PEOPLE...
...WANT TO KILL ME...!
HUFF
NO...
FLAP
THIS...
...IS...
...NOT GOOD!

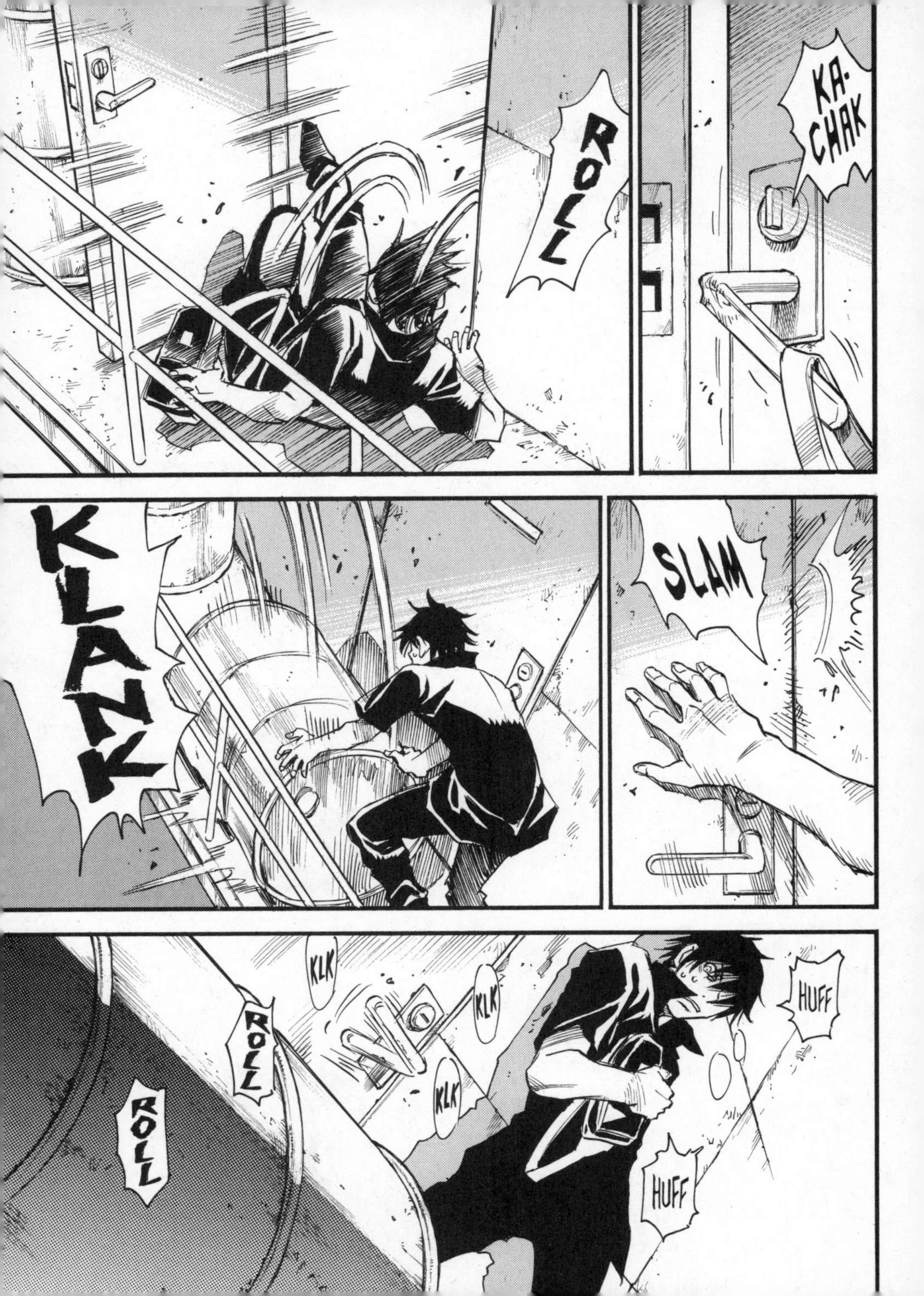
KA-CHAK
ROLL
SLAM
KLANK
HUFF
KLK
KLK
KLK
ROLL
HUFF
ROLL

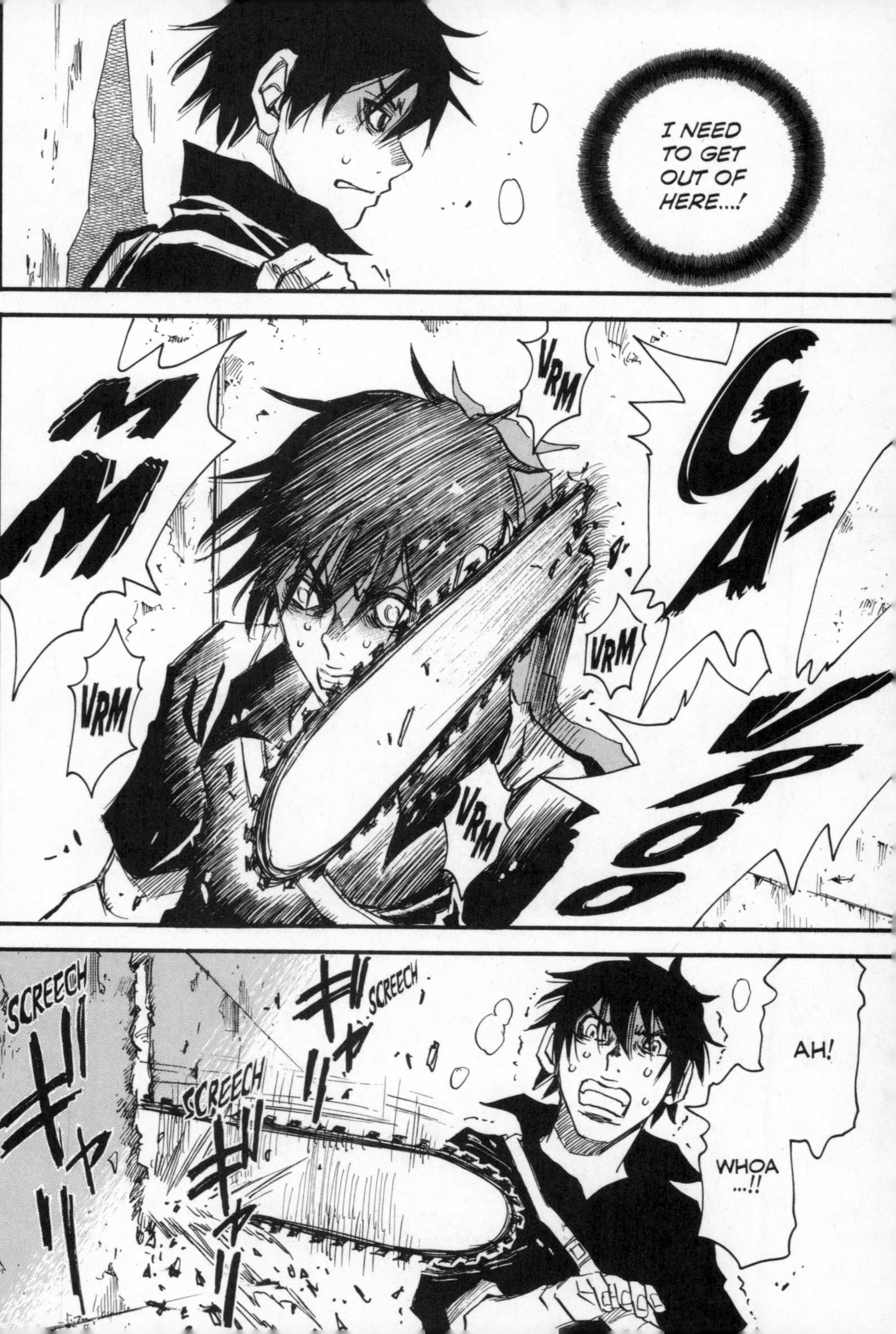
I NEED TO GET OUT OF HERE...!
VRM
VRM
VRM
VRM
AH!
WHOA ...!!
SCREECH
SCREECH
SCREECH

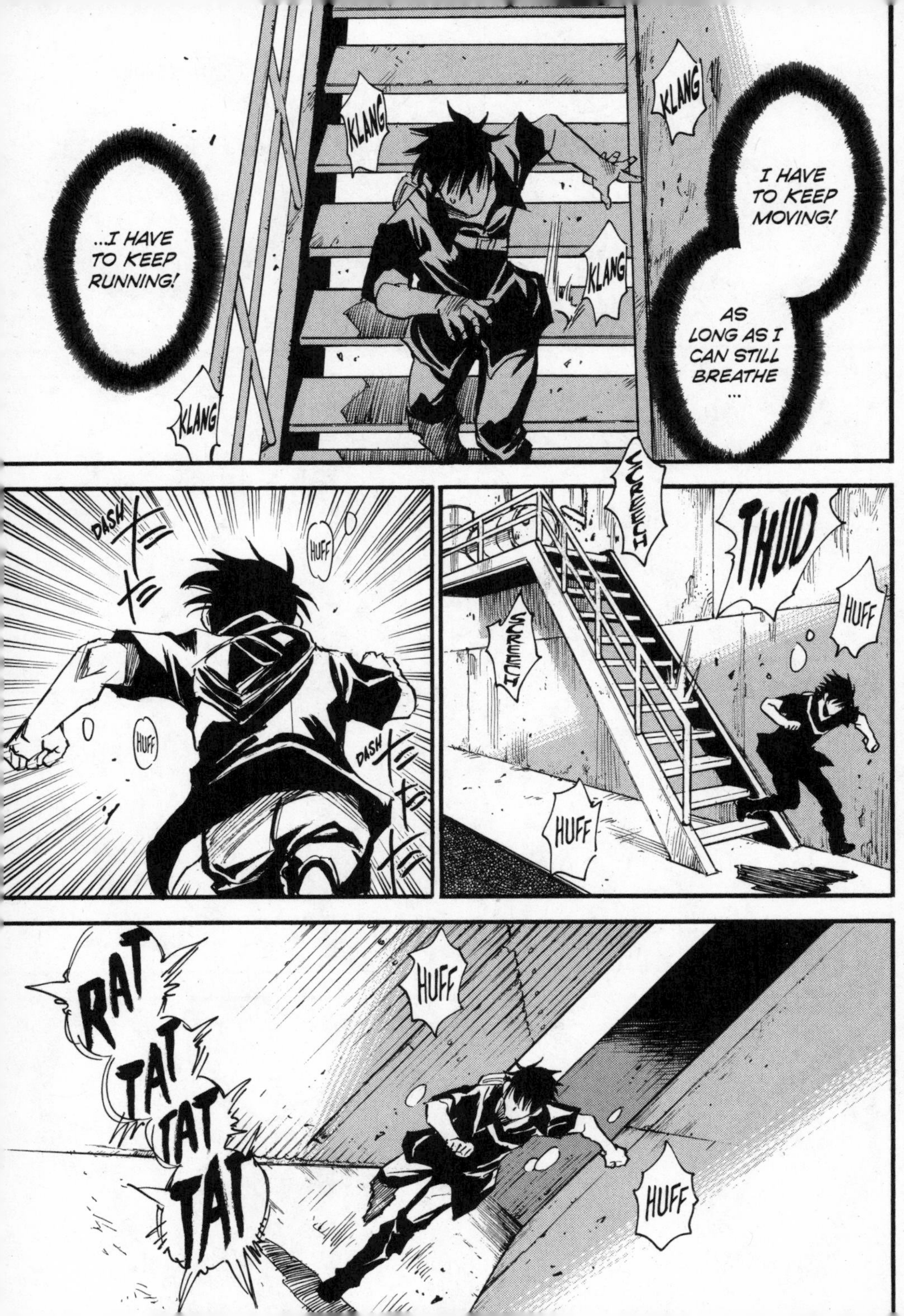
KLANG
I HAVE TO KEEP MOVING!
AS LONG AS I CAN STILL BREATHE ...
KLANG
KLANG
...I HAVE TO KEEP RUNNING!
KLANG
THUD
SCREECH
HUFF
SCREECH
HUFF
HUFF
DASH
DASH
HUFF
HUFF
HUFF
RAT TAT TAT TAT

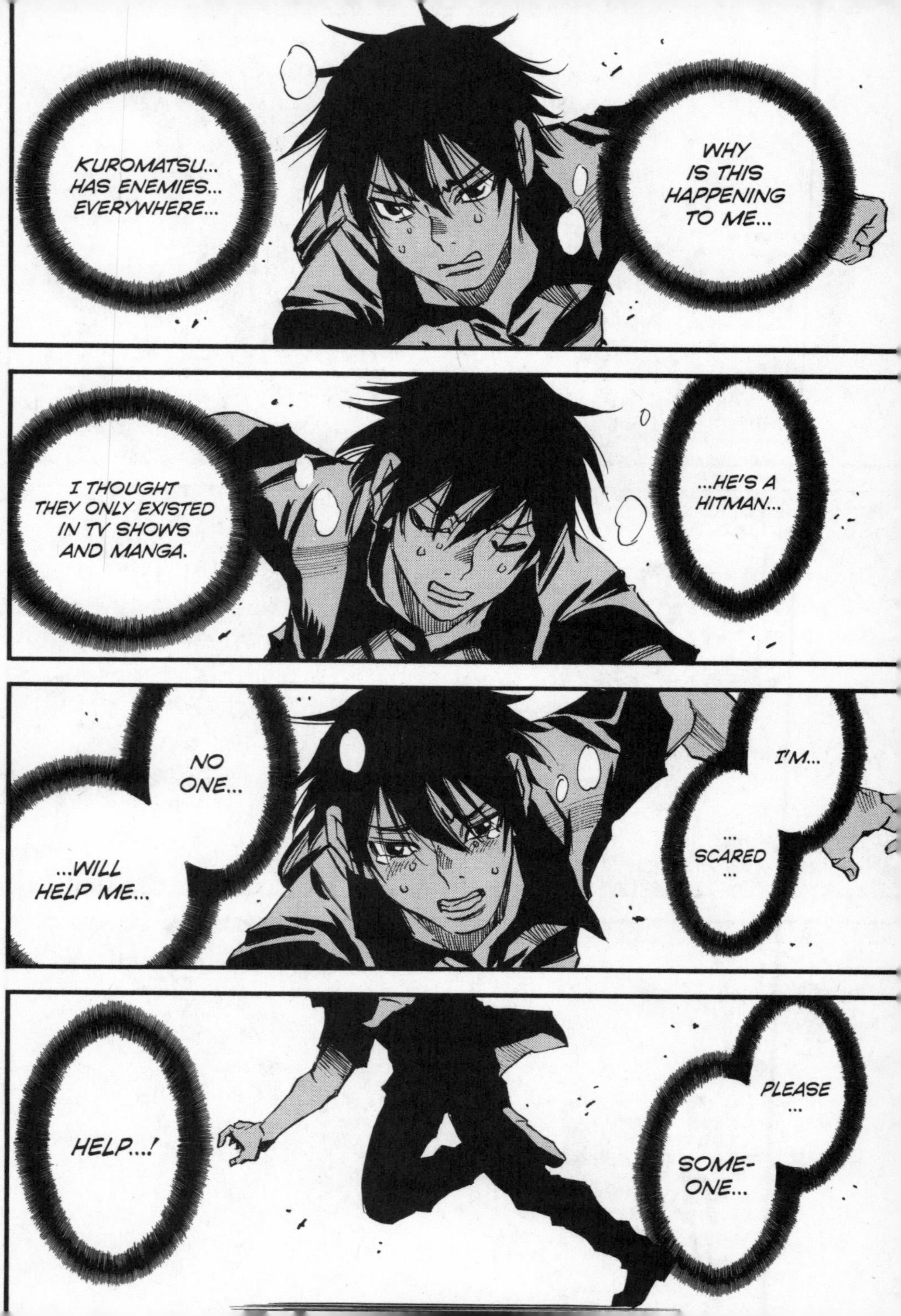
WHY IS THIS HAPPENING TO ME...
KUROMATSU... HAS ENEMIES... EVERYWHERE...
...HE'S A HITMAN...
I THOUGHT THEY ONLY EXISTED IN TV SHOWS AND MANGA.
I'M... ...SCARED...
NO ONE...
...WILL HELP ME...
PLEASE... SOME-ONE...
HELP...!

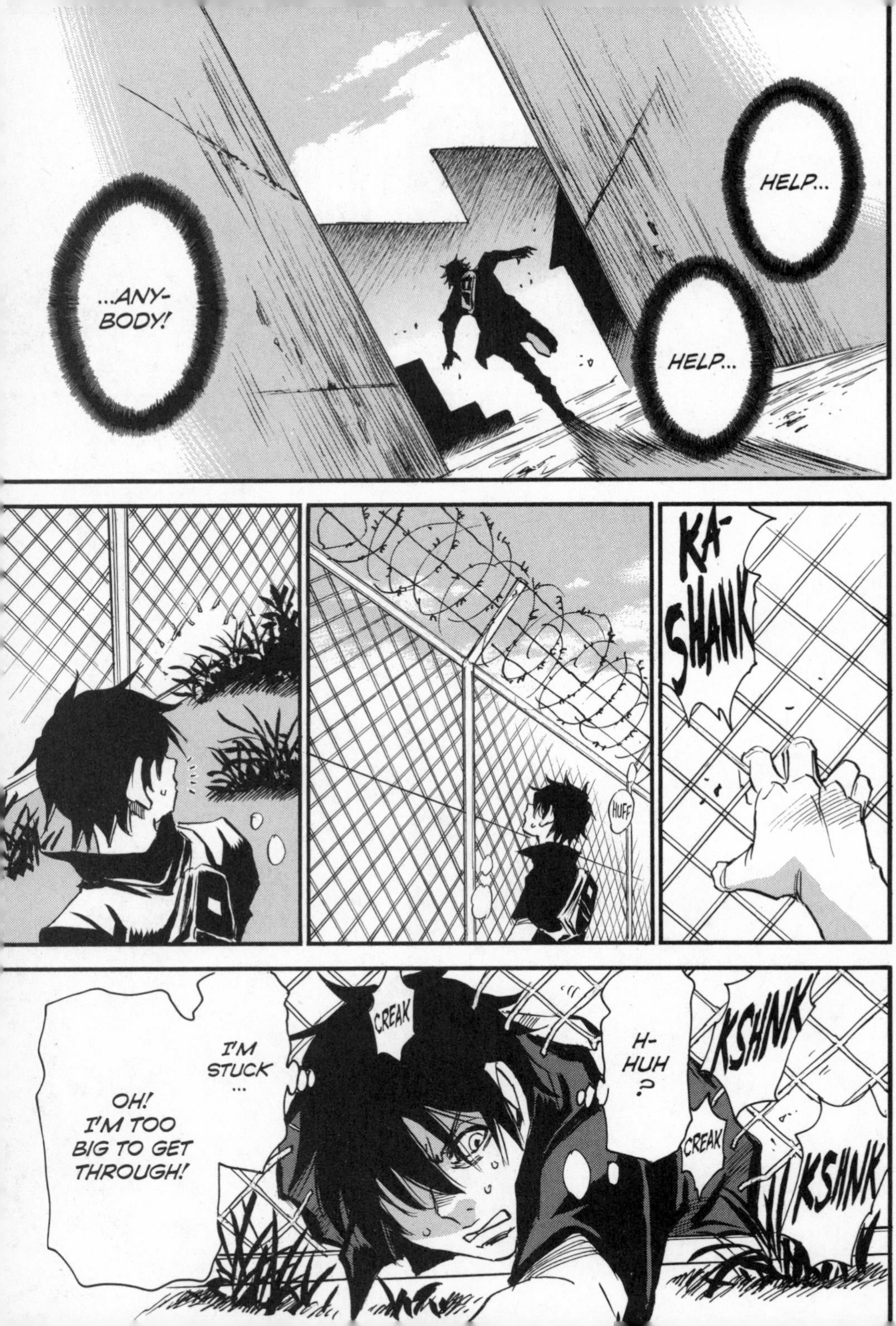
HELP...
HELP...
...ANY-BODY!
KA-SHANK
HUFF
KSHNK
H-HUH?
CREAK
I'M STUCK...
KSHNK
CREAK
OH! I'M TOO BIG TO GET THROUGH!

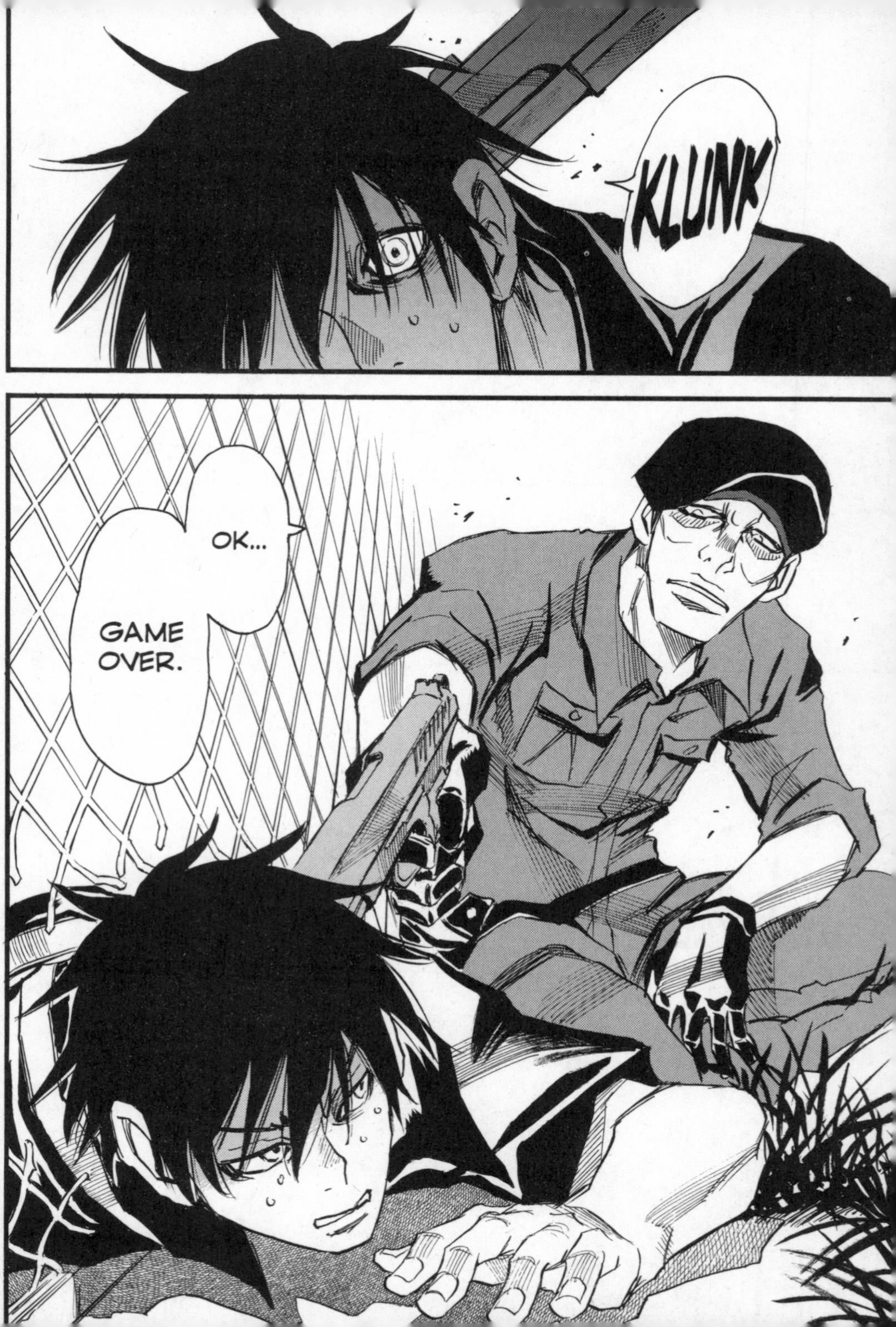
KLUNK
OK...
GAME OVER.

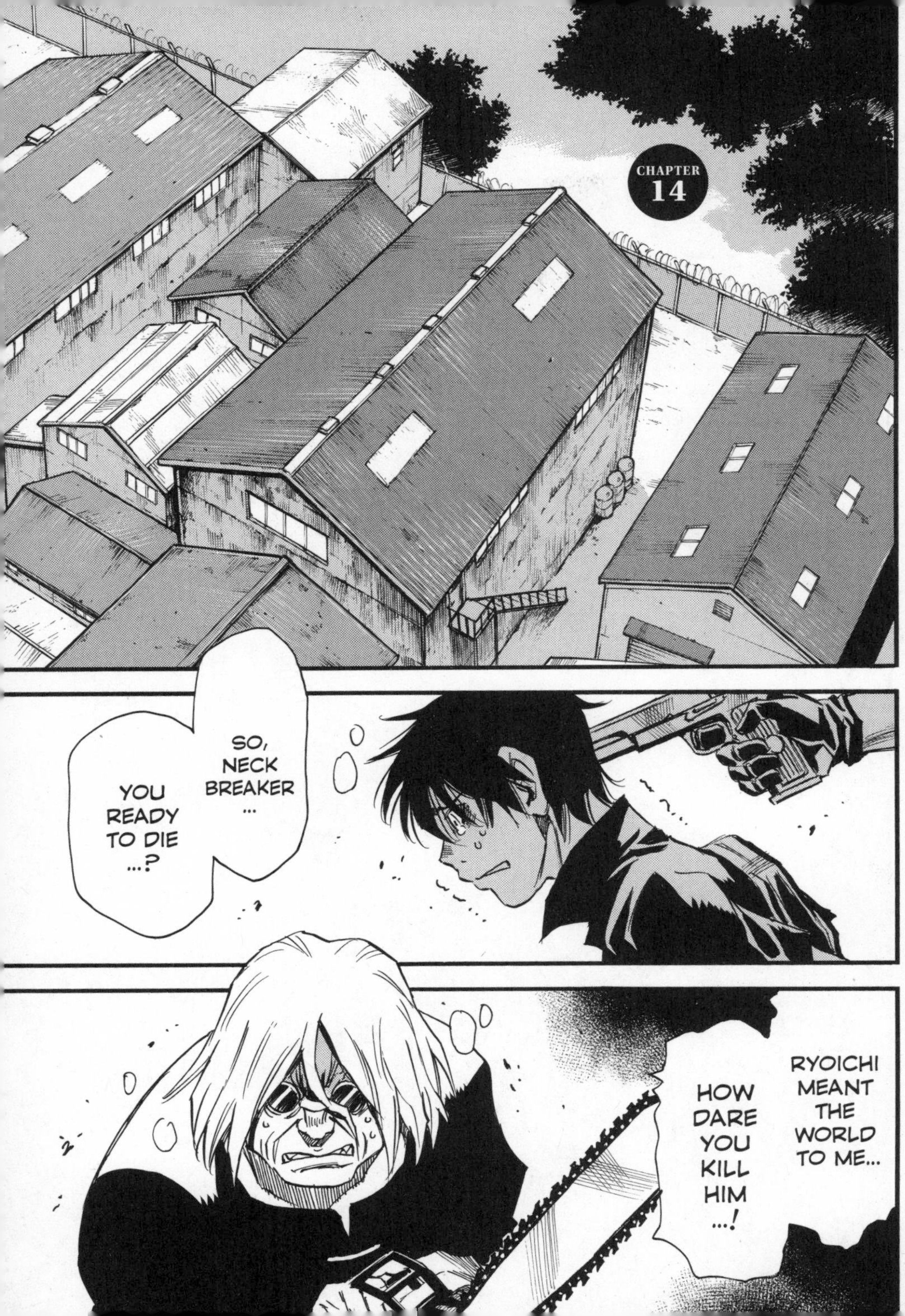
CHAPTER 14
SO, NECK BREAKER ...
YOU READY TO DIE ...?
RYOICHI MEANT THE WORLD TO ME...
HOW DARE YOU KILL HIM ...!

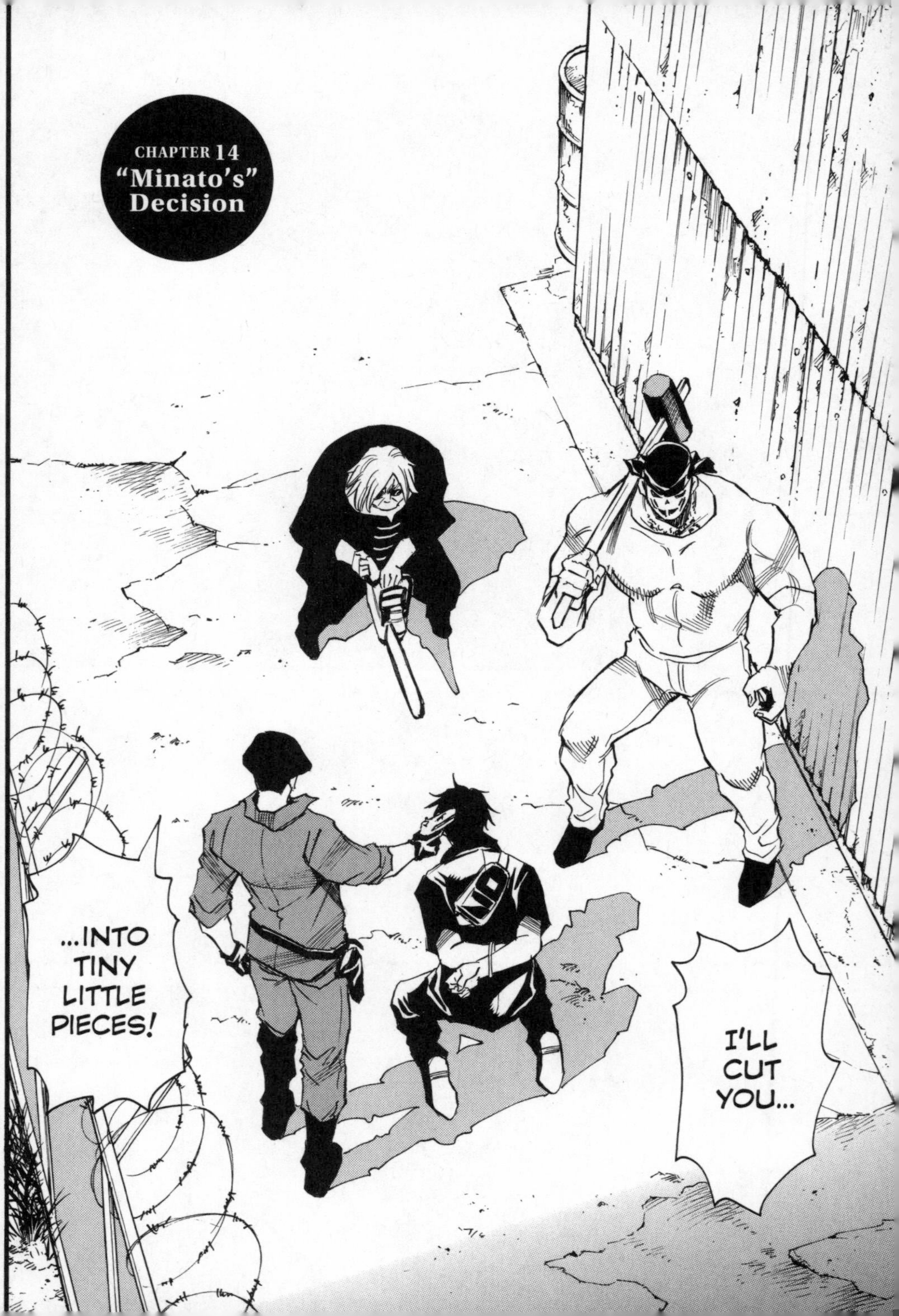
CHAPTER 14
"Minato's" Decision
I'LL CUT YOU...
...INTO TINY LITTLE PIECES!

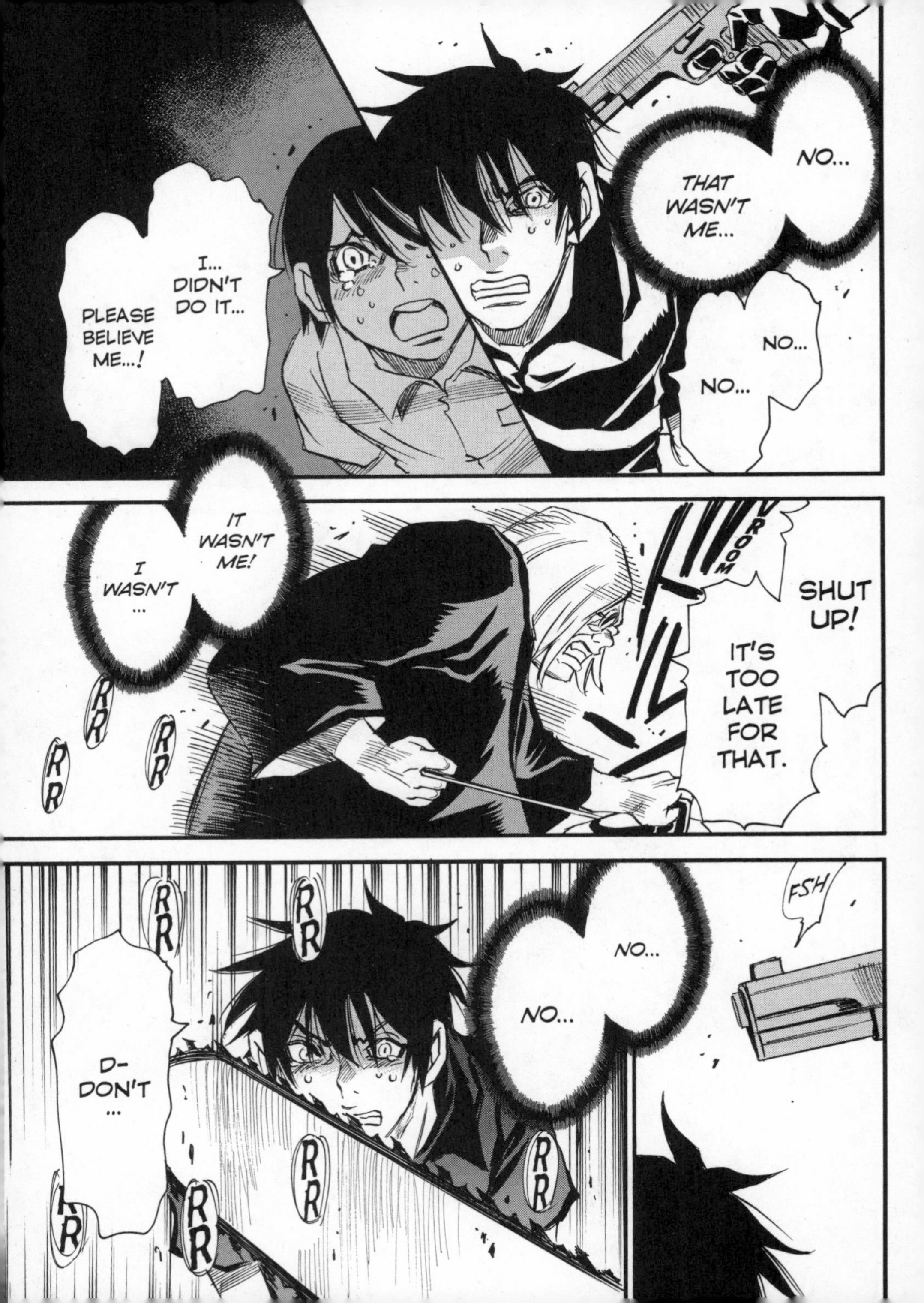
NO...
THAT WASN'T ME...
NO...
NO...
I... DIDN'T DO IT...
PLEASE BELIEVE ME...!
SHUT UP!
IT'S TOO LATE FOR THAT.
VROOM
IT WASN'T ME!
I WASN'T ...
RR
RR
RR
FSH
NO...
NO...
RR
RR
RR
D- DON'T ...
RR
RR
RR

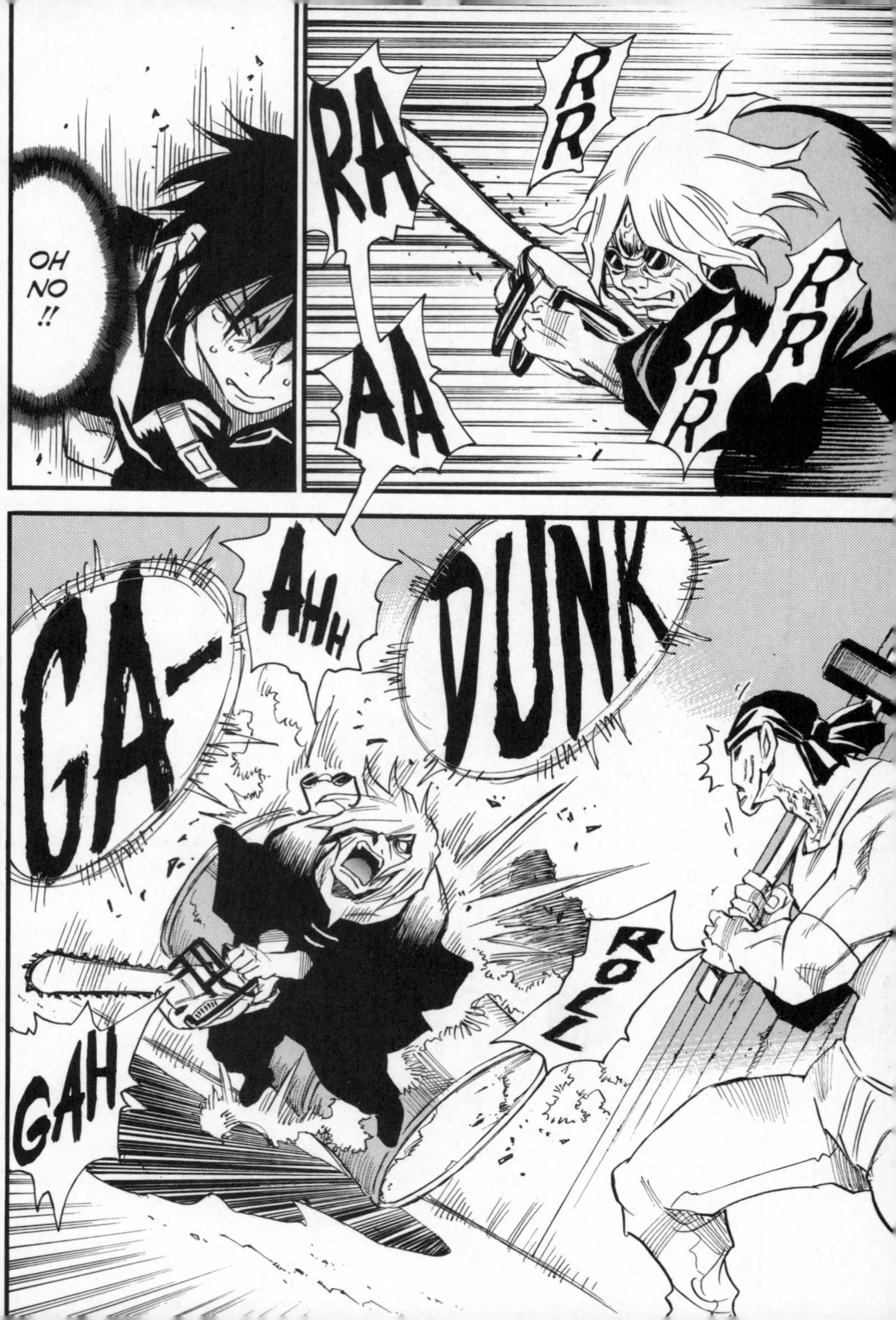
RR
RAAAAHH
RRRR
OH NO !!
CA-DUNK
ROLL
GAH

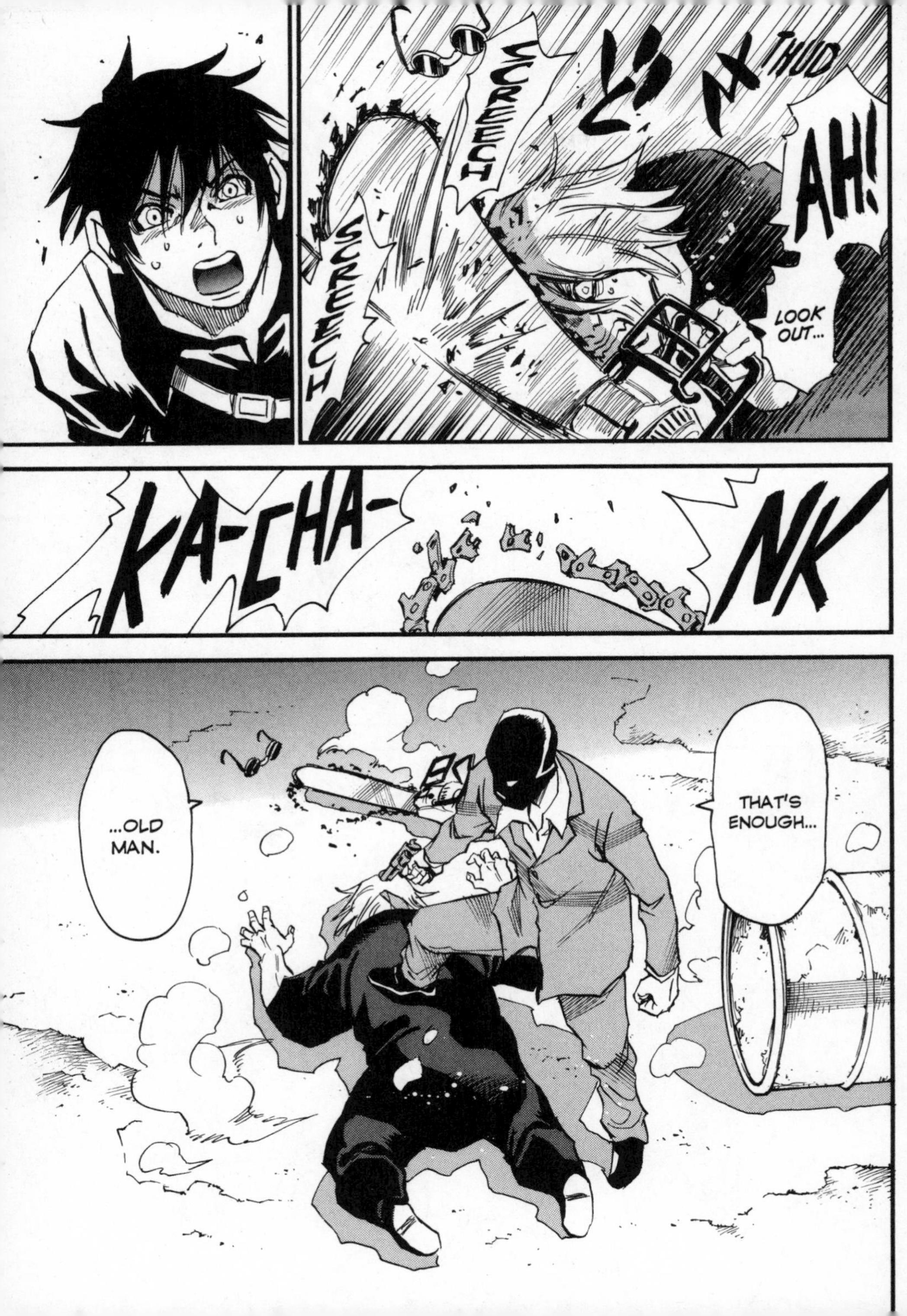
THUD
どッ
AH!
LOOK OUT...
SCREECH
SCREECH
KA-CHA-NK
THAT'S ENOUGH...
...OLD MAN.

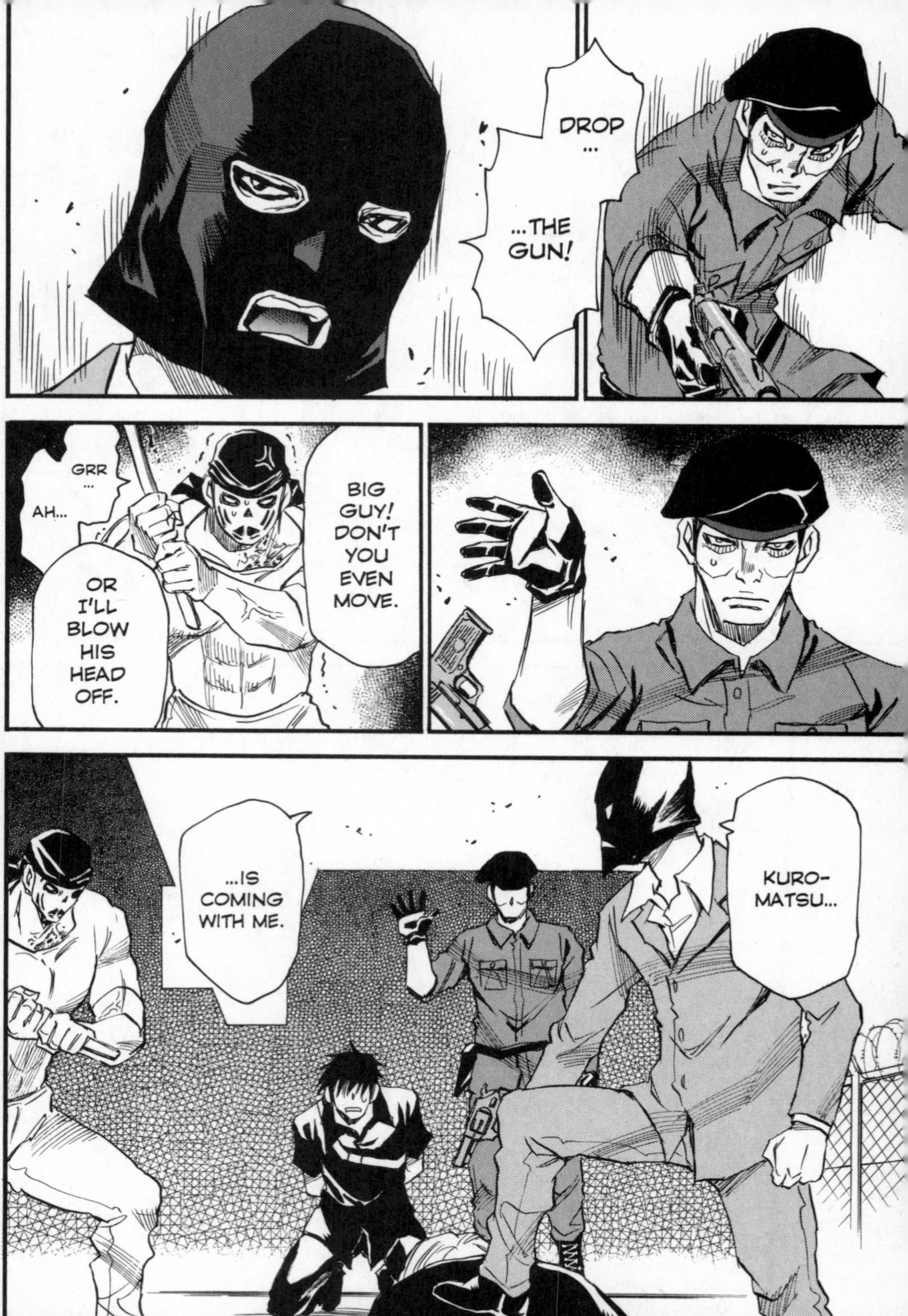
DROP ... ...THE GUN!
BIG GUY! DON'T YOU EVEN MOVE.
GRR ... AH...
OR I'LL BLOW HIS HEAD OFF.
KURO-MATSU...
...IS COMING WITH ME.

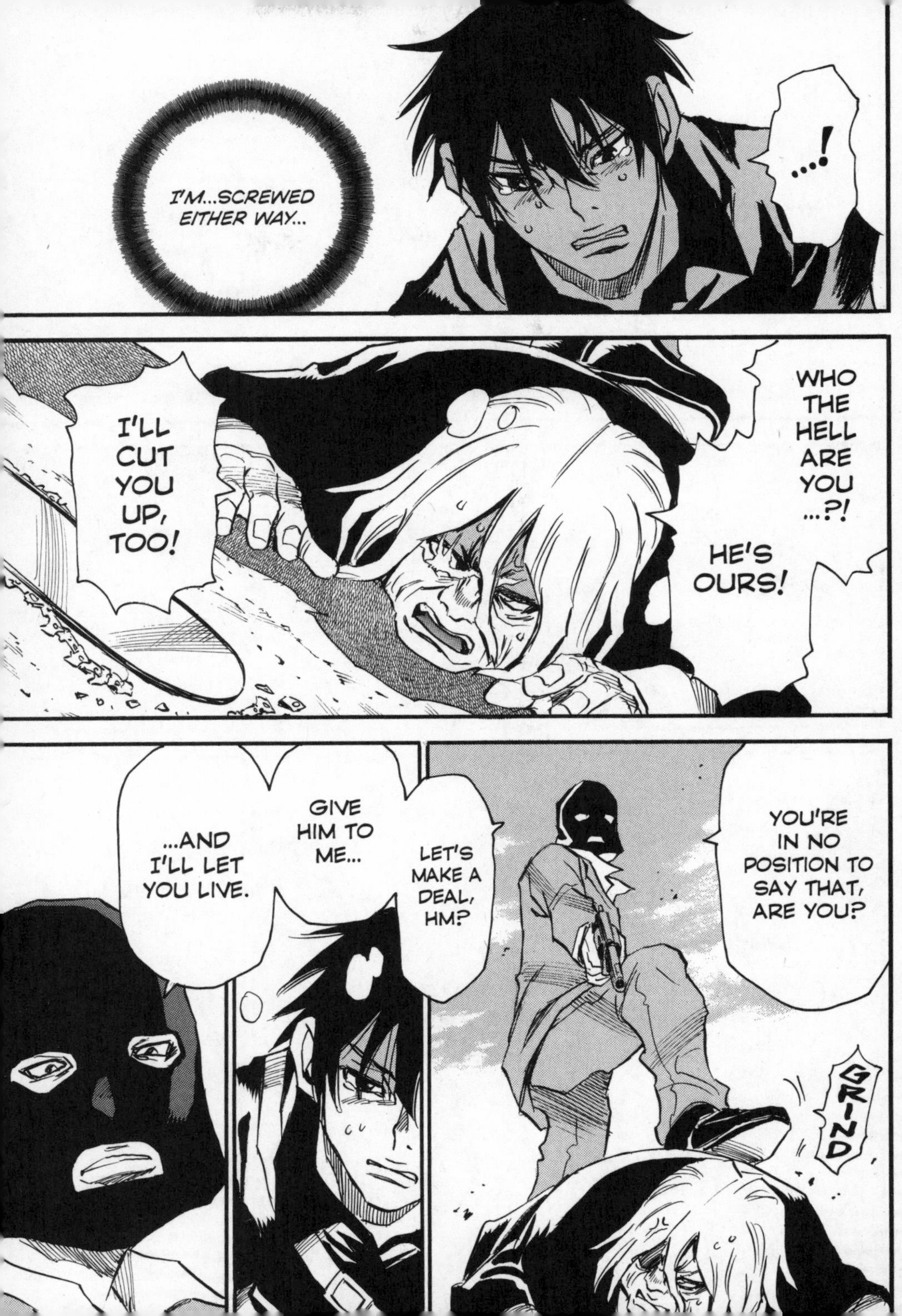
...!
I'M...SCREWED EITHER WAY...
WHO THE HELL ARE YOU ...?!
HE'S OURS!
I'LL CUT YOU UP, TOO!
YOU'RE IN NO POSITION TO SAY THAT, ARE YOU?
GRIND
LET'S MAKE A DEAL, HM?
GIVE HIM TO ME...
...AND I'LL LET YOU LIVE.

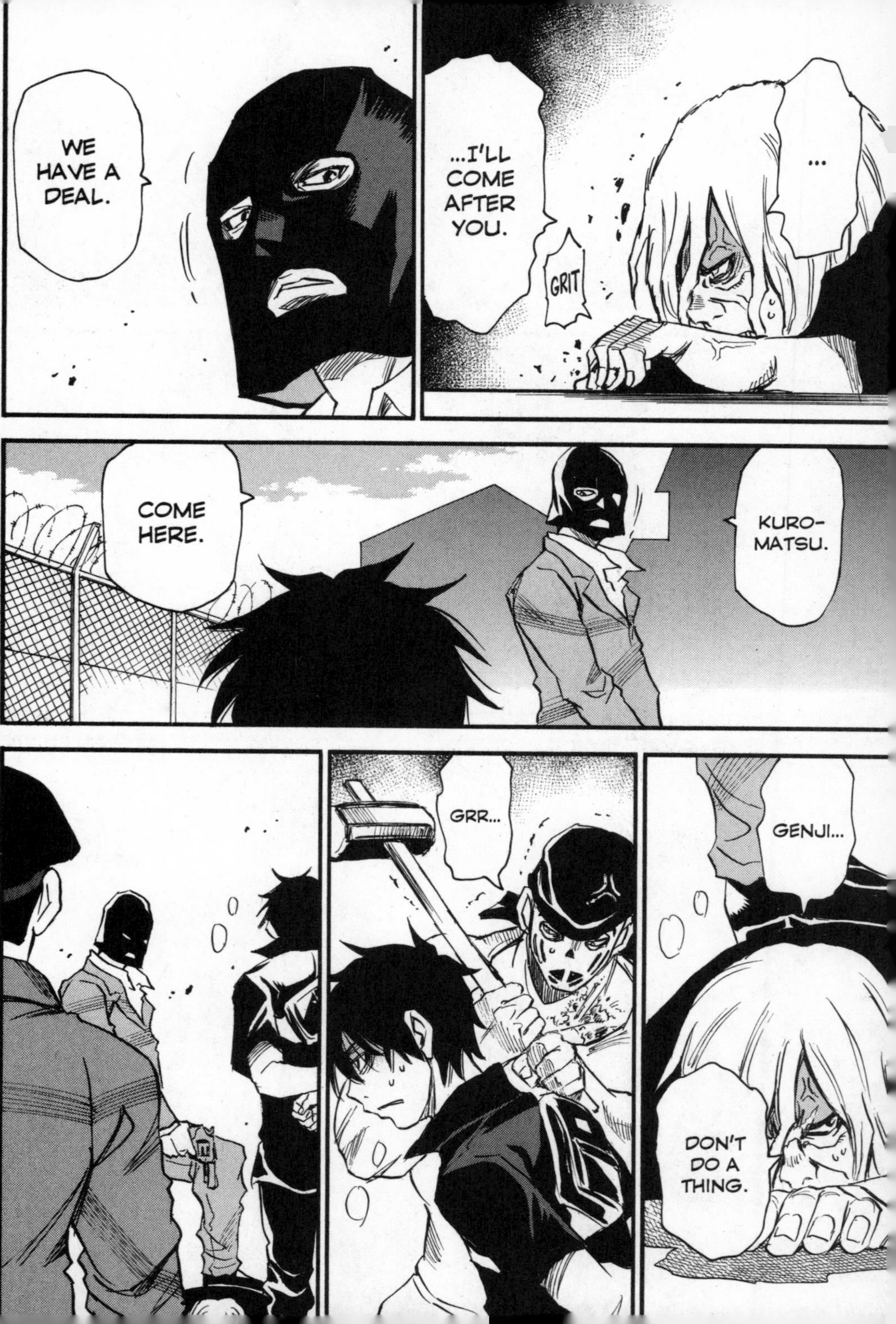
...
...I'LL COME AFTER YOU.
GRIT
WE HAVE A DEAL.
KURO-MATSU.
COME HERE.
GENJI...
DON'T DO A THING.
GRR...

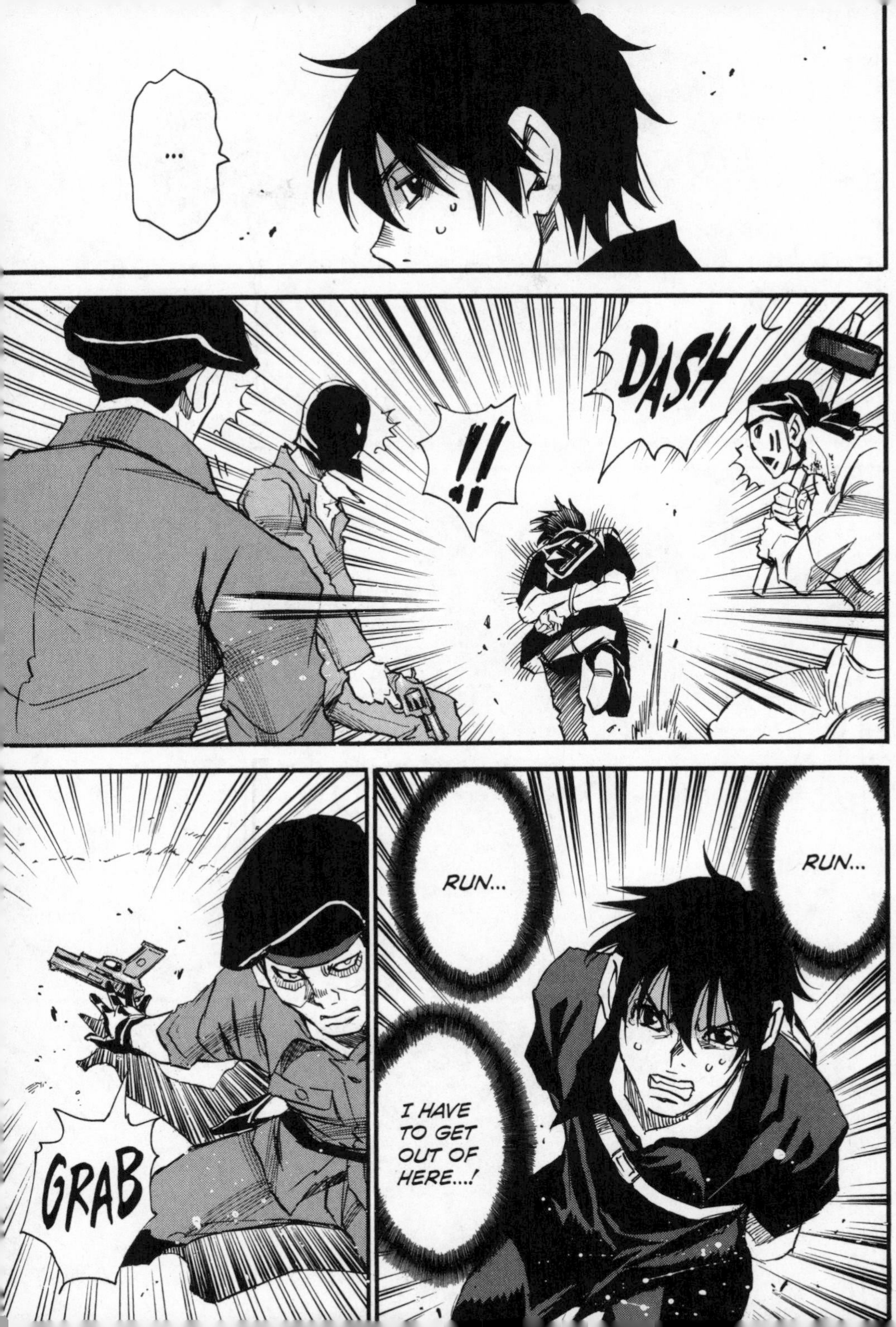
...
DASH
!!
RUN...
RUN...
I HAVE TO GET OUT OF HERE...!
GRAB

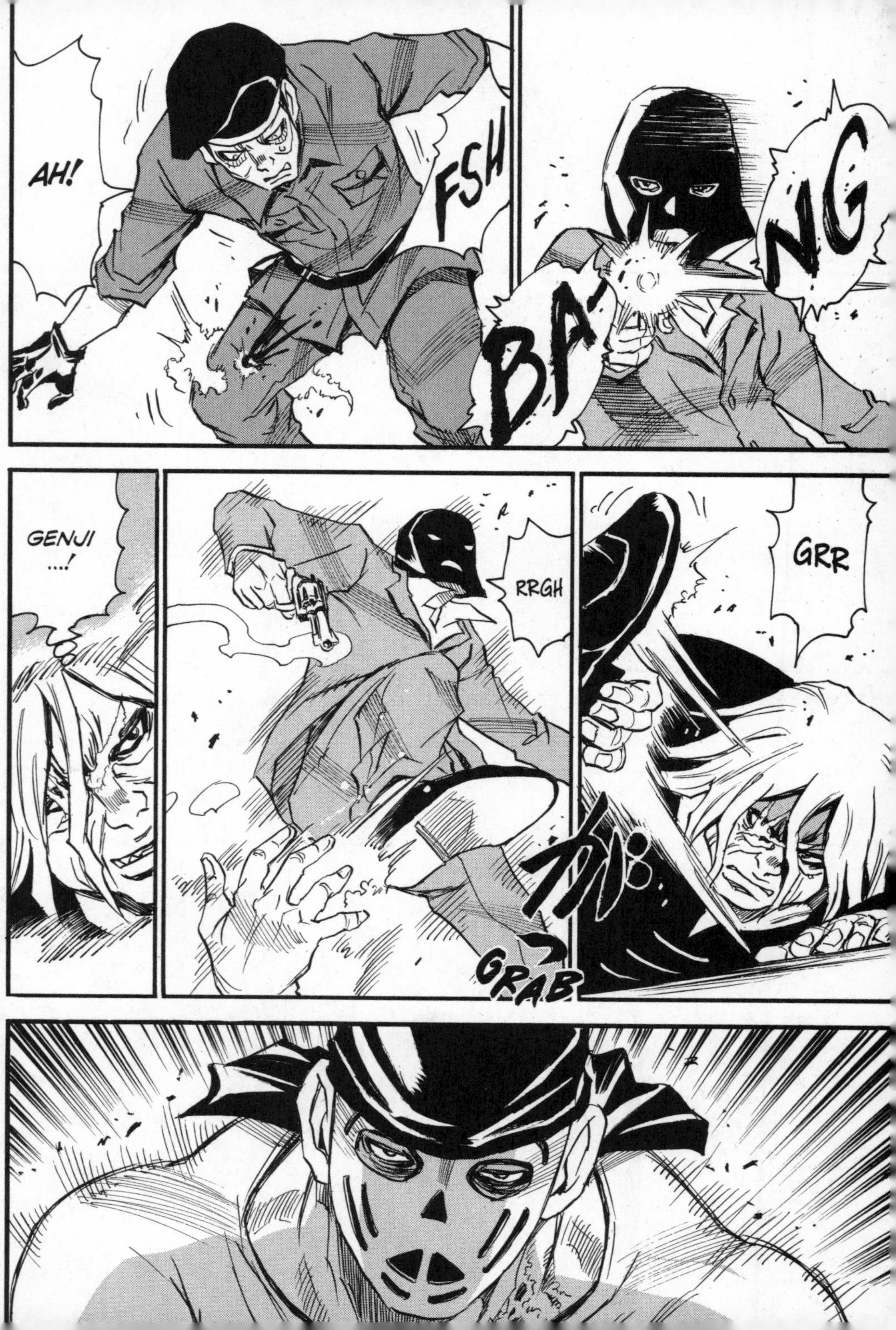
BA-NG
FSH
AH!
GRR
RRGH
GRAB
GENJI ....!

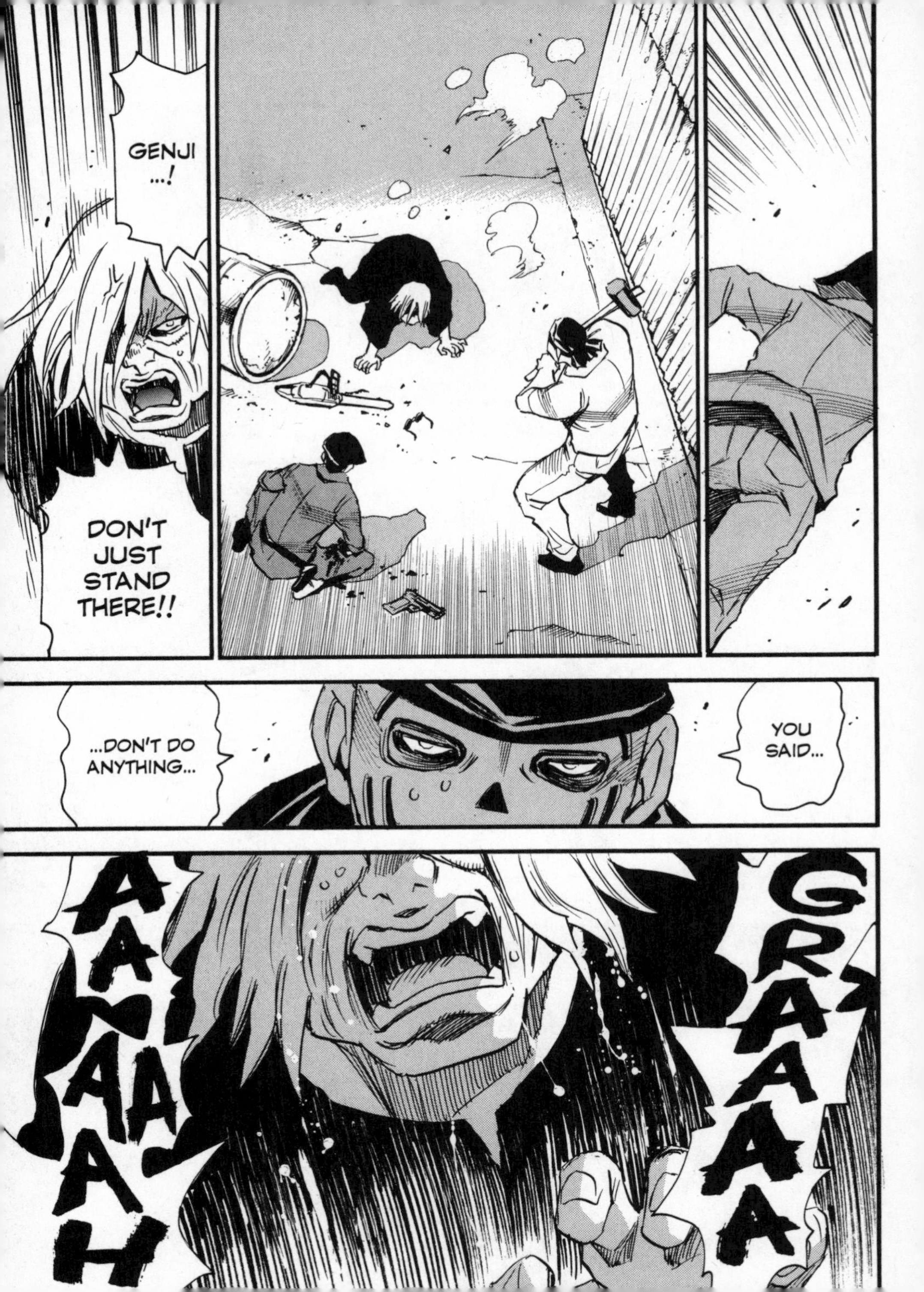
GENJI ...!
DON'T JUST STAND THERE!!
YOU SAID...
...DON'T DO ANYTHING...
GRAAAAAA
AAAAAAH

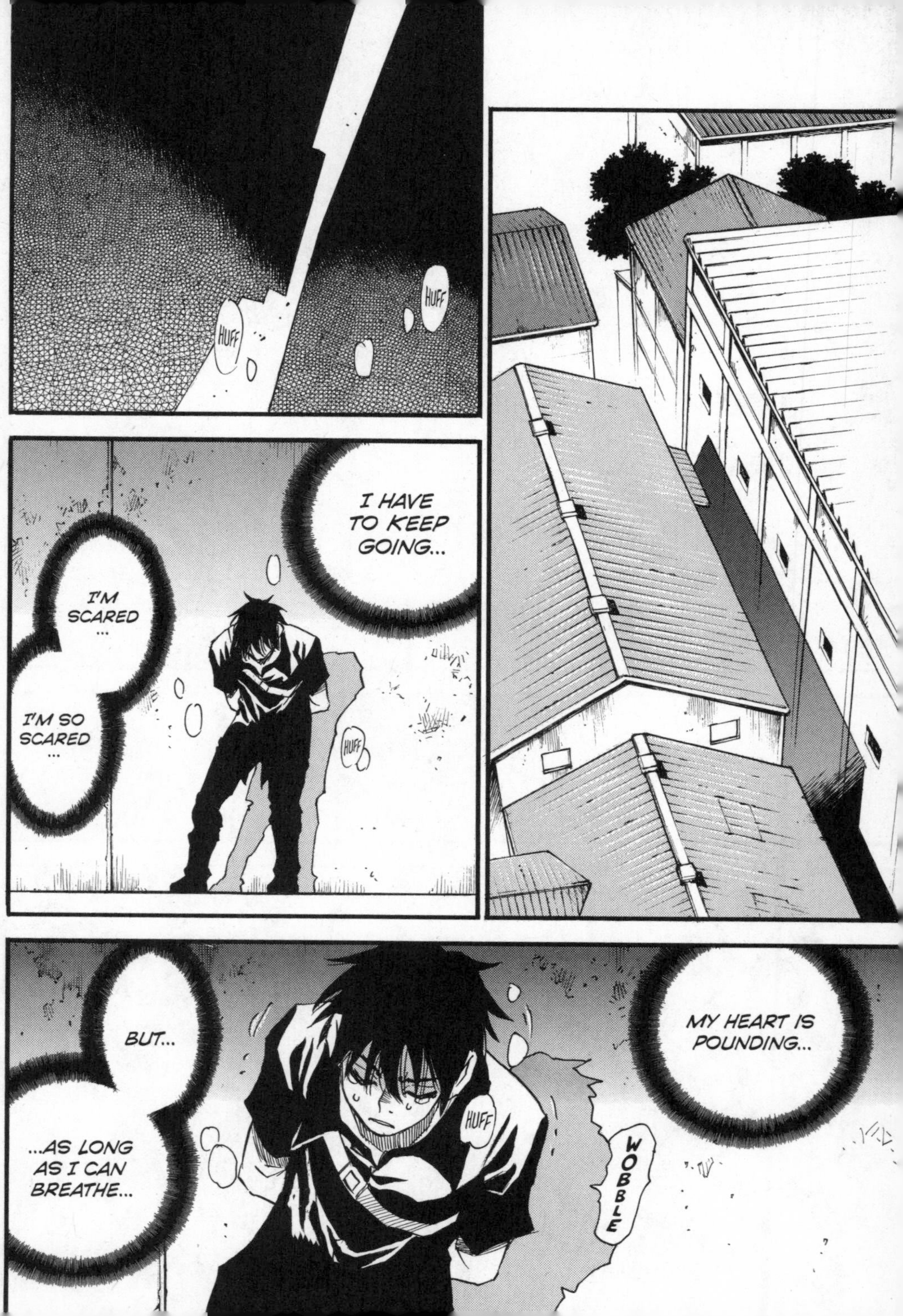
HUFF
HUFF
I HAVE TO KEEP GOING...
I'M SCARED ...
I'M SO SCARED ...
HUFF
MY HEART IS POUNDING...
HUFF
WOBBLE
BUT...
...AS LONG AS I CAN BREATHE...

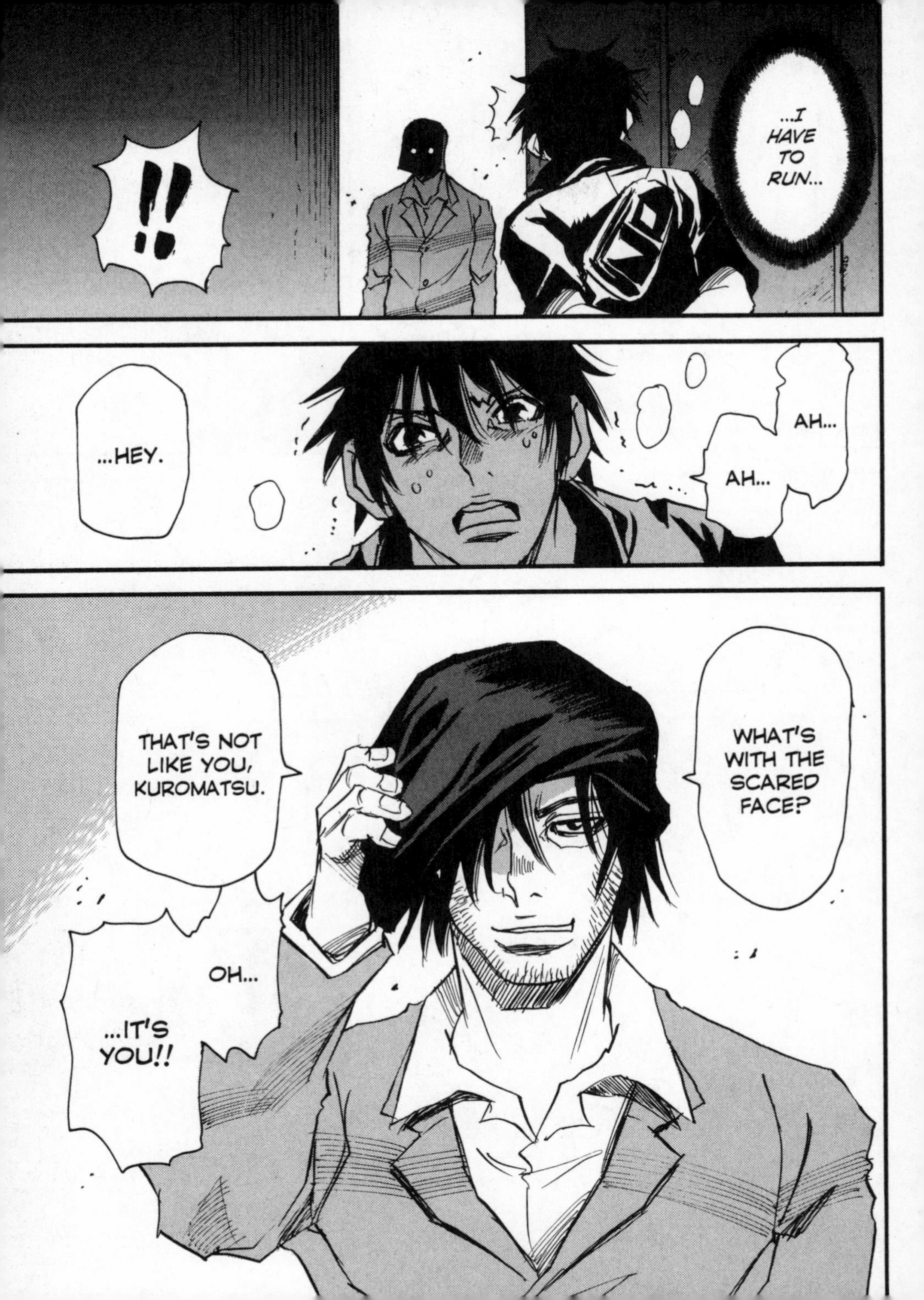
...I HAVE TO RUN...
!!
AH... AH...
...HEY.
WHAT'S WITH THE SCARED FACE?
THAT'S NOT LIKE YOU, KUROMATSU.
OH... ...IT'S YOU!!

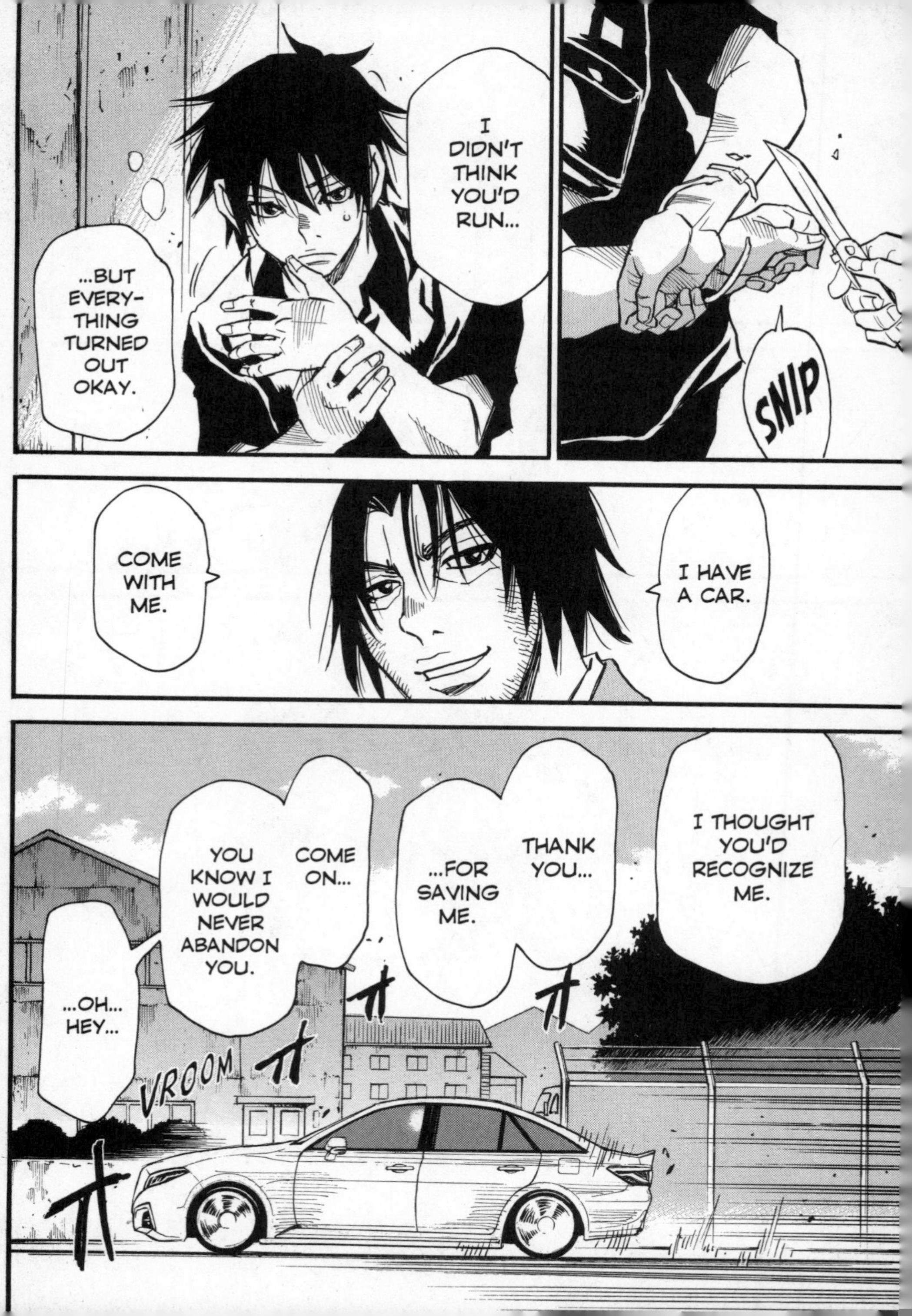
SNIP
I DIDN'T THINK YOU'D RUN...
...BUT EVERY-THING TURNED OUT OKAY.
I HAVE A CAR.
COME WITH ME.
I THOUGHT YOU'D RECOGNIZE ME.
THANK YOU...
...FOR SAVING ME.
COME ON...
YOU KNOW I WOULD NEVER ABANDON YOU.
...OH... HEY...
VROOM

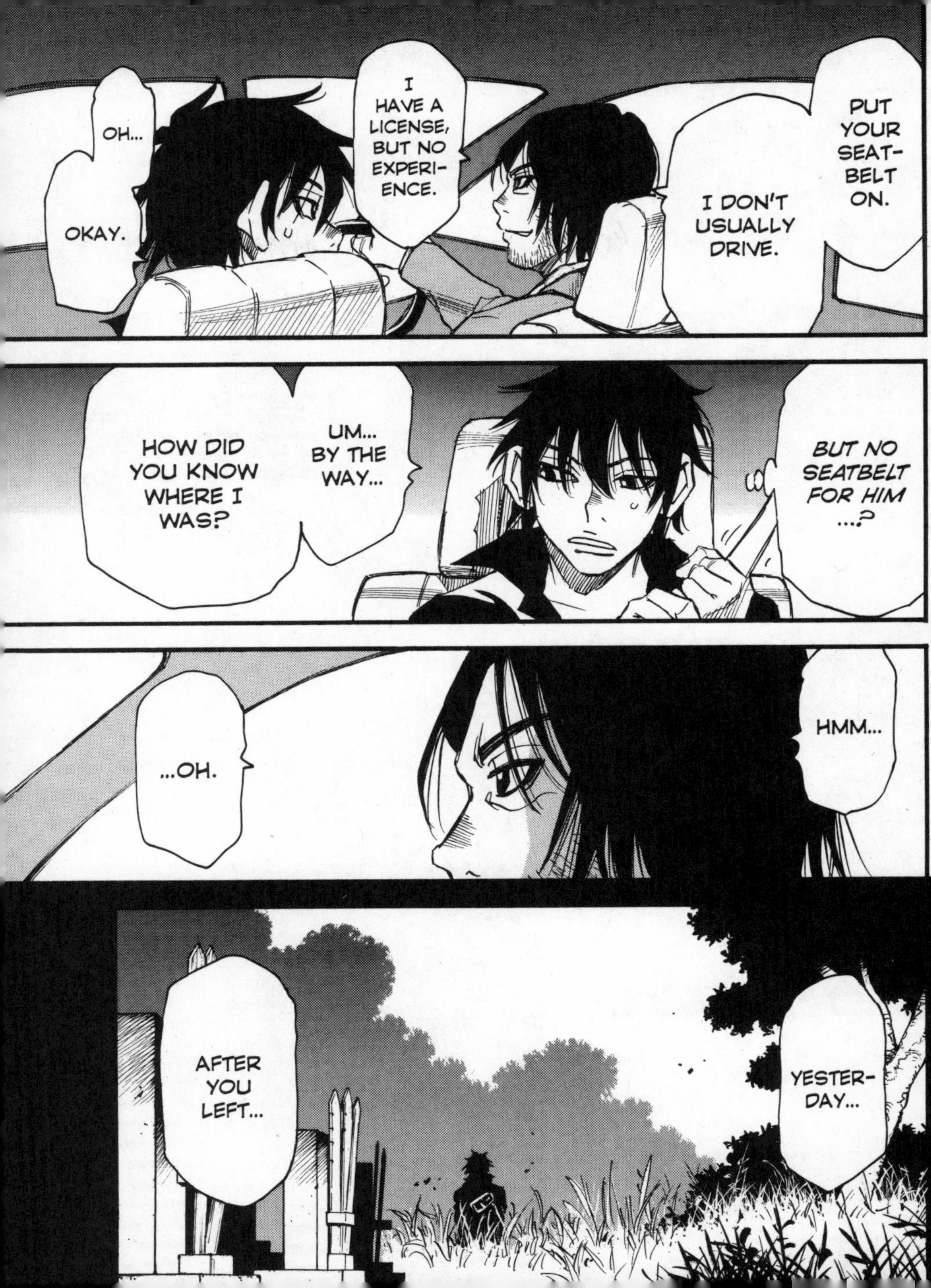
PUT YOUR SEATBELT ON.
I DON'T USUALLY DRIVE.
I HAVE A LICENSE, BUT NO EXPERIENCE.
OH... OKAY.
BUT NO SEATBELT FOR HIM ...?
UM... BY THE WAY...
HOW DID YOU KNOW WHERE I WAS?
HMM...
...OH.
YESTERDAY...
AFTER YOU LEFT...

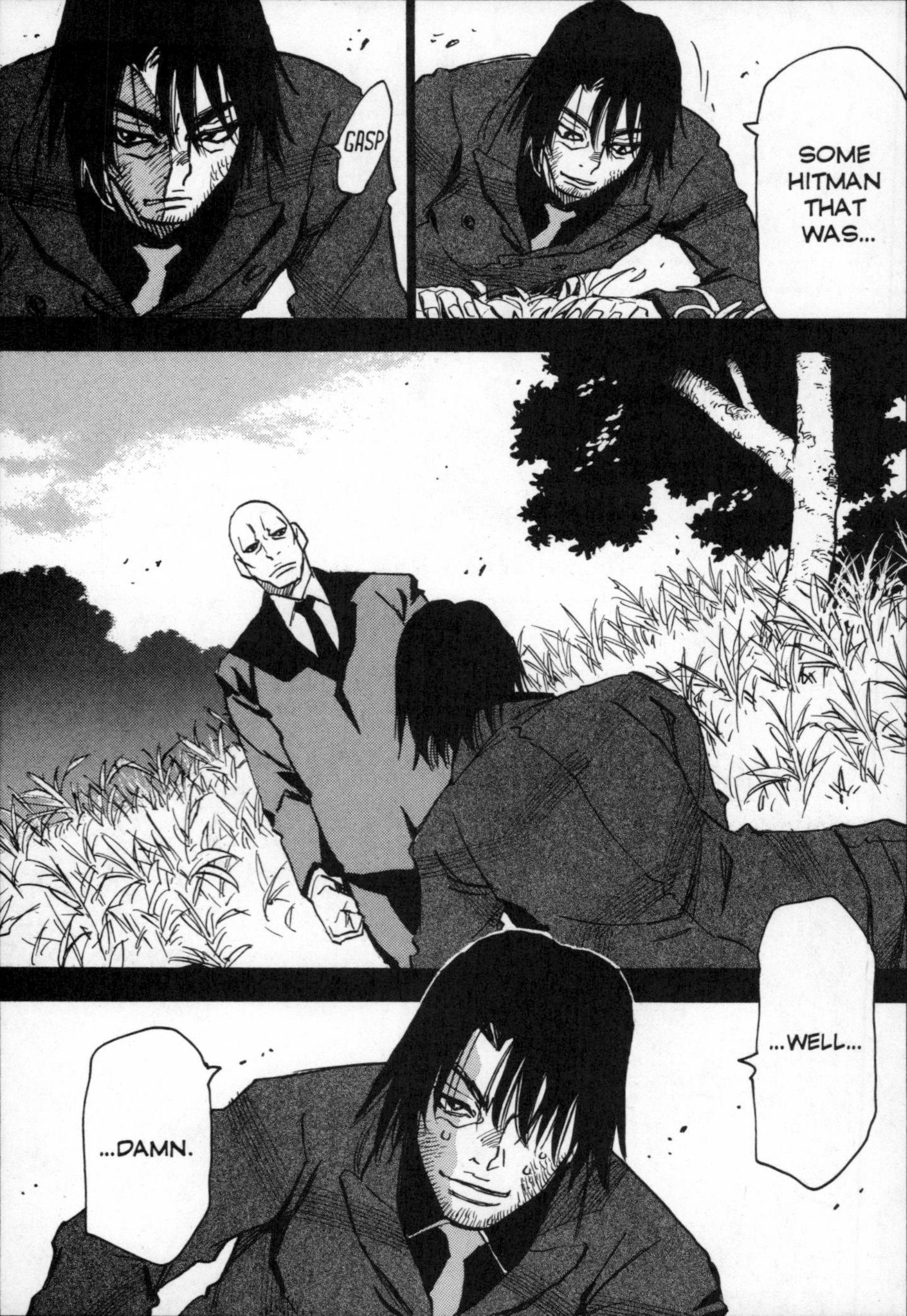
SOME HITMAN THAT WAS...
GASP
...WELL...
...DAMN.

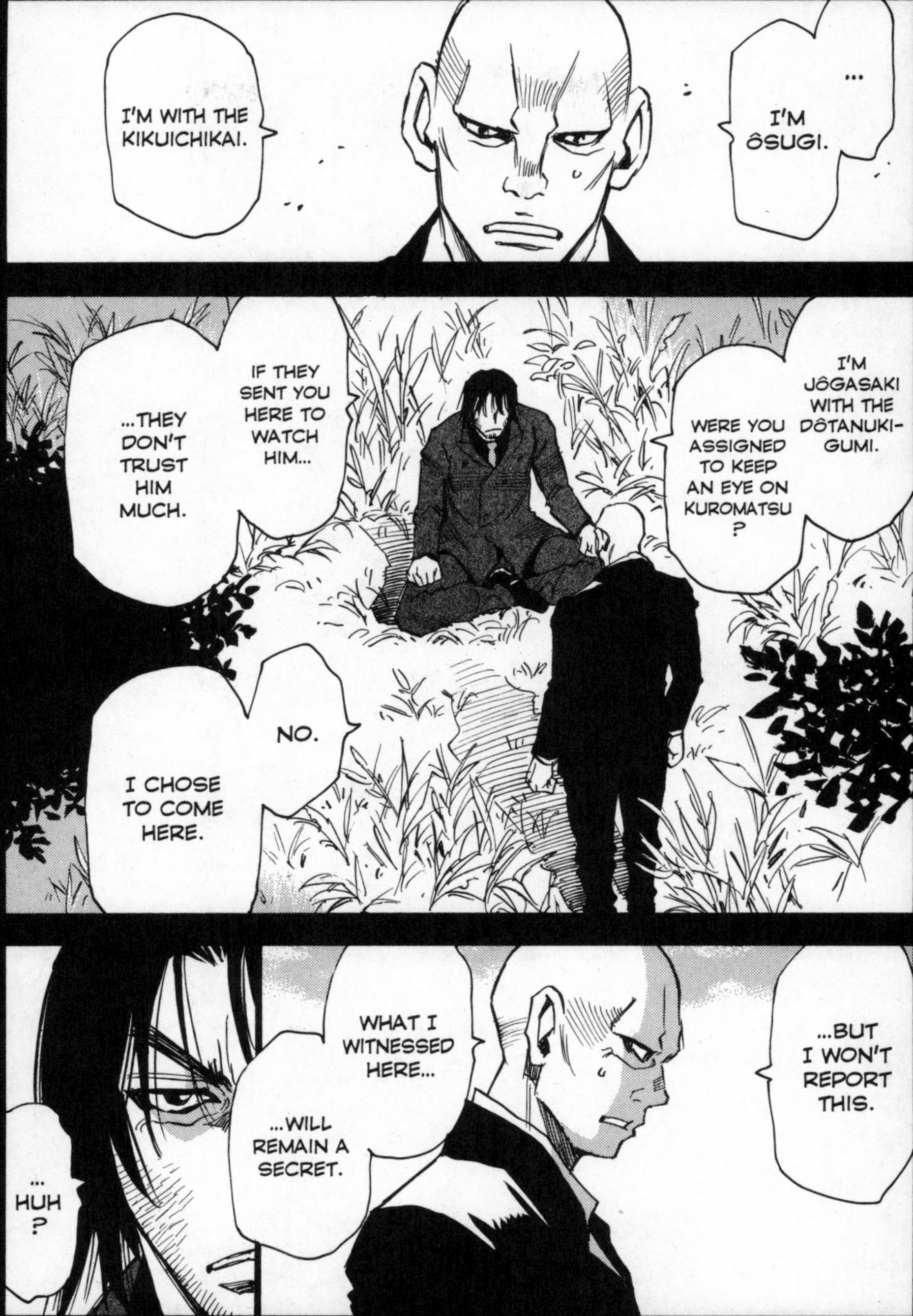
...
I'M ÔSUGI.
I'M WITH THE KIKUICHIKAI.
I'M JÔGASAKI WITH THE DÔTANUKI-GUMI.
WERE YOU ASSIGNED TO KEEP AN EYE ON KUROMATSU?
IF THEY SENT YOU HERE TO WATCH HIM...
...THEY DON'T TRUST HIM MUCH.
NO.
I CHOSE TO COME HERE.
...BUT I WON'T REPORT THIS.
WHAT I WITNESSED HERE...
...WILL REMAIN A SECRET.
... HUH?

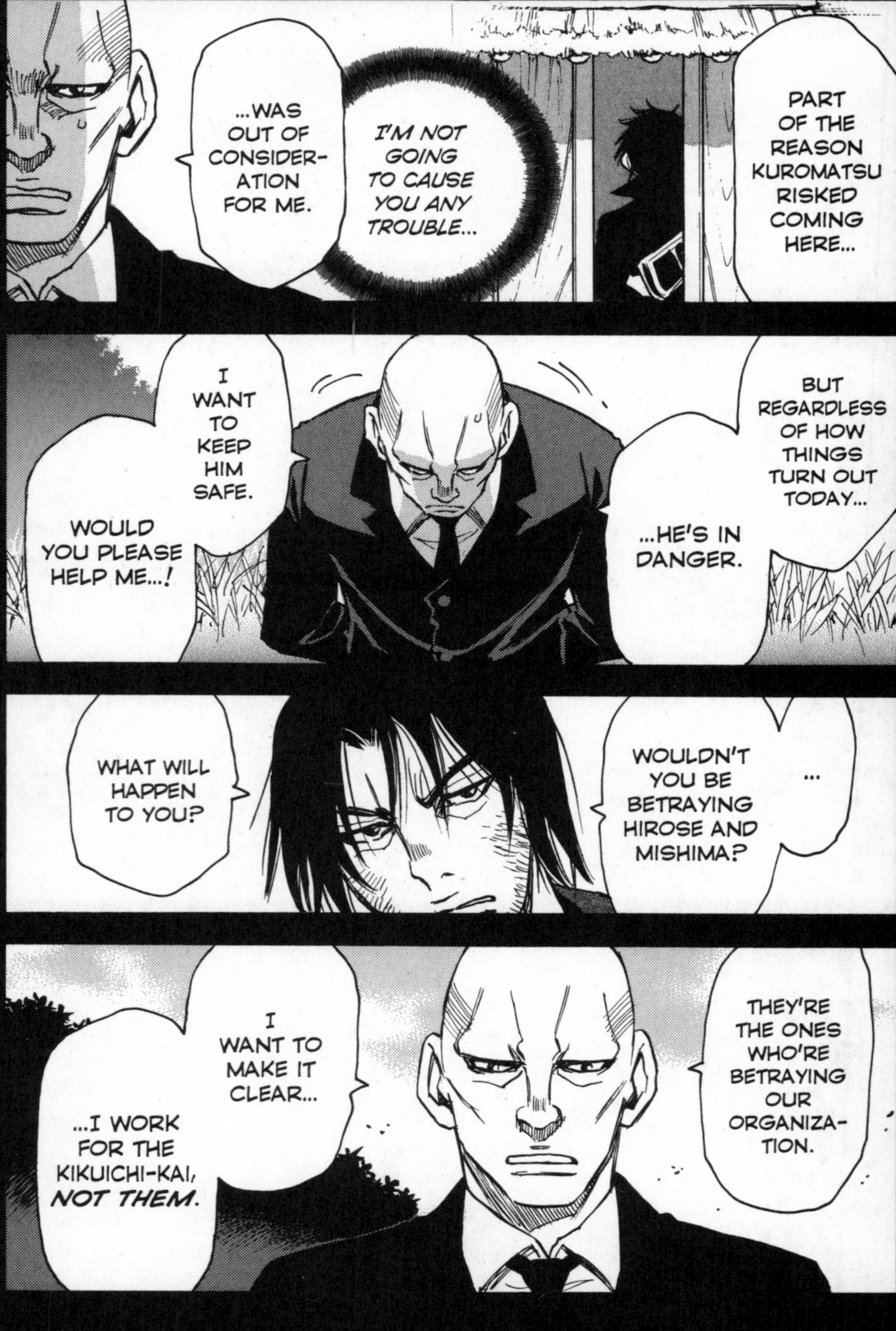
PART OF THE REASON KUROMATSU RISKED COMING HERE...
I'M NOT GOING TO CAUSE YOU ANY TROUBLE...
...WAS OUT OF CONSIDER-ATION FOR ME.
BUT REGARDLESS OF HOW THINGS TURN OUT TODAY...
...HE'S IN DANGER.
I WANT TO KEEP HIM SAFE.
WOULD YOU PLEASE HELP ME...!
...
WOULDN'T YOU BE BETRAYING HIROSE AND MISHIMA?
WHAT WILL HAPPEN TO YOU?
THEY'RE THE ONES WHO'RE BETRAYING OUR ORGANIZA-TION.
I WANT TO MAKE IT CLEAR...
...I WORK FOR THE KIKUICHI-KAI, NOT THEM.

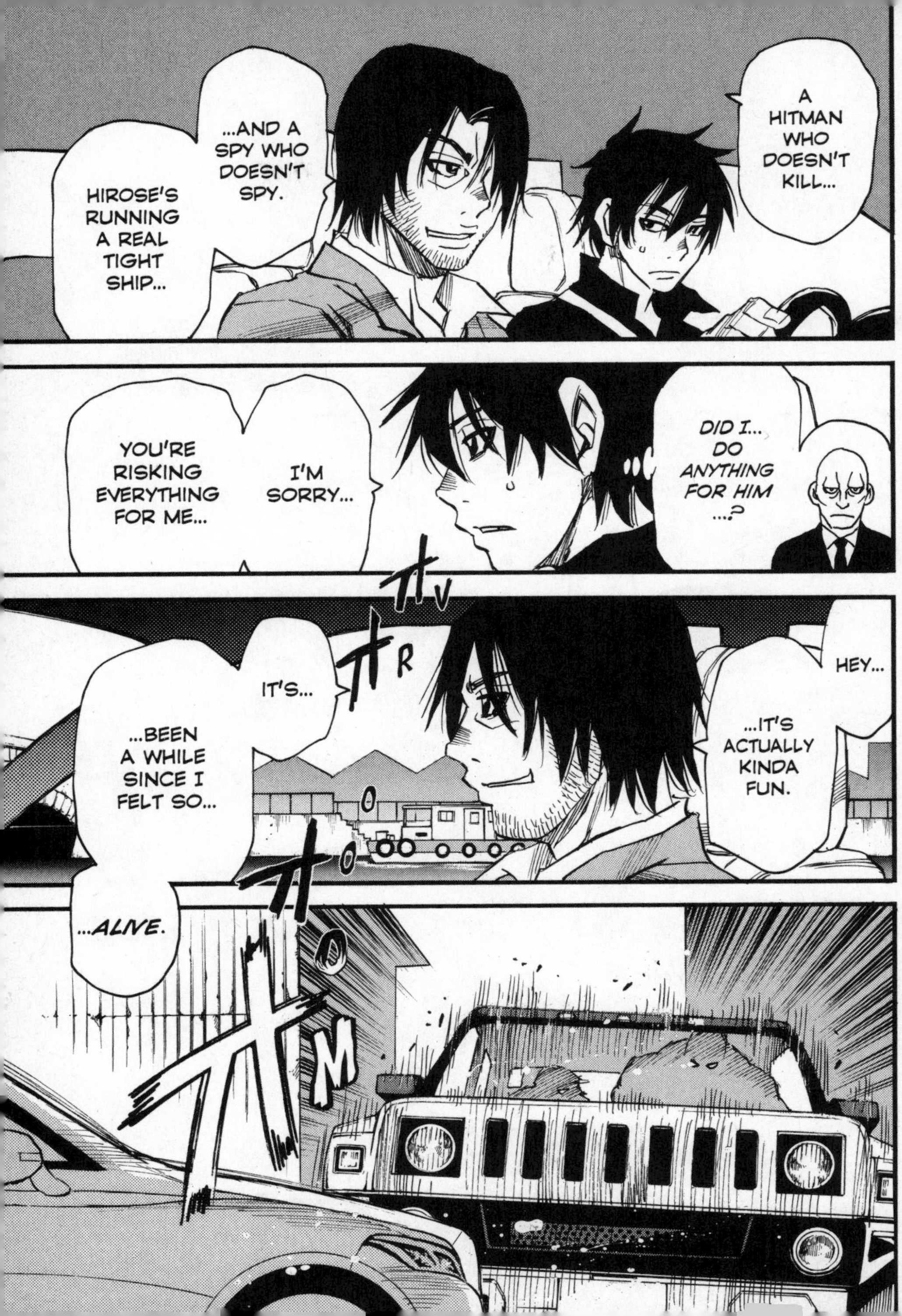
A HITMAN WHO DOESN'T KILL...
...AND A SPY WHO DOESN'T SPY.
HIROSE'S RUNNING A REAL TIGHT SHIP...
DID I... DO ANYTHING FOR HIM ...?
I'M SORRY...
YOU'RE RISKING EVERYTHING FOR ME...
HEY...
...IT'S ACTUALLY KINDA FUN.
IT'S...
...BEEN A WHILE SINCE I FELT SO...
...*ALIVE*.

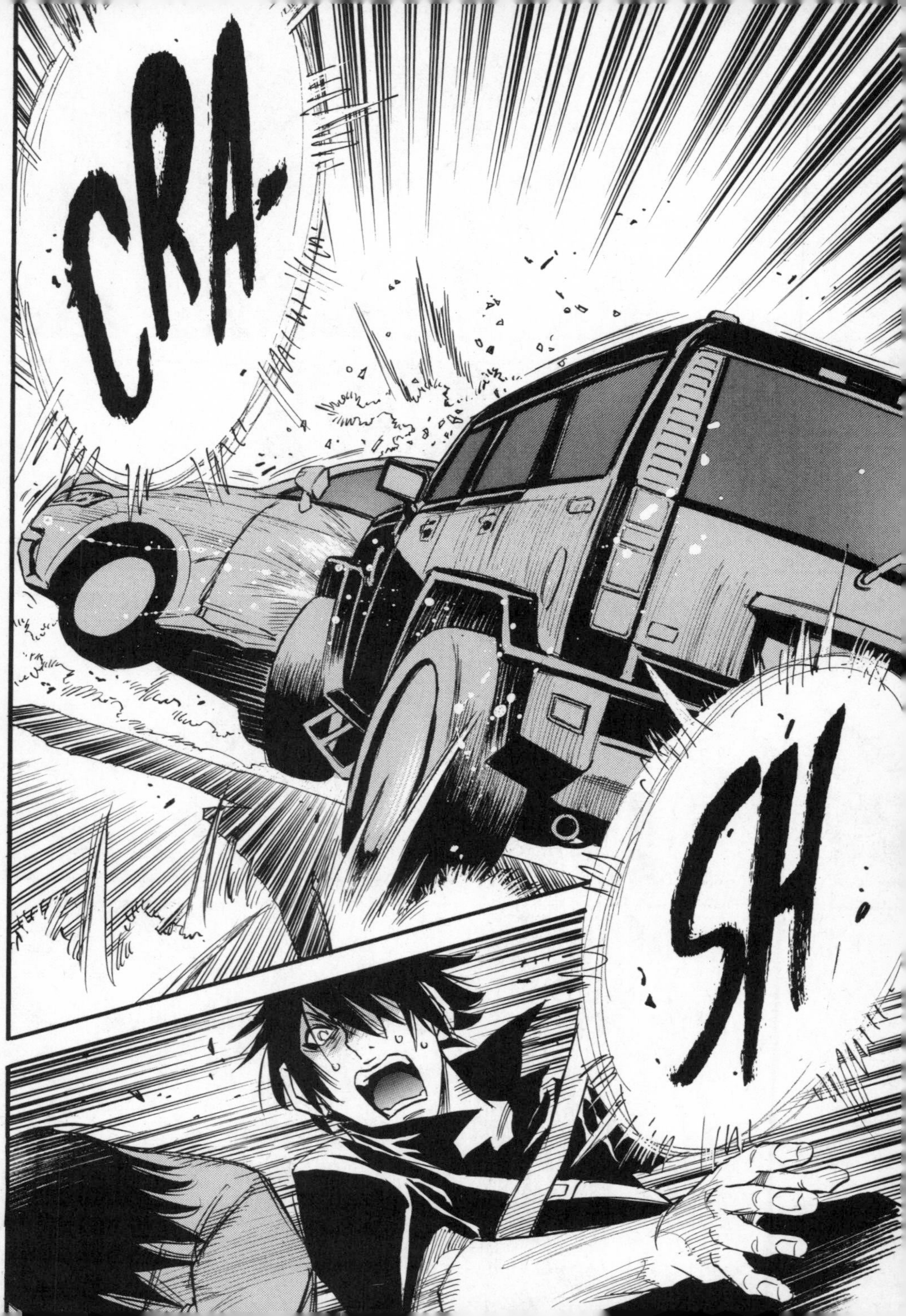
CRA-
SH

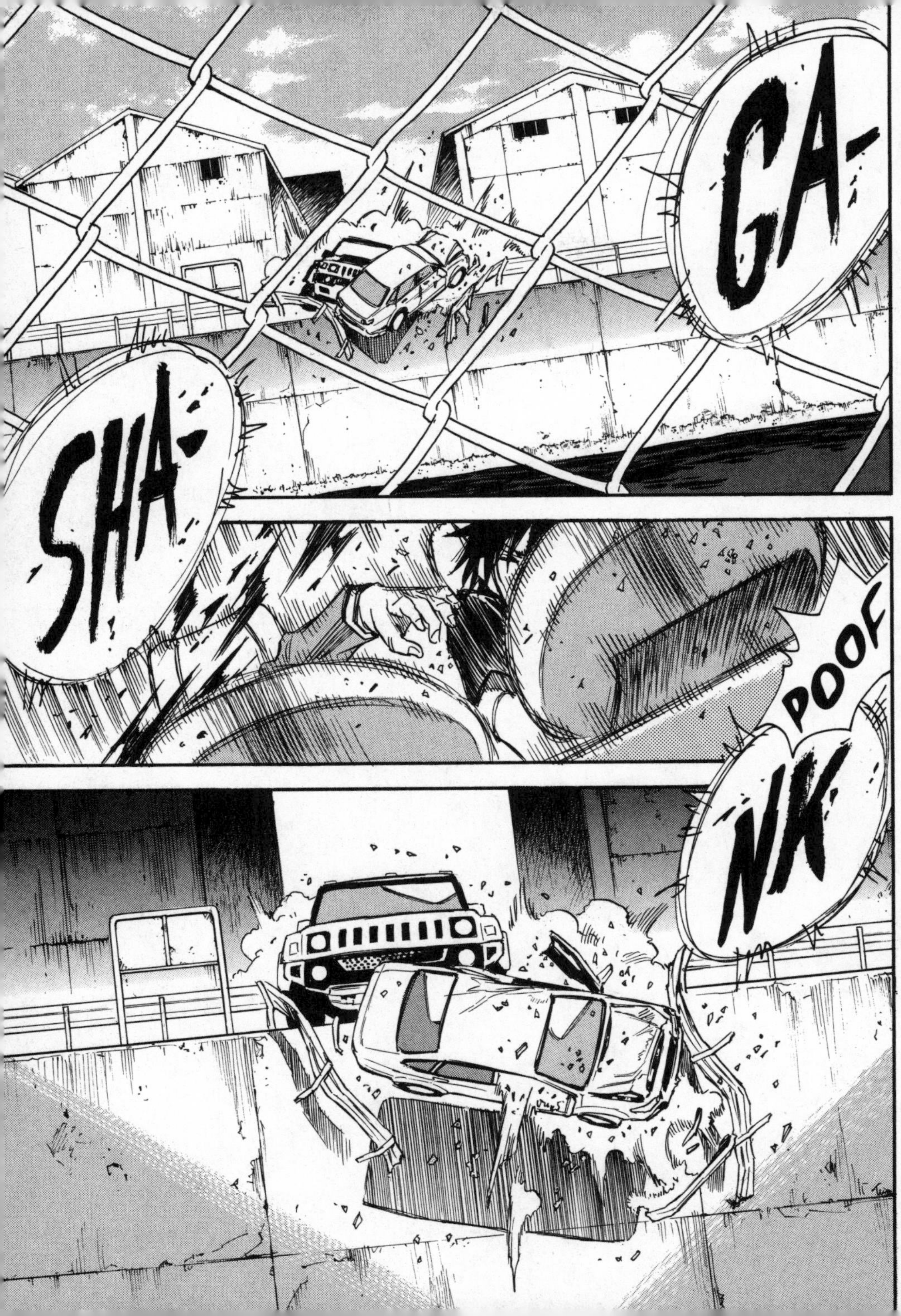
GA-
SHA-
POOF
NK

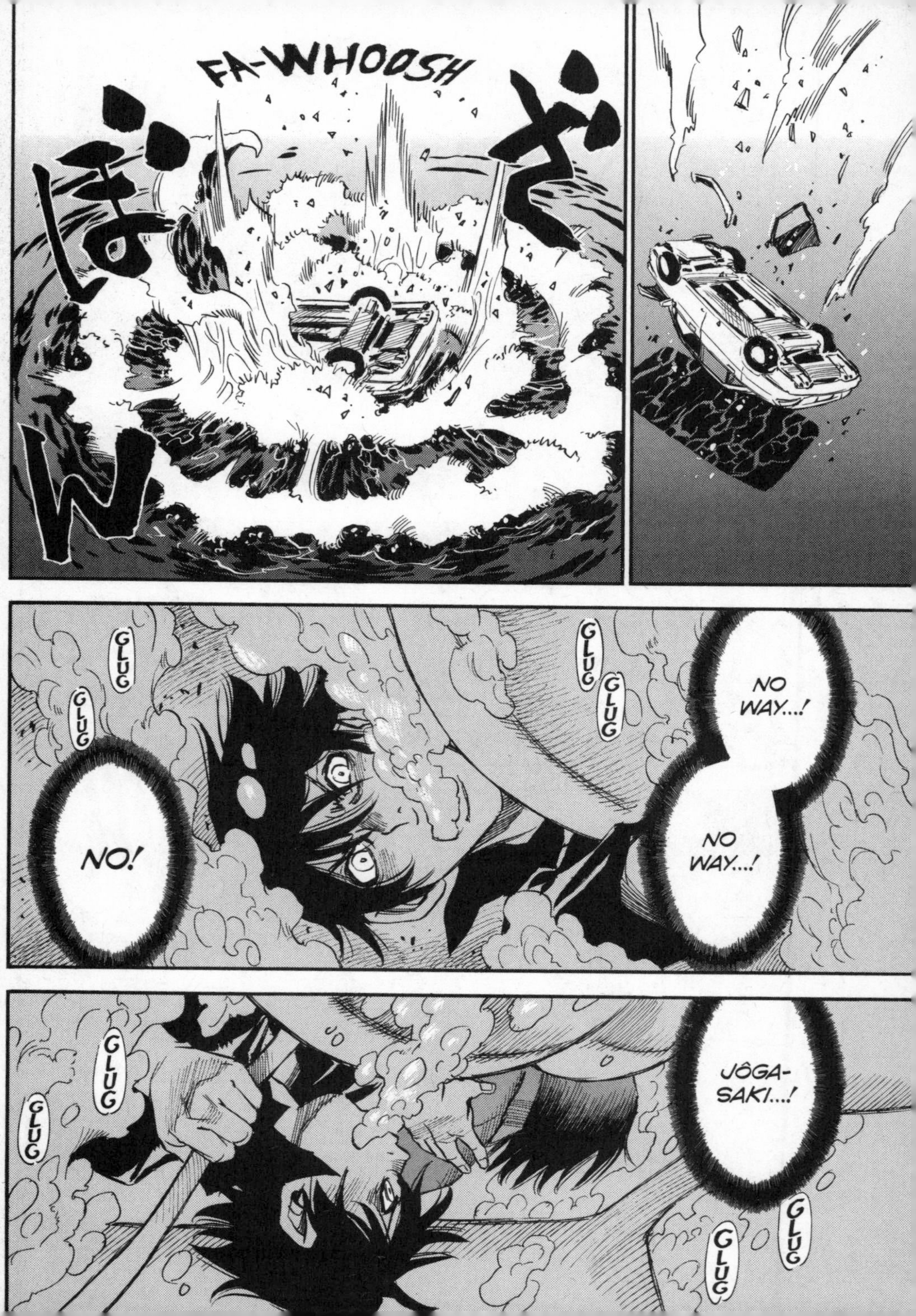
FA-WHOOSH
NO WAY...!
GLUG
GLUG
NO WAY...!
GLUG
GLUG
NO!
JÔGA-SAKI...!
GLUG
GLUG
GLUG
GLUG

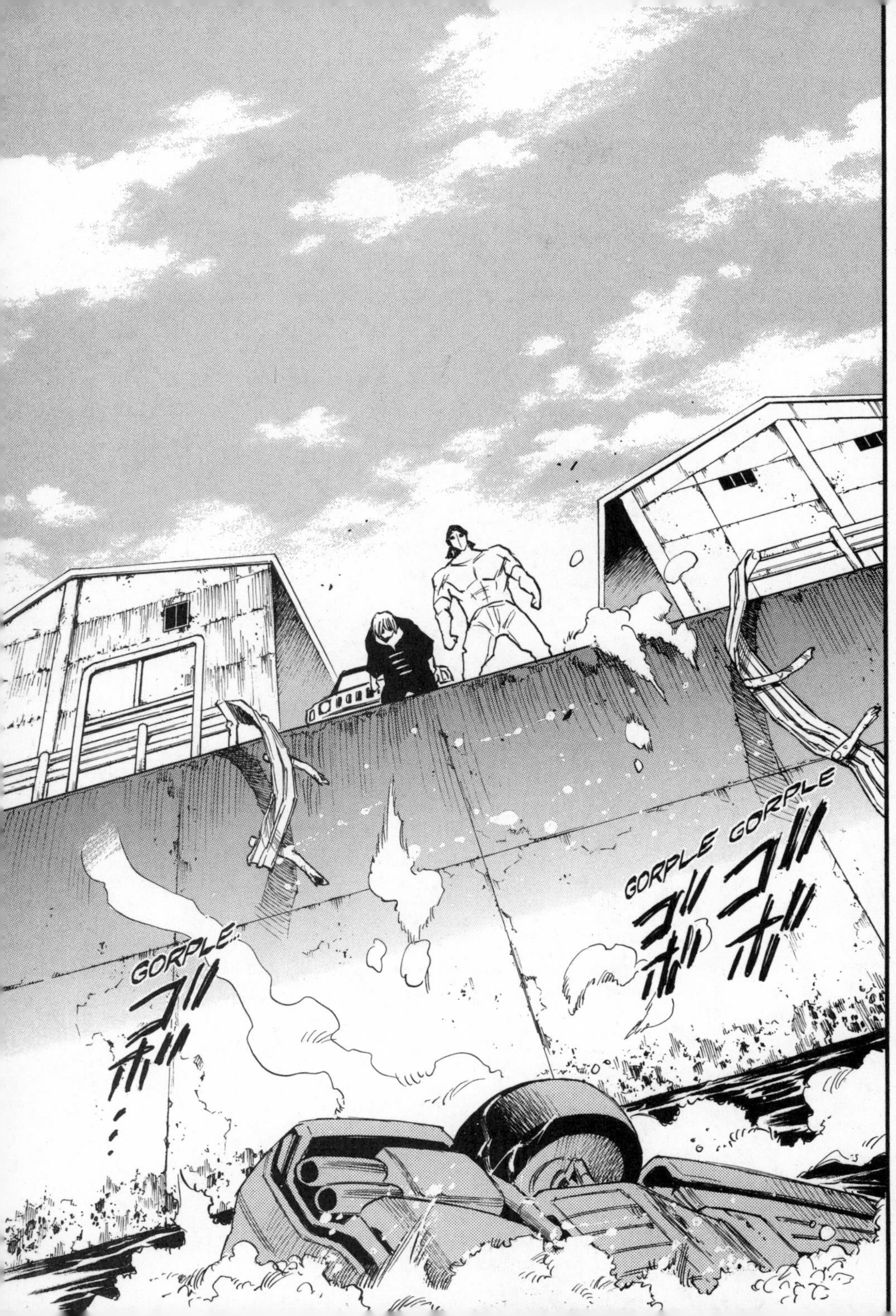
GORPLE GORPLE
ゴボゴボ
GORPLE...
ゴボ…

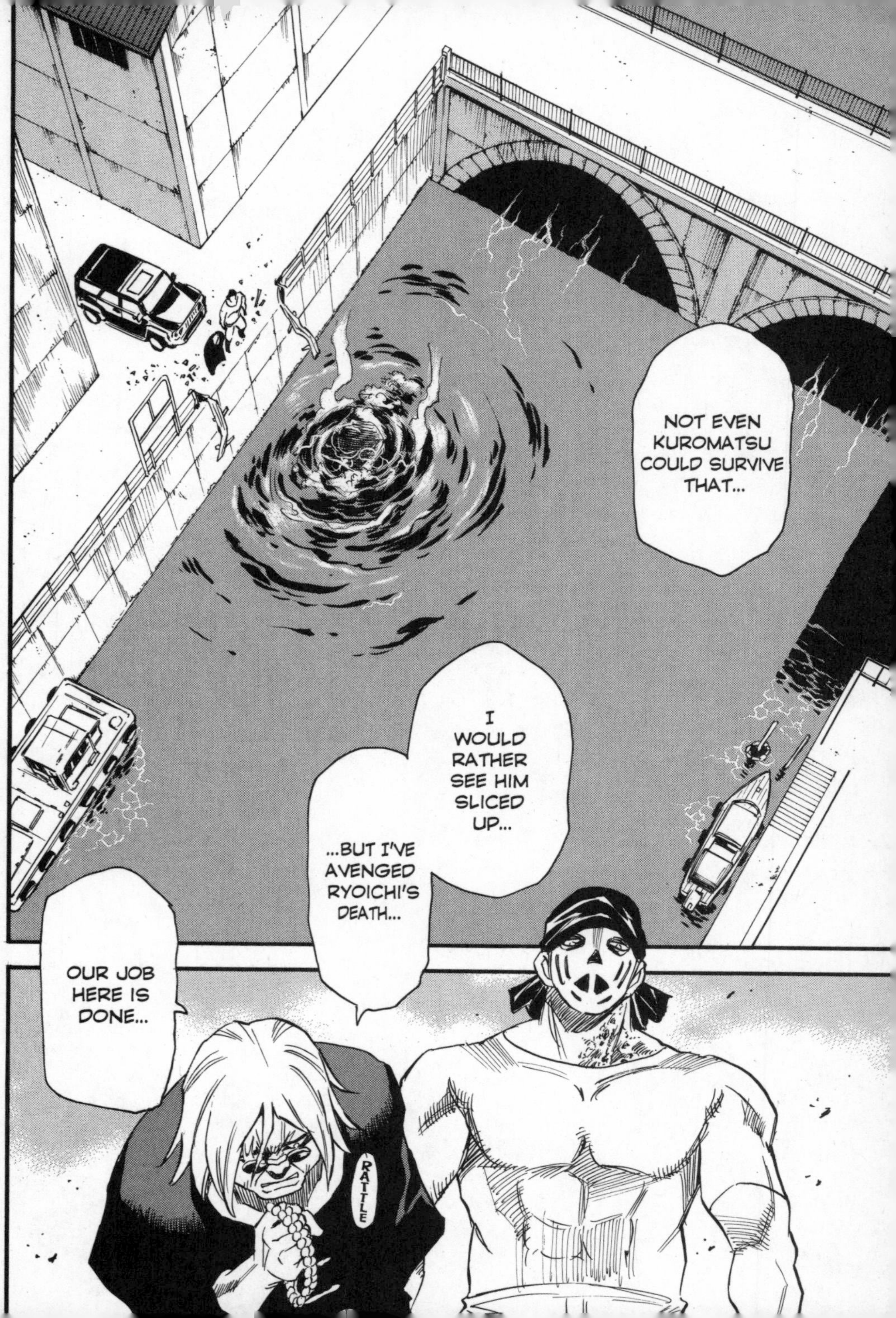
NOT EVEN KUROMATSU COULD SURVIVE THAT...
I WOULD RATHER SEE HIM SLICED UP...
...BUT I'VE AVENGED RYOICHI'S DEATH...
OUR JOB HERE IS DONE...
RATTLE

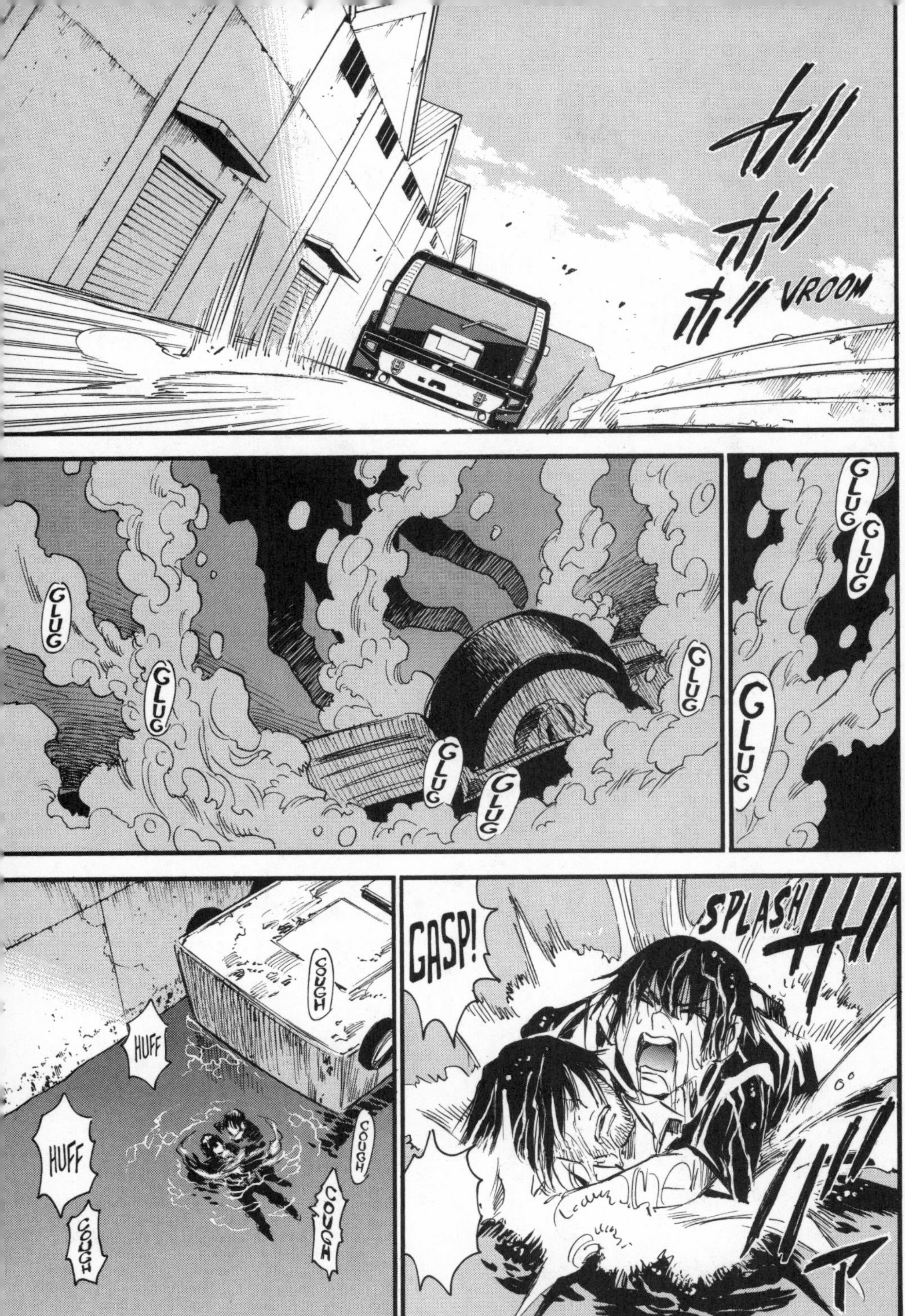
VROOM
GLUG
GLUG
GLUG
GLUG
GLUG
GLUG
GLUG
GLUG
SPLASH
GASP!
COUGH
HUFF
HUFF
COUGH
COUGH
COUGH

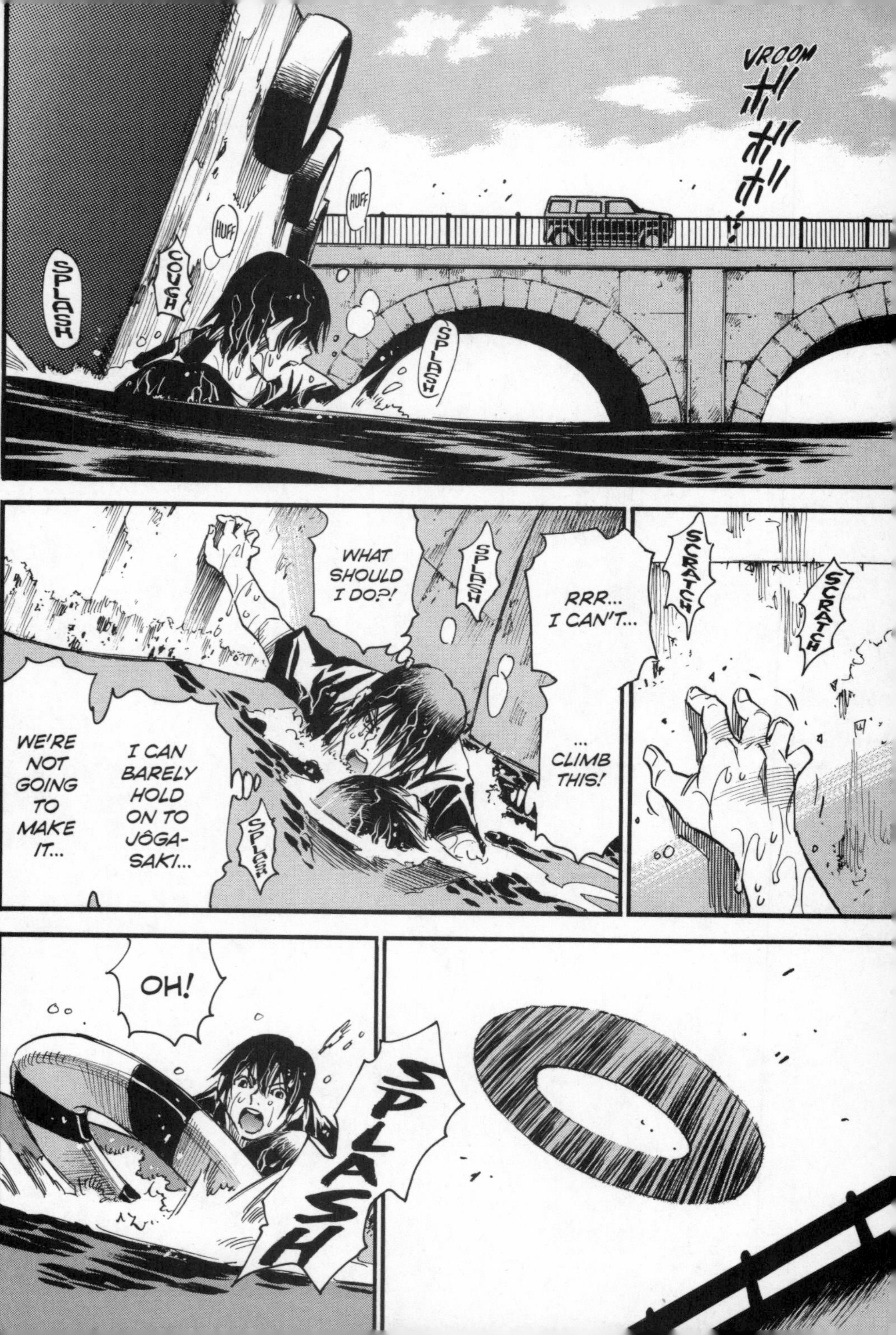
VROOM
ボボボボ!
HUFF
HUFF
SPLASH
COUGH
SPLASH
SCRATCH
SCRATCH
RRR... I CAN'T...
... CLIMB THIS!
SPLASH
WHAT SHOULD I DO?!
I CAN BARELY HOLD ON TO JÔGA-SAKI...
SPLASH
WE'RE NOT GOING TO MAKE IT...
OH!
SPLASH

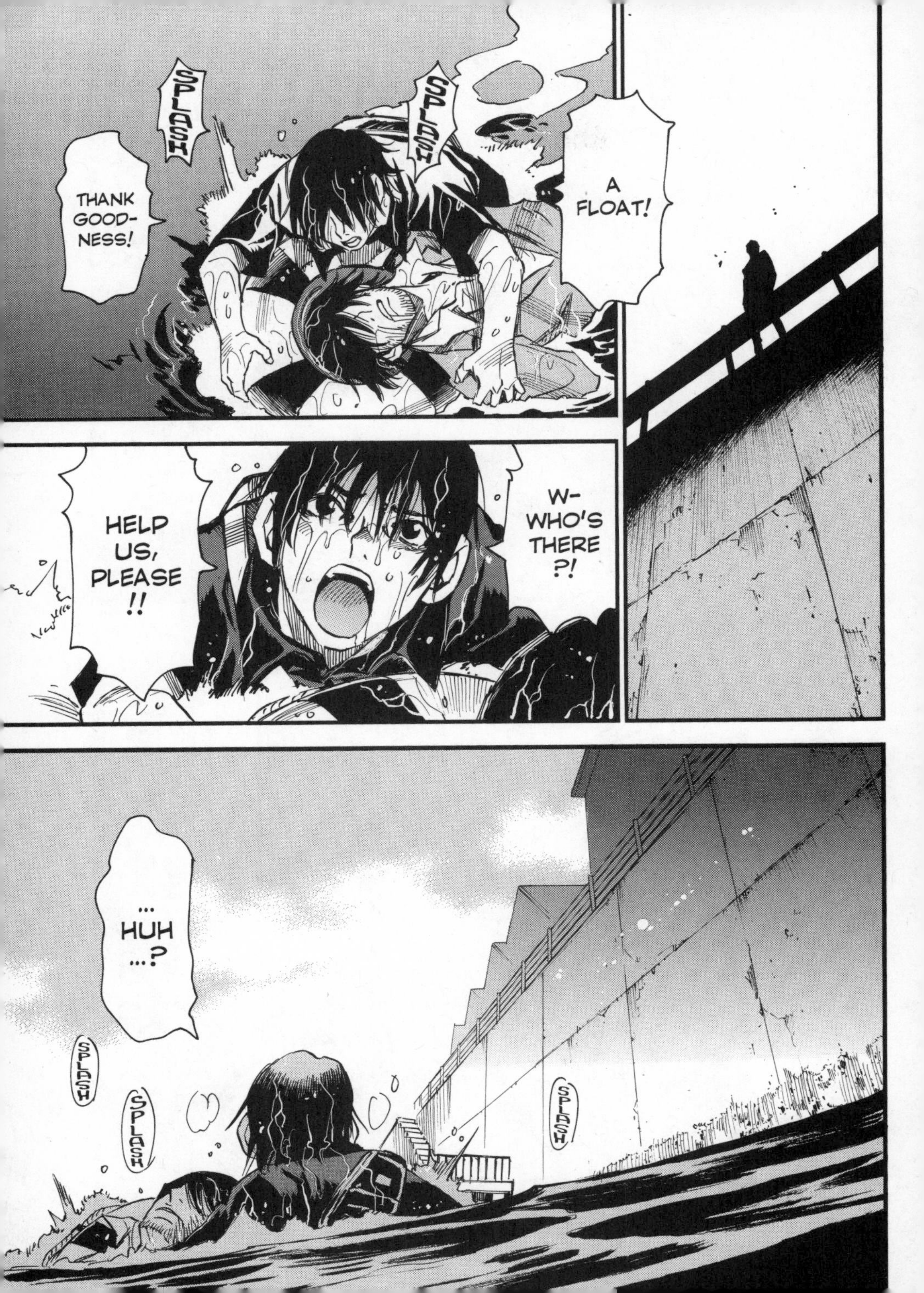
A FLOAT!
SPLASH
SPLASH
THANK GOOD-NESS!
W-WHO'S THERE?!
HELP US, PLEASE!!
SPLASH
... HUH ...?
SPLASH
SPLASH

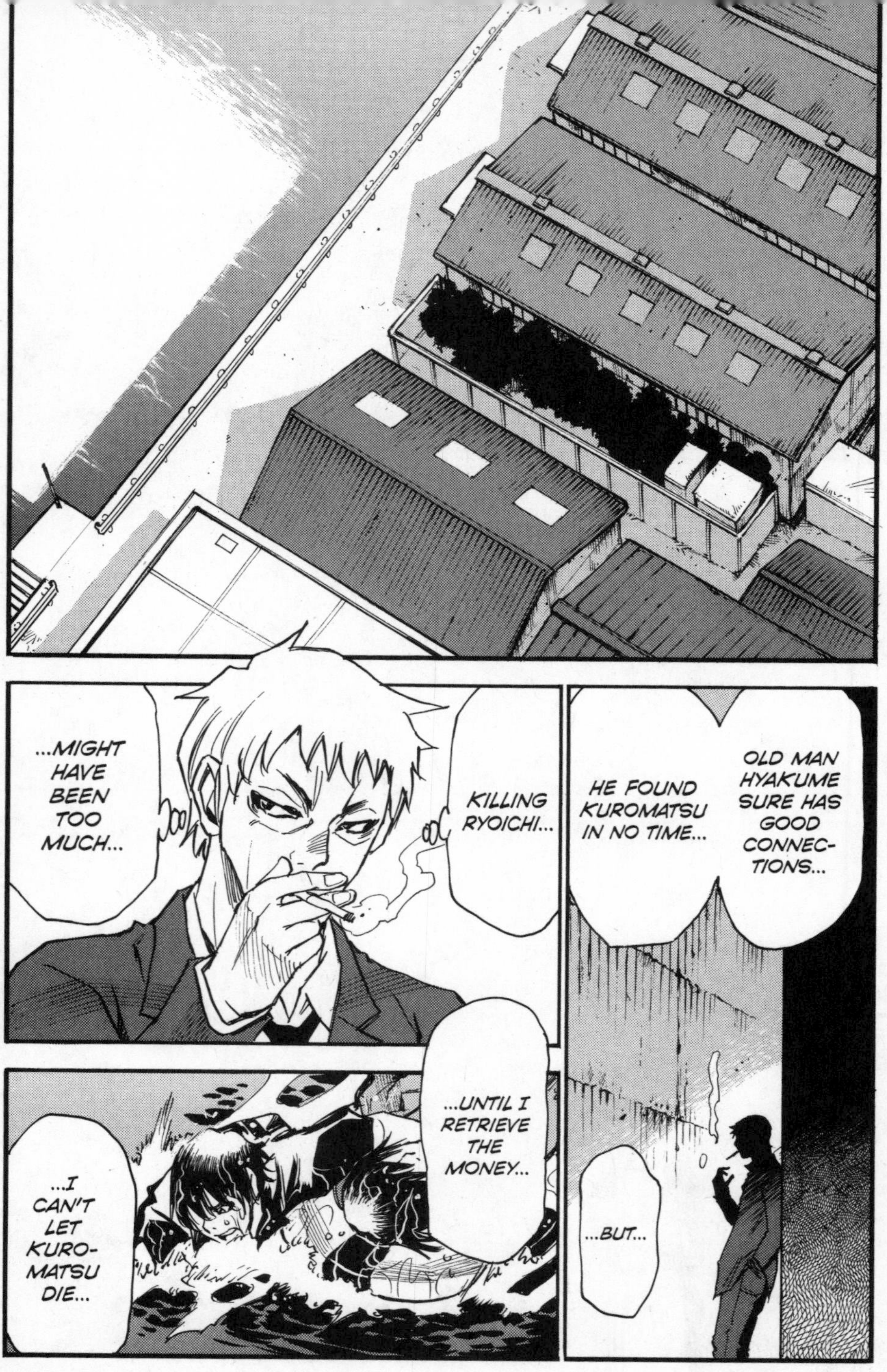
OLD MAN HYAKUME SURE HAS GOOD CONNECTIONS...
HE FOUND KUROMATSU IN NO TIME...
...BUT...
KILLING RYOICHI...
...MIGHT HAVE BEEN TOO MUCH...
...UNTIL I RETRIEVE THE MONEY...
...I CAN'T LET KUROMATSU DIE...

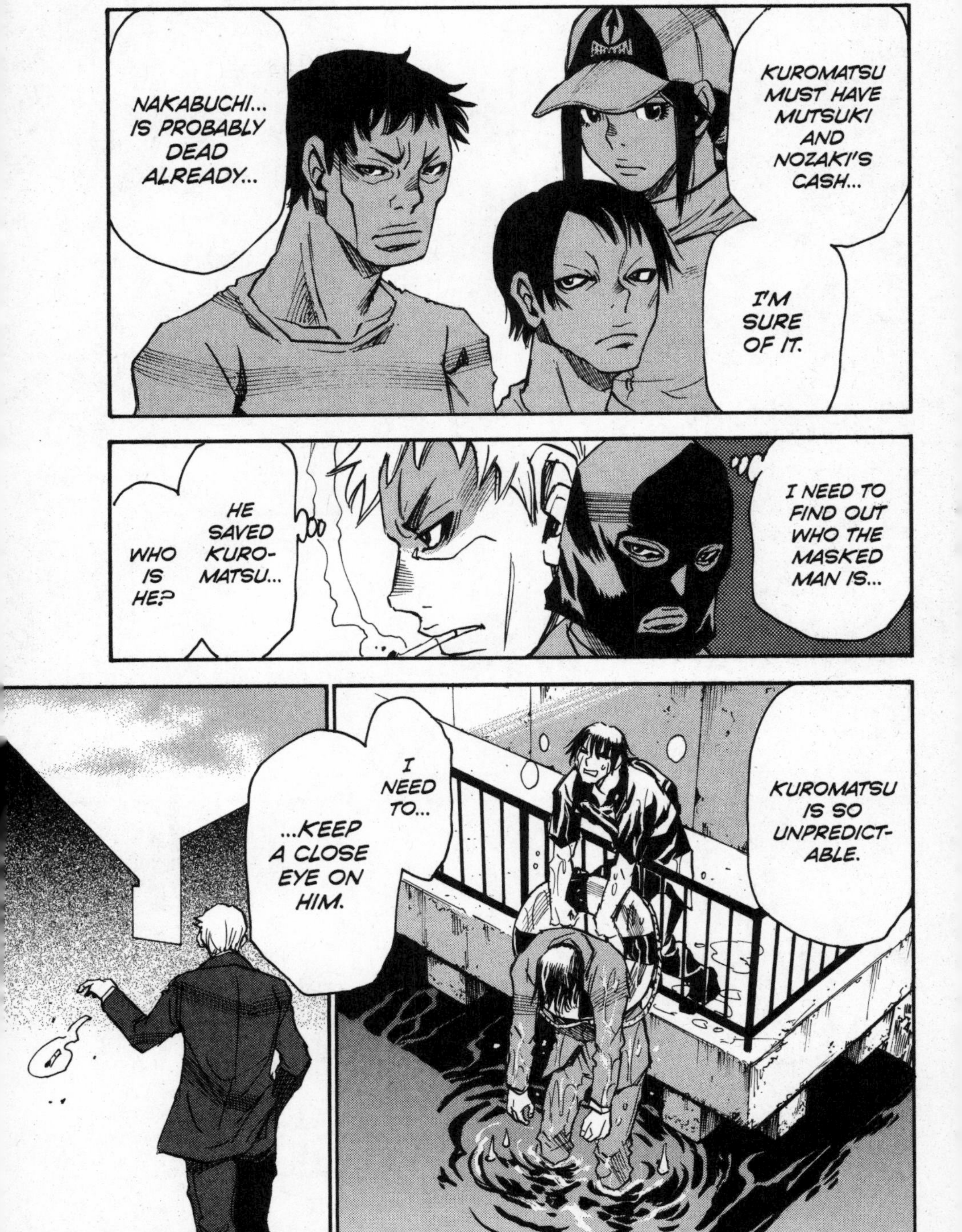
KUROMATSU MUST HAVE MUTSUKI AND NOZAKI'S CASH...
I'M SURE OF IT.
NAKABUCHI... IS PROBABLY DEAD ALREADY...
I NEED TO FIND OUT WHO THE MASKED MAN IS...
HE SAVED KURO-MATSU...
WHO IS HE?
KUROMATSU IS SO UNPREDICT-ABLE.
I NEED TO...
...KEEP A CLOSE EYE ON HIM.

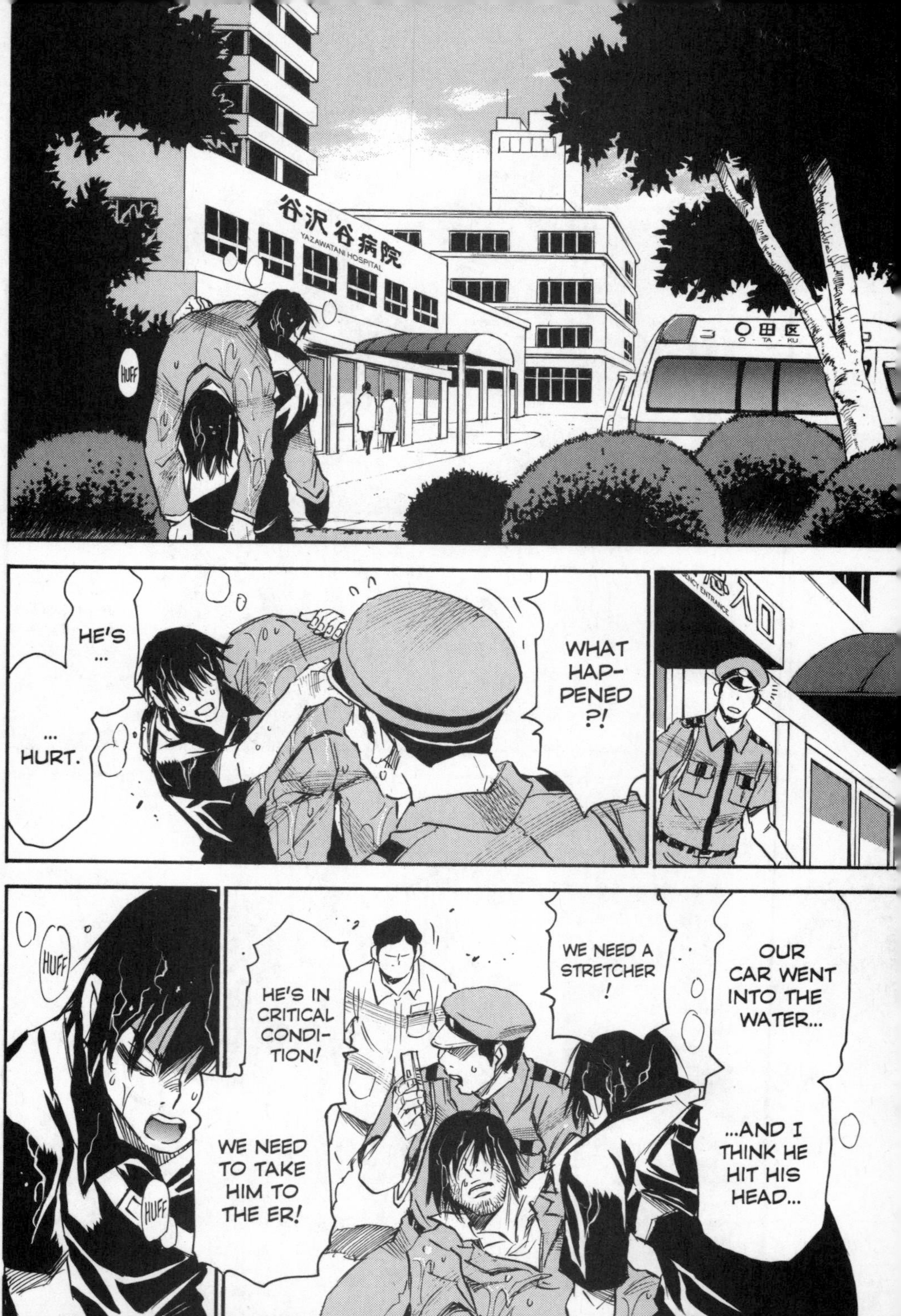

谷沢谷病院
YAZAWATANI HOSPITAL
O-TA-KU
HUFF
WHAT HAP-PENED?!
HE'S ...
... HURT.
OUR CAR WENT INTO THE WATER...
...AND I THINK HE HIT HIS HEAD...
WE NEED A STRETCHER!
HE'S IN CRITICAL CONDI-TION!
WE NEED TO TAKE HIM TO THE ER!
HUFF
HUFF

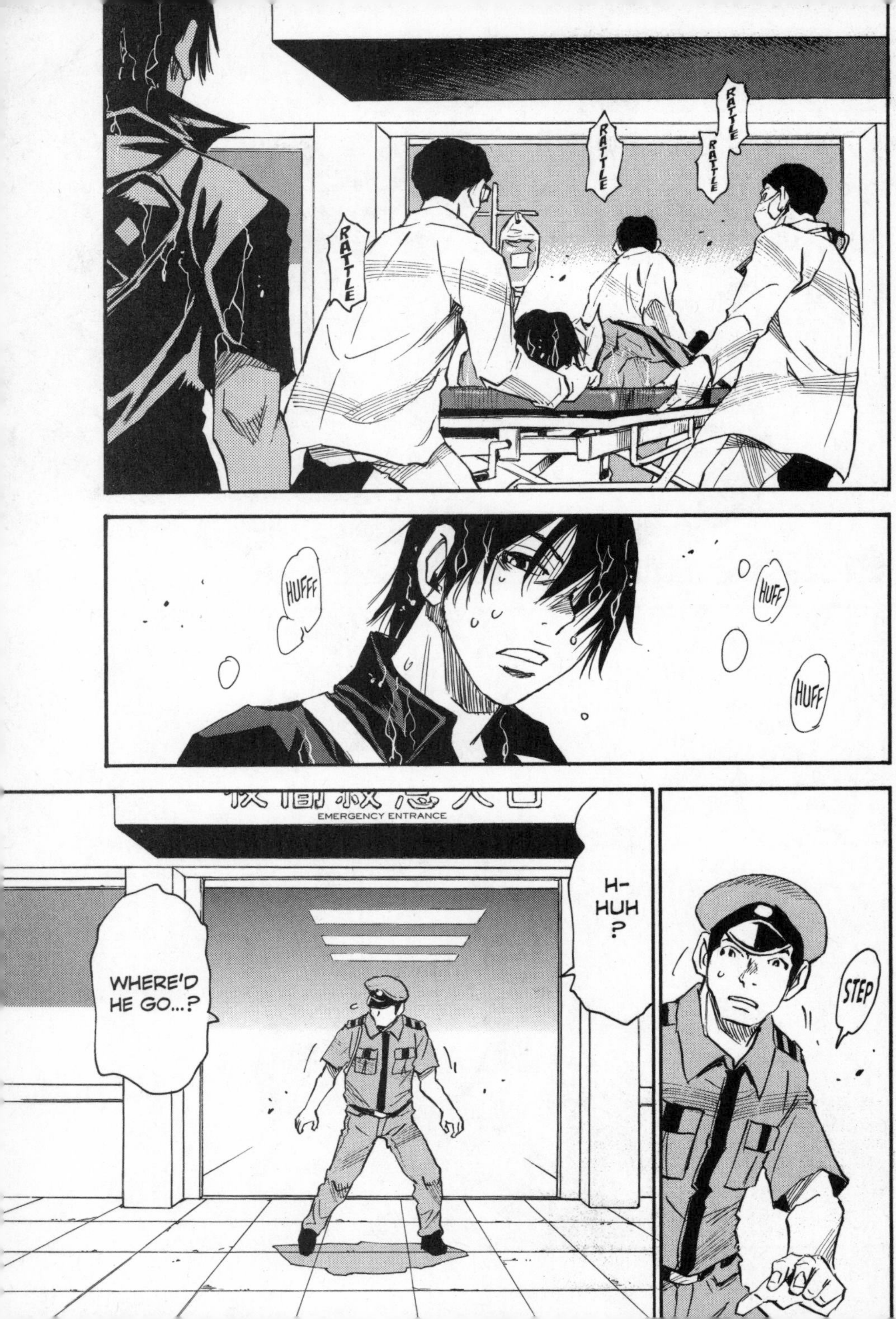
RATTLE
RATTLE
RATTLE
RATTLE
HUFF
HUFF
HUFFF
STEP
EMERGENCY ENTRANCE
H-HUH?
WHERE'D HE GO...?

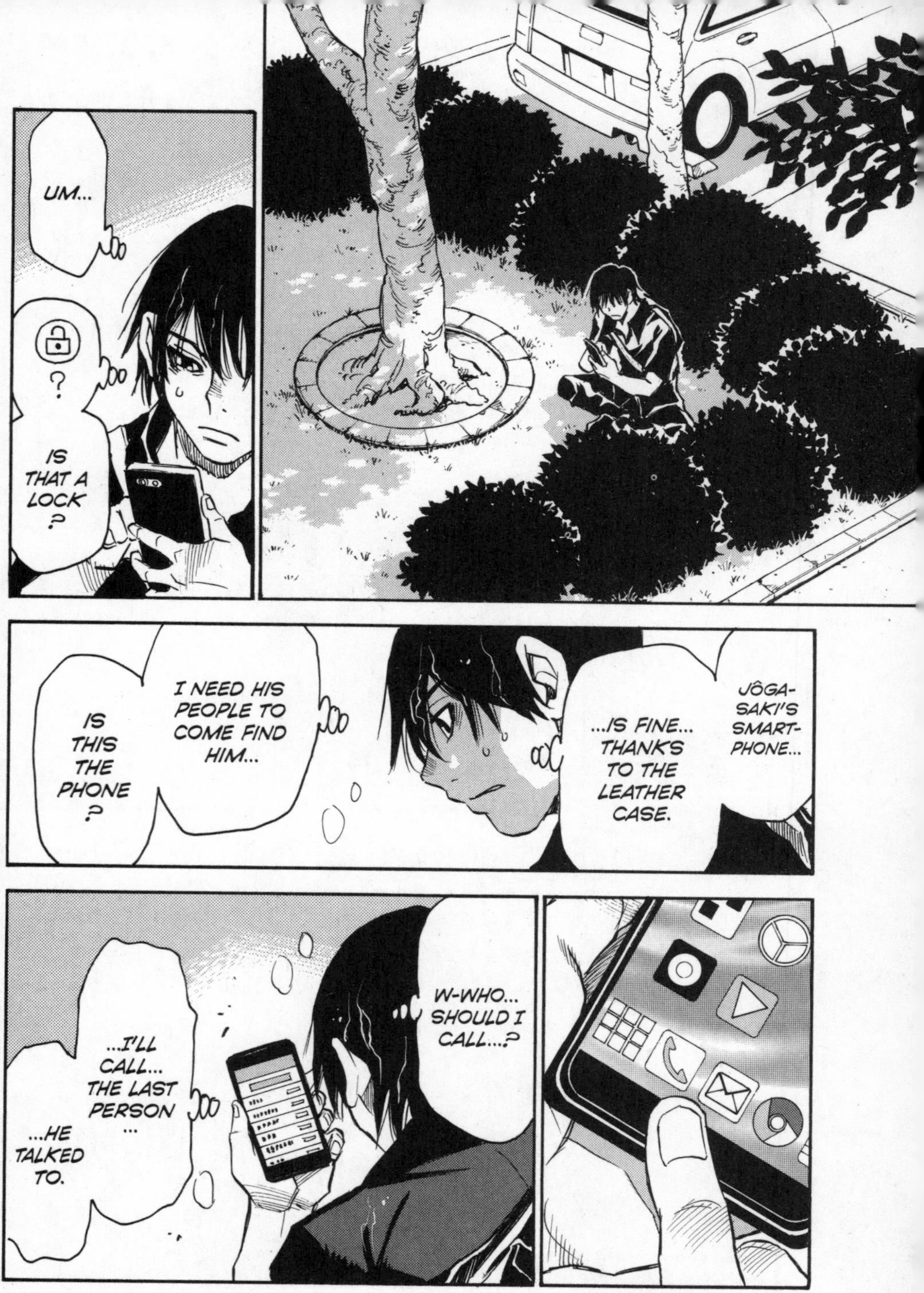
UM...
?
IS THAT A LOCK?
JÔGA-SAKI'S SMART-PHONE...
...IS FINE... THANKS TO THE LEATHER CASE.
I NEED HIS PEOPLE TO COME FIND HIM...
IS THIS THE PHONE?
W-WHO... SHOULD I CALL...?
...I'LL CALL... THE LAST PERSON...
...HE TALKED TO.

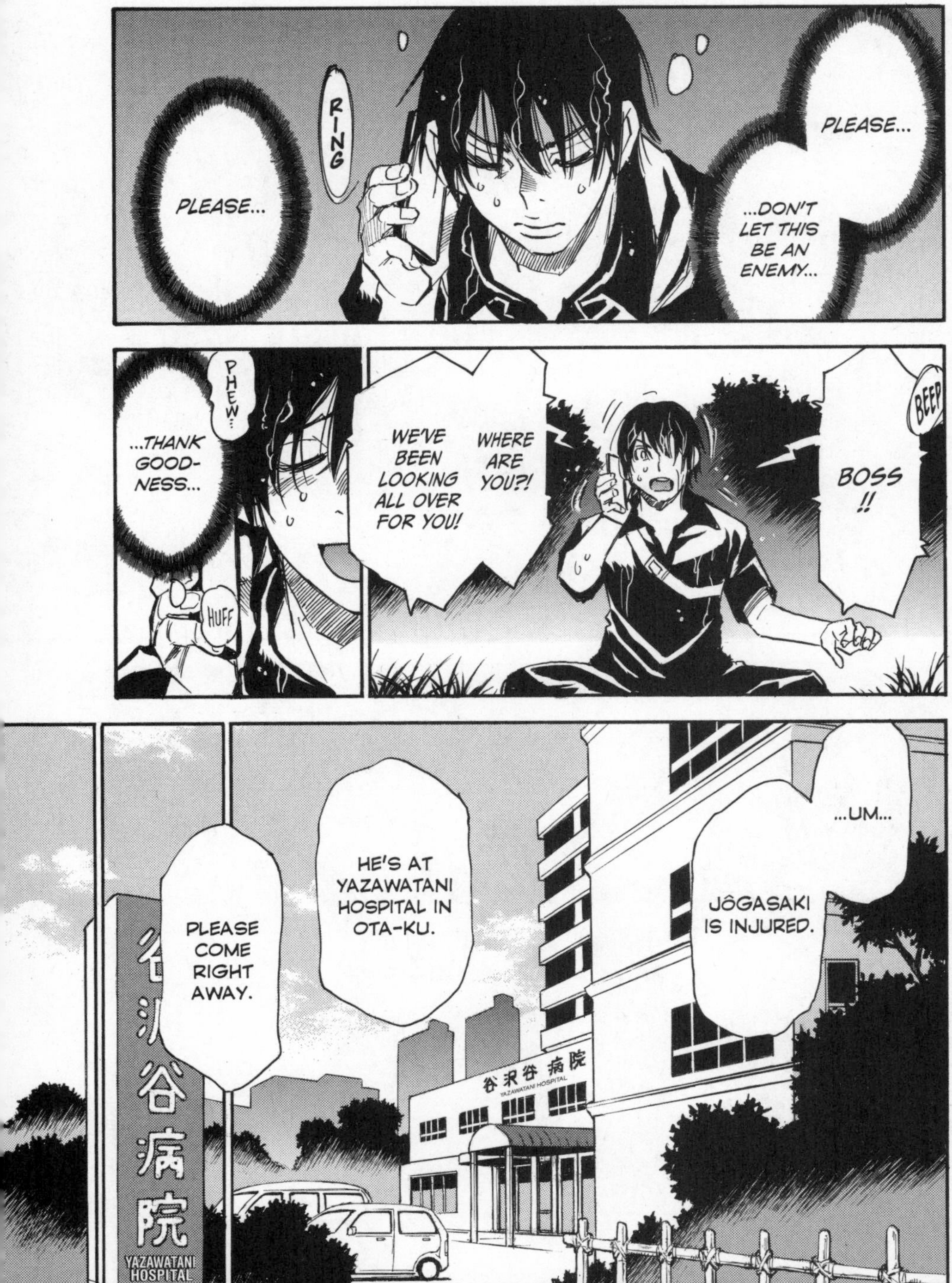
PLEASE...
...DON'T LET THIS BE AN ENEMY...
RING
PLEASE...
BEEP
BOSS!!
WHERE ARE YOU?!
WE'VE BEEN LOOKING ALL OVER FOR YOU!
PHEW...
...THANK GOODNESS...
HUFF
...UM...
JÔGASAKI IS INJURED.
HE'S AT YAZAWATANI HOSPITAL IN OTA-KU.
谷沢谷病院
YAZAWATANI HOSPITAL
PLEASE COME RIGHT AWAY.
谷沢谷病院
YAZAWATANI HOSPITAL

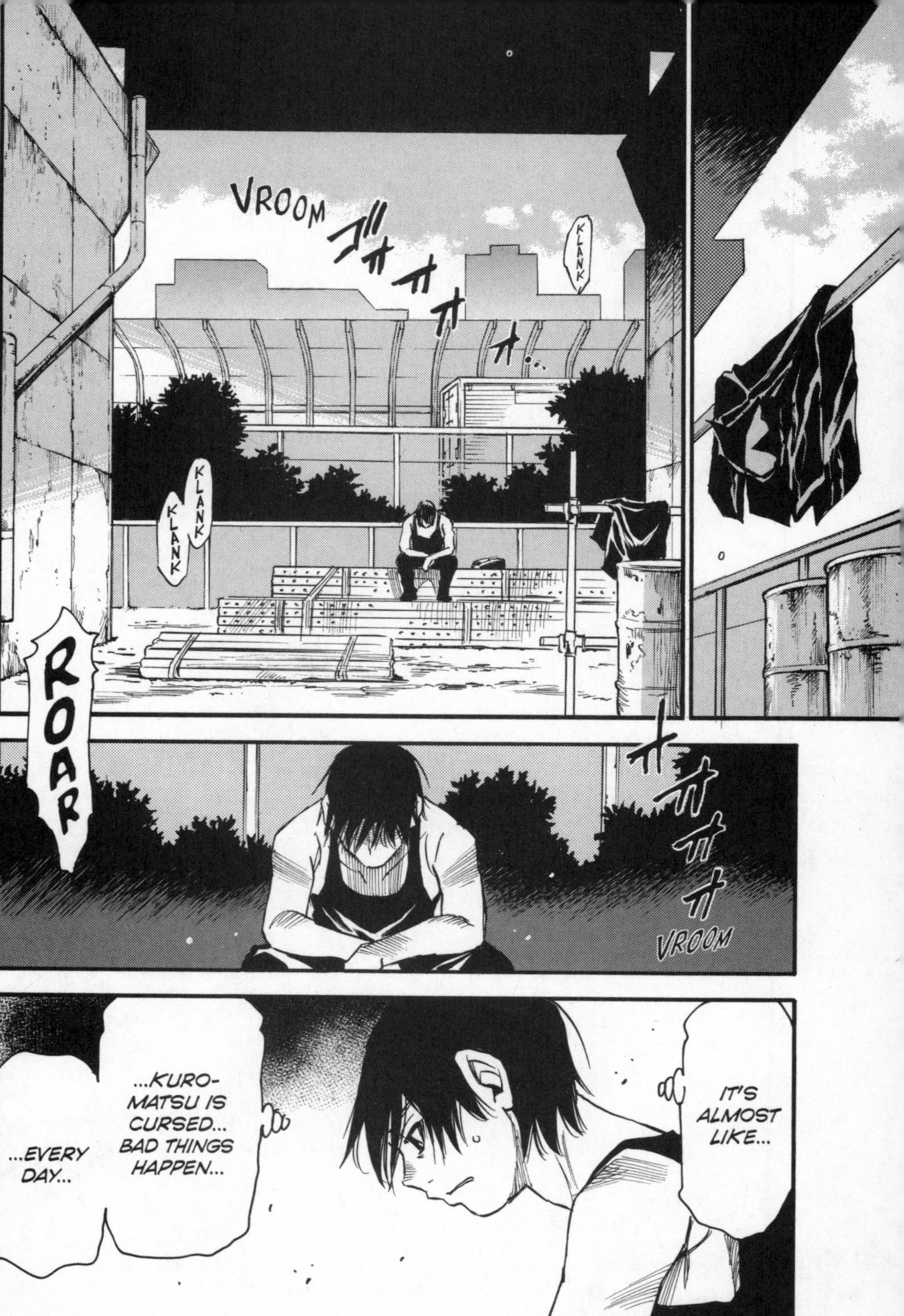
KLANK
VROOM
ゴォォォォォ...
KLANK KLANK
ォォォォ
VROOM
ROAR
IT'S ALMOST LIKE...
...KURO-MATSU IS CURSED... BAD THINGS HAPPEN...
...EVERY DAY...

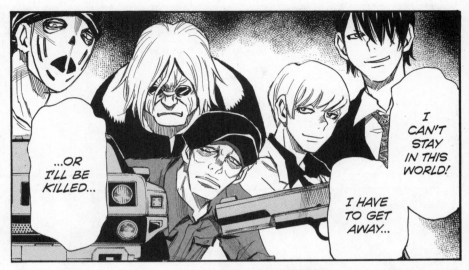

I CAN'T STAY IN THIS WORLD!
I HAVE TO GET AWAY...
...OR I'LL BE KILLED...
JÔGASAKI IS NICE...
...BUT HE'S A PART OF THIS UNDER-WORLD...
HE...
...ALSO LIVES THIS WAY...
HE...
... HAPPENS TO LOOK LIKE A KID NOW... BUT...
...

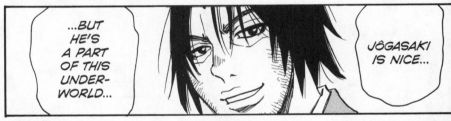

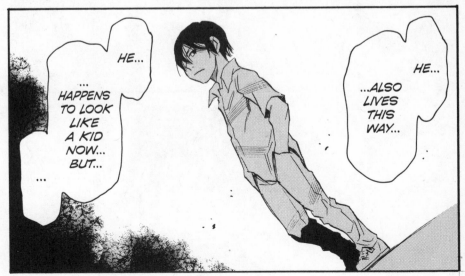

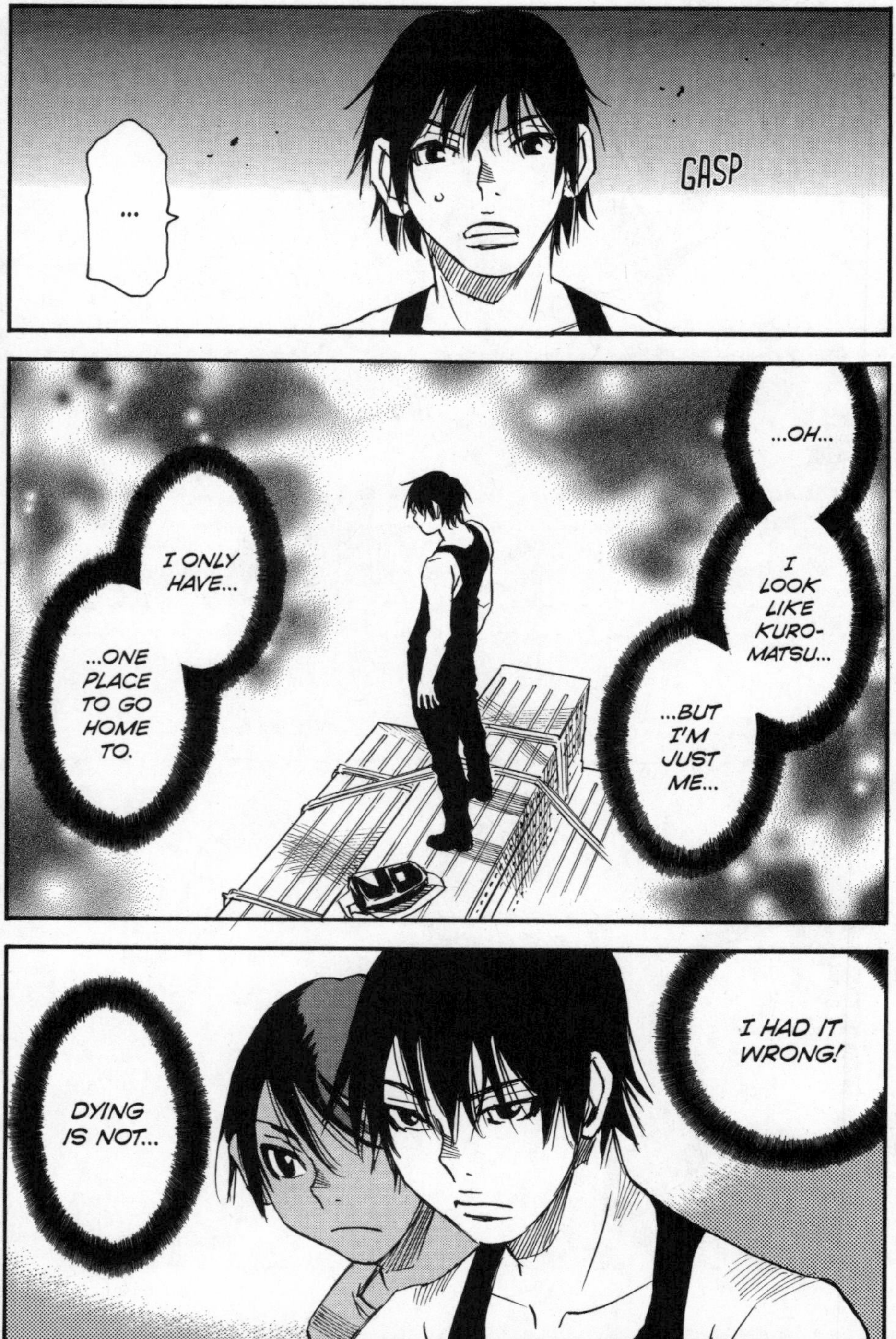
GASP
...
...OH...
I LOOK LIKE KURO-MATSU...
...BUT I'M JUST ME...
I ONLY HAVE...
...ONE PLACE TO GO HOME TO.
I HAD IT WRONG!
DYING IS NOT...

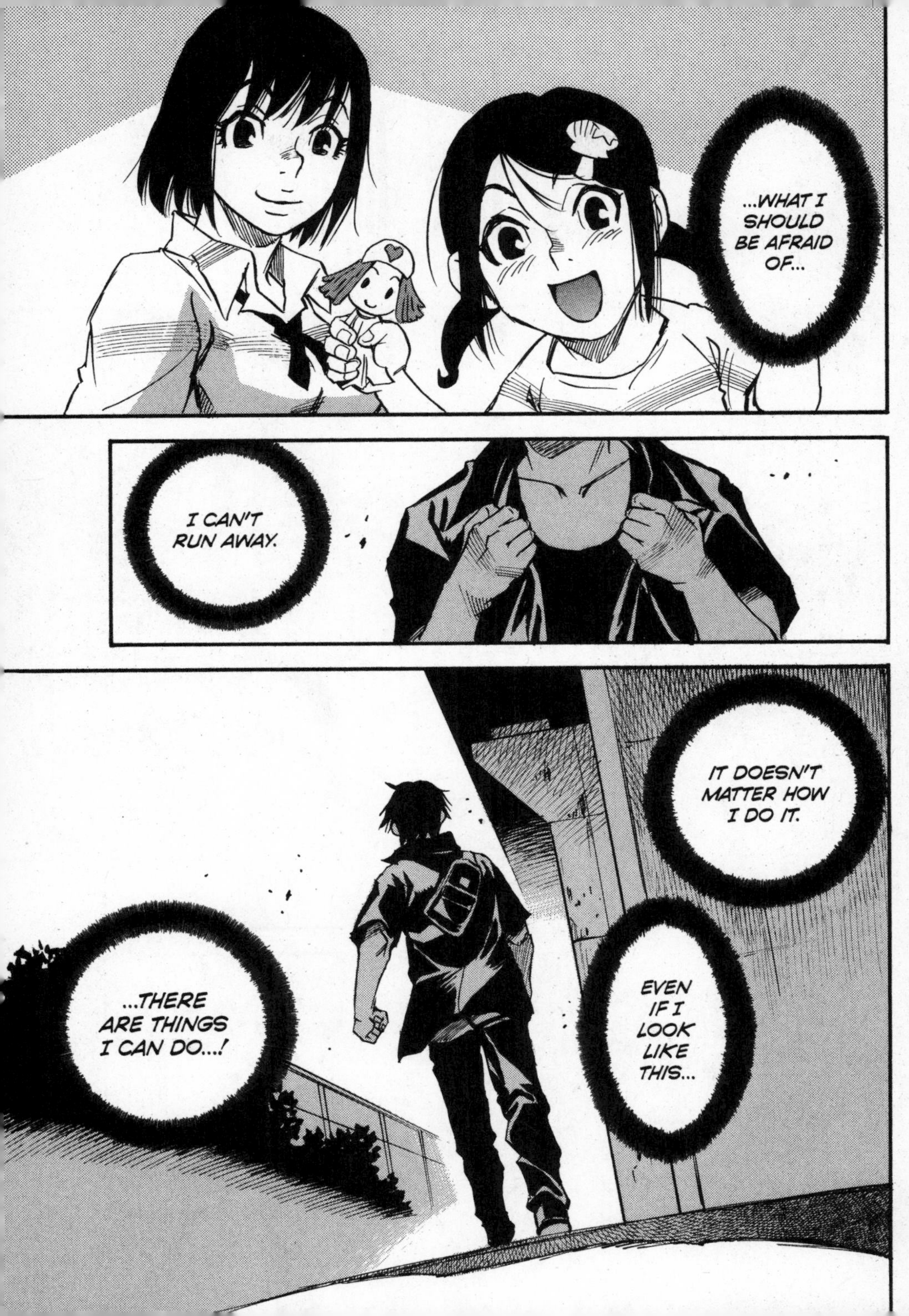
...WHAT I SHOULD BE AFRAID OF...
I CAN'T RUN AWAY.
IT DOESN'T MATTER HOW I DO IT.
EVEN IF I LOOK LIKE THIS...
...THERE ARE THINGS I CAN DO...!

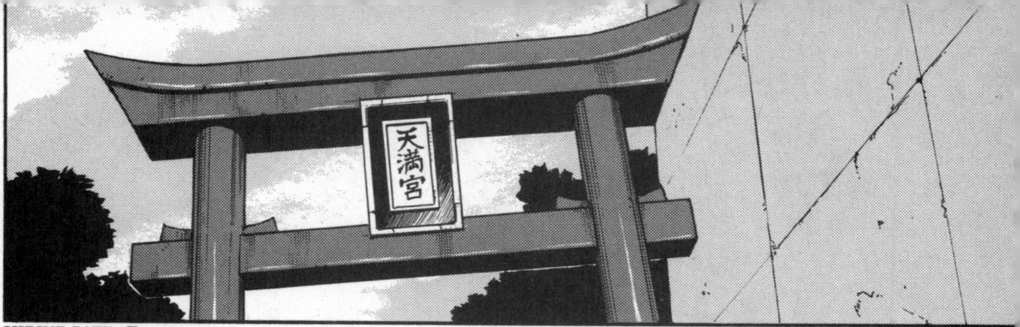

SHRINE GATE: *Tenmangu.*

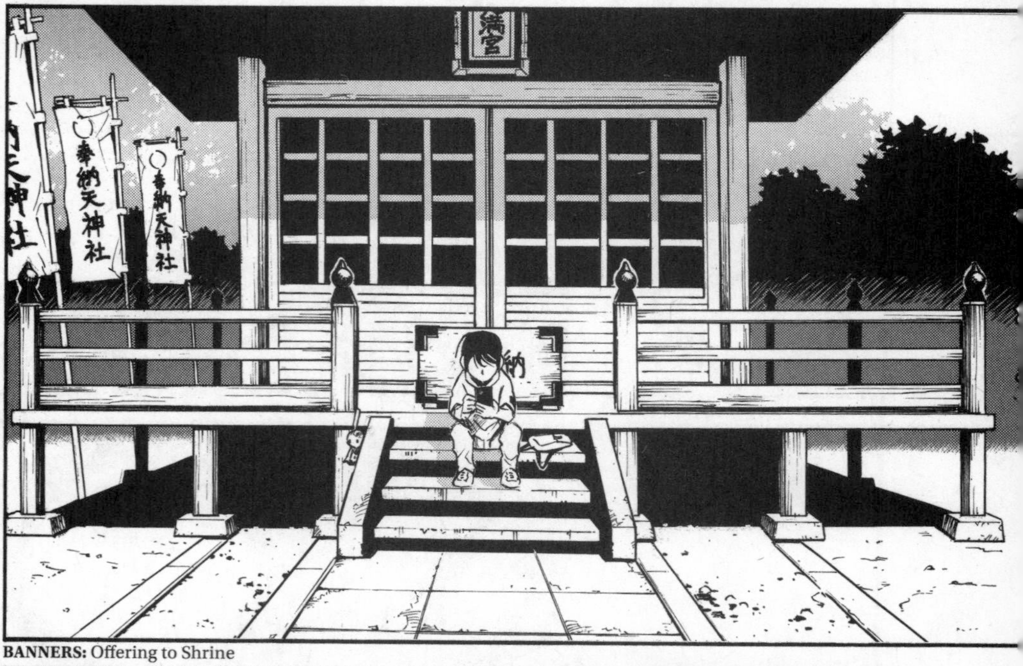

BANNERS: Offering to Shrine

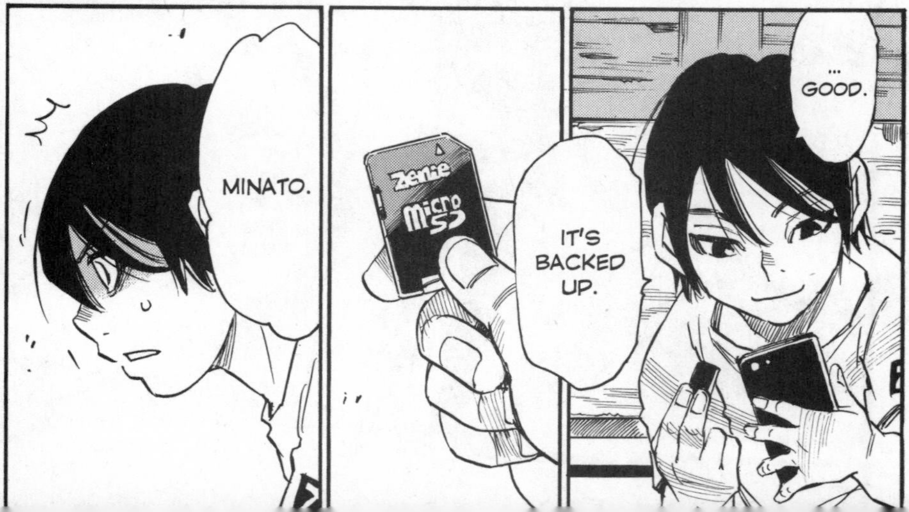
...GOOD.
IT'S BACKED UP.
MINATO.

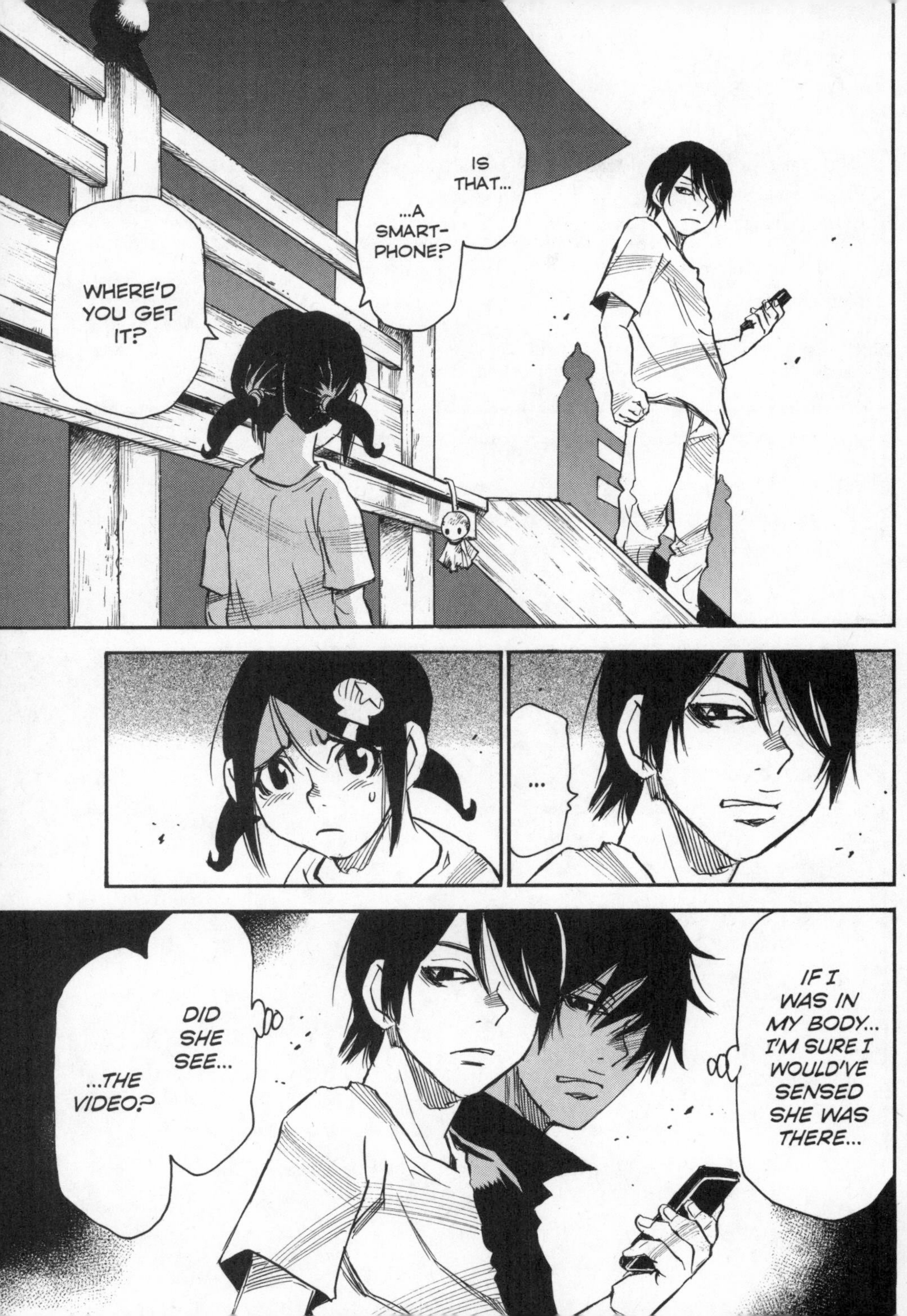
IS THAT... ...A SMARTPHONE?
WHERE'D YOU GET IT?
...
IF I WAS IN MY BODY... I'M SURE I WOULD'VE SENSED SHE WAS THERE...
DID SHE SEE... ...THE VIDEO?

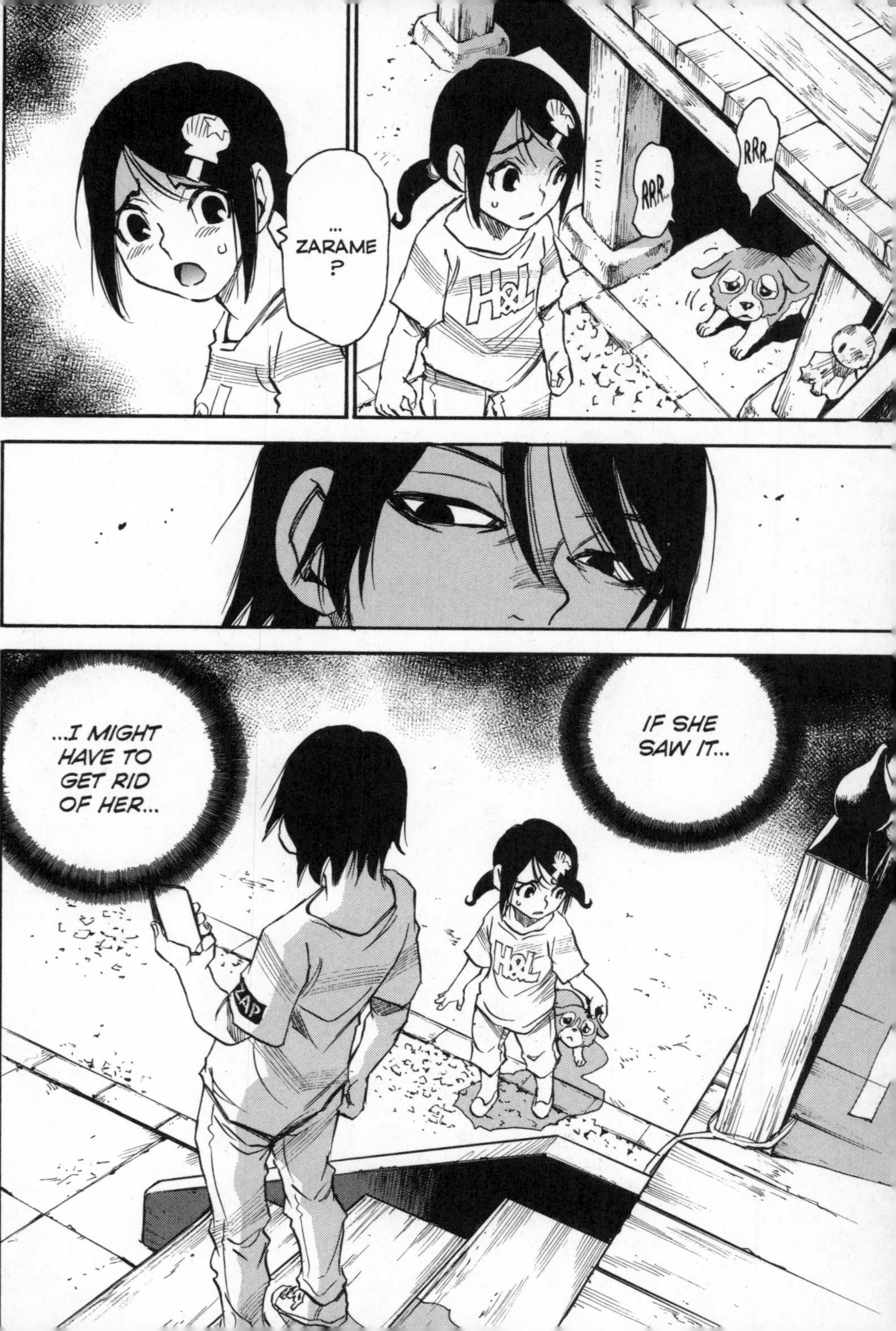
RRR...
RRR...
... ZARAME ?
IF SHE SAW IT...
...I MIGHT HAVE TO GET RID OF HER...

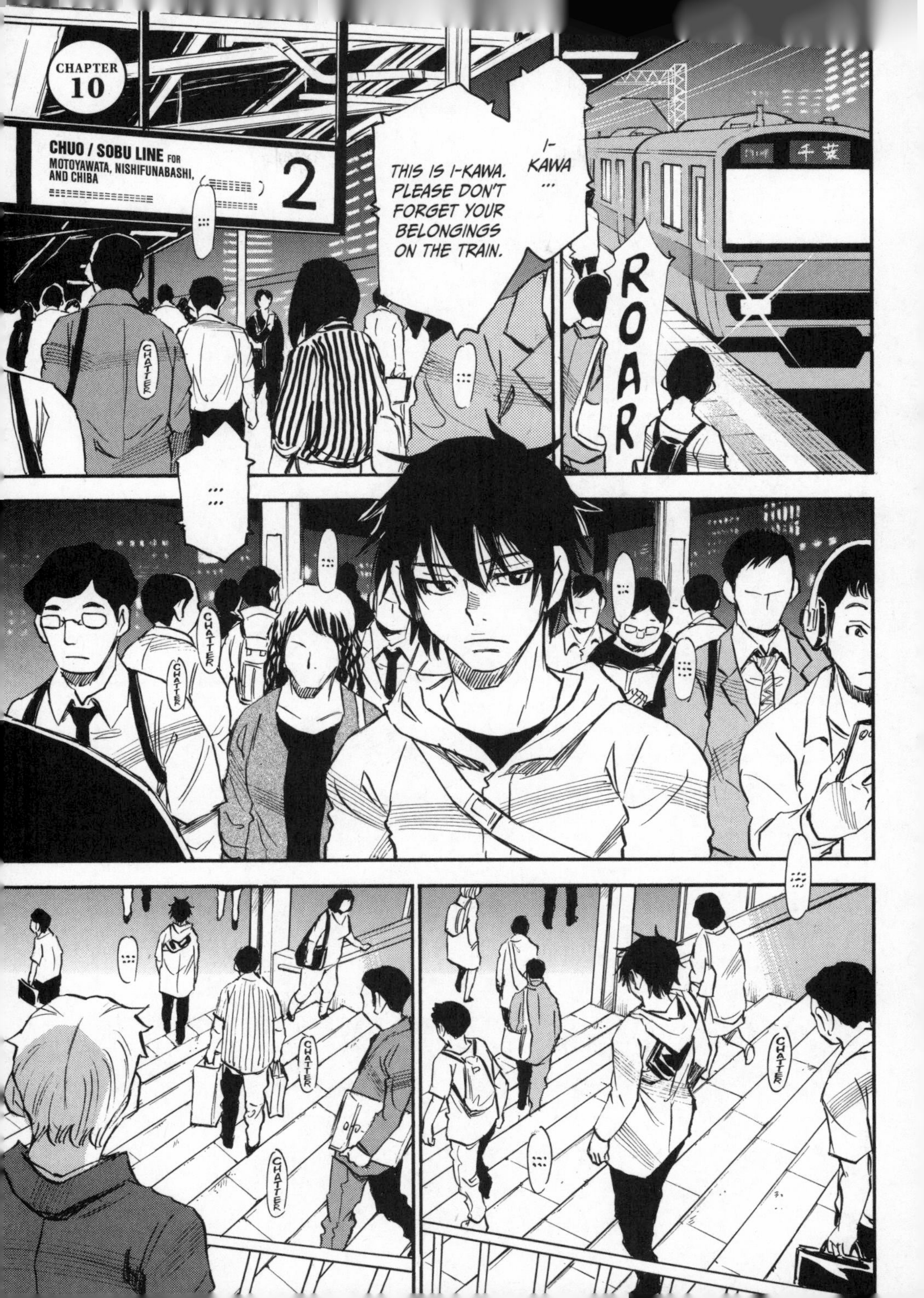
CHAPTER 10
I-KAWA ...
THIS IS I-KAWA. PLEASE DON'T FORGET YOUR BELONGINGS ON THE TRAIN.
ROAR
...
CHUO / SOBU LINE FOR MOTOYAWATA, NISHIFUNABASHI, AND CHIBA
2
千葉
...
CHATTER
...
...
...
CHATTER
CHATTER
...
...
CHATTER
...
CHATTER
CHATTER
...

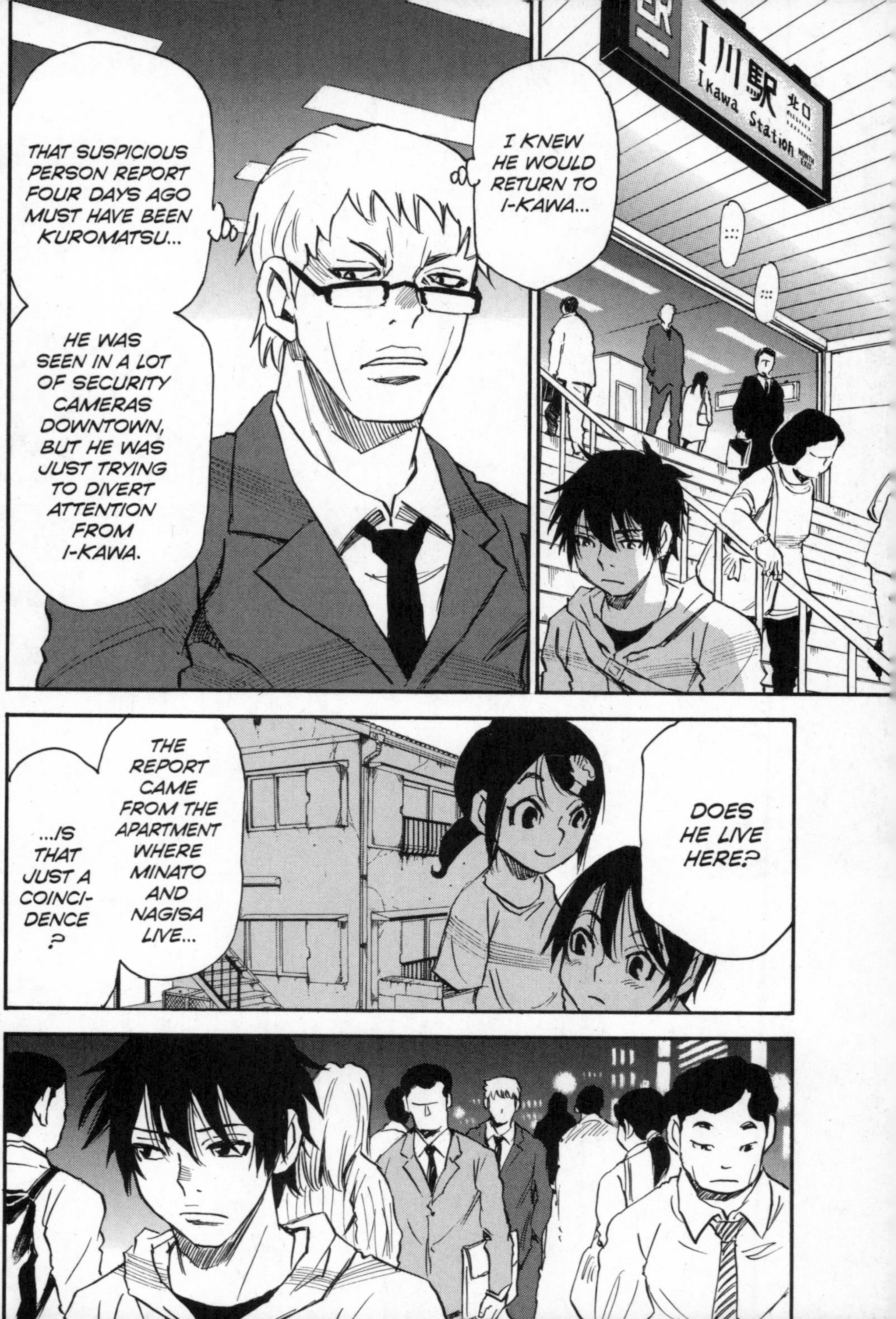
I川駅
Ikawa Station
北口
NORTH EXIT
I KNEW HE WOULD RETURN TO I-KAWA...
THAT SUSPICIOUS PERSON REPORT FOUR DAYS AGO MUST HAVE BEEN KUROMATSU...
HE WAS SEEN IN A LOT OF SECURITY CAMERAS DOWNTOWN, BUT HE WAS JUST TRYING TO DIVERT ATTENTION FROM I-KAWA.
DOES HE LIVE HERE?
THE REPORT CAME FROM THE APARTMENT WHERE MINATO AND NAGISA LIVE...
...IS THAT JUST A COINCI-DENCE?

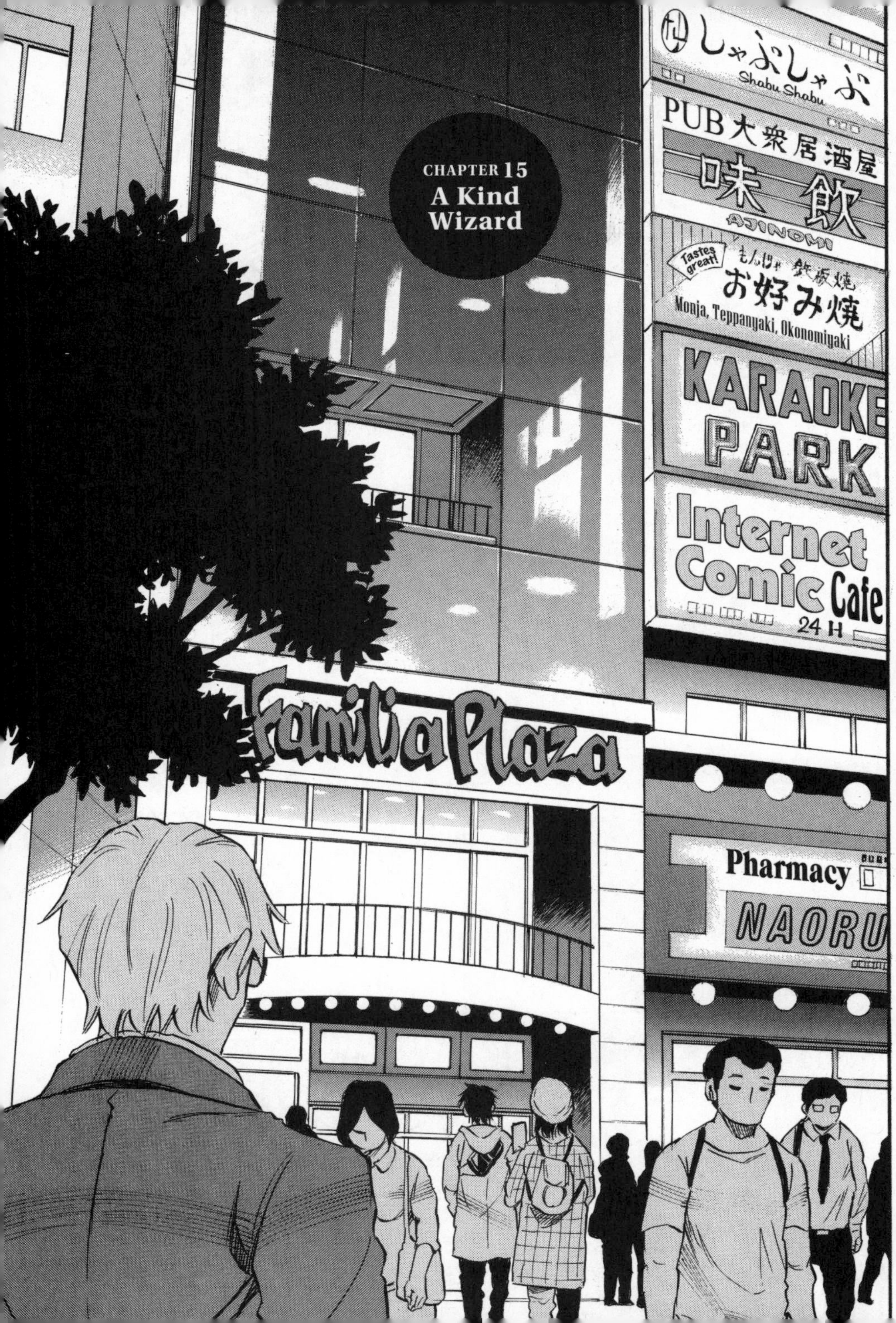
CHAPTER 15
A Kind Wizard
しゃぶしゃぶ
Shabu Shabu
PUB 大衆居酒屋
味飲
AJINOMI
Tastes great!
もんじゃ 鉄板焼
お好み焼
Monja, Teppanyaki, Okonomiyaki
KARAOKE PARK
Internet Comic Cafe
24 H
Familia Plaza
Pharmacy
NAORU

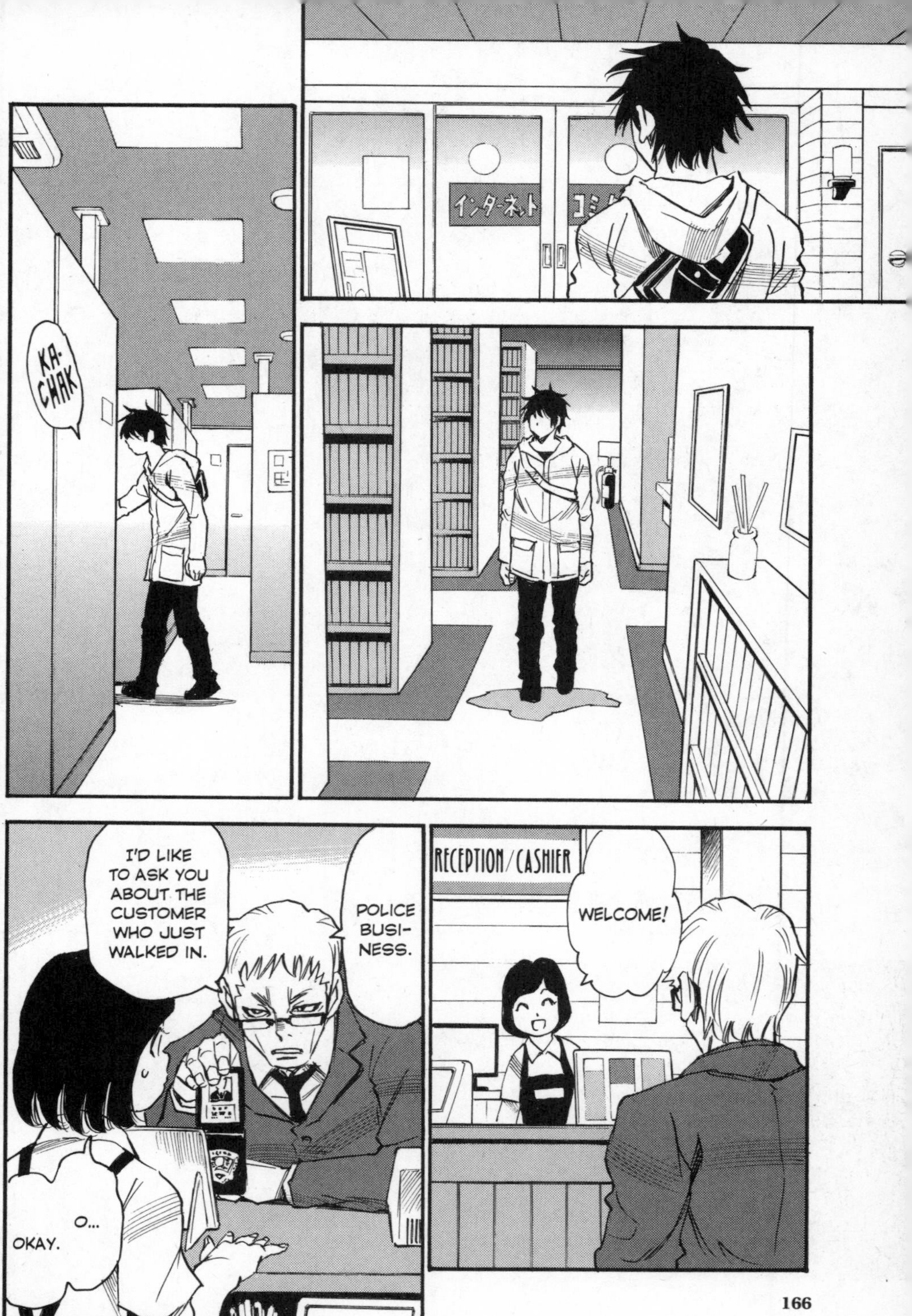
インターネット コミ
KA-CHAK
RECEPTION/CASHIER
WELCOME!
POLICE BUSI-NESS.
I'D LIKE TO ASK YOU ABOUT THE CUSTOMER WHO JUST WALKED IN.
O... OKAY.

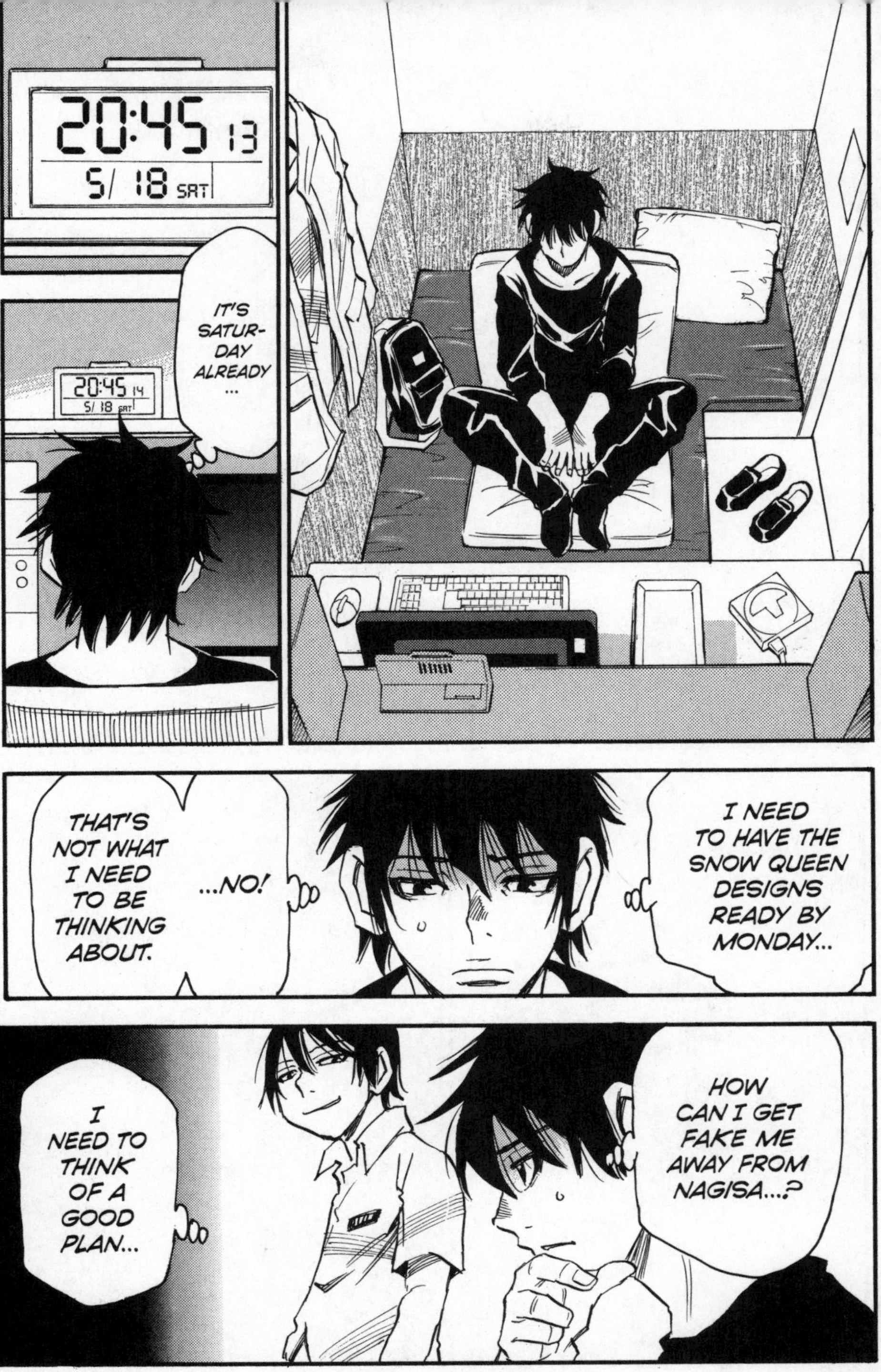
20:45 13
5/ 18 SAT
20:45 14
5/ 18 SAT
IT'S SATURDAY ALREADY...
I NEED TO HAVE THE SNOW QUEEN DESIGNS READY BY MONDAY...
...NO!
THAT'S NOT WHAT I NEED TO BE THINKING ABOUT.
HOW CAN I GET FAKE ME AWAY FROM NAGISA...?
I NEED TO THINK OF A GOOD PLAN...

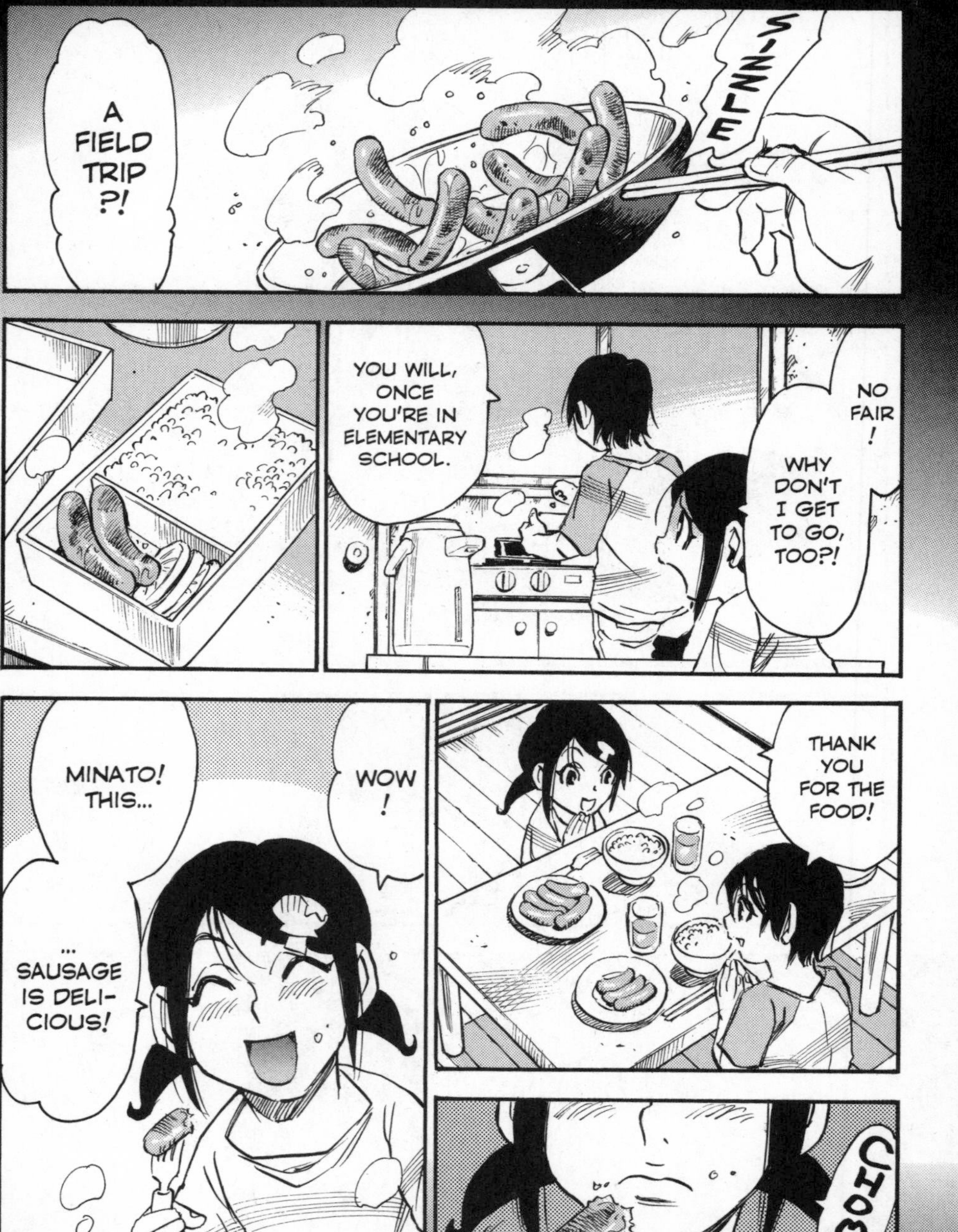
SIZZLE
A FIELD TRIP?!
NO FAIR!
WHY DON'T I GET TO GO, TOO?!
YOU WILL, ONCE YOU'RE IN ELEMENTARY SCHOOL.
THANK YOU FOR THE FOOD!
CHOMP
WOW!
MINATO! THIS...
...SAUSAGE IS DELICIOUS!

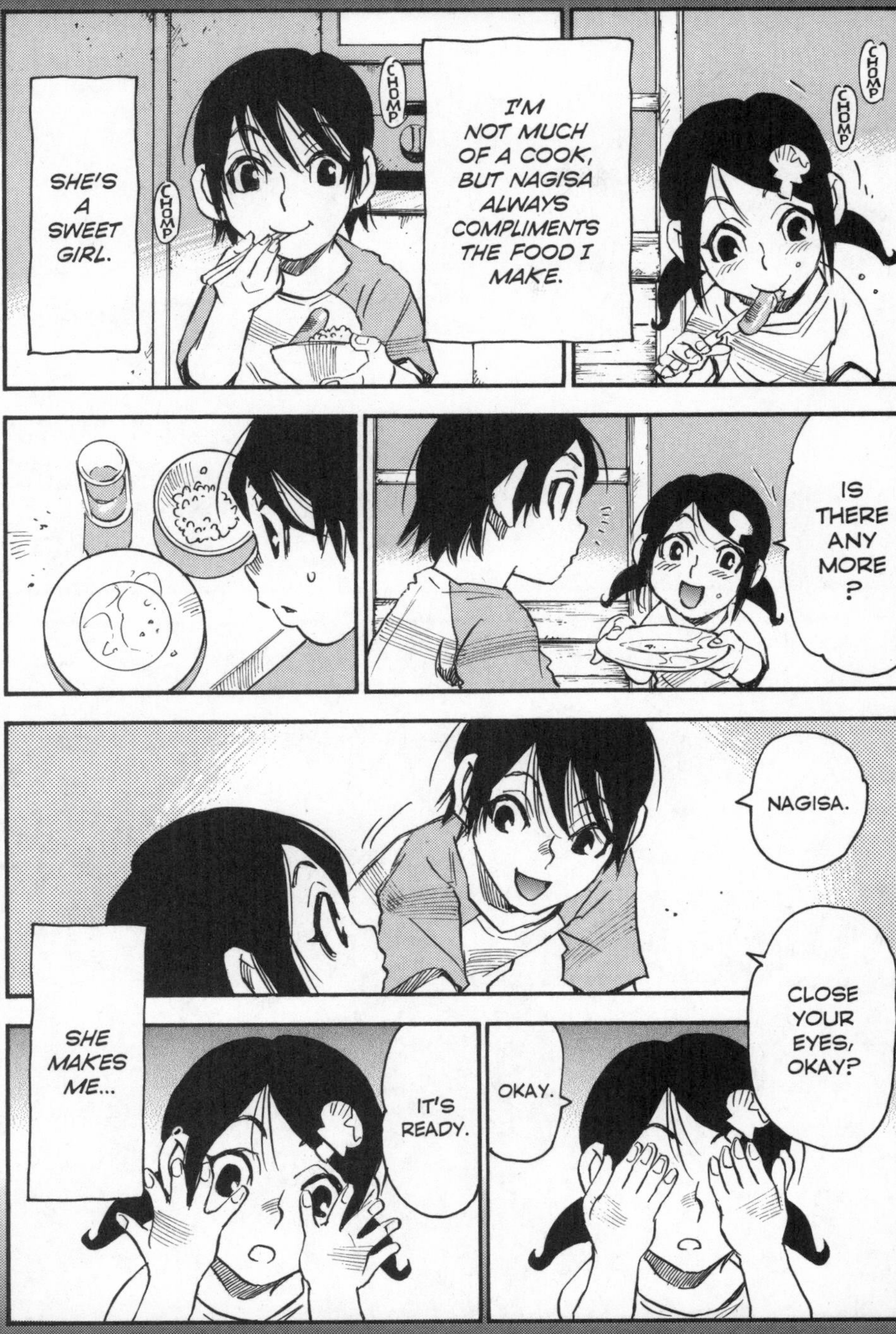
CHOMP
CHOMP
I'M NOT MUCH OF A COOK, BUT NAGISA ALWAYS COMPLIMENTS THE FOOD I MAKE.
CHOMP
CHOMP
SHE'S A SWEET GIRL.
IS THERE ANY MORE?
NAGISA.
CLOSE YOUR EYES, OKAY?
OKAY.
IT'S READY.
SHE MAKES ME...

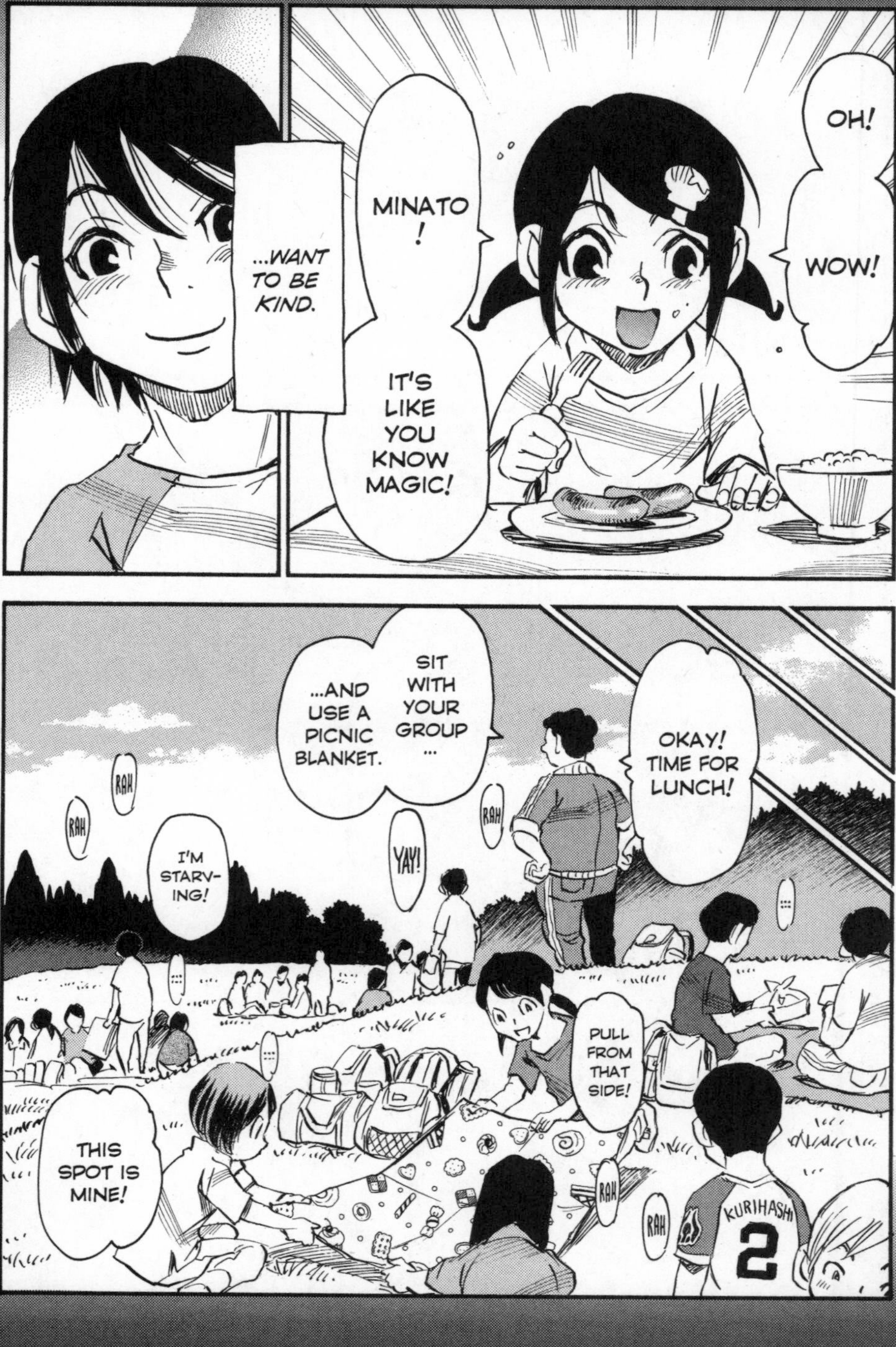
OH!
WOW!
MINATO!
IT'S LIKE YOU KNOW MAGIC!
...WANT TO BE KIND.
OKAY! TIME FOR LUNCH!
SIT WITH YOUR GROUP ...
...AND USE A PICNIC BLANKET.
RAH
YAY!
RAH
RAH
I'M STARVING!
...
...
PULL FROM THAT SIDE!
...
THIS SPOT IS MINE!
RAH
RAH
KURIHASHI
2

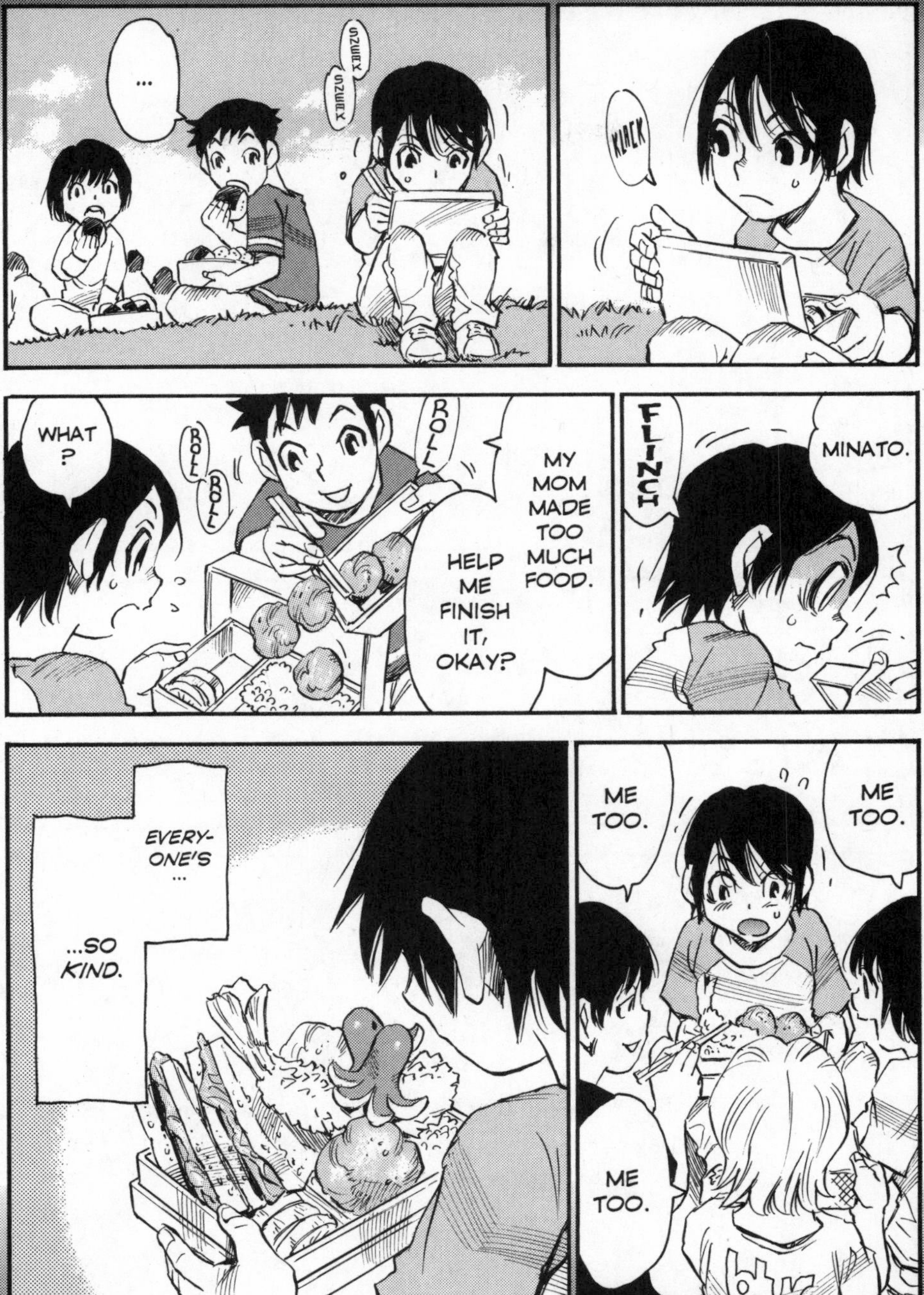
KLACK
SNEEK SNEEK
...
MINATO.
FLINCH
ROLL
MY MOM MADE TOO MUCH FOOD.
HELP ME FINISH IT, OKAY?
ROLL ROLL
WHAT?
ME TOO.
ME TOO.
ME TOO.
blur
EVERY-ONE'S ...
...SO KIND.

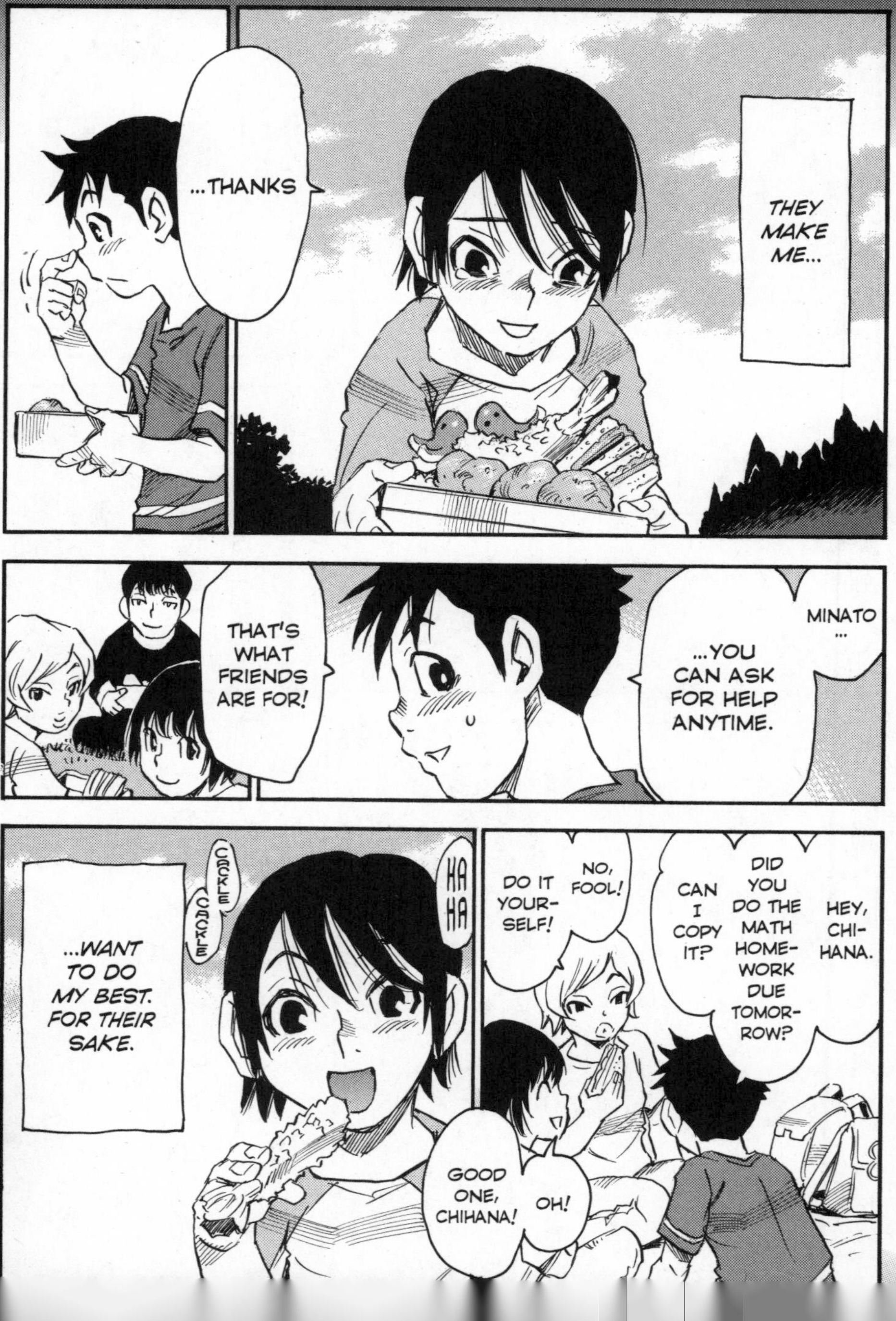
THEY MAKE ME...
...THANKS
MINATO ...
...YOU CAN ASK FOR HELP ANYTIME.
THAT'S WHAT FRIENDS ARE FOR!
HEY, CHI-HANA.
DID YOU DO THE MATH HOME-WORK DUE TOMOR-ROW?
CAN I COPY IT?
NO, FOOL!
DO IT YOUR-SELF!
HA HA
CRACKLE CRACKLE
...WANT TO DO MY BEST. FOR THEIR SAKE.
OH!
GOOD ONE, CHIHANA!

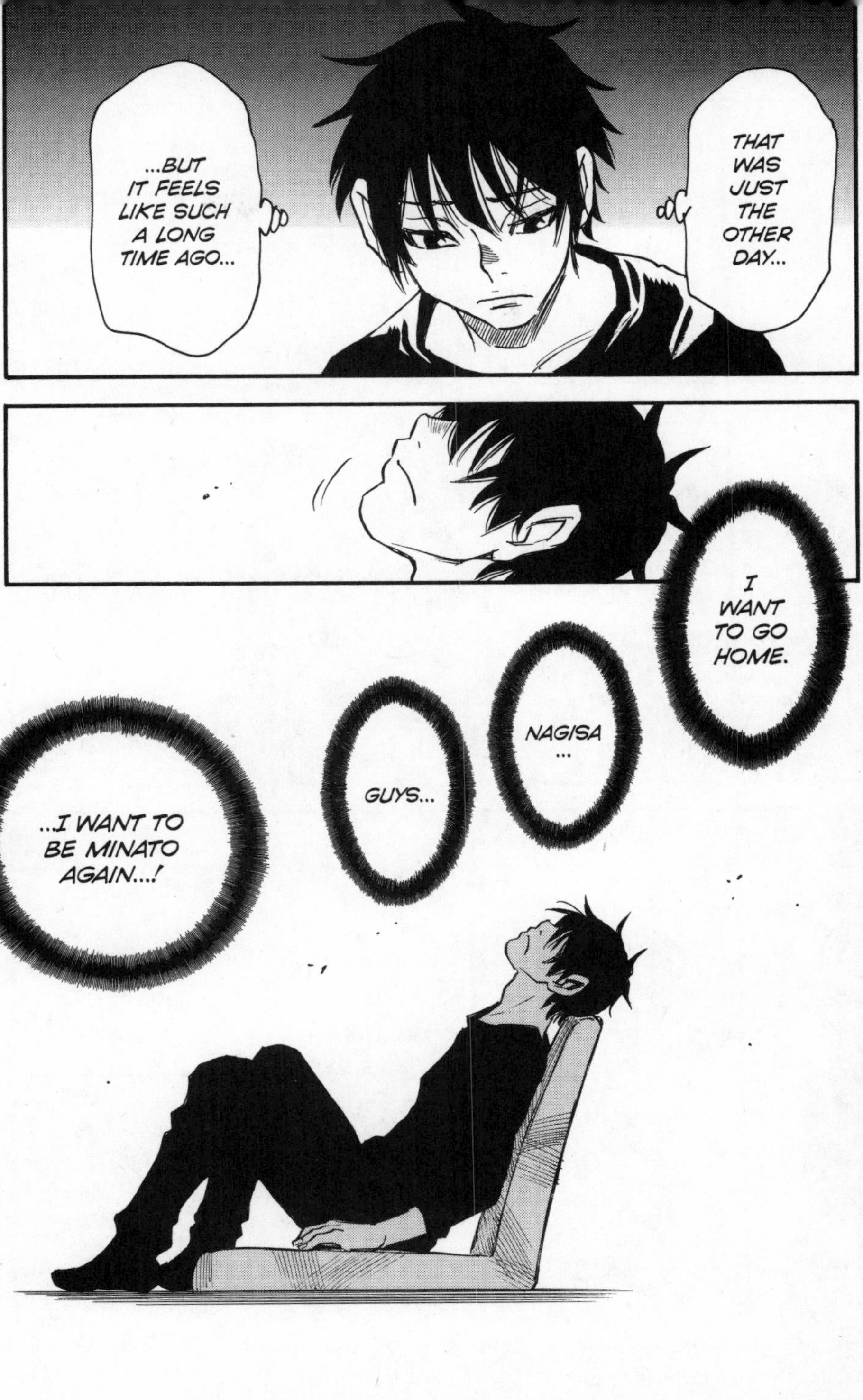
THAT WAS JUST THE OTHER DAY...
...BUT IT FEELS LIKE SUCH A LONG TIME AGO...
I WANT TO GO HOME.
NAGISA...
GUYS...
...I WANT TO BE MINATO AGAIN...!

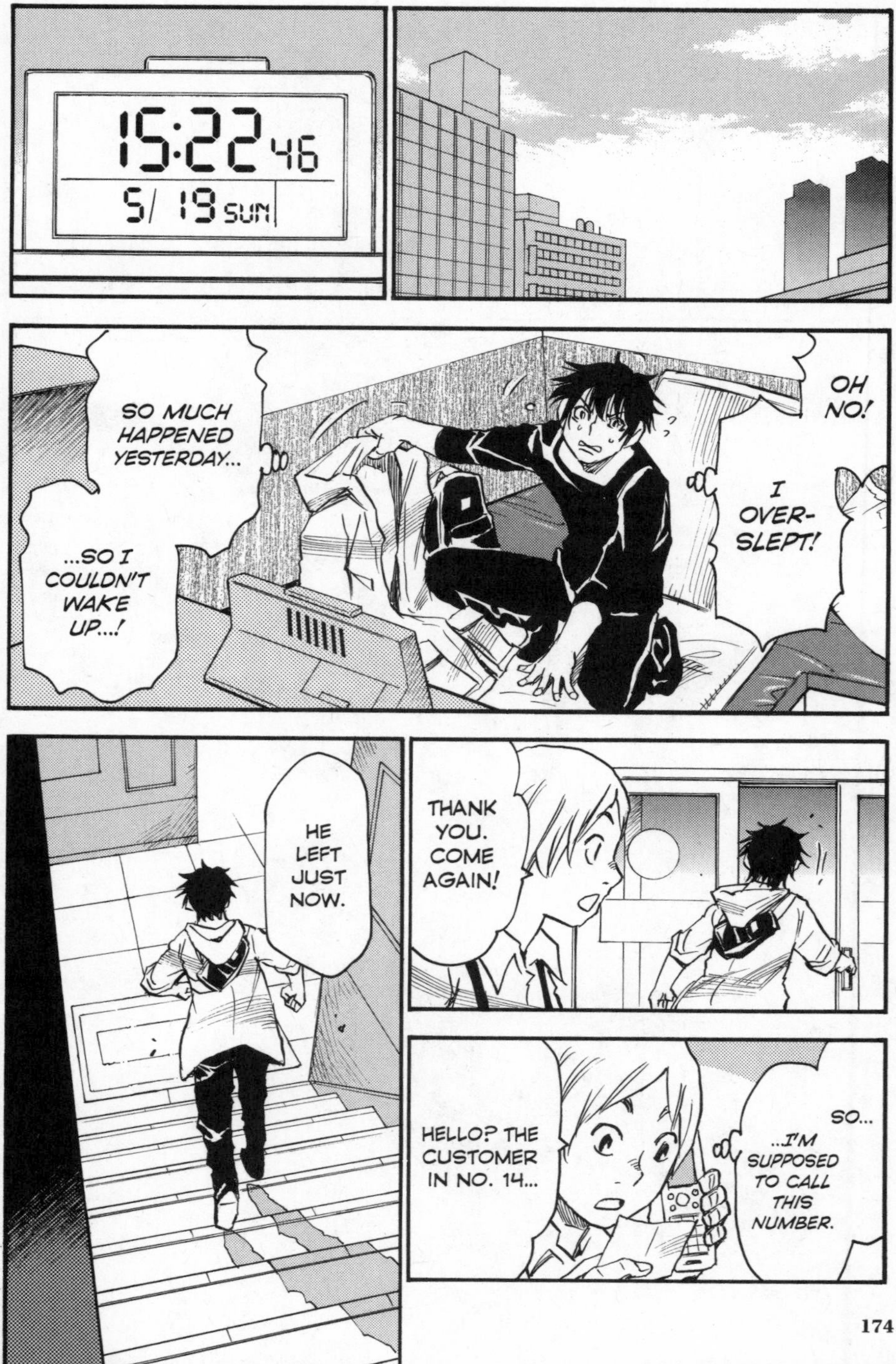
15:22 46
5/ 19 SUN
OH NO!
I OVER-SLEPT!
SO MUCH HAPPENED YESTERDAY...
...SO I COULDN'T WAKE UP...!
THANK YOU. COME AGAIN!
SO...
...I'M SUPPOSED TO CALL THIS NUMBER.
HELLO? THE CUSTOMER IN NO. 14...
HE LEFT JUST NOW.

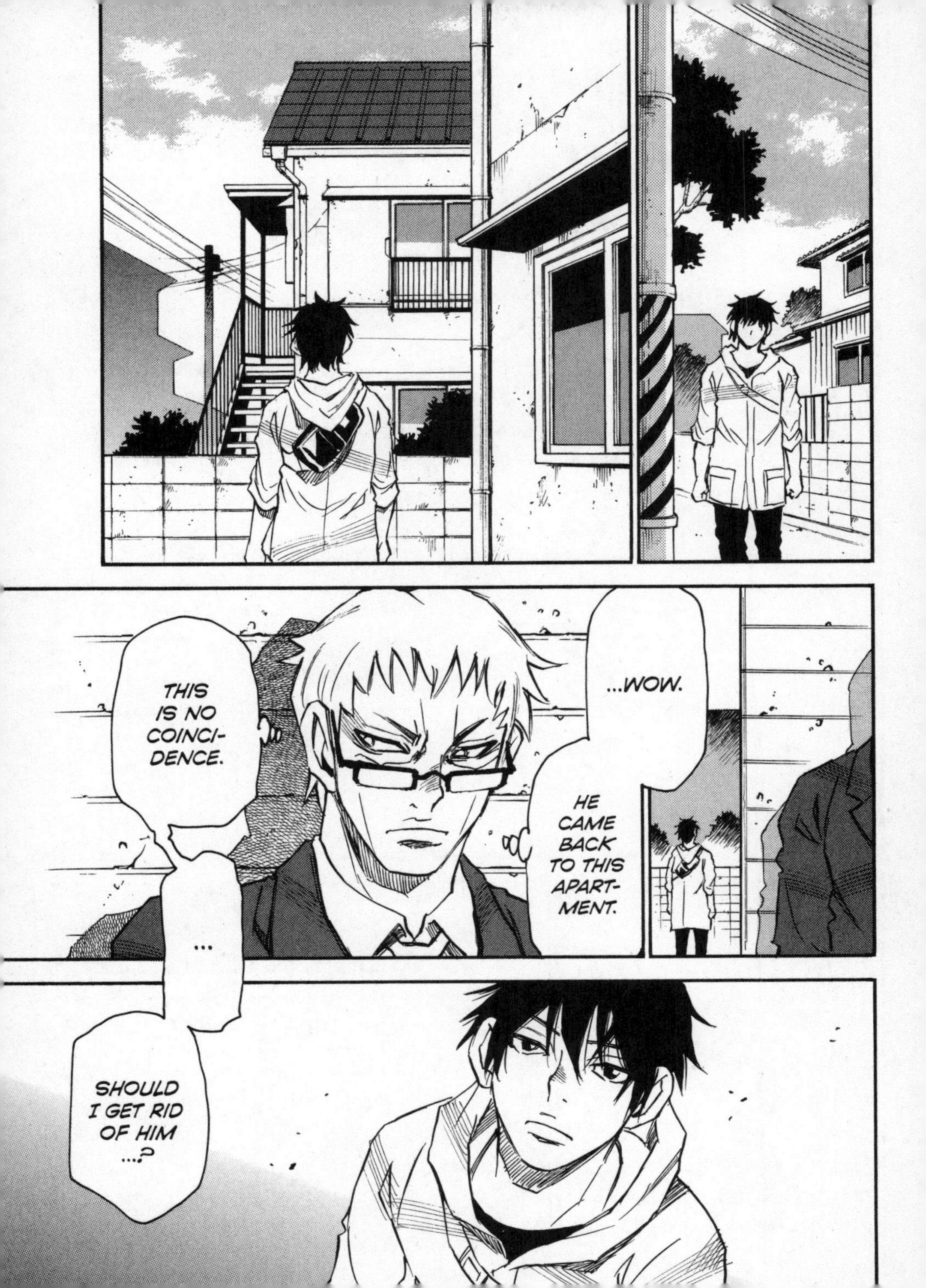
...WOW.
HE CAME BACK TO THIS APARTMENT.
THIS IS NO COINCIDENCE.
...
SHOULD I GET RID OF HIM ...?

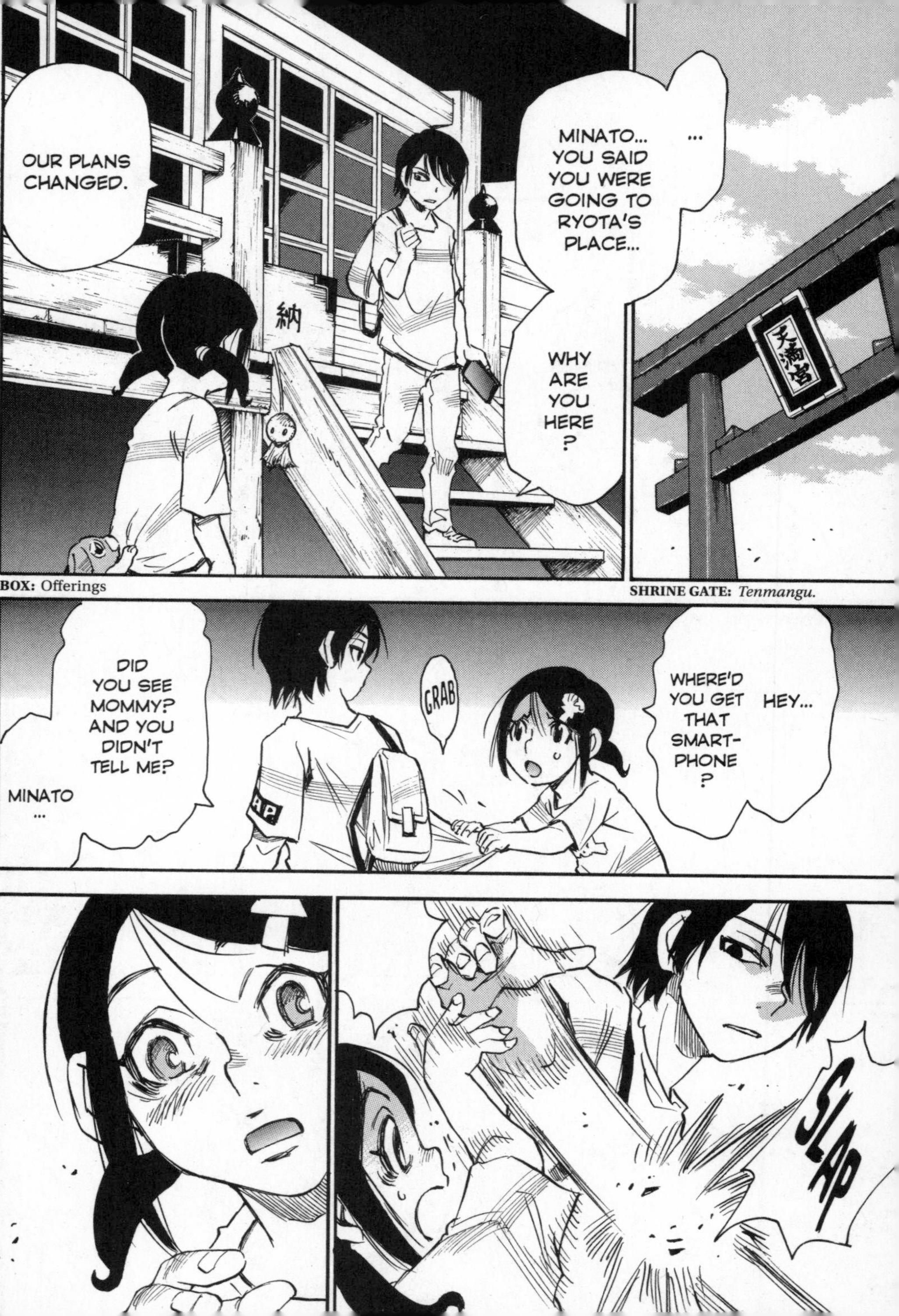
...
MINATO... YOU SAID YOU WERE GOING TO RYOTA'S PLACE...
WHY ARE YOU HERE ?
OUR PLANS CHANGED.
HEY...
WHERE'D YOU GET THAT SMART-PHONE ?
GRAB
DID YOU SEE MOMMY? AND YOU DIDN'T TELL ME?
MINATO ...
SLAP

BOX: Offerings

SHRINE GATE: *Tenmangu.*

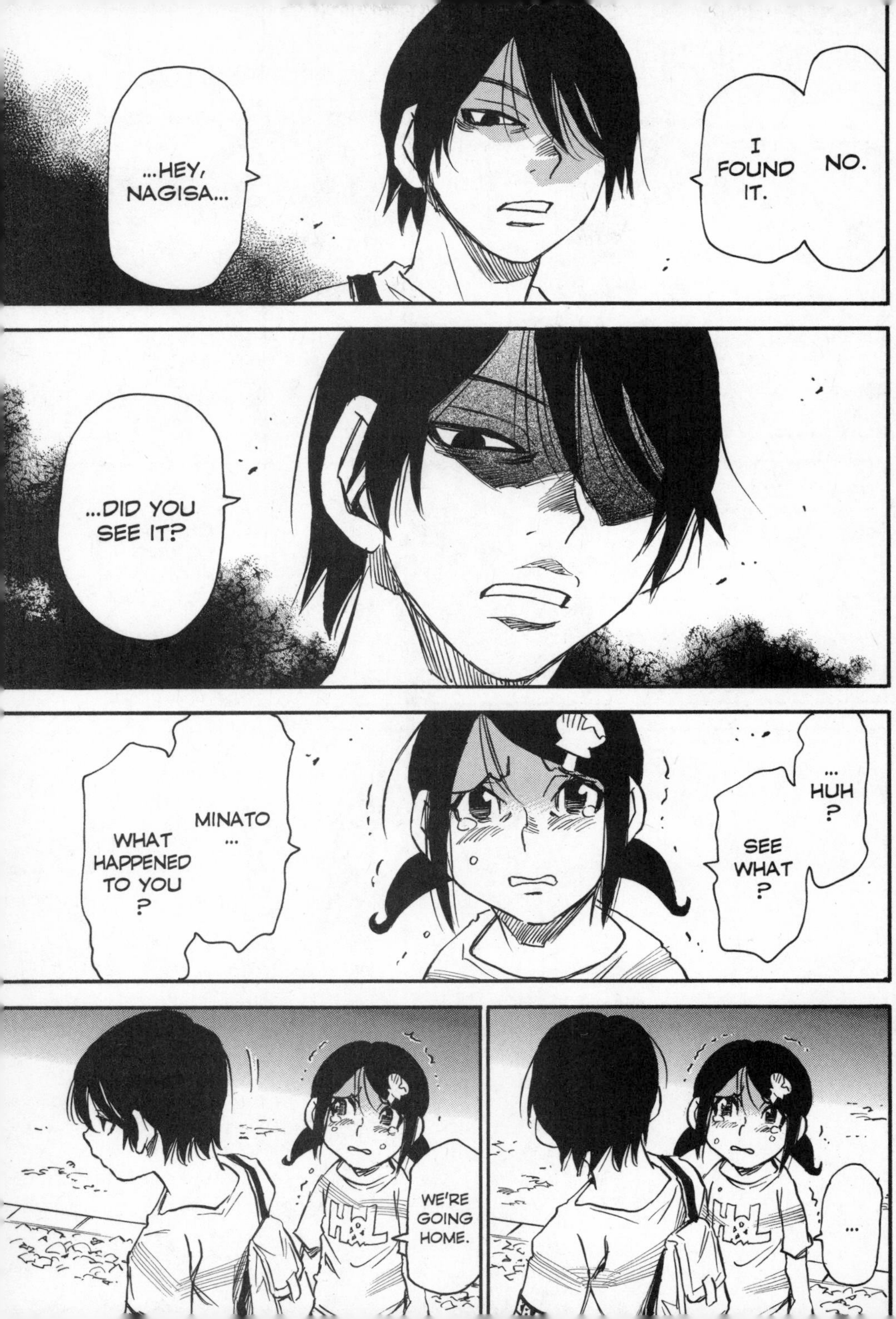
NO.
I FOUND IT.
...HEY, NAGISA...
...DID YOU SEE IT?
...HUH?
SEE WHAT?
MINATO...
WHAT HAPPENED TO YOU?
...
WE'RE GOING HOME.

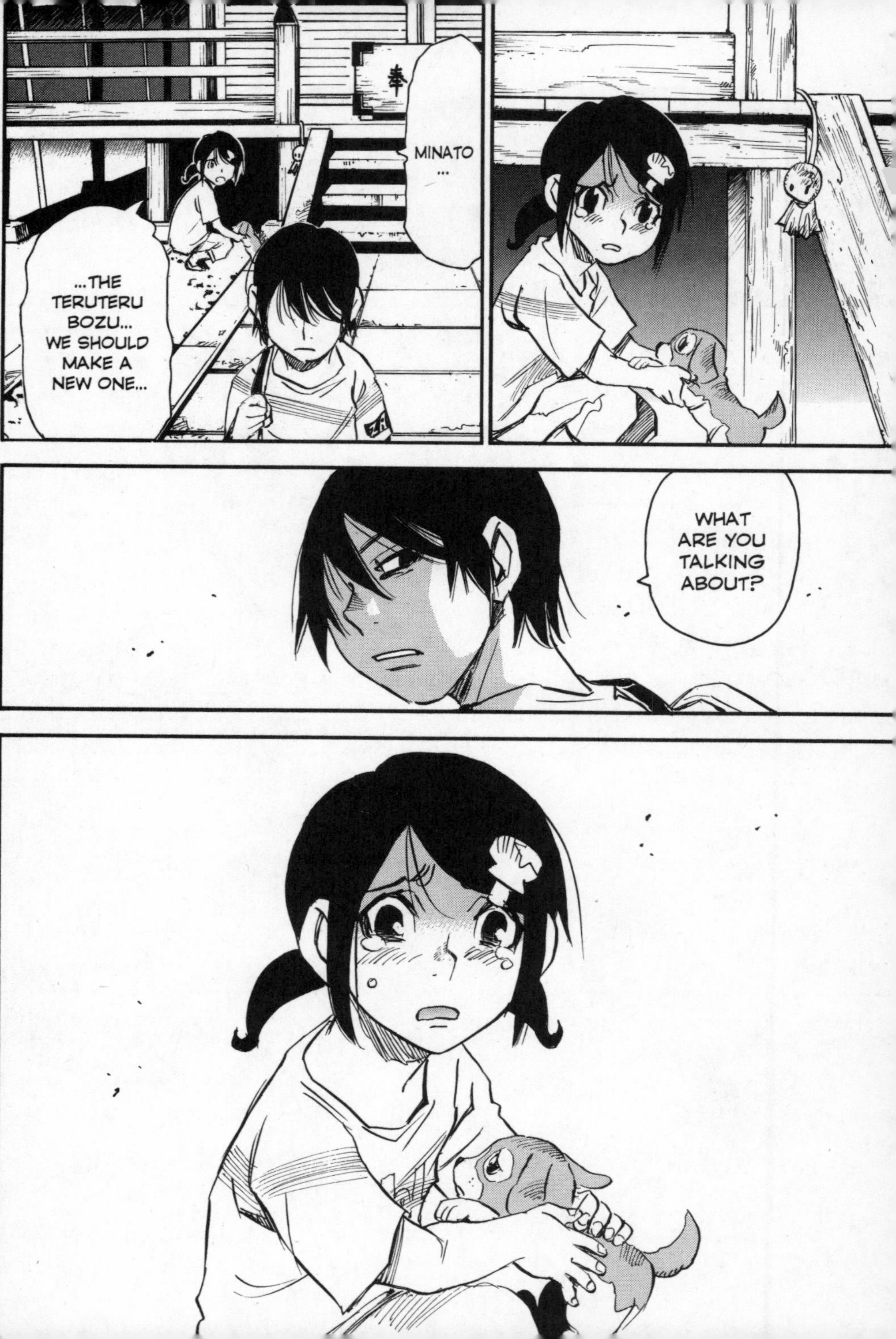
MINATO ...
...THE TERUTERU BOZU... WE SHOULD MAKE A NEW ONE...
WHAT ARE YOU TALKING ABOUT?

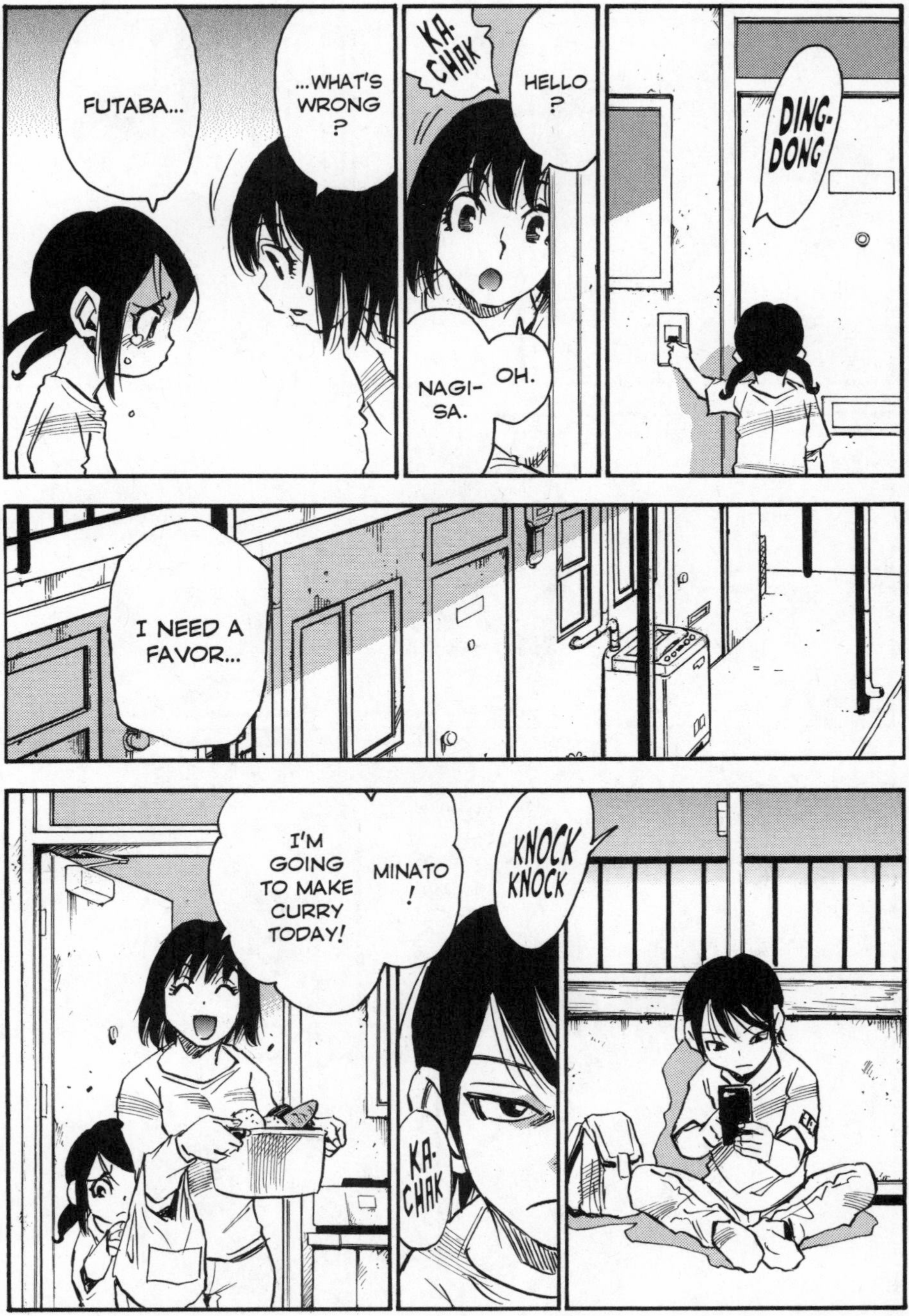
DING-DONG
KA-CHAK
HELLO?
OH. NAGISA.
...WHAT'S WRONG?
FUTABA...
I NEED A FAVOR...
KNOCK KNOCK
KA-CHAK
MINATO!
I'M GOING TO MAKE CURRY TODAY!

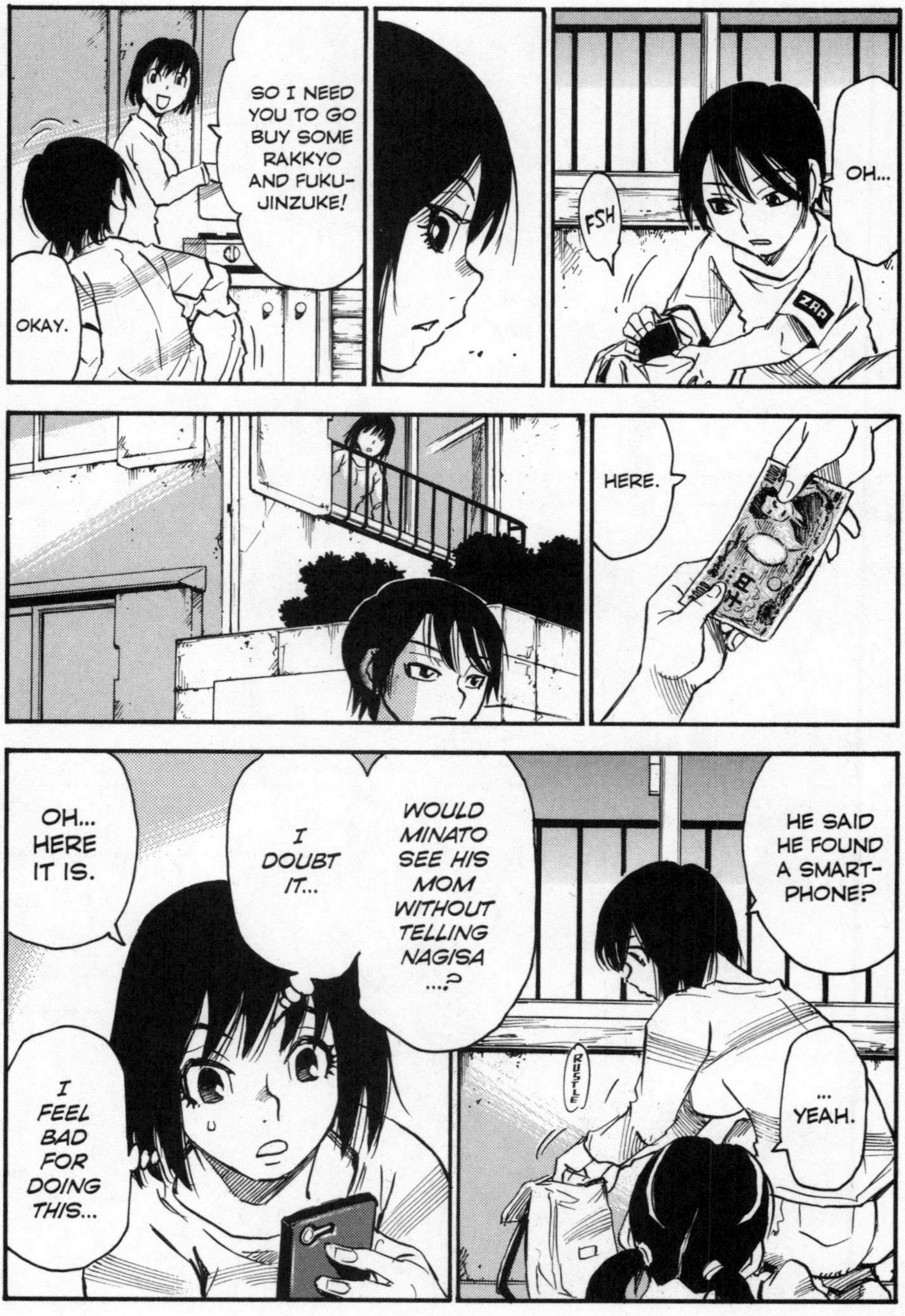
OH...
FSH
SO I NEED YOU TO GO BUY SOME RAKKYO AND FUKU-JINZUKE!
OKAY.
HERE.
HE SAID HE FOUND A SMART-PHONE?
RUSTLE
... YEAH.
WOULD MINATO SEE HIS MOM WITHOUT TELLING NAGISA ...?
I DOUBT IT...
OH... HERE IT IS.
I FEEL BAD FOR DOING THIS...

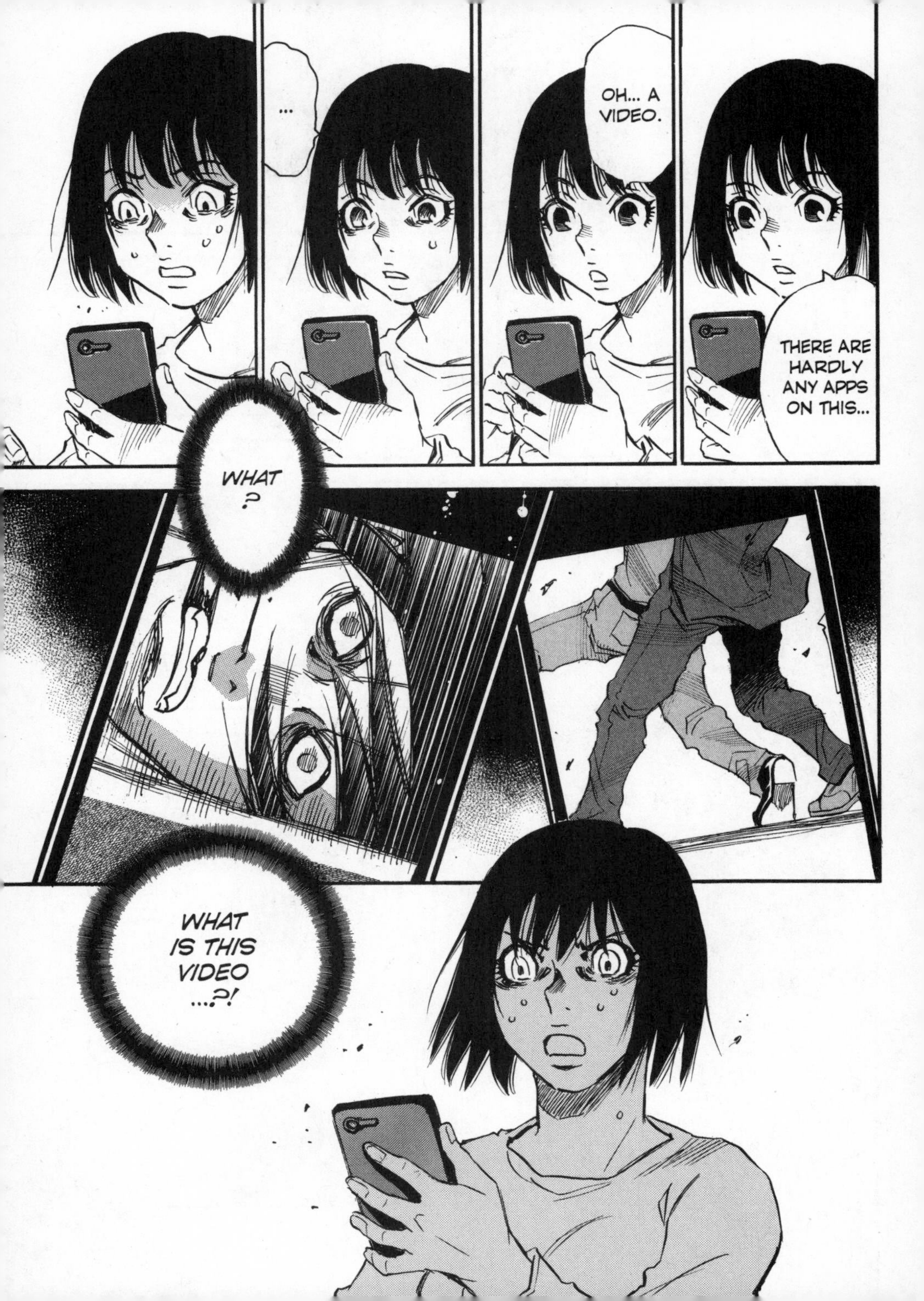
THERE ARE HARDLY ANY APPS ON THIS...
OH... A VIDEO.
...
WHAT ?
WHAT IS THIS VIDEO ...?!

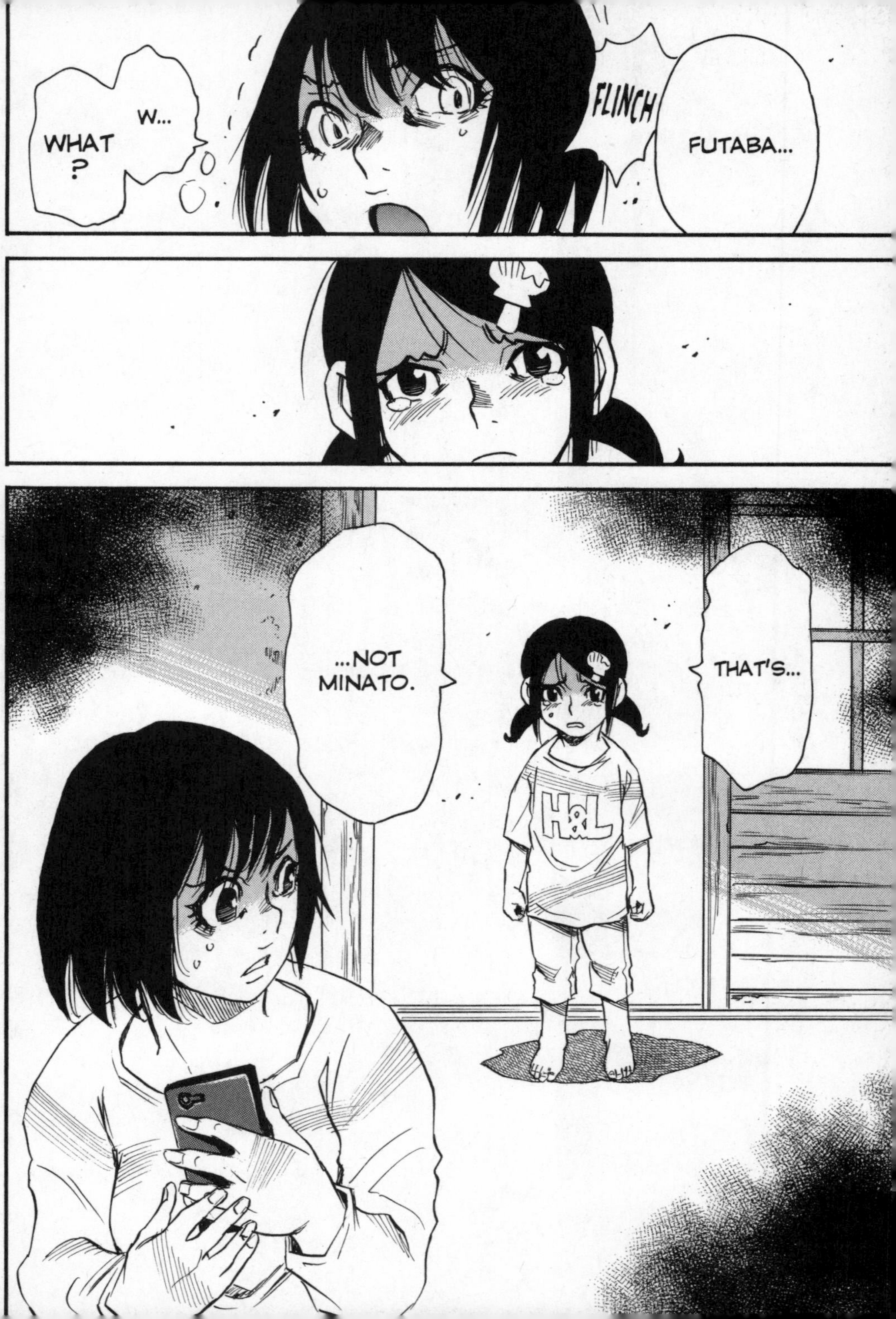

FUTABA...
FLINCH
W... WHAT?
THAT'S...
...NOT MINATO.
H&L

STAFF

Kei Sanbe

Yoichiro Tomita
Manami, 18 years old
Koji Kikuta
Yasunobu

Keishi Kanesho

SPECIAL THANKS
Nagīnyo

BOOK DESIGN
Yukio Hoshino
VOLARE inc.

EDITORS
Naofumi Muranaka
Hiroshi Nishimura
Toshihiro Tsuchiboshi

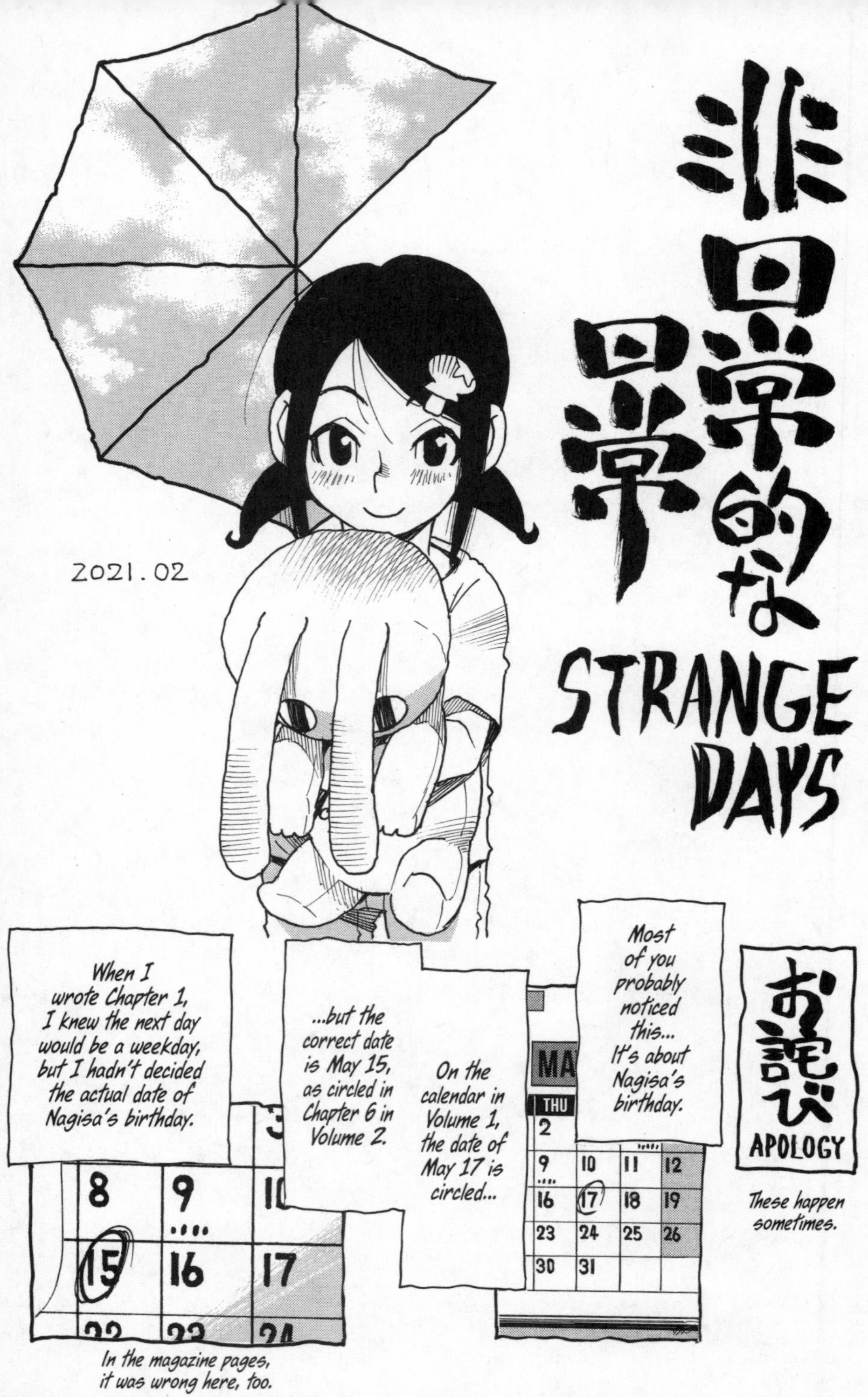

非日常的な日常
STRANGE DAYS
2021.02
お詫び
APOLOGY
These happen sometimes.
Most of you probably noticed this... It's about Nagisa's birthday.
On the calendar in Volume 1, the date of May 17 is circled...
...but the correct date is May 15, as circled in Chapter 6 in Volume 2.
When I wrote Chapter 1, I knew the next day would be a weekday, but I hadn't decided the actual date of Nagisa's birthday.
In the magazine pages, it was wrong here, too.

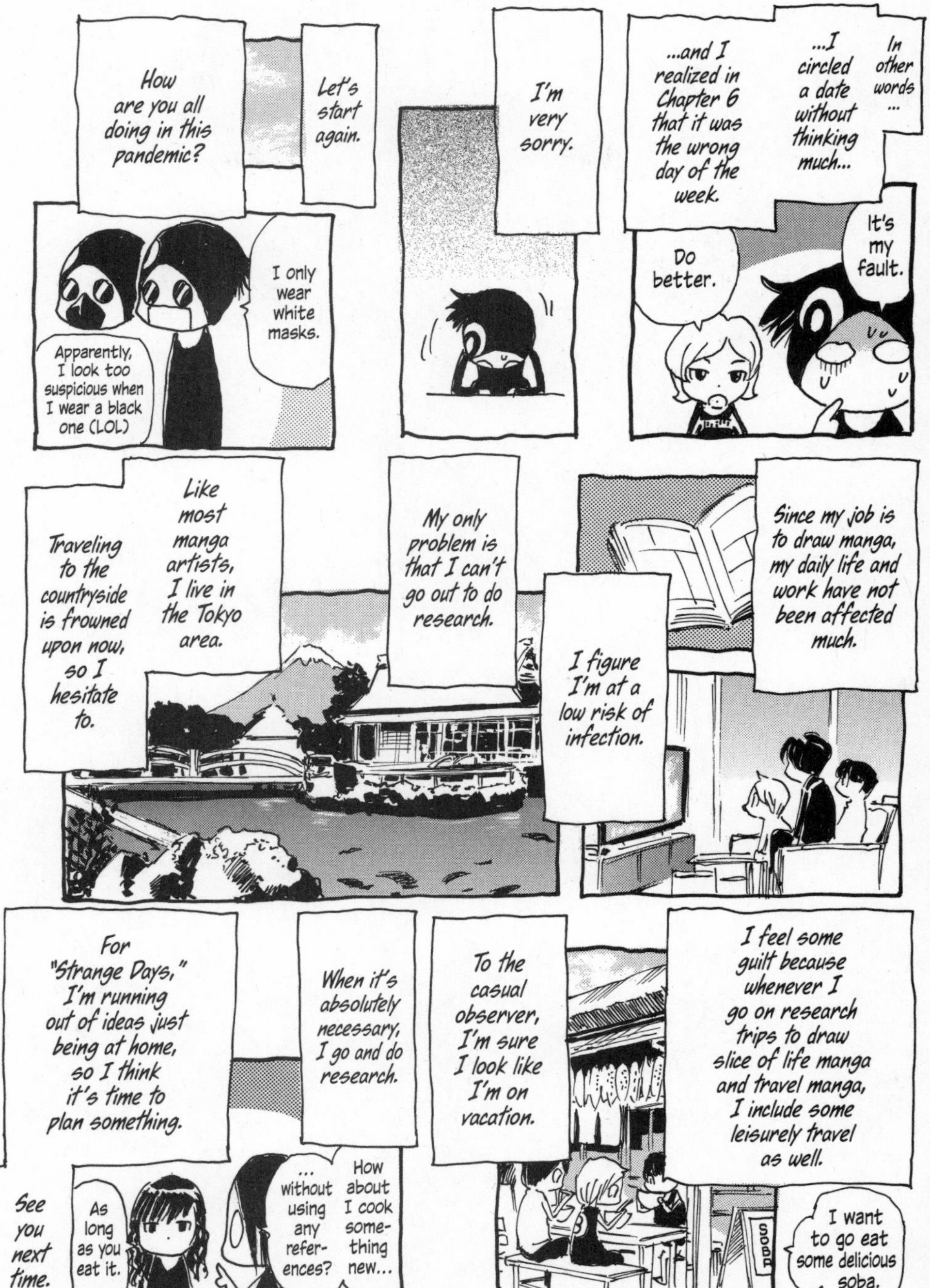
In other words...
...I circled a date without thinking much...
...and I realized in Chapter 6 that it was the wrong day of the week.
It's my fault.
Do better.
I'm very sorry.
Let's start again.
How are you all doing in this pandemic?
I only wear white masks.
Apparently, I look too suspicious when I wear a black one (LOL)
Since my job is to draw manga, my daily life and work have not been affected much.
I figure I'm at a low risk of infection.
My only problem is that I can't go out to do research.
Like most manga artists, I live in the Tokyo area.
Traveling to the countryside is frowned upon now, so I hesitate to.
I feel some guilt because whenever I go on research trips to draw slice of life manga and travel manga, I include some leisurely travel as well.
To the casual observer, I'm sure I look like I'm on vacation.
SOBA
I want to go eat some delicious soba.
When it's absolutely necessary, I go and do research.
For "Strange Days," I'm running out of ideas just being at home, so I think it's time to plan something.
How about I cook something new...
...without using any references?
As long as you eat it.
See you next time.

A Kodansha Trade Paperback Original

Island in a Puddle 3 copyright © 2021 Kei Sanbe
English translation copyright © 2022 Kei Sanbe

Published in the United States by
Kodansha USA Publishing, LLC, New York.

Publication rights for this English edition arranged through
Kodansha Ltd., Tokyo.

First published in Japan in 2021 by Kodansha Ltd., Tokyo
as *Mizutamari ni ukabu shima*, volume 3.

ISBN 978-1-64651-458-8

Printed in the United States of America.

9 8 7 6 5 4 3 2 1

Translation: Iyasu Adair Nagata
Lettering: Evan Hayden
Editing: Nathaniel Gallant
Kodansha USA Publishing edition cover design by Adam Del Re

Publisher: Kiichiro Sugawara

Director of Publishing Services: Ben Applegate
Director of Publishing Operations: Dave Barrett
Associate Director, Publishing Operations: Stephen Pakula
Publishing Services Managing Editors: Madison Salters, Alanna Ruse
Production Managers: Emi Lotto, Angela Zurlo

KODANSHA.US

KODANSHA